A Brief History
of South Africa

First published by Jacana Media (Pty) Ltd in 2021

10 Orange Street
Sunnyside
Auckland Park 2092
South Africa
+2711 628 3200
www.jacana.co.za

ISBN 978-1-928232-95-7

Cover design by publicide
Editing by Russell Martin
Proofreading by Lara Jacob
Indexing by Christopher Merrett
Set in Crimson Text 10/13pt
Printed by ABC Printers, Cape Town
Job no. 003835

A Brief History
of South Africa

*From the Earliest Times to the
Mandela Presidency*

John Pampallis
and
Maryke Bailey

Fanele

(Zul; Xho; Tso): necessary.
This is a necessary book.

Contents

Part B: Themes in South African History

Foreword

We cannot really understand the world without understanding history. The present is a product of the past and we can have no deep appreciation of our current circumstances and the challenges that face us without knowing how we got here. The inequalities, injustices, friendships, enmities, conditions of life and the institutions that provide the structure of our world are all products of the history that has culminated in the society and the nation that we live in today.

History is not just an account of past events. It is also an interpretation of those events and developments; it underpins our identities as individuals, as societies and as nations. It is for this reason that history is deeply political. How people understand their past determines to a large extent how they understand themselves, their role in the world and the nature of their challenges.

The powerful have always understood this and have manipulated it to ensure acceptance of the status quo. Colonial and apartheid historians in South Africa did this largely by ignoring the history of black people or by portraying them as obstacles to the spread of order and civilisation or merely as a threat that needed to be managed – through 'native policy' or 'bantu administration'. One or other version of this history was taught in schools to bolster and justify white supremacist rule. Since 1994, we have been in an extended period of defining – through the work of historians, the mass media and popular culture – how South African history should be understood in a democracy.

Progressive writers of South African history, dating back to the nineteenth century, have long provided perspectives that differ from the dominant narrative. In the last forty years, such voices have become quite common. School curricula have been adjusted and now reflect a more inclusive view of South African history. Despite this, many South African adults and youth today still find themselves with a very superficial knowledge of the country's history or awareness that its interpretation and meaning are up for debate. This book plays an important role in developing that awareness.

A Brief History of South Africa has a few distinctive features. First, it is designed to be used primarily in study circles or reading groups. Each chapter is followed by a set of questions to stimulate critical discussion as well as a list of suggested readings to enhance the groups' deliberations. The purpose is to extend readers' knowledge of the subject matter and to expose them to other viewpoints. Second, the book contains two sections: one dealing with the unfolding narrative of South African history and one examining specific themes in a little more depth. Third, the book is aimed at an audience of adults and youth who may not be history specialists but whose understanding of history will enhance their role as important influencers of society through their work in organisations or as teachers of the younger generation.

This book makes an important contribution to understanding how our country came to be where it is. It assists readers to face both the present and the future.

Kgalema Motlanthe
Former President of South Africa
Board Chairperson, Oliver Tambo School of Leadership

Preface

WHAT THE BOOK IS ABOUT

This short book has been written to present a progressive introduction to South African history and to encourage critical thinking about it. It does not aim to be comprehensive, but rather to provide an overall outline of the contry's history to introduce readers to a 'big picture' that can be supplemented by further readings, some of which are recommended at the end of each chapter.

Effective history teaching has not been prioritised in South African schools since 1994. This fact, together with the appallingly distorted version of history taught before 1994, means that most South Africans – young and old – have scant knowledge of the country's past. Poorly informed interpretations of the past – often based on racist, sexist and ethnic mythologies – continue to bedevil social interaction and are seldom examined closely. In such circumstances, populist sentiments are more likely to gain traction, leading to uninformed public discussions around complex issues.

While presenting an account of South Africa's experiences of colonisation, segregation and successive governments, this book seeks to portray the central role of the resistance to colonialism and racist rule over the years: resistance to colonial invasion and occupation as well as the struggle against oppression waged by political, social and trade union movements in the modern era. Many actors were engaged in resistance to oppression, and it is not possible to include all movements in equal depth. Preference has been given to dominant organisations, while the authors have alerted readers to lesser-known resistance movements and at the same time hope that the suggested additional readings will enrich their knowledge of different organisations and individuals in a specific time period.

A key purpose of the book is to provide a study guide for both formal and non-formal adult education. It offers an opportunity to adults, post-school students and out-of-school youth to expand and enrich their knowledge of South African history.

An equally important purpose is to assist in strengthening history teaching in schools. Many history teachers, especially those who do not have a specific higher-education qualification in history, feel that they need additional support. The book will give all history teachers the opportunity to expand their own knowledge, provide them with source material for their learners, and point them to a range of other sources with a variety of historical interpretations.

We believe that such a book, when properly used, can play a small but important role in the development of a more informed, critical and respectful public discourse, rooted in real historical knowledge and characterised by a willingness to engage thoughtfully, if robustly, with diverse views.

The book is divided into two parts. Part A is a narrative history from the earliest times until the end of the Mandela presidency while Part B deals with the historical development of nine themes: the economy, the bantustans, the history of schooling, poverty and inequality, life under apartheid, women's struggles, the trade union movement, South Africa's successive constitutions, and the international solidarity movement against apartheid. This will enable readers who want a quick overview of a particular theme, to access the relevant material easily. Each chapter or theme is followed by further readings and discussions or activities to assist learners in engaging with the text. All narrative chapters and themes are relatively short and can be read by most readers in less than half an hour. It is expected that the knowledge gained from the book will be supplemented by the additional readings.

For most of the period covered by the book, South Africa was under colonial and racist rule, and much of the text covers the nature of this rule and the opposition to it from the political and trade union organisations of black people, supported by some anti-racist whites. The book examines political developments, the nature of racist rule, the development of the economy, the exploitation of workers and their resistance through trade unions, and the resistance to oppression by communities and women's and youth organisations.

How to use the book

The book is designed specifically to be used in small study circles in various settings, formal and non-formal. The formal settings could be education programmes of political organisations, trade unions, and church or community organisations, while non-formal settings could be groups of friends, fellow students or workplace colleagues. School history teachers will be able to use the book in the same way or adapt it to their own contexts. It could also be a useful introduction to South African history for the interest and pleasure of individual readers, both youth and adults.

It is envisaged that study circles will meet periodically, preferably weekly, at a time that suits its members to discuss each chapter or theme. Before every meeting, each member should read a chapter and one or more of the additional readings on her or his own. At the meeting of the study circle the chapter would be discussed by using the questions for discussion and the text engagement activities. Study circle members may find it useful to divide the additional readings among themselves so that all, or at least most, of them are covered and their information and perspectives can contribute to discussions at their next meeting. Other readings that do not appear in the lists could, of course, also deepen the discussions by providing other perspectives. Similarly, study circles could add or omit discussion questions as they see fit.

Study circle facilitators, who might rotate from meeting to meeting, should try to ensure that all members are drawn into the discussion. All views should be listened to and discussed respectfully; interpretations of history are seldom entirely right or wrong.

We trust that the book, together with the additional readings, will prove an interesting and useful introduction to the history of South Africa and that it will inform a deeper understanding of our history and better-informed public discourse and debate on contemporary challenges.

A Note on Terminology

RACE

Racial terminology in South Africa has a convoluted and complicated history. The use of the word *African* has long been used by indigenous black people in South Africa to refer to themselves. This is illustrated, for example, by the adoption of the name African National Congress (ANC) in 1923 to replace the organisation's original name, South African Native National Congress, under which it was established in 1912. Until the late 1960s, the words *non-European* or *non-white* were widely used to refer collectively to all those groups that were oppressed by colonialism and apartheid. Oppressed groups other than indigenous Africans have generally been described (by themselves and others) as *coloured* or *Indian*, and these terms are still generally accepted. The word *native* was also widely used both by white governments and by Africans until the 1950s but fell into disuse after that. From the early 1960s the government began to use the word *Bantu*, but this was largely rejected by Africans.

From the 1960s, the emerging Black Consciousness Movement, and in particular the South African Students' Organisation under the leadership of Steve Biko, began to assert the use of the word *black* to refer collectively to Africans, coloureds and Indians. This was partly a rejection of words that described people in negative terms (i.e. *non-European* or *non-white*) and also in support of the political objective of asserting the unity of those who were oppressed under apartheid and to encourage a broad and more united struggle to oppose it. This usage was quickly adopted by other formations of the liberation movement including the largest one, the African National Congress. Ironically, in the 1980s, the apartheid government also adopted the use of the word *black* but used it to refer only to Africans since it was obviously not interested in using language that would help unify its opponents.

In the post-apartheid period, the word *black* began to replace *African* in common usage for various reasons. A more inclusive use of the word *African* was perhaps best crystallised by then Deputy President Thabo Mbeki in his famous 'I Am an African' speech. The speech was delivered on behalf of the ANC when Parliament adopted the new Constitution on 8 May 1996, and referred to all South Africans as *Africans*.

We have had to make a choice and have opted to use the word *black* to refer collectively to all oppressed groups and *African* to refer to indigenous black people throughout the book.

STUDENTS

Before 1994 those attending primary or secondary schools were officially referred to as *pupils*. However, from the mid-1970s the word *students* came to be used more frequently and the Soweto Uprising was widely described as a student uprising. Both words were used until 1994 when the new Department of Education introduced the word *learners* as the official term; but in everyday usage both *pupil* and *student* were still widely used. Those studying in post-school institutions such as universities and colleges were, and still are, referred to as *students*.

In this book we have chosen to use the word *student* to refer to anybody attending an educational institution.

Acknowledgements

The authors wish to thank the following:

Former President Kgalema Motlanthe who initiated the project of writing this book and gave generously of his time to discuss various aspects of it with the authors during the writing process.

The OR Tambo School of Leadership whose commitment to purchase a number of books helped make this publication possible.

Michelle Friedman who wrote the first draft of Theme 7 on the history of trade unions in South Africa.

The following people suggested readings, gave us useful advice regarding available literature, and provided a sounding board for ideas and interpretations: Catherine Burns, David Masondo, Zandisile Pase, Nafisa Essop Sheik and Steven Sparks.

Luli Callinicos and Irene Pampallis for reading and commenting usefully on a number of chapters.

Karin Pampallis for her immense support including editing the book and providing her expertise in guiding us through the publication process.

On a more personal level, Maryke's whole family, and particularly Mark Bailey and Netty Nameso, for their constant support, and (again) Karin for similar support to John.

Last but not least, the staff and consultants at Jacana Media for their work and support during the publication process. Aimee Armstrong in particular has been a pleasure to work with; she has been efficient, quick and, as her name suggests, amiable throughout.

Part A
Chronological Narrative

One

Southern African Societies up to the Seventeenth Century

BEFORE WE START

We do not know what the early residents of southern Africa[1] called themselves and so we often refer to the various people by their linguistic group. A 'linguistic group' refers to a group of languages that share similar features because they developed from the same language root. For example, Zulu and Xhosa are from the Nguni linguistic group. The Nguni linguistic group is part of the broader Bantu linguistic group, and is very different from the Khoesan linguistic group. In academic language, the word 'Bantu' does not have the racist connotations that it had under apartheid, but is the term given to the language groups that are spread across central and southern Africa.

THE FIRST INHABITANTS OF SOUTHERN AFRICA: THE SAN

Modern humans (*Homo sapiens*) are a type of hominin. The hominin group embraces all human species, modern and extinct, and their ancestors. The Cradle of Humankind, north of Johannesburg, contains some of the earliest fossils of extinct human species, as well as about 40 per cent of the world's hominin fossils. The name 'Cradle of Humankind' can be slightly misleading. While the Cradle clearly proves the presence of early hominins in southern Africa, it does not indicate that *Homo sapiens* first developed in the Cradle area. Humans did, however, first develop in Africa between 100 000 to 200 000 years ago

---

1   In this chapter we use modern-day place names. We also refer to southern Africa rather than South Africa. 'Southern Africa' in this chapter ignores political borders and includes areas of neighbouring countries that are now known as Botswana, Lesotho, Mozambique, Namibia, eSwatini and Zimbabwe.

before spreading out through the rest of the world.

Early modern humans were present in southern Africa over 100 000 years ago. Owing to a lack of evidence, we know very little about these early residents. However, we do know that they lived a hunter-gatherer lifestyle and that by 10 000 years ago various hunter-gatherer communities were spread throughout southern Africa. Some of these groups were the ancestors of the modern San.

Different San groups had different languages, skills and knowledge, although their lifestyles and the tools they used were broadly similar. They moved around in search of food, and therefore their groups remained quite small. Groups usually ranged from 20 to 70 people, but they could become as large as 250 people. The San were quite egalitarian, which meant there was not much difference in status between individuals. They also had a sharing ethic. This meant that individuals did not gather food or wealth for themselves, but shared it with the group.

KHOE HERDERS IN SOUTHERN AFRICA

About 2 500 years ago some hunter-gatherers living in northern Botswana acquired sheep-herding and pottery-making skills from Bantu-language-speaking farming communities who came from further north in Africa. The introduction of sheep herding changed the lifestyle and culture of these hunter-gatherers and they became herders, known today as the Khoe or Khoekhoen.[2] As time went on, Khoe culture spread from Botswana into Namibia and the Cape.

The Khoe were not crop farmers and needed to move around to find grazing for their livestock. Given the difference between herding and hunter-gatherer lifestyles, however, the San and the Khoe organised their societies differently. As herding provided a more predictable food supply than hunting and gathering, Khoe societies could provide for more people. Herders also practised private ownership. Individuals could accumulate personal wealth, mainly in the form of livestock. Richer herders had more power and status. Khoe groups were therefore much larger and more hierarchical than the egalitarian San. Some Khoe groups were as large as 2 500 people and had clear leaders such as chiefs.

Interactions between the San and the Khoe varied. Some San served Khoe groups as hunters, guides or even soldiers. The Khoe looked down on the San. 'San' appears to have been a derogatory word used by the Khoe, but it now seems to be accepted as a term for South Africa's first people.

By the 1400s there were about fifteen major Khoe groups stretching south from Namibia to the Western Cape, and eastwards from the Western Cape to the Great Fish River in the Eastern Cape.

The Khoe were the first people from southern Africa to make contact with the Europeans when Portuguese sailors stopped for water at Mossel Bay in 1488. The first contact resulted in fighting, with one Khoe person dying. Yet interactions were not always hostile. In the first half of the 1600s, before Dutch colonisation, it was common

---

2   Khoe and Khoekhoen are sometimes written as Khoi and Khoikhoi respectively.

San Rock Art, Cederberg, South Africa

for the Khoe groups around Table Bay to trade sheep and cattle with European sailors in exchange for iron, brass and copper.

The richest Khoe group around the time of European contact was the Inqua. This was because they held some of the best grazing land, and controlled the trade in copper from the Orange River, which was exchanged for produce grown by the southern Nguni-speakers of the Eastern Cape. The Nguni-speakers, like all Bantu-language-speakers, were farmers. While the Nguni-speakers had probably settled in the Eastern Cape around the 1300s or 1400s, Bantu-language-speakers had arrived much earlier. Their arrival brought crop farming to southern Africa.

ARRIVAL OF THE FIRST FARMERS IN SOUTHERN AFRICA

Unlike the hunter-gathering San and the herding Khoe, the Bantu-language-speakers were farmers. One of the most important differences between farmers and herders is that the farmers lived in permanent settlements instead of always moving in search of good hunting or grazing land. Since farming societies stayed in one place and had a predictable food supply, they could sustain much bigger populations than the San and Khoe. The farmers planted crops such as sorghum and millet, and kept livestock such as sheep, goats, chickens and cattle. These early farmers also had knowledge of mining and metallurgy.[3]

---

3   Metal-working.

Group	San	Khoe	Early Bantu-language-speakers
Economic activity	Hunter-gatherers	Pastoralists	Farmers
Movement	Nomadic	Nomadic	Settled/stationary
Group size	Usually between 20 and 70 people	Larger groups, usually a few hundred people	Usually a few hundred people; later, powerful settlements could contain a few thousand
Presence in South Africa	About 10 000 years ago, various San communities spread across southern Africa	Emerged about 2 500 years ago[4]	Settled in north-eastern South Africa around AD 250
Social structure	Egalitarian	Hierarchical	Hierarchical
Relationship to property	Sharing ethic	Private ownership	Private ownership

Early Bantu-language-speakers expanded southwards from eastern Africa (the Great Lakes region) and western Africa (probably around Angola). The earliest farmers settled around the Kruger National Park, eSwatini and Mozambique in about AD 250. Settlements spread south along the coast of KwaZulu-Natal over the next 500 years. By AD 700 some farmers had settled as far south as modern-day East London. While the Khoe were able to survive in the drier, winter rainfall areas of southern Africa, the Bantu-language-speaking farmers needed fertile land and better rainfall for their crops. Farmers therefore settled in the northern and eastern areas of southern Africa, which experience higher rainfall.

The various farming groups responded differently to their environment and resources. Most planted sorghum and millet. While cattle were important, some groups had more cattle than others, and there were others who needed to rely more on hunting for meat. Groups close to the sea also fished and collected shellfish.

We need to be careful about assuming that the early farmers settled on 'empty land'. San groups were spread across southern Africa and there is evidence that the early farmers interacted with the San. Some San groups may have felt threatened and moved away, whereas others may have lived in close proximity to the farmers.

Early farming appears to have followed similar settlement patterns. The cattle kraal stood in the centre of the homestead, and the huts and granaries of the various wives were built around the kraal. This shows that cattle held an important position in the

---

4   There is a debate among historians as to whether the Khoe emerged as a result of some San communities becoming pastoralists, or whether they are a different ethnic group altogether. This is why we have used the word 'emerged' rather than 'arrived'.

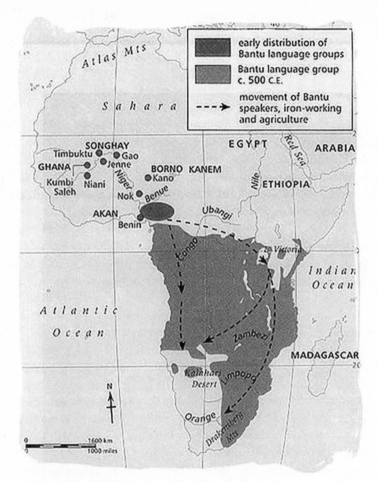

Map showing origination and southward migration of the black people in Africa. Source: South African History Online

world-view of early Bantu-language-speaking farmers. In early farming societies across southern Africa, this settlement pattern was followed by everybody, whether chiefs or commoners.

There is evidence of consistent farming activity around the Shashe–Limpopo basin from about AD 900. About this time early Bantu-language-speakers, called Zhizho by archaeologists, settled in the area. A settlement known as Schroda to archaeologists developed and grew in size and importance, eventually housing about 500 people. This was much larger than other farming settlements of the time. But why did Schroda grow in size, power and status? The answer possibly lies in its links with the Indian Ocean trade, which also contributed to the rise of Mapungubwe, Great Zimbabwe and Khami.

GROWTH OF TRADE AROUND THE SHASHE–LIMPOPO BASIN

Two thousand years ago there was a thriving trade network across the Indian Ocean between Asia and the African coast around Kenya and Tanzania. By AD 900 Arab and Swahili merchants had travelled further south and were trading from the Mozambican ports of Sofala and Inhambane. They traded items like glass beads, shells, cloth and ceramics in exchange for goods like ivory and gold.

It seems that Zhizho settlers were originally attracted to the Shashe–Limpopo basin by the opportunities to hunt elephants for ivory, which they could trade with the merchants on the east coast. The Zhizho settlers appear to have dominated the Shashe–Limpopo basin area and disrupted the lifestyles of the hunter-gatherers that lived there. However, as trade with the east coast grew, the Zhizho were displaced by a new group of Bantu-language-speakers from the north, who arrived in the early 1000s.

When the newcomers settled around the Shashe–Limpopo basin, many Zhizho moved away. The newcomers established their capital, called K2 by archaeologists, a few kilometres away from Schroda. The K2 settlers were probably attracted by the wealth that the trade links provided, and wanted to control the trade themselves.

Some scholars think that the early Bantu-language-speakers, like the Zhizho, probably spoke an early form of Shona. There is much greater certainty that the people who displaced the Zhizho were ancestral Shona-speakers.

K2, MAPUNGUBWE, GREAT ZIMBABWE AND KHAMI

Glass beads, which were commonly used in Indian Ocean trade, have been found at various settlements around Schroda, not just at Schroda itself. This shows that different Zhizho settlements were involved in trade and that it wasn't strictly controlled by the people living at the large Schroda capital itself. However, the people of K2 appear to have been organised into stronger hierarchies than the Zhizho had been. Ivory, gold and glass beads have been found only in the settlements where the elite and powerful K2 people lived, not in those of the commoners. This suggests that the elite controlled access to trade and certain goods.

Around 1220 the residents of the K2 capital moved about a kilometre away to Mapungubwe, which became the new capital. The king and the elite lived at the top of the hill, away from the commoners and their cattle. Other settlements in the Mapungubwe kingdom copied the pattern of the capital.

This change in settlement pattern is very significant. While there were certainly hierarchies in early farming societies, these communities did not have such distinct social classes as we see in Mapungubwe. The elite clearly separated themselves from the commoners. The various classes also appear to have had different values and beliefs about the role of cattle, since cattle were more important than trade for the livelihoods of commoners.

Mapungubwe is significant in southern African history because it is the earliest example of a powerful, centralised state with clear class distinctions. While the K2 capital housed about 1 500 people, Mapungubwe's capital housed about 5 000 people.

Mapungubwe settlements stretched into the north of South Africa, into eastern Botswana and north of the Limpopo into Zimbabwe. The people at the various settlements all obeyed the king of Mapungubwe Hill and paid tribute to the elite at the capital.

Mapungubwe's power ended around 1290 and a new, larger and more powerful kingdom emerged. A group of people who lived further north in Zimbabwe (who were also early Shona-speakers) were able to take control of the east coast trade away from the Mapungubwe elite. As the new group's wealth and power increased, they established their capital at Great Zimbabwe.

The Great Zimbabwe kingdom dominated from roughly 1300 until about 1450. Then Great Zimbabwe's power also waned and a new kingdom, known as Khami, emerged. Located near modern-day Bulawayo, it grew in strength and was able to take control of the trade, particularly in gold, with the east coast.

Some Shona-speaking Khami groups migrated southwards towards the Soutpansberg, where they interacted with two new Bantu-language groups in southern Africa, the Sotho–Tswana and the Nguni. Their interactions played a role in the creation of the early Venda culture.

ANCESTRAL SOTHO–TSWANA AND NGUNI SETTLERS

During the rise of Mapungubwe, Great Zimbabwe and Khami, other changes were taking place in South Africa. Two new groups of Bantu-language-speakers, Nguni and Sotho–Tswana groups, migrated south from east Africa and settled south of the Limpopo.

The first Nguni farmers arrived around AD 1000 and settled along the KwaZulu-Natal coast. By the 1400s some Nguni settlements had reached the Pondoland coast and the area around modern-day Makhanda (Grahamstown). The Sotho–Tswana arrived in South Africa around 1300 and originally settled around the Soutpansberg. By the early 1600s, Sotho–Tswana groups had expanded further south into northern KwaZulu-Natal and the eastern Free State.

The Sotho–Tswana and the Nguni did not settle on empty land. Unfortunately we do not know much about the interactions between the newcomers and the earlier Bantu-language-speaking farmers, except that the Nguni and Sotho–Tswana eventually became the dominant groups.

The presence of Khoesan clicks in various Nguni languages shows that Nguni-speakers often interacted with the San and Khoe. For example, the southern Nguni, ancestors of people like the Xhosa, interacted intensively with the Khoe groups in the Eastern Cape. The northern Nguni had more limited interactions with the Khoe and San, but there is evidence that some San shamans living in the Drakensberg were paid in livestock by the northern Nguni for rainmaking rituals.

Not all San benefited from the expansion of farming societies. Traditional San hunting grounds were lost, and their communities were disrupted as a result. There is evidence of San abandoning their lifestyle and independence and taking on a subservient and dependent status among farming groups, particularly around the Kalahari.

SOUTHERN AFRICA IN THE 1600S: AN OVERVIEW

By the 1600s the landscape and population of southern Africa were very different from what they had been 2 000 years previously. The changes were partly due to the arrival of herding in the Cape, farming in the east, and the growth of trade routes to the east coast of Africa. Equally important were the changes that had taken place at the trading ports in modern-day Mozambique and Tanzania, where Europeans had begun gradually to displace the Arab and Swahili traders.

The populations of the Nguni and Sotho–Tswana continued to expand in the 1700s. In the next chapter we will focus more exclusively on some of the Nguni and Sotho–Tswana societies and the changes they experienced in the 1700s and 1800s.

CHAPTER 1: DISCUSSION QUESTIONS

1. What was your view of pre-colonial southern African history before you read this chapter? Did reading this chapter change your view? If so, how? If not, how did it confirm any views you held?

2. Why is the introduction of herding and farming considered to mark two turning points in southern African history?

3. What role did the Indian Ocean trade network play in the development of various societies in southern Africa? Did it affect all societies equally?

4. The San are without a doubt South Africa's first people, and this is recognised in South Africa by having the San on our national coat of arms. Yet, no San language is recognised as an official language of South Africa. Furthermore, land restitution claims date back only to 1913. The San had lost their traditional hunting grounds long before this time. Many South Africans do not realise that we have San people living in South Africa today. In a country based on the values of social justice and restitution, should the San be compensated for the losses they have suffered historically? If so, how can South Africans ensure that this happens?

5. We see many African groups arriving throughout the history of southern Africa. These groups are now considered the indigenous people of southern Africa. When does a group shed its newcomer or settler status and become part of the indigenous population?

6. Different people were displaced by new groups of settlers. Can we compare the settlement and expansion of early African farmers to European settlement and colonialism? What are the similarities and what are the differences?

CHAPTER 1: ADDITIONAL READINGS

Online readings

Daggett, Adrienne (2016) The Indian Ocean: A Maritime Trade Network History Nearly Forgot. Discover, 20 October 2016. http://discovermagazine.com/2016/nov/trading-places.

Guy, Jeff (2007) The First Farmers. In *Ancient Civilizations and Global Trade.* Turning Points in History Series, Book 1. Johannesburg: STE. http://www.sahistory.org.za/archive/book-1-ancient-civilizations-and-global-trade-commissioned-department-education.

Guy, Jeff (2007) The Beginnings of Globalisation. In *Ancient Civilizations and Global Trade.* Turning Points in History Series, Book 1. Johannesburg: STE. http://www.sahistory.org.za/archive/book-1-ancient-civilizations-and-global-trade-chapter-2-beginnings-globalisation-jeff-guy.

Huffman, T.N. (2011) Prehistory: Pre-colonial Farmers in Gauteng. *South African History Online*, 29 March 2011, updated 15 June 2012. http://www.sahistory.org.za/topic/prehistory-pre-colonial-farmers-gauteng.

Jolly, Peter (2015) Early Contact between Southern San and Khoe and Bantu-Speaking Groups. *UPSpace Institutional Repository.* http://repository.up.ac.za/bitstream/handle/2263/44058/003_Chapter%201.pdf?sequence=3&isAllowed=y.

McKenna, Amy (ed.) (2011) Early History. In *The History of Southern Africa.* Britannica Educational Publishing in association with Rosen Education Services. http://www.sahistory.org.za/sites/default/files/file%20uploads%20/amy_mckenna_editor_the_history_of_southern_afrbook4you.pdf.

Online visual resources

https://he.palgrave.com/companion/Shillington-History-Of-Africa/resources. This website offers various maps relating to African history such as migrations, trade routes, language groups and kingdoms. Click on the 'Maps' button and you can explore some of the maps yourself. (Two maps, 10.2 and 10.3, have been included in the list below.)

https://he.palgrave.com/resources/CW%20resources%20(by%20Author)/S/Shillington/Maps/Map10_2.jpg. Map 10.2 shows the kingdoms of Mapungubwe, Great Zimbabwe and Khami.

https://he.palgrave.com/resources/CW%20resources%20(by%20Author)/S/Shillington/Maps/Map10_3.jpg. Map 10.3 shows the general settlement of Sotho–Tswana and Nguni chiefdoms.

http://www.sahra.org.za/sahris/sites/default/files/heritagereports/Mapungu-
bwe%20Powerpoint%20Presentation.pdf. This slideshow on Mapungubwe
includes maps and images of artefacts.

Books

Diamond, Jared (2005) *Guns, Germs and Steel: A Short History of Everybody for the Last 13,000 Years.* London: Vintage Books.

Giliomee, H. and B. Mbenga (eds) (2007) *New History of South Africa.* Cape Town: Tafelberg. (See Chapter 1: From the First People to the First Settlements)

Two

State Formation in Southern Africa, 1760–1840

The previous chapter dealt with the arrival, settlement and expansion of Sotho–Tswana and Nguni farmers in southern Africa. This chapter focuses on the political changes that took place among the Sotho–Tswana and Nguni groups from the late 1700s to the early 1800s.[5]

THE TIME OF TROUBLES

In the 1600s and early 1700s the Nguni and Sotho–Tswana chiefdoms were generally decentralised and their homesteads scattered. But by the 1830s the southern African interior was dominated by large, centralised kingdoms.

In the late 1700s and early 1800s social, political and economic instability increased for Sotho–Tswana and Nguni farming societies in southern Africa. This period of upheaval is sometimes referred to as 'the time of troubles'. It has also been called the *mfecane* or the *difaqane*.[6] There were increased tensions and conflict between competing chiefdoms. Sometimes independent chiefdoms united to form large, centralised kingdoms. At other times weaker kingdoms broke apart when they were defeated, or moved away to avoid clashes with more powerful neighbours. This migration fuelled further conflicts while also creating new kingdoms.

---

5   In the Online Visual Resources list at the end of this chapter, there is a link to two maps that show the names of groups and places mentioned in this chapter.

6   There are debates among historians about the use and definitions of these two terms, partly because writers who used them tended to focus on the rise of the Zulu kingdom as the only cause of the disruptions. More recent historians reject this idea, and therefore some writers also reject the use of the two terms.

This chapter examines some examples of the kingdoms formed during the time of troubles. While it is not possible to provide detailed accounts of all the political changes in this era, we will briefly examine some of the changes that took place in southern Africa. We will then briefly consider some of the causes of conflict in this area.

LARGER STATES EMERGE

Various societies experienced different processes of state formation. The Zulu, Sotho and Ndebele kingdoms are three examples of the very different ways in which chiefdoms expanded and exerted their power. In this section we will briefly look at the role that the *amabutho* system played in the northern Nguni kingdoms before moving on to the three kingdoms mentioned above.

Amabutho

Some northern Nguni chiefdoms developed a system known as *amabutho*. Groups of young men of the same age would be put into age sets. While the original purpose of the age sets appears to have been connected to circumcision rituals, their roles changed over time as members became elephant hunters, cattle raiders and, eventually, soldiers.

The *amabutho* system is not really a cause of the conflict in this period, but it is worth mentioning because it played a large role in the power of the kingdoms that eventually dominated. Groups that used the system had a definite military advantage over those that did not, for it helped them to increase and maintain their power.

Many people believe that Shaka created the *amabutho*. Although the *amabutho* system expanded and became more centralised under Shaka, evidence shows that by the 1790s the Ndwandwe, Ngwane and Mthethwa all had a system of *amabutho*. This was before Shaka came to power.

The Zulu kingdom

By the early 1800s there were already some powerful kingdoms along the northern coast of KwaZulu-Natal. Two of the most powerful were the Ndwandwe under Zwide and the Mthethwa under Dingiswayo. The two kingdoms clashed and Zwide defeated Dingiswayo in about 1818. The Ndwandwe became the most powerful force in the region.

Kingdoms were created when many different chiefdoms were brought under the power of the most powerful chief or king. However, if a king was defeated in battle, the kingdom could break up if the chiefdoms asserted their independence again. Dingiswayo's defeat caused the Mthethwa kingdom to break up and allowed the Zulu chiefdom to develop its own power.

The Zulu had been part of the Mthethwa kingdom. When Dingiswayo was defeated, the Zulu chiefdom under Shaka began conquering and assimilating the chiefdoms that had previously been under Mthethwa control.

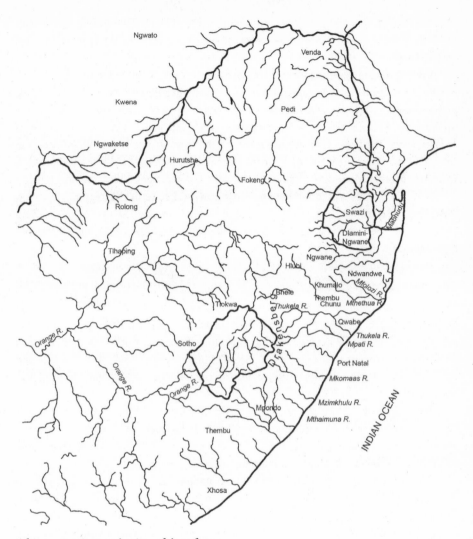

African groupings at the time of the mfecane

Zwide realised that the biggest threat to the Ndwandwe was the growing Zulu chieftaincy and so he launched an attack on the Zulu in about 1819. However, the Zulu retaliated and defeated Zwide. He moved further north into southern eSwatini and rebuilt his kingdom there. The Ndwandwe grew in power once more but were finally defeated completely by the Zulu in 1826.

Throughout the 1820s Shaka's Zulu kingdom expanded its control and consolidated its power. The Zulu were a strong military force, but the power of the Zulu kingdom was not only due to its military prowess. Shaka also used diplomacy to bring chiefdoms under his control. He recognised the value of European trade and maintained trade links with the Portuguese at Delagoa Bay (now Maputo). He also established relationships

29

with the British, who had set up a trading station at Port Natal (later known as Durban) in 1824. Shaka hoped to increase his access to European goods, including guns, through these traders.

Shaka's kingdom dominated the area between the Mkhuze and Thukela rivers in northern KwaZulu-Natal, although his influence extended beyond its borders to include places like Port Natal (Durban). Shaka's reign ended in 1828 when he was assassinated on the orders of his half-brother Dingane, who succeeded Shaka as king. After the defeat of his army by the Boers (Dutch settlers) at the Battle of Ncome River (Blood River) in 1838, Dingane fled north. He was pursued by the Boers, who had allied themselves with Dingane's brother Mpande. Dingane was defeated and Mpande became the new king.

By 1835 the Zulu kingdom was the most powerful state in the region. However, from the 1830s, the arrival of the Boers and the British saw the power of the Zulu kingdom diminish and it lost much land in the following years. Chapter 3 describes this process further.

The Sotho kingdom

The modern kingdom of Lesotho has its roots in the 1820s. Moshoeshoe became chief of the Bamokotedi in 1820. He expanded his chiefdom, partly by offering protection to refugees and vulnerable groups who sought refuge from the conflicts and disruptions of the time of troubles. By 1836 Moshoeshoe's kingdom had about 25 000 people and by 1848 it had 80 000. By 1853, after defeating the Tlokwa, he had 100 000 people as his subjects.

Moshoeshoe's kingdom was not a centralised state like the Zulu kingdom, and he did not use the northern Nguni *amabutho* system. Smaller chiefdoms that joined Moshoeshoe for protection were given a certain amount of independence. They could run their own affairs, provided they remained loyal to him.

Moshoeshoe used the *mafisa* system, which attracted many people to his kingdom. Poor men who joined his kingdom would become clients. They would be lent cattle if they did not have their own, and they were allowed to keep some of the offspring and build up their own herd. In return, they were expected to offer complete loyalty to the king.

Moshoeshoe is often remembered for his diplomatic skill. He made important alliances with kingdoms like the Pedi under Sekwati and he avoided confrontation as much as possible with powerful rivals. He sent gifts to Shaka and paid tribute to the Ngwane. However, he used force when necessary to ward off his enemies. He successfully defeated attacks by the Ngwane, Ndebele, Tlokwa and the Orange Free State Boers. Moshoeshoe also conducted cattle raids on the Thembu to the south so that he would have enough cattle for the *mafisa* system.

Moshoeshoe's state also developed relationships with the expanding Cape Colony and with the Boer trekkers. He valued the trade with the Cape, particularly in horses, blankets and guns. Moshoeshoe encouraged European missionaries to settle in his kingdom and often drew on their knowledge and advice in dealing with the Cape. However, his relationship with the missionaries deteriorated by the 1840s as he lost more and more land to the colonisers.

Conflict between the Boers and the Sotho kingdom increased from the 1840s onwards. The Basotho were originally settled in the Caledon River Valley but lost much of their land to the better-armed Boers; eventually they were limited to the mountainous region that Lesotho occupies today. In 1868, two years before his death, Moshoeshoe appealed to the British for protection from the Boers. The British took control of his country and by 1885 Basutoland (as it was called by the British) had become a British protectorate.

The Ndebele kingdom

Mzilikazi's Ndebele kingdom was Nguni in origin, and he used the *amabutho* system of the northern Nguni. However, it was very different from the Zulu and Sotho kingdoms in that he moved several times before he finally settled in present-day Matabeleland in Zimbabwe.

Mzilikazi was a chief of the Khumalo, part of the Ndwandwe kingdom. When the Zulu defeated the Ndwandwe in 1819, Mzilikazi moved towards the Vaal River. Here he raided the Vaal communities for cattle and food. Refugees from other conflicts joined his chiefdom. By 1823 his people had become known as the Matabele in Sotho and the Ndebele in the Nguni languages. Mzilikazi moved several times. His raiding and conquest affected many Sotho–Tswana communities. In 1823 he settled along the Vaal. In about 1827–8 he moved further north to the Magaliesberg and later, around 1833, he moved further west to the upper Marico River.

The Ndebele often raided far from their settlements, attacking the Venda kingdom in the Soutpansberg and the Sotho kingdom further south. He raided, conquered and defeated many prominent southern Tswana chiefdoms during the 1820s and 1830s. Defeated groups were either absorbed into his kingdom, or they broke apart and scattered.

By 1836 the Boers had moved onto the Highveld. They joined forces with the Griqua and Tswana-speaking Barolong and attacked the Ndebele. Defeated, the Ndebele fled north, and by 1840 had established themselves in south-western Zimbabwe. When Mzilikazi died in 1868, his son Lobengula became king and maintained Ndebele independence until 1893, when his army succumbed to the armed force of the British in their northward expansion. Matabeleland, as the area was then named, became a base for British colonial conquest of the territory that would soon become Rhodesia (and later Zimbabwe).

SOUTHERN TSWANA SOCIETIES

The southern Tswana societies occupied the area between the Vaal River and the Kalahari. Some of the major kingdoms in this area were the Ngwaketse, Hurutshe, Tlhaping, Rolong, Kwena and Fokeng. These groups had existed before the 1700s, but the end of the eighteenth century saw the growth of large towns, sometimes made up of more than a hundred homesteads, often inhabited by more than 10 000 people. By the first decades of the 1800s the Kwena capital of Molokwane had about 12 000 people, the Tlhaping's capital of Dithakong had about 15 000 and the Hurutshe's capital of Kaditshwene, had about 20 000 people. Kaditshwene was about the same size as Cape Town at the time.

While the power of the southern Tswana kingdoms was already declining by 1820, the arrival of Mzilikazi's Ndebele accelerated this process. He raided and conquered many prominent southern Tswana groups during the 1820s and 1830s. Defeated people were either absorbed into his kingdom or else they scattered. The Kwena and the Hurutshe were entirely defeated by Mzilikazi, and the city of Kaditshwene was completely destroyed and abandoned. The Rolong chiefdoms were among those who scattered after their defeat. This helps to explain why the Rolong were willing to ally with the Boers against Mzilikazi in the mid-1830s.

The Gaza kingdom

South African historians have neglected the Gaza kingdom because most of its territory lay in modern-day Mozambique. The Gaza kingdom was the biggest state in the region during the mid-1800s.

Soshangane broke away from the Ndwandwe kingdom after its defeat by the Zulu. He moved further north, settled around Delagoa Bay and established the Gaza kingdom there. His followers included both Nguni- and Tsonga-speakers; they became known as the Shangaan.

The Gaza kingdom rose to prominence during the 1820s and 1830s. Its strength was based on control of the ivory and slave trade at Delagoa Bay and Inhambane in Mozambique. Soshangane used *amabutho* to conduct raids. By 1837 the Gaza dominated the region from Delagoa Bay to as far north as the Zambezi. They were finally defeated by the Portuguese in 1895.

The Swazi kingdom

The Ndwandwe (also known as the Swazi) defeated the Ngwane under Sobhuza I in 1815. Sobhuza fled to present-day eSwatini, where he brought smaller groups of Tsonga, Nguni and Sotho under his influence. He avoided conflict with his more powerful neighbours. At first, while the state was small, the Swazi were well organised and made use of the mountainous terrain to their advantage.

Sobhuza managed to resist major attacks by the powerful Zulu and Gaza kingdoms. He was succeeded by his son, Mswati II, from whom eSwatini took its name. Both Sobhuza and Mswati extended Swazi territory. When Mswati died in 1868, his kingdom covered an area twice its present size and spread into Mozambique and present-day Mpumalanga.

The Pedi kingdom

In about 1800, Thulare established the Pedi kingdom on the Steelpoort River, near present-day Burgersfort. After a conflict with the Ndwandwe, the Pedi under Sekwati established a capital at the mountain stronghold of Phiring around 1828.

Sekwati has been compared to Moshoeshoe, who was his ally. He did not confront more powerful chiefdoms and used diplomacy successfully to maintain peaceful relations with many neighbours. Like Moshoeshoe, he allowed missionaries to settle in his territory. He also made use of the *mafisa* system, and this attracted many followers, particularly people seeking protection from the wars of the Swazi and Gaza. By 1837 Sekwati's kingdom extended from the Steelpoort River to the Olifants River.

In 1840, Sekwati allowed some Boers to settle on Pedi land, but he subsequently prevented further settlement despite three armed raids by the Boers in the 1850s and 1860s. The Bapedi were powerful partly because they built up a large stockpile of arms. These were obtained from trade with the Portuguese in Mozambique, and, after the discovery of diamonds at Kimberley, guns were bought back home by migrant Pedi mine workers (see Chapter 4).

In 1861, Sekwati was succeeded by his son Sekhukhune, who made peace with the Boers to avoid further conflict. However, when the British briefly took over the Transvaal in 1877 they were determined to destroy the Pedi kingdom. In late 1879, a British force armed with modern weapons attacked and defeated the Pedi forces. They captured Sekhukhune and effectively ended Pedi independence.

CAUSES OF CONFLICT DURING THE TIME OF TROUBLES

We know that political changes in southern Africa happened as a reaction to growing conflict and instability in the late 1700s and early 1800s. But what caused the growing conflict in the first place? Several factors contributed to the upheavals of the period.

Population growth and competition for resources

The populations of Sotho–Tswana and Nguni societies grew throughout the 1700s, but there was not enough space to expand their settlements. This was partly owing to the environmental limits of farming as well as the pressures placed on communities bordering on the expanding Cape Colony. Furthermore, by the early 1800s there were droughts across southern Africa. This led to food shortages and competition between chiefdoms for fertile land, cattle and food.

Trade

Chiefdoms competed for control over trade. For example, trade routes ran from the Portuguese colonial trading ports in the north-west (Angola) and on the east coast (Mozambique) to the upper Marico district. The Hurutshe had long controlled this trade but by the early 1800s their power had weakened and the Ngwaketse assumed control of the trade in that area. Another trade route ran south from the northern interior occupied by the southern Tswana chiefdoms to the Cape Colony. The Tlhaping gained control of trade with the Cape, and thus grew in power. A number of chiefdoms vied for control of the sources of trade goods like the copper mines in the Dwarsberg.

Nguni chiefdoms also competed with one another for trade with Delagoa Bay. Here

Europeans exchanged iron and cloth for ivory and cattle. The chiefdoms that controlled some of this trade, such as the Ndwandwe and Mthethwa, were able to increase their wealth and power as a result.

Colonial expansion and raiders

The expansion of the Cape Colony (see Chapter 3) caused many groups to lose their land and livestock and move away from the colonisers. The dispossessed people often came together to form new communities and identities, such as the Kora and the Griqua, and they settled beyond the borders of the colony.

The Kora were groups consisting of Khoe, San and Tswana, as well as runaway slaves from the Cape. The Griqua were made up of Khoe herders as well as people of 'mixed' descent from the Cape Colony. The Kora and Griqua often conducted trade between the southern Tswana and the Cape settlers, but some groups also took part in raiding.

Kora, Griqua and Boer raiders often attacked the Tswana and Sotho chiefdoms. The Kora and Griqua had access to guns and horses (which they obtained from the Cape) and they raided the Tswana for cattle and people, which they sold to the Cape Colony. Boer settlers also raided the southern Tswana territories, looking for San women and children to work on their farms, as well as livestock. This increased the instability of the area and fuelled further conflicts.

Chiefdoms also raided one another for cattle and women. Cattle obviously increased individual wealth, but cattle raids were also conducted so that chiefdoms did not have to sell their own cattle to traders along the Cape trade route and at Delagoa Bay.

The role of slavery and slave raids south of Delagoa Bay is rather contested. Evidence suggests that before the 1820s slave trading did not play a large role in Delagoa Bay. However, after 1820, as slave trading increased in Delagoa Bay, some larger states, like the Gaza, came to control the slave trade.

CONCLUSION

By the 1830s southern Africa's political landscape looked very different from what it had been a hundred years before. There were fewer scattered chiefdoms and many more centralised kingdoms. These had to deal not only with rival kingdoms, but also with a growing colonial presence. Some kingdoms managed to maintain their independence until the second half of the 1800s, when colonial power began to dominate the interior of southern Africa.

In the next chapter we will explore the beginning and spread of colonialism in South Africa.

CHAPTER 2: DISCUSSION QUESTIONS

1. What was the most interesting information you learned from this chapter? Did it change any ideas you had about South African history in the 1700s and 1800s?

2. The *mafisa* system is an example of a patronage system. Great wealth was needed for the system to continue, which resulted in cattle raids on weaker groups. It also demanded complete loyalty from clients. Yet, the system was valued by those who benefited from the loan of the cattle and were thus able to survive and possibly even prosper. Patronage systems are not seen as compatible with modern, democratic values. Should we reject patronage systems as outdated, corrupt systems that take advantage of vulnerable and desperate people, or should we value African patronage systems as humane welfare systems that help the poor and vulnerable?

3. It has been suggested that South Africa needs to look to an earlier date than 1913 for land restitution claims. The Sotho kingdom claimed areas of the Caledon River Valley, which forms part of the southern Free State today. They lost this land to Boer settlers. In the interest of land restitution, would Lesotho have a claim on this land in the Free State? Furthermore, would the descendants of the Ndebele, who eventually settled in Zimbabwe, have a claim on South African land on the Highveld or in KwaZulu-Natal? How far back should we look for legitimate land claims?

4. The break-up of the Ndwandwe led to a group under Soshangane settling in Mozambique. Another group under Zwangendaba (who was not mentioned in the chapter) fled further north and finally settled in Tanzania. The Sotho–Tswana and Nguni groups who settled in southern Africa were originally from east Africa. Should we abandon identities like 'South African', 'Zimbabwean' and 'Tanzanian' and embrace a more pan-African identity? What are the practical implications for border control? Would a pan-African identity help in fighting xenophobia?

CHAPTER 2: ADDITIONAL READINGS

Please note that there is very limited reliable information about the time of troubles, the *mfecane* or *difaqane*, available on the internet. Much of the information is either factually incorrect or relies on outdated theories. Reliable texts tend to be restricted to academic books and journal articles. For this reason, try to get hold of Giliomee and Mbenga's *New History of South Africa*, which is available at bookstores and in good libraries. It is written for the general public and has valuable maps and visuals that will help you to understand the period in greater depth.

Online readings

People of South Africa: Griqua (2011). *South African History Online*, 21 March 2011. http://www.sahistory.org.za/article/griqua.

Political Changes from 1750–1835. *South African History Online*, 24 November 2011, updated 8 May 2017. http://www.sahistory.org.za/topic/political-changes-1750-1835.

Seleti, Yonah (2004) State Formation in Nineteenth-Century South Africa. In *Migration, Land and Minerals in the Making of South Africa.* Turning Points in History Series, Book 3. Johannesburg: STE Publishers. http://www.sahistory.org.za/archive/chapter-1-state-formation-nineteenth-century-south-africa.

The Struggle over Land: Basotho Lose Out (n.d.). *South African History Online*. http://www.sahistory.org.za/archive/struggle-over-land-basotho-lose-out.

Online visual resources

https://he.palgrave.com/resources/CW%20resources%20(by%20Author)/S/Shillington/Maps/Map15_3.jpg. The map shows some of the chiefdoms and kingdoms in southern Africa in the 1700s.

http://huntershistoricalhome.weebly.com. The map shows the migration of various groups during the time of troubles.

Books

Giliomee, H. and B. Mbenga (eds) (2007) *New History of South Africa.* Cape Town: Tafelberg. (See Chapter 4: A Time of Trouble and Rapid Transformation)

Wright, John (2011) Turbulent Times: Political Transformations in the North and East, 1760s–1830s. In *The Cambridge History of South Africa*, Volume 1, *From Early Times to 1885,* edited by C. Hamilton, B. Mbenga and R. Ross. New York: Cambridge University Press.

Three

Colonial Expansion and African Resistance

Establishment and Expansion of the Cape Colony

The Dutch East India Company (or the VOC, its Dutch acronym)[7] set up a refreshment station at Table Bay in 1652 so that Dutch ships could obtain fresh fruit, vegetables and meat for the sailors on their way from Europe to the trading ports and Dutch colonies in Asia. The Dutch did not originally intend to establish a colony at the Cape. However, in 1657 nine VOC employees were released from their contracts and were granted private farms. This set a trend of expanding European settlement and colonialism in the Cape.

For the first fifty years the Dutch slowly entrenched themselves at the Cape. By the early 1700s the Cape Colony extended about eighty kilometres from the original trading fort in Cape Town. Expansion happened much faster during the 1700s, largely because of the movement of Dutch pastoralists known as trekboers. Unlike the wealthier Dutch settlers living in Cape Town and on the wheat and wine farms close by, the trekboers were poor European farmers who did not own farms, but who herded cattle and hunted for survival. In their search for grazing for their cattle, the trekboers often roamed beyond the established borders of the colony, and so claimed more and more land for European occupation. In this way, the growth of the colony was unplanned and happened much faster as the trekboers increased in numbers. By the late 1700s the Cape Colony extended about eight hundred kilometres from the original fort.

In 1795, during the Napoleonic Wars in Europe, the British took over the Cape from the Dutch; in 1803 the Dutch once again regained control. However, in 1806 the British took control of the Cape permanently and it became part of the British colonial empire.

---

7   VOC stands for the Vereenigde Oostindische Compagnie.

The changeover to British control brought important policy changes. For example, the British handled the frontier clashes with the Khoe and Xhosa very differently from the Dutch. Furthermore, the arrival of the British sparked the migration of Dutch-speakers into the interior of southern Africa in the 1830s, thereby expanding the colonial presence significantly throughout the region.

SLAVERY IN THE CAPE

Before we examine indigenous responses to colonial expansion, it is important to recognise the role played by slaves in the Cape Colony. A slave is a person who is treated as a slave-owner's private property. Slaves were treated as trade goods and could be bought and sold like cattle. Enslaved people had very few human rights. Their children were considered the property of the master too, and could be sold or given away without their parents' consent. Slaves were not equal to free citizens in the eyes of the law. They could receive brutal punishment from their masters or the government, particularly if they ran away.

Cape settlers used slaves for labour on their farms and in their homes. Slaves made up about half of the population of the Cape Colony. Between 1652 and 1808 about 63 000 slaves were transported to the colony from Asia, east Africa and Madagascar. Before the abolition of slavery, less than two per cent of slaves were freed during their lifetime. Wealthy settlers in towns and farmers closer to Cape Town relied mostly on slaves for their labour, while poorer farmers and trekboers employed impoverished Khoe.

Slaves from different parts of the world brought a variety of cultural influences to the Cape. Islam was introduced through the importation of Muslim slaves from Dutch Indonesia; other slaves also converted to Islam. The earliest Afrikaans texts are written in Arabic script.

In 1838, all slaves in the British Empire were freed. Unfortunately, freedom did not bring prosperity for many ex-slaves. They still suffered racial discrimination and often had to work for very low wages. The descendants of slaves, Khoe, San and 'mixed race' people would come to make up what was later known as the coloured community of the Cape.

KHOE AND SAN RESPONSES TO CAPE COLONIAL EXPANSION

As the Dutch settlement at the Cape expanded, the Khoe around Table Bay lost their grazing lands. Trading for cattle continued, but raiding and counter-raiding for cattle became common between the settlers and Khoe.

Khoe societies were not large, centralised farming societies. Nor were they united as one group. Nevertheless, the Khoe resisted Dutch expansion. The first Khoe–Dutch war took place in 1659 and lasted about a year. Neither side could claim a decisive victory. The Khoe kept the cattle they had raided, but accepted Dutch claims to their land. A second Khoe–Dutch war erupted in 1673 and lasted until 1677. After this war, Khoe societies began to weaken and the Dutch expanded further afield.

A smallpox epidemic hit the Cape in 1713. It killed many settlers and slaves, and it

Map of southern African in the 18th century. Source: History of Africa by Kevin Shillington. Published by Palgrave Macmillan Higher Education.

also killed many Khoe. As Khoe societies became weaker, more and more impoverished Khoe began working for Dutch farmers. Throughout the 1700s the working conditions and rights of the Khoe workers deteriorated.

The San were also affected by colonial expansion. As early as 1700 the San had resisted Dutch expansion into the interior around Tulbagh. Widespread San resistance to colonial expansion took place between 1770 and 1810 on the north-eastern frontier of the Cape Colony, contributing to the instability of the region. The San attacked frontier farms, causing some settlers to abandon their farms completely.

Colonial reaction to San resistance was harsh. Commandos – fighting groups made up of settlers and often including Khoe workers – attacked the San, killing men, women and children. The women and children were also often captured and used as virtual slave labour on the frontier farms.

Events like these caused new communities like the Griqua to emerge beyond the Cape frontier, where groups of displaced Khoe, San, 'mixed race' people and runaway slaves could merge into a community. Some San groups moved further north to escape the violence and instability, while some Khoe moved east and were absorbed by the southern Nguni.

THE COLONY'S EASTERN FRONTIER AND THE XHOSA

The Zuurveld is an area that stretches along the coast for about 150 kilometres between the Fish and Sundays rivers in the Eastern Cape. During the 1600s it was mainly occupied by the Gona, a Khoe group, as well as the Gqunukwebe, a group with some Khoe ancestry. By the 1700s the southern Nguni farmers, now also known as the Xhosa, had settled in the Zuurveld. By the 1770s, trekboers had expanded into the Zuurveld as well.

When the trekboers and the Xhosa first came in contact with each other in the Zuurveld, they managed to coexist. As Xhosa chiefdoms expanded, they had often absorbed groups such as the San, Khoe, Thembu and Bhaca. The Xhosa originally assumed that they would absorb the Dutch as well. This did not happen, and cattle-raiding and competition for grazing land increased between the Xhosa and the Dutch.

Farming societies like the Xhosa were organised differently from the hunter-gatherer and herding societies. They were not nomadic and could sustain larger populations. This meant that their resistance to the European settlers would be much more powerful than that offered by the Khoe or the San. The first frontier war between the settlers and the Xhosa broke out in 1779. Over the next hundred years another eight frontier wars were fought. The third frontier war (1799–1803) saw the Khoe and Xhosa unite to fight against colonial power. Many frontier farms were evacuated. The revolt ended when it was agreed that the Xhosa would remain in the Zuurveld. However, when the British took permanent control of the Cape in 1806, their policies regarding the frontier became more aggressive.

The conflict between the Xhosa and the British was very different from the earlier conflicts with the Dutch, and the scale of devastation was much larger. The British aimed to expel the Xhosa completely from the Zuurveld. They did so in 1812, killing many, including women and children, and destroying homesteads and fields. The British then set up military forts along the Fish River and strengthened the frontier even further by settling about 4 000 British settlers in the area in 1820.

The Xhosa kingdoms did not make up a strong, centralised, unified state like some of the northern Nguni kingdoms, and groups of Xhosa were often in conflict with one another. At times during the hundred years of the frontier wars some groups and chiefs remained neutral or sometimes worked in alliance with the colonists. The Mfengu developed a particularly strong alliance with the British, although this weakened as Britain gained greater control in the area and proved less in need of allies. Over time, the Mfengu lost trust in Britain's good faith as an ally.

The arrival of the British settlers in 1820 intensified the battle for land. They pressured the British government to take control of Xhosa land. The Xhosa resisted and the British authorities tried various ways to impose their control. The conflicts intensified in the 1840s and 1850s. By the late 1850s the Xhosa had lost much of their power and land. The ninth, and last, frontier war took place between 1877 and 1878. In 1894, the last independent chiefdom in the Eastern Cape, Pondoland, was finally annexed to the Cape Colony.

A detail from the Keiskamma tapestry, which was created by over 100 women from Hamburg and neighbouring villages in the Eastern Cape. It is 120 metres in length and depicts scenes from the history of South Africa, including pre-colonial history. It now hangs in the Parliament buildings in Cape Town. Source: Keiskamma Trust

COLONIAL EXPANSION AND RESISTANCE BEYOND THE CAPE COLONY

The changeover from Dutch to British colonial control in 1806 brought a new culture, language and many legal changes to Cape colonial society. Importantly, the British made slavery illegal in 1833. Some of the Dutch-speaking settlers resented this and other policies of the British. They chose to escape British control and set up independent republics in the interior of South Africa. The migration of these Boers (which literally means 'farmers') took place in the mid-to-late 1830s. Later, Afrikaner nationalists would name this migration the 'Great Trek', and those who took part were called Voortrekkers. Over a period of ten years about 15 000 trekkers, together with 5 000 servants, took part in the mass migration.

The Great Trek can be seen as the start of systematic white settlement in the interior of southern Africa, but it is important to realise that white dominance over the land and its people did not happen all at once. Originally, the trekkers settled on land with the permission of the local chief or king. Later, the Boers claimed permanent rights to the land.

For most African communities, the Boers were simply another group who were competing for land and cattle. In the same way that chiefs would ally with other chiefs to defeat their enemies, African leaders sometimes allied with the Boers, or the British, in order to defeat a common enemy. For example, Chief Moroka II of the Rolong allowed the Voortrekkers to retreat to Thaba Nchu after they were attacked by his enemy, Mzilikazi, in 1836. Together with the Griqua, the Rolong fought with the Boers against Mzilikazi in 1837. However, while the Boers were willing to draw up treaties and trade with African groups, they saw themselves as racially superior and the Boer republics that were set up in the 1850s privileged white people in their laws and policies.

The Voortrekkers were not united, and various groups of Voortrekkers settled in different areas. The Boers also had to contend with the British, who were quick to assert control over the Voortrekkers if they believed it was in Britain's interest. Boer access to guns gave them an advantage over the African chiefdoms, but for many years they were unable to defeat the more powerful kingdoms, which remained independent until the late 1800s.

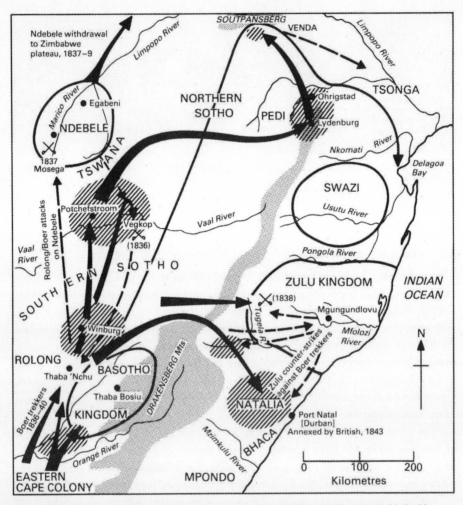

Boer expansion into the interior. Source: History of Africa by Kevin Shillington. Published by Palgrave Macmillan Higher Education.

THE SOTHO KINGDOM AND THE ORANGE FREE STATE

By the 1830s, the land across the Orange River and in the Caledon River Valley was jointly inhabited by the Griqua, Moshoeshoe's Sotho kingdom, the Tlokwa and the Rolong, as well as some trekboers. The Voortrekkers who settled in the area, which became known as Transorangia in the 1830s, rented farms from the Griqua or were granted permission to settle on the land by Moshoeshoe. However, whereas Moshoeshoe saw the use of the land as temporary, the settlers later claimed he had given it to them permanently.

In 1848 the British annexed all the land between the Orange and Vaal rivers. They drew up the boundaries of the new territory, called the Orange River Sovereignty, and as a result the Sotho lost land they had originally occupied. Moshoeshoe decided to maintain his diplomatic relations with the British and accepted the new boundaries, but

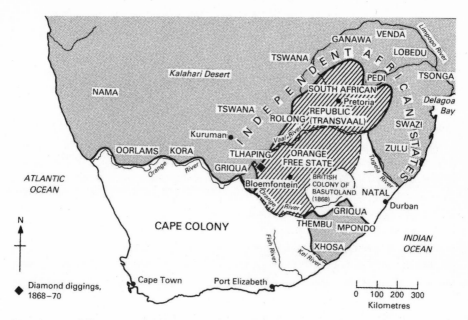

Map showing different states in South Africa circa 1870. Source: History of Africa by Kevin Shillington. Published by Palgrave Macmillan Higher Education.

not everybody in the kingdom agreed. Conflict broke out and the British were defeated both at the Battle of Viervoet in 1851 and at the Battle of Berea in 1852. However, Moshoeshoe made peace with the British, preferring to stay on good terms with them. The Sotho defeat of the British played a role in the British withdrawing from the Orange River Sovereignty and granting the Boers self-government in 1854. The new Boer republic was called the Orange Free State.

Tensions increased between the Sotho kingdom and the Orange Free State throughout the 1850s. By the mid-1860s the two groups were at war, which ended with the Treaty of Thaba Bosiu in 1866. According to this treaty, the Sotho lost two-thirds of their arable land. However, it was difficult for the Orange Free State government to find Boer settlers willing to settle so close to the Sotho, and the Sotho started moving back again. This sparked yet more conflict in 1867 and 1868.

Moshoeshoe decided to appeal to the British for protection against the Boers in 1868 to prevent even further land losses. Britain agreed and the Sotho kingdom came under British control. The boundaries of the kingdom were set and remained in place until 1966, when it gained its independence and became the modern country of Lesotho.

THE ZULU KINGDOM AND NATAL

The Zulu kingdom responded to colonial expansion differently from the Sotho kingdom. In 1837 a party of Boers under the leadership of Pieter Retief moved into modern-day KwaZulu-Natal. They tried to get permission from Dingane to settle in the area, but Dingane was aware of the land dispossession and wars experienced by the Xhosa chiefdoms further south and felt threatened by the Boers.

In 1838 Dingane killed Retief and attacked a camp of Boers and their servants. The Voortrekkers responded by sending a force against the Zulu in December 1838. Dingane attacked the trekkers on the banks of the Ncome River, where he was badly defeated. After Dingane's defeat his half-brother Mpande, together with 17 000 followers, broke away. Mpande made an alliance with the Voortrekkers and went to war against Dingane. Dingane was defeated and Mpande ruled the Zulu until 1872 when his son Cetshwayo succeeded him. In 1839, the trekkers had established the independent republic of Natalia, incorporating the southern regions of Zululand. In 1843, the British annexed the republic and it became the British colony of Natal.

Although the Zulu kingdom had lost a significant amount of power and land to the colonisers, it maintained its independence until the late 1870s. In January 1879, the British set out to conquer it. However, they had underestimated Zulu military power; the army of King Cetshwayo, armed mainly with assegais, spears and shields, defeated a British force equipped with modern firearms at the Battle of Isandlwana. However, six months later the British army launched another military expedition to Cetshwayo's capital at Ulundi, where they finally defeated the Zulu force. By August 1879 Cetshwayo was captured and exiled to Cape Town, bringing a final end to the war. Zululand was divided into thirteen chiefdoms by the British, who also imposed taxes on the Zulu.

INDIANS IN NATAL

There were various reasons for the Anglo-Zulu War. One was that settler farmers resented the fact that they could not draw on Zulu men to work on their farms. This is why Indians first came to Natal in 1860. Impoverished Indian labourers agreed to exploitative work contracts (called indentures) that bound them to work for white Natal farmers for up to ten years. Thereafter they could either return to India or remain in Natal. About half chose to stay. Between 1860 and 1912 about 150 000 Indian labourers travelled to Natal to work on the farms there. By the 1870s wealthier Indians also began to travel to Natal on their own initiative in search of new economic opportunities.

THE PEDI AND THE SOUTH AFRICAN REPUBLIC

After the Boers defeated Mzilikazi in 1837, they claimed the land in the region as their own by right of conquest, and demanded tribute from African groups living on the land. The region north of the Vaal, known as the South African Republic (the ZAR or the Transvaal), was recognised as an independent Boer republic by the British in 1852 according to the Sand River Convention.

The ZAR was not strong enough to control all the land it claimed. The Boers had to make treaties and agreements with the more powerful kingdoms to the north and east, such as those of the Swazi and Pedi. The Boers in the ZAR resented the existence of the independent Pedi state, which they could not defeat. When the British annexed the ZAR in 1877, they finally defeated the Pedi kingdom in December 1879 with the help of the Swazi (a rival of the Pedi).

THE BRITISH CONSOLIDATE CONTROL

The last war of armed resistance to colonial occupation was conducted by the Venda people under King Mphephu, who were defeated by the Boers in 1898. Across southern Africa, the entire process of conquest and tenacious resistance had taken 246 years. This was the inevitable result of a clash between agrarian societies armed with only rudimentary weapons and the world's most industrialised power. It mirrored Europe's subjugation of much of the rest of the world in the same era.

By 1899 the territory of today's South Africa was divided into two British colonies (the Cape and Natal) and two Boer republics (the Orange Free State and ZAR). The discovery of gold in the ZAR and Britain's desire to control the goldfields would lead to the Anglo-Boer War of 1899–1902. The British victory over the Boer republics would complete British territorial control of South Africa, and lead to the Union of South Africa in 1910. This is the subject of the next two chapters.

CHAPTER 3: DISCUSSION QUESTIONS

1. What was the most interesting information you learned in this chapter? Provide a reason for your answer.

2. Various African kingdoms responded differently to colonial expansion. Consider the responses of the Sotho and Zulu kingdoms. Why do you think their responses were different? What were the short-term and long-term effects of these responses?

3. The actions of our ancestors can make us very uncomfortable and may result in present-day emotions such as anger, guilt, shame or frustration. They may also lay the foundations for stereotypes that are projected onto groups as a whole. The history of colonial expansion in South Africa can be an emotional topic. How should we confront this history? How should we react, as individuals and as a society, to the actions of generations who came before us?

4. If you managed to read some of the additional readings, you will notice that the names of modern towns are often based on the names of British colonial officials, such as Harrismith and Grahamstown, or those of Voortrekkers, such as Pietermaritzburg or Pretoria. Is it time for us to give up the debate

on name changes and focus our energy and resources on more practical issues? Or is it important that, as a society, we pursue name changes as we come to terms with South Africa's heritage?

CHAPTER 3: ADDITIONAL READINGS

Online readings

Anglo-Zulu Wars, 1879–1896 (2011). *South African History Online*, 21 March 2011. http://www.sahistory.org.za/article/anglo-zulu-wars-1879-1896.

Bhebhe, N. (1989) The British, Boers and Africans in South Africa, 1850–80. In *Africa in the Nineteenth Century until the 1880s*, edited by J.F. Ade Ajayi. UNESCO General History of Africa Series, Volume VI. London, Berkeley, CA, and Paris: Heinemann, University of California Press, and UNESCO. http://unesdoc.unesco.org/images/0018/001842/184295eo.pdf.

Bonner, Philip (1983) *Kings, Commoners and Concessionaries: The Evolution and Dissolution of the Nineteenth-Century Swazi State*. African Studies Series 31. Cambridge: Cambridge University Press. http://www.sahistory.org.za/sites/default/files/file%20uploads%20/philip_bonner_kings_commoners_and_concessionairbook4you.pdf.

Conquest of the Eastern Cape, 1779–1878 (2011). *South African History Online*, 21 March 2011. http://www.sahistory.org.za/article/conquest-eastern-cape-1779-1878.

Delius, Peter (1984) The Imperial Factor and the Destruction of Pedi Independence. In *The Land Belongs to Us: The Pedi Polity, the Boers, and the British in the Nineteenth-Century Transvaal*. Perspectives on Southern Africa 35. Berkeley, CA: University of California Press. http://www.ucpress.edu/op.php?isbn=9780520051485.

Great Trek, 1835–1846 (2011). *South African History Online*, 21 March 2011. http://www.sahistory.org.za/article/great-trek-1835-1846.

The Impact and Limitations of Colonialism (2004) Turning Points in History Series, Book 2. Johannesburg: STE Publishers. http://www.sahistory.org.za/archive/book-2-impact-and-limitations-colonialism-commissioned-department-education.

The Indian Community in SA (n.d.). O'Malley Archive, hosted by the Nelson Mandela Centre of Memory. https://www.nelsonmandela.org/omalley/index.php/site/q/03lv02424/04lv03370/05lv03414.htm.

The Struggle over Land: Basotho Lose Out (n.d.). *South African History Online*. http://www.sahistory.org.za/archive/struggle-over-land-basotho-lose-out.

Webb, Denver A. (2015) Kraals of Guns: Fortifications in the Wars of Resistance and Dispossession in the Eastern Cape, 1780–1895. Alice: University of Fort

Hare. http://v1.sahistory.org.za/pages/library-resources/articles_papers/forts_of_ec/menu.htm.

Online visual resources

This link will take you to a website with free downloadable maps: https://he.palgrave.com/companion/Shillington-History-Of-Africa/resources/. Click on the 'Maps' icon and look at the following maps. Individual URLs have also been provided for the different maps:

- 15.1 South-western Cape, 1650–1700: https://he.palgrave.com/resources/CW%20resources%20(by%20Author)/S/Shillington/Maps/Map15_1.jpg.
- 15.2 The expansion of Boer settlement in the eighteenth century: https://he.palgrave.com/resources/CW%20resources%20(by%20Author)/S/Shillington/Maps/Map15_2.jpg.
- 15.3 Southern Africa in the eighteenth century: https://he.palgrave.com/resources/CW%20resources%20(by%20Author)/S/Shillington/Maps/Map15_3.jpg.
- 18.2 The Cape Colony and Xhosa resistance, 1811–1836: https://he.palgrave.com/resources/CW%20resources%20(by%20Author)/S/Shillington/Maps/Map18_2.jpg.
- 18.3 The Boer Trek and African resistance, 1836–1840: https://he.palgrave.com/resources/CW%20resources%20(by%20Author)/S/Shillington/Maps/Map18_3.jpg.
- 18.4 Southern Africa in 1870: https://he.palgrave.com/resources/CW%20resources%20(by%20Author)/S/Shillington/Maps/Map18_4.jpg.

Books

For information about the Cape Colony, slavery and the Cape frontier wars, read Chapters 2 and 3 in *New History of South Africa*, edited by H. Giliomee and B. Mbenga, Cape Town: Tafelberg, 2007.

For information about colonial expansion into the interior, read Chapters 5 and 6 in *New History of South Africa*, edited by H. Giliomee and B. Mbenga, Cape Town: Tafelberg, 2007.

For information about land struggles, read Chapter 7 in T.R.H. Davenport and C. Saunders, *South Africa: A Modern History*, 5th edn, London: Palgrave Macmillan, 2000.

Four

Diamonds, Gold and the Reshaping of South Africa

In 1867 the first diamond was found in Griqualand West (the area around present-day Kimberley). Before long, other diamonds were discovered in the area and it became apparent that this was part of a very large deposit of diamonds. Almost twenty years later, gold was discovered on a farm called Langlaagte, now part of Johannesburg. Other deposits were also discovered along the length of the Witwatersrand, running east and west from Johannesburg. Gold was the basis of the most of the world's monetary systems and was also highly prized in the form of jewellery. Developments arising from the diamond and gold discoveries were to lead to a truly radical transformation of South Africa, in respect of its social, political and cultural life, as well as its economy.

As soon as it became clear that the diamond-bearing territory would bring enormous wealth to those who controlled it, a dispute developed between various parties. Aside from the Griquas, who were the main occupants of the area, it was claimed by the Orange Free State and the South African Republic (the ZAR,[8] or the Transvaal). Some of the northern parts of the area were regarded by Tswana-speaking and Khoe chiefs as theirs. The British authorities, who had made no claim to the area, managed to have the Lieutenant Governor of Natal Colony appointed to arbitrate in the dispute. In 1871, he awarded the entire territory to the Griqua chief Nicholas Waterboer, although the Orange Free State did not accept the decision. Later in the same year, the British annexed the area as the colony of Griqualand West, supposedly to protect the rights of the Griquas. It was later incorporated into the Cape Colony.

---

8   ZAR is derived from the Dutch name for the South African Republic: the Zuid-Afrikaansche Republiek.

The Witwatersrand was already an accepted part of the South Africa Republic and so sovereignty was not immediately an issue. However, Britain later established its authority here in 1902 after victory in the Anglo-Boer War. Britain was keen to establish control of these territories not only for economic reasons, but also for reasons related to its international political strategy; at the time, European powers were involved in an intense contest to acquire territory on the African continent. More will be said about this in Chapter 5.

CONTROL OF THE MINING INDUSTRY

The discovery of diamonds and gold attracted large numbers of people in search of their fortunes – or, at least, for a way to improve their lives. The newcomers, black and white, came from many parts of southern Africa as well as from countries such as Britain, Australia, Canada and the United States. In Kimberley they became small-scale diamond diggers, prospectors, engineers, diamond traders, shopkeepers, labourers and canteen keepers.

Eventual ownership of the mining industry was partly determined by the geological nature of the mineral deposits. In Griqualand West, the bulk of the diamonds were found in pipes of blue ground (later known as Kimberlite), which had a fairly small surface area and ran deep into the earth. Diggers generally owned claims to small plots of land – some as small as three square metres – where the Kimberlite pipes reached the surface. Mining on such plots rapidly became impractical as the mines became deeper. Periodic slumps in the price of diamonds forced some diggers to sell their claims to more successful miners. The result was the emergence of larger companies who could afford expensive machinery and employed large numbers of workers. As more and more diamonds were produced, prices were driven down. Competition between the diamond producers was fierce, and eventually in 1890 one large company emerged with a monopoly. This was De Beers Consolidated Mines; its chairman, Cecil John Rhodes, had the backing of the Anglo-French Rothschild Bank.

On the Witwatersrand, the gold deposits were the largest ever discovered in the world. However, the average gold content of each ton of earth was very small and most of the gold lay deep beneath the surface. This meant that the mining process required expensive machinery and expensive methods of extracting the ore from the ground. The result was that, from the start, gold mining was controlled by companies with large amounts of capital. Much of the capital invested in the first mines came from Rhodes and others who had become rich in the diamond industry, as well as from wealthy individuals and financial institutions in Britain, France, Germany and the United States. The owners of the mines accumulated vast wealth. They lived in luxury in grand mansions erected in the suburbs to the north of Johannesburg, particularly in Parktown. They became known as the Randlords and exercised great power and influence over the economic and political life of South Africa and its neighbouring territories.

Cecil John Rhodes

Non-mining Activities

The wealth created by mining stimulated other economic activities. In addition to mine owners and workers, the new towns filled up with a range of people: hotel, restaurant and bar operators, traders, workers in small factories and workshops, transport riders, commercial farmers, bakers and other food processors, professionals and tradespeople, and many others. The business owners were mainly, but not entirely, white; black people were generally excluded from business ownership either by law or by racist practices and by the fact that many were migrants who worked on the mines for a few months at a time and then left again.[9] Most businesses employed white workers, many of whom made their permanent homes in the towns and cities that sprung up in the interior. Virtually all businesses and all white homes employed black workers – usually at wage levels that left their living standards well below those of most whites.

Workers in the Mines

Black mine workers

In line with the existing monetary system (the gold standard), the price of gold was fixed. In addition, the mining capitalists could do nothing to influence the prices of imported machinery and supplies. So the most important way for them to maintain or increase

---

9   A small number of Indians, especially in Natal Colony, did manage to open successful businesses although they also suffered discrimination from white suppliers and customers.

their profit levels in a labour-intensive industry was to keep wages as low as possible. This mainly applied to the wages of black people,[10] who constituted the vast majority of the workforce. (The position of white workers is discussed separately below).

The mine owners' economic power gave them strong political influence. Moreover, the bulk of the ZAR government's supporters – the white landowners – benefited from the expanding mining industry, which provided a large market for produce from the farms. The government was thus willing to assist the mine owners to obtain cheap labour by providing anti-worker legislation, infrastructure and policing.

A system of migrant labour became entrenched for African workers in the mining industry, as they left their rural homes for periods of several months to work on the mines. This made it possible for them to earn money to buy consumer goods, farming implements or guns (for hunting or defence) without abandoning their ties with their old ways of life. The mine owners soon discovered that the migrant labour system had big advantages for them, and they became committed to entrenching it as the norm in the industry. Migrant labour was cheaper for employers than settled labour. In the workers' rural homes, women and children remained active, growing crops and raising livestock, and so contributed to the family income. If they lived in the towns, they would most likely be dependent on the income of the male mine workers and would be unable to contribute to sustaining the family. By insisting on migrant labour, the mines were able to keep their wages to a minimum.

In order to establish tight control over the workers and keep the cost of workers' food and accommodation as low as possible (and thus allow the mines to keep their wages correspondingly low), the compound system of accommodation was developed, first in Kimberley and then on the gold mines in the Transvaal. Under this system workers were confined to the compounds for the entire period of their contracts. Living conditions were hard, with up to twenty men sharing a room. In general, compound life was unpleasant and unhygienic and placed great psychological stress on workers. They had no privacy and found it difficult to adjust to the abnormal life they led, far from family and friends.

One problem that the mine owners encountered was that if wages were too low, workers would stay away from the mines or leave before their contracts were finished. The owners therefore adopted strategies to persuade or, more frequently, coerce Africans to become low-paid migrant workers.

The Chamber of Mines, set up to represent the interests of all the mine owners, created special recruitment organisations – the Native Recruiting Association (NRA) and the Witwatersrand Native Labour Association (WNLA) – to recruit labourers from all parts of South Africa and its neighbouring territories as far north as Malawi and Zambia. The most important source of mine labour was Mozambique.

Recruitment alone was not enough to persuade young men to leave their homes and go to the mines and towns as low-paid workers. Consequently, more coercive methods were used with the cooperation of the colonial governments. One of the most

---

10 The overwhelming majority were Africans from Mozambique, Lesotho and the Eastern Cape. A small number of coloured workers were also employed by the mines.

important of these was taxation. Most Africans still lived off the land and participated only marginally in the money economy. Governments began to impose taxes to force them to become wage workers so as to earn the money to pay these obligations. For example, a tax on each hut in the rural settlements (the so-called hut tax) was introduced first in Lesotho in 1870 and then in various parts of South Africa. The average worker had to work for about three months in order to pay the tax for himself and his family. After the Anglo-Boer War, the British colonial administration in the Transvaal imposed a poll tax of two pounds (£2) on each adult African male as well as on his second and each additional wife. These and other forms of taxation remained in place after the Union of South Africa was formed in 1910.

Another factor pressuring rural Africans to become wage workers was their growing inability to make a decent living out of farming. The whole process of foreign conquest had gradually deprived Africans of most of their land over more than two centuries. As land was seized, it was mainly transferred into the ownership of individual white farmers. While the process of colonial conquest continued, new means of dispossession were developed in the late nineteenth and early twentieth centuries. By this time, many Africans lived on white-owned farms as low-paid farm workers or labour tenants. Others – cash tenants – rented land from white landowners or became sharecroppers who gave part of their crop to the owner. Many cash tenants and sharecroppers sold their produce in urban markets and contributed to agricultural exports; they enjoyed a much higher standard of living than wage workers or labour tenants. These arrangements were opposed by the white farmers, especially the wealthier ones. As a result of their pressure – and that of the mining companies – the Union government passed the Natives Land Act in 1913. This set aside less than 7.5 per cent of the country's land as 'native reserves' – areas reserved for African occupation.[11] This severely restricted Africans' ownership and use of agricultural land outside the reserves. The Land Act and its consequences are examined more fully in Chapter 7.

After the mineral discoveries, pass laws were introduced to control the movement of workers. A pass was a document allowing the bearer to be present in a particular area or to move from one area to another. Passes were meant to control workers' movements for various purposes: to prevent workers 'deserting' from the mines before their contracts expired; to channel them to areas with labour shortages; and to put them at a disadvantage in their relations with their employers.

White mine workers

Aside from the large number of blacks, the mines also employed a smaller, but still sizeable, number of white workers. Because of the difficulty involved in mining gold so deep underground, skilled as well as unskilled workers were needed. Some miners, both black and white, had learned mining skills in Kimberley, but there were not enough of them. Most skilled workers thus came from the tin, coal and gold mines of Britain

---

11 These areas coincided largely with those already set aside by the pre-Union colonial governments in the Cape and Natal.

Underground miners pose with an early drilling machine. Source: UWC Robben Island Mayibuye Archive

and Australia. Because their skills were in short supply, they could demand fairly high wages. Many had belonged to trade unions in their home countries and soon organised themselves into strong unions in South Africa.

To defend the interests of skilled white workers, these unions were prepared to take militant action, including strikes. One of their greatest fears was that African workers would learn their skills and replace them at lower rates of pay. As a result and because they shared the racist prejudices of most other whites in the colonies, the South African working class remained divided along colour lines. There were, however, a small number of white workers who came to South Africa with socialist ideas and helped to develop trade unions for both white and black workers. They were instrumental in establishing socialist organisations, in particularly the Communist Party of South Africa, which was later to play an important role in the national liberation and working-class movements.

HOW THE MINERAL REVOLUTION CHANGED SOUTH AFRICA

The mines, their owners and their political allies did not introduce racial inequality or racial oppression into South Africa – colonisation and the colonial governance systems had long since done that. However, the mining industry rearranged the racist social order and provided it with institutions that met the needs of an industrial society that was thoroughly unequal, racist and repressive.

The growth of new towns in the mining areas set South Africa on the path to becoming a predominantly urban society, where power and wealth resided mostly in the

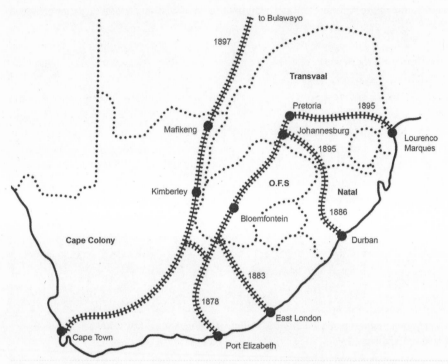

South Africa's railways in the 1890s. Railways revolutionised South Africa's transport and communications.

cities and towns. However, although the urban population did grow quickly, it would take almost a century before urban residents outnumbered those of the rural areas, largely because the migrant labour system continued to provide rural-based workers to the urban areas.

The cheap labour system became entrenched beyond the mining industry – in manufacturing, commerce and domestic service. In the beginning, most non-mining workers were also migrants although some settled more permanently in the towns. The pattern of a racially divided labour force was reinforced by the migrant labour system, the pass laws and the job reservation laws; these are examined in future chapters. The rapidly emerging pattern of racially separate living areas added to the oppression of black people.

The population of the towns provided a vast market and stimulated the growth of industries producing consumer goods such as clothing, leather, food and liquor, as well as printing and construction. The mining industry also stimulated growth in the production of specific goods that it required, such as explosives, machinery and tools. While growing steadily, manufacturing remained for decades a rather small sector of the South African economy compared with mining and agriculture.

Non-urban economic development was also affected by the mining industry. The East Rand coal deposits were developed to provide fuel for the gold mines, and forestry expanded significantly to grow the timber that was required for props in the mines. More important was the stimulus that the growth of towns gave to agriculture, as they provided an increasingly large market for produce such as maize, wheat, sugar and fruit. At first many African farmers were able to take advantage of the opportunities for commercial agriculture, but these were soon closed to them through legal prohibitions, including the Natives Land Act of 1913 (see Chapter 7).

The mines stimulated the development of railways to link the mining areas with the port cities of Cape Town, Durban, Port Elizabeth, East London and Lourenco Marques (Maputo). The railways made possible the growth of imports and exports of various kinds, opened up markets for agricultural produce, and made personal transport faster and more convenient. New roads were also built and old ones improved.

Overall, the mineral revolution diminished the cultural and social distance between South Africa and rest of the world. It transformed the country from a relatively isolated agricultural society to a country well on its way to becoming a modern industrial economy with the potential to provide a decent life for all, a promise that sadly has not been fulfilled to this day.

CHAPTER 4: DISCUSSION QUESTIONS

1. Do you think South Africa would be very different today if gold and diamonds had never been discovered? If so, in what ways would it be different?

2. People from other African countries have travelled to work in the South African mines and other industries for over a century. Discuss what impact you think this has had on the South African economy and to what extent it has affected politics, trade unionism and culture in South Africa. How do you think migrant labour going to South Africa affected the neighbouring countries from which the workers came?

3. Many workers also came to South Africa from non-African countries, especially Britain. They also worked on the mines and in various other industries. Why do you think they came here? What impact did this have on South African society?

4. Since the beginning of the mineral revolution, South Africa has had a racially divided working class with regard to wages, organisation, and relations with employers and government. Even though this division has become less rigid since 1994, it is still characteristic of the South African workforce in mining and many other industries. What were the main reasons for the development of racial divisions among workers, and why do you think they have persisted into the democratic era?

5. Many migrant mine workers came from rural areas of South Africa. What do you think the effect was on rural life, including the lives of mine workers' families?

Chapter 4: Additional Readings

Online readings

Callinicos, Luli (1987) *Gold and Workers.* Johannesburg: Ravan Press. http://www.sahistory.org.za/archive/gold-and-workers-1886-1924-luli-callinicos.

First, Ruth (circa 1960) The Gold of Migrant Labour. http://www.sahistory.org.za/sites/default/files/DC/asapr61.3/asapr61.3.pdf.

McKenna, A. (2011) *The History of Southern Africa.* New York: Britannica Educational Publishing. (Chapter 2, especially the section on Minerals and the Scramble for Southern Africa, pp. 39–43). http://www.sahistory.org.za/sites/default/files/file%20uploads%20/amy_mckenna_editor_the_history_of_southern_afrbook4you.pdf.

Migration, Land and Minerals in the Making of South Africa (2004) Turning Points in History Series, Book 3. Johannesburg: STE Publishers. (Chapters 2 and 3). https://www.sahistory.org.za/archive/book-3-migration-land-and-minerals-making-south-africa-commissioned-department-education.

Pampallis, John (1991) *Foundations of the New South Africa.* Cape Town: Maskew Miller Longman. (Chapter 2). https://www.sahistory.org.za/sites/default/files/file%20uploads%20/foundation_of_the_new_south_africa_original_final.pdf.

Potenza, Emilia (1996) All That Glitters: The Glitter of Gold. In *All That Glitters: An Integrated Approach to South African History*, edited by E. Potenza, R. Versfeld and P. Delius. Cape Town: Maskew Miller Longman. https://www.sahistory.org.za/archive/all-glitters-glitter-gold-emilia-potenza.

Simons, Jack and Ray Simons (1983) *Class and Colour in South Africa, 1850–1950.* London: International Defence and Aid Fund. (Chapter 3). https://www.sahistory.org.za/sites/default/files/file%20uploads%20/class_and_colour_-_harold_jack_simons_r.e._simons.pdf.

Books

Beinart, W. (2001) *Twentieth Century South Africa.* Oxford: Oxford University Press.

Morris, M. (2004) *Every Step of the Way: The Journey to Freedom in South Africa.* Cape Town: HSRC Press. (Chapter 6)

Giliomee, H. and B. Mbenga (eds) (2007) *New History of South Africa.* Cape Town: Tafelberg. (Chapter 8: The Story of Gold)

Richards, P. and J.J. Van-Helten (1980) The Gold Mining Industry in the Transvaal 1886-99. In *The South African War: The Anglo-Boer War, 1899–1902,* edited by P. Warwick. London: Trewin Copplestone Books.

Thompson, L. (1990) *A History of South Africa.* New Haven: Yale University Press. (Chapter 4, especially the section on Diamonds, Gold and the Mining Cities)

Worden, N. (2012) *The Making of Modern South Africa: Conquest, Apartheid, Democracy.* Hoboken, NJ: Wiley-Blackwell. (Chapter 3)

Five

Anglo-Boer Relations to 1910: War and Union

GROWING TENSIONS

From the time that Britain captured the Cape Colony from Holland in 1806, relations between the British administration and the Dutch-speaking farmers (known to themselves and others as Boers) were strained. During the late 1830s thousands of so-called Voortrekkers, accompanied by their servants, left the Cape because of their dissatisfaction with British rule in general and the abolition of slavery in particular. In what came to be known as the Great Trek, they journeyed into the interior of South Africa where they fought several wars in which their superior weapons helped them to dispossess African people of much of their land and cattle. They settled on the land, dividing it into large farms owned by individual families. (This process is described in more detail in Chapter 3.) Most of the indigenous Africans who remained in the conquered areas became labourers or tenants on the settlers' farms. The Boers established two republics – the Orange Free State and the South African Republic (often referred to as the Transvaal). Both republics acted oppressively towards the indigenous populations. The constitution of the Transvaal, for example, stated that there was 'no equality in church or state' between white and black people.

From the time of the Great Trek, the Boers had gradually started to develop an identity and understanding of themselves as a separate nation or people (*volk*). This was based on the evolving Afrikaans language (as a distinct language rather than just a dialect of Dutch) and the Christianity of the Dutch Reformed churches. They found religious justification for their belief in white racial superiority and the divinely ordained role of Afrikaners in Africa. The Boers (or Afrikaners) saw the British as a hostile force that had to be resisted. Afrikaner nationalism would grow into a strong influence shaping the two Boer republics and would be a major factor in the history of twentieth-century South Africa.

Much of today's KwaZulu-Natal was brought under British rule in 1843 and Boer influence in much of that area was consequently limited. While much of the land in the colony of Natal was settled by white farmers, the area north of the Thukela River remained under the control of the Zulu kings until the conquest of the Zulu kingdom in 1879. By that time most of present-day South Africa had been conquered by either the Boers or the British.

The two Boer republics were recognised by Britain in the 1850s. However, in 1877 Britain decided to annex the Transvaal; this was part of a British plan to create a federation of South African states. But the annexation was resisted by the Transvaal Boers, who rose up in arms against Britain in 1880. After a short war (sometimes referred to as the First Anglo-Boer War), Britain was forced to recognise the independence of the Transvaal once again, but imposed certain conditions that limited the Transvaal's control over foreign policy. Britain was unwilling to devote resources to a larger military effort because it felt that there was not enough at stake.

This attitude did not last. The development of gold mining from the mid-1880s resulted in growing strains between the Transvaal and Britain. The Transvaal's new-found wealth made it more determined to resist British influence over its affairs. Britain, on the other hand, became more interested in extending its power over the affairs of the Transvaal. The resulting tensions would reach boiling point with the outbreak of the second Anglo-Boer War[12] in 1899.

Towards War

Most of the money invested in the gold mines and other businesses on the Witwatersrand initially came from Britain or from British capitalists who had made their fortunes on the diamond fields around Kimberley. The Transvaal government, led by Paul Kruger, tried with some success to attract more investment from various European countries, especially France and Germany. The most important investments involved the Netherlands–South African Railway Company and the German–Swedish company Nobel, which produced dynamite, an essential product for the mining industry. These companies were granted legal monopolies to operate in the Transvaal, resulting in increased mining costs, which led to fierce protests from the mine owners. They also complained about Kruger's

---

12 In recent years it has become common among many in South Africa to refer to this second Anglo-Boer War as the South African War in recognition of the fact that many of the participants were black and neither British nor Boer. The terms South African War or Boer War have long been used by many British writers and the British media. We have decided here to use the term Anglo-Boer War. The British and the Boers were the main protagonists and the war was fought largely to sort out differences between them. Moreover, although black people participated on both sides and suffered greatly, whether they were participants or civilians, victory was unlikely to benefit them. Indeed it did not, even for those who supported the winning (British) side.

customs policy, which they claimed had the effect of pushing up the price of imports unreasonably. In addition, they accused the government of not doing enough to help them recruit and control African workers.

For these and other reasons, powerful mine owners and their financial backers in Britain were eager to overthrow the Kruger government and replace it with a British administration, which they believed would look after their interests. Britain's ambitions were also being fuelled at the time by fierce competition with other European countries to acquire colonies in Africa – the so-called Scramble for Africa. Britain feared that as the Transvaal became richer, it would grow to dominate South Africa economically and politically, and would align itself with Britain's rivals, especially Germany, which had already annexed Namibia in 1884.

With the opening of the gold mines and the development of towns and cities, thousands of white people from other parts of South Africa and abroad came to the Witwatersrand. Most were English-speaking and of British origin. The mining capitalists used their wealth and their control of the press to exercise a strong influence over these new settlers, who soon began to rival the Boers in numbers. The Boers felt threatened; to maintain their control of the government, they increased the qualifications required for citizenship and voting rights to make it difficult for non-Boers to acquire the vote. Blacks had no citizenship or voting rights in the Transvaal. The new laws led to angry protests from the white immigrants, whom the Boers called Uitlanders (foreigners). These protests were strongly supported by most mine owners and by powerful British politicians who believed that the dissatisfaction of the Uitlanders could create the conditions for a British takeover of the Transvaal.

With the support of the British Colonial Secretary, Joseph Chamberlain, some of the leading mining capitalists resolved to use Uitlander grievances to assist them to capture control of the Transvaal. They smuggled arms to a committee of Uitlanders in Johannesburg who were busy organising an uprising that was to take place on an appointed day. They were to be supported by a force of 500 armed men entering the Transvaal from British Bechuanaland (now Botswana) under the command of Dr L.S. Jameson, a leading British colonial politician and associate of Cecil Rhodes. The poorly organised uprising never materialised. Jameson's raiders were ambushed and captured by Boer troops, who had found out about the plan to overthrow their government.

After the failure of the Jameson Raid, Britain became intent on provoking a war to take over the Transvaal. Kruger's government could see this and began to prepare itself. Large quantities of modern weapons were imported from Germany and France. Boer officers were sent to Germany for training and some German instructors were brought in to help train troops in the Transvaal. Britain shipped more soldiers to South Africa and posted some on the border of the Transvaal. Kruger demanded the withdrawal of these troops and, when Britain refused, the Transvaal declared war on 11 October 1899. The Orange Free State government realised that the defeat of the Transvaal would mean the end of their own independence, and joined the war on the side of their fellow Boers.

By May 1900 British forces had captured Bloemfontein, Johannesburg and Pretoria.

Boer commando with African labourers, most likely workers on Boer farms. Source: UWC
Robben Island Mayibuye Archive

But the Boers refused to surrender and fought a guerrilla war for another two years. To
deny them support, the British army burned farms and moved Boer women and children
into concentration camps whose conditions were wretched: they were overcrowded,
unhygienic, disease-ridden, and short of medical supplies and food. About 28 000 people,
85 per cent of them children, died in these camps. African farm labourers and tenants
were herded into separate camps where conditions were even worse. By the end of
the war, 115 000 Africans had been interned in these camps; over 14 000 deaths were
recorded, but many thousands more probably died.

Though the British and Boers were the main protagonists in the war, black troops –
both Africans and coloureds – were drawn in to participate on both sides. They worked
mainly (though not entirely) in a non-combatant capacity, as labourers, stretcher-
bearers, transport riders, intelligence scouts and so on. Altogether 100 000 black people
were employed on the British side and about 10 000 on the Boer side. In Natal, Mohandas
Gandhi (later to become the leader of the independence movement in India) organised
the Indian Ambulance Corps of over a thousand men who served on the British side.

Eventually the Boer armies surrendered and signed the Treaty of Vereeniging on
31 May 1902. The Transvaal and Orange Free State became British colonies but were
promised responsible government (that is, limited self-government) in the near future.
Britain would also give them financial assistance to help restore their economies.

Britain abandoned its war-time promises to protect the rights of black people.

The first cabinet of the Union of South Africa. Prime Minister Louis Botha is at the centre in the front row.

Regarding the rights of Africans, the treaty stated, 'The issue of the franchise to natives will not be decided until after the introduction of self-government.' African leaders raised their voices strongly against this. Self-government, of course, meant government by the white minority, which was certain to reject rights for blacks. In fact, the condition of black people became worse after the war. For example, in Natal large areas of land were confiscated from Africans and turned over to white farmers. In the Transvaal the pass laws were made stricter, punishment for breaking a labour contract was made more severe, and taxes for blacks were increased. In rural areas British soldiers helped the Boers evict Africans who had taken over their farms during the war. Unlike the Boer farmers, Africans whose land and cattle had been seized by British troops during the war got no compensation.

THE UNION OF SOUTH AFRICA

Although Boer resentment against the British inevitably remained strong after the war, the most prominent Boer leaders came to terms with the fact that their independence was a lost cause. They now sought reconciliation with Britain and with the English-speaking whites and resolved to promote their own culture, language and identity within the British Empire. For its part, the British government realised that if it was to continue to dominate South Africa, it would need the cooperation of the Boers. The period was not without its contradictions, however. Although the British government had resolved to work more closely with the Boers, Lord Milner, the post-war British Governor of the former Boer republics, attempted to anglicise the Boer population by making English the language of instruction in all public schools; he also promoted large-scale immigration from Britain. The Boers resented this policy of anglicisation and it became a major issue fuelling the growth of Afrikaner nationalism.

After the Anglo-Boer War, many colonial leaders began to consider uniting South Africa's four British colonies to create a single country. This would assist them to deal better with the economic tensions between the colonies around trade tariffs and railway policy.

There were also political reasons for uniting the colonies. The Bambatha Rebellion in Natal in 1906 had alarmed many whites, and encouraged them to unite against any further African uprisings. Britain supported such a union because a single, strong government would be better able to serve British interests in the region. African leaders in all the colonies were generally supportive of a union, but insisted that it should have a constitution that did not discriminate on the basis of race.

A meeting of white representatives from all four colonies – known as the South African National Convention – met from October 1908 to February 1909 and negotiated a Draft Act of Union that was then submitted to the British Parliament for approval. In the new Union, the four colonies were to become provinces: the Cape, the Orange Free State, the Transvaal and Natal. Political power would be exercised largely at the national level, with few responsibilities allocated to the provinces, which were to be mainly administrative structures.

Power remained entirely in the hands of whites. Only they were allowed to become members of parliament. In the Transvaal, Natal and the Orange Free State no blacks would be allowed to vote. In the Cape the existing qualified franchise would remain; a few property-owning blacks would be allowed to vote, but only for white candidates. Blacks could, however, be elected as members of the Cape Provincial Council. (The issue of the black franchise is discussed in more detail in Chapter 6.)

It was also agreed that English and Dutch were to be the official languages with equal status. In order to settle a dispute over where the capital would be located, it was decided that Pretoria would be the administrative capital, Cape Town the legislative capital and Bloemfontein the location of the appellate division of the Supreme Court, the country's highest court. Pietermaritzburg, the capital of Natal, was given financial compensation.

Africans, bitterly opposed to the racist nature of the Draft Act of Union, called a counter-gathering in March 1908 – the South African Native National Convention. They decided to join with others, including the largely coloured African People's Organisation (APO), and send a delegation to London to try to persuade Britain not to adopt the Draft Act of Union. The mission proved unsuccessful. (See Chapter 6 for a fuller description of the activities of black political organisations at this time.)

In London, the black delegation was largely ignored and the British Parliament passed the Draft Act of Union unchanged as the South Africa Act. When the Act took effect on 31 May 1910, the Union of South Africa came into existence – the first unitary state within South Africa's present borders.

The first general election was won by the South African Party, led by Louis Botha, who became the first Prime Minister of the Union. His close colleague, Jan Smuts, was given three ministries (Defence, Mines and the Interior) and became the second most powerful politician in the country. Despite their background as Boer generals, both Botha and Smuts now embraced the British Empire and sought to strengthen unity between Dutch-speaking and English-speaking whites. In 1914, a group of Afrikaner politicians led by General J.B.M. Hertzog, who resented Botha and Smuts's increasingly pro-British stance, left the South African Party to form the National Party, which came to represent Afrikaner nationalist interests.

CHAPTER 5: DISCUSSION QUESTIONS

1. In the lead-up to the 1910 Act of Union, what positions did the following groups take and why?
   a. The British and the leaders of the white English-speaking colonists;
   b. The Boer leaders (represented mainly by Louis Botha and Jan Smuts);
   c. Black South Africans as represented by the leaders of the 1909 Native Convention and the African People's Organisation.

2. Why were the British so generous to the defeated Boers? Why did they not honour their promises to blacks?

3. Consider the name of the war of 1899–1902 and discuss the most appropriate term for it. Bear in mind that wars are often called by different names by different participants. (For example, the war that Americans refer to as the Vietnam War is called the American War or the Resistance War against America by the Vietnamese.)

4. For a century, the Afrikaner nationalist movement used the experience of the Anglo-Boer War as a way to mobilise Afrikaners against British dominance in South Africa's economic and political life – at least until the achievement of the Republic in 1961. Discuss what you think the reasons for this were.

5. Many progressive people in Europe supported the Boers, viewing them as a small, oppressed nation defending their freedom against British imperialism. Volunteers from a number of countries such as the Netherlands, Sweden, Norway, Italy and Russia fought on the Boer side. Do you agree that Boer freedom was being threatened by Britain? Were the Boers an oppressed nation or an oppressor nation? Is it possible to both anti-imperialist and an oppressor?

Chapter 5: Additional Readings

Online readings

Keegan, T. (2004) Imperialism and the Union of South Africa. In *Migration, Land and Minerals in the Making of South Africa*. Turning Points in History Series, Book 3. Johannesburg: STE Publishers. https://www.sahistory.org. za/archive/book-3-migration-land-and-minerals-making-south-africa-commissioned-department-education.

Pampallis, J. (1991) *Foundations of the New South Africa*. Cape Town: Maskew Miller Longman. (Chapter 3). https://www.sahistory.org.za/sites/default/files/file%20uploads%20/foundation_of_the_new_south_africa_original_final.pdf.

Simons, Jack and Ray Simons (1983) *Class and Colour in South Africa 1850–1950*. London: International Defence and Aid Fund. (Chapter 3). https://www.sahistory.org.za/sites/default/files/file%20uploads%20/class_and_colour_-_harold_jack_simons_r.e._simons.pdf.

Second Anglo-Boer War 1899–1902. *South African History Online* (n.d.). http://www.sahistory.org.za/article/second-anglo-boer-war-1899-1902.

Yekela, D.N. (2004) The Socio-economic Impact of the Mineral Revolution on South African Society. In *Migration, Land and Minerals in the Making of South Africa*. Turning Points in History Series, Book 3. Johannesburg: STE Publishers. https://www.sahistory.org.za/archive/book-3-migration-land-and-minerals-making-south-africa-commissioned-department-education.

Books

Giliomee, H. and B. Mbenga (eds) (2007) *New History of South Africa*. Cape Town: Tafelberg. (Chapter 8: The Story of Gold, pp. 199–206, and The Second Line of War: Black Involvement, pp. 218–23)

Hyam, Ronald (1980) Afrikaner Nationalism 1902–14. In *The South African War: The Anglo-Boer, 1899–1902*, edited by P. Warwick. London: Trewin Copplestone Books.

Meredith, M. 2007. *Diamonds, Gold and War*. London: Simon and Schuster UK.

Morris, M. (2004) *Every Step of the Way: The Journey to Freedom in South Africa*. Cape Town: HSRC Press. (Chapters 7 and 8)

Nasson, W. (2010) *The War for South Africa: The Anglo-Boer War 1899–1902*. Cape Town: Tafelberg.

Pretorius, F. 2013. *The Anglo-Boer War, 1899–1902*. Cape Town: Don Nelson.

Thompson, L. (1990) *A History of South Africa*. New Haven: Yale University Press. (Chapter 4, especially the sections on British Imperialism and the

South African War, pp. 132–41, and War, Peace and the Transfer of Power (pp. 141–53)

Warwick, P. (1980) Black People and the War. In *The South African War: The Anglo-Boer, 1899–1902*, edited by P. Warwick. London: Trewin Copplestone Books.

Six

Early Black Political Organisations

NEW FORMS OF RESISTANCE

From 1652 up to the end of the nineteenth century, Africans in South Africa resisted colonial domination mainly by military or diplomatic means (see Chapter 3). Resistance was carried out by the existing chiefdoms and kingdoms, in various parts of the country where people endeavoured to maintain their independence and avoid coming under colonial domination. Because the unified colonial forces (first Dutch and then British) met with a divided and uncoordinated response, they were able to defeat the indigenous resistance. Colonial troops with modern rifles, machine guns and cannons faced Africans with spears and shields. Despite brave resistance and even a few heroic victories – such as at Isandlwana – the outcome was inevitable. By 1899, the whole of South Africa consisted of two British colonies and two Afrikaner, or Boer, republics. As described in the previous chapter, this was followed soon after the Anglo-Boer War by the establishment of the Union of South Africa in 1910.

From the mid-nineteenth century, Africans in the Cape Colony began to participate in electoral politics. In 1854, the colony introduced a qualified franchise. This meant that people, irrespective of race, qualified to vote on the basis of the property that they owned or rented. In practice the voters' roll was made up overwhelmingly of whites, who were wealthier, but some coloured and African voters did qualify and they formed significant minorities in some constituencies in Cape Town and in the Transkei.

By the late nineteenth century, blacks had begun to form modern political organisations. The first of these were established in the 1880s in the Eastern Cape – then part of the Cape Colony – and included Imbumba yama Afrika, the Native Electoral Association and the Native Educational Association. These organisations participated in elections, usually supporting liberal white candidates. They also held meetings and conferences to discuss matters of concern to Africans, and sent petitions and delegations

Abdullah Abdurahman. Source: UWC Robben Island
Mayibuye Archive

to the colonial authorities to present their ideas and grievances.

In 1892, the Coloured People's Association was established in Kimberley and it also developed support in Cape Town. Its initial purpose was to oppose the Franchise and Ballot Act, which raised the property qualification for voters in the Cape. The Act was also opposed by various Eastern Cape organisations; one of their main concerns was defending their already limited franchise rights. The African Political (later People's) Organisation (APO), whose most important leader was Dr Abdullah Abdurahman, was established in 1902. Although it was open to all blacks and did attract some African members, its membership was predominantly coloured, and it became the leading party representing coloured people for the next fifty years.

New newspapers – in both English and indigenous languages – were established to express African political views. They also printed educational pieces and articles of general interest. John Tengo Jabavu started *Imvo Zabatsundu* in King William's Town, and a group of three leading intellectuals (Walter Rubusana, Alan Soga and Meshack Pelem) established *Izwi Labantu* in East London. Other important newspapers established around this time included *Koranta ea Becoana* in Mafikeng and *Tsala ea Becoana* (later renamed *Tsala ea Batho*) in Kimberley, both founded by Sol Plaatje. In Natal, John Dube established *Ilanga lase Natal*.

These men were also among the most prominent black political leaders in their communities. They – and others like them in various parts of South Africa – were generally Christians and had been well educated in mission schools; some had studied

1888: Indian labourers cutting sugar cane, Natal colony. Source: Photo by Robert Harris/Henry Guttmann Collection/Getty Images

or travelled abroad, particularly to Britain and the United States. They formed part of a small elite of men and women who owed their status not to tradition or birthright but to their education. They were mostly professionals – teachers, ministers, lawyers, doctors, nurses and journalists – as well as owners of small businesses and, on occasion, traditional leaders. They generally advocated loyalty to the British crown and the Empire, and looked to Britain for protection against the local settlers, especially the Boers.

Most Indian South Africans had initially come to South Africa as indentured labourers on the sugar cane plantations in Natal. Others came from India and Mauritius as independent merchants. Indian communities organised themselves to resist various forms of racist oppression including the threat of deportation, restrictions on freedom of movement, a special poll tax applying only to Indians, and restrictions on their business activities. In 1894 they formed the Natal Indian Congress (NIC) and in 1904 the Transvaal Indian Congress (TIC). These organisations made representation to the colonial authorities, organised petitions, and even sent a delegation to London to protest against unfair discrimination and harsh legislation. The NIC and TIC were the first political movements in South Africa to use mass non-violent resistance, inviting arrest and imprisonment. In 1919 they came together with the smaller Cape Indian Congress to form the South African Indian Congress (SAIC) although the constituent organisations retained their own identities. The most prominent leader of the early Indian resistance (until 1914) was Mohandas Gandhi, who later went on to lead the independence struggle in India, where he acquired the honorific title of Mahatma.

THE NATIVE CONGRESSES

After the Anglo-Boer War, with the defeat of the Boer republics, the entire country consisted of four separate British colonies. As a result all blacks fell ultimately under the same ruler: the British government. This strengthened the realisation among blacks that they would need to unite in order to fight more effectively against oppression. During the war, Britain had claimed that one of its aims was to free blacks in the Transvaal and Orange Free State from 'Boer slavery'. The British also undertook to extend the Cape franchise system to the former Boer republics. These promises were not kept after the Boers surrendered in 1902.

In the years following the war, the main aim of black politicians – who had long known and communicated with one another – was to extend franchise rights to the Transvaal, the Orange Free State and Natal (franchise rights in Natal were so negligible as to be almost non-existent). Native Congresses were established in all the four British colonies, led by men such as Sefako Makgatho (Transvaal), Walter Rubusana (the Cape), Thomas Mapikela (Orange Free State) and John Dube (Natal). In addition to their campaigns for the extension of franchise rights, these congresses protested against the pass laws, excessive taxation, segregation on trains, the prohibition on Africans holding public meetings in the Transvaal, and the brutal suppression of the Bambatha Rebellion in Natal. Their methods included organising petitions, sending delegations to colonial authorities, and passing resolutions at their meetings. None of these were effective, a fact that reflected the weak position in which black people found themselves in the economy, education and the political sphere, including the public service and the courts.

Towards Greater Unity

In the years following the war, the British government and the leaders of the four colonies began to consider uniting the colonies into one country (see also Chapter 5). They called the South African National Convention to discuss these matters in 1908–9. The most sensitive issue discussed was the matter of whether the Cape's non-racial qualified franchise would be extended to the other provinces. It was finally decided that only white males would be allowed to vote, except in the Cape, where black men with the necessary property qualifications would have the vote in parliamentary elections, but only for white candidates. African and coloured candidates would be allowed in elections for the Cape Provincial Council.

Even before the National Convention had finished its business, African politicians summoned a South African Native Convention in Bloemfontein in March 1909. The Convention was widely representative, and included delegates from all four colonies as well as Botswana (Bechuanaland), intellectuals and traditional leaders. They accepted the principle of a single South African Union, but called for equal rights for all South Africans regardless of colour. When the racist intentions of the National Convention became clear, the Native Convention joined with the APO and sympathetic whites and sent a delegation to London to protest to the British government. Their protests were ignored, and the Union of South Africa came into being on 31 May 1910, on the terms proposed by the white colonial leaders.

The South African Native Convention marked the beginning of a growing unity among Africans across South Africa and was one indication of the national, rather than ethnic or regional, consciousness that had been developing over the previous three decades. Although the political organisations for Africans were led primarily by a mission-educated, liberal middle class, non-political processes were also stimulating the growth of a national awareness among broader sections of the population. With the industrialisation and urbanisation that began with the discovery of diamonds and gold, many thousands of black people from all over South Africa were attracted – or pushed – into the new urban areas. They lived together in the same neighbourhoods, socialised together, and worked together in the same factories, mines and other workplaces. They were all subjected to job discrimination, exploitative wages, pass laws and constant police harassment. More and more, they saw themselves as having a great deal in common.

Another factor contributing to the gradual growth of a national identity was religious activity. From the 1880s, some Africans had begun to establish new churches independent of white control. These were often referred to as Ethiopian churches, reflecting the fact that Ethiopia was the only truly independent country in Africa at that time. Some churches affiliated to black American faith communities such as the African Methodist Episcopal (AME) Church. The independent movement grew as more people were attracted to it, and some new churches emerged out of splits within existing ones. By 1912 there were 76 independent churches in South Africa. Ethiopianism connected Africans in the various colonies to one another and promoted the growth of national awareness.

THE AFRICAN NATIONAL CONGRESS

The new Union government lost no time in passing a range of very repressive laws. Within less than two years, it became illegal for African workers in the mines and factories to strike; certain skilled jobs were reserved only for whites; and an all-white defence force was established. A Squatters Bill (the predecessor of the 1913 Land Act) was also presented to Parliament.

Confronted by the post-1910 political dispensation, most black political leaders realised that they would need a national organisation to provide a voice for their people. The initiative was taken by Pixley ka Isaka Seme, a lawyer originally from Natal, who published in *Imvo Zabantsundu* a call for the formation of a National Congress. He and other leaders of the Native National Convention then organised a national meeting of provincial and local organisations, traditional leaders and prominent individuals from all four provinces as well as neighbouring protectorates and colonies such as Swaziland (eSwatini), Basutoland (Lesotho), Bechuanaland and Rhodesia (Zimbabwe). Women, however, were not even invited, reflecting the male-centric values of the time.

This meeting, held in Bloemfontein (today's Mangaung), decided to establish the South African Native National Congress (renamed the African National Congress in 1923).[13] John Dube was elected president and Sol Plaatje the secretary general. Although the meeting took place without much fanfare or publicity, it proved to be one of the seminal events in South African history; its significance was possibly not recognised even

---

13 Although the organisation assumed the name African National Congress (ANC) only in 1923, it is much better known by this name today. To avoid any confusion, this book uses the name even for the period 1912–23.

Sol Plaatje and Pixley ka Isaka Seme, two of the prominent founders of the ANC

by those who founded the organisation. For over a century, the Congress would be the leading voice of Africans in the country. Ninety-two years after its establishment, it would lead South Africa to democracy and form its first democratically elected government.

Chapter 6: Discussion Questions

1.   Why did Africans and coloured leaders look to Britain for protection from local white settlers and their governments? To what extent were these hopes justified and to what extent were they successful?

2.   The Indian Congresses were more confrontational towards the governments of the time than either the Native Congresses or the African People's Organisation. Discuss the effectiveness of non-violent resistance and whether it was an appropriate form of struggle at this time.

3.   Discuss the historical significance of the early African newspapers, both at the time they were formed and over the long term in relation to their political and cultural influence.

4.   Evaluate the historical importance of the formation of the African National Congress in 1912.

Chapter 6: Additional Readings

Online readings

African National Congress (n.d.) *A Brief History of the African National Congress.* http://www.anc.org.za/content/brief-history-anc or https://www.

anc1912.org.za/brief-history-anc.

African People's Organisation. *South African History Online* (n.d.) http://www.sahistory.org.za/organisations/african-peoples-organisation-apo.

Natal Indian Congress. *South African History Online* (n.d.) http://www.sahistory.org.za/organisations/natal-indian-congress-nic.

Pampallis, J. (1991) *Foundations of the New South Africa.* Cape Town: Maskew Miller Longman. https://www.sahistory.org.za/sites/default/files/file%20uploads%20/foundation_of_the_new_south_africa_original_final.pdf.

The Formation of the SANNC/ANC. *South African History Online* (n.d.) https://www.sahistory.org.za/article/formation-sanncanc.

Transvaal Indian Congress. *South African History Online* (n.d.) http://www.sahistory.org.za/organisations/transvaal-indian-congress-tic.

Books

Giliomee, H. and B. Mbenga (eds) (2007) *New History of South Africa.* Cape Town: Tafelberg. (Chapter 9: The Road to Union, and Launching the Union)

Meli, F. (1989) *A History of the ANC: South Africa Belongs to Us.* London: James Currey. (Chapters 1 and 2)

Odendaal, A. (1984) *Vukani Bantu: The Beginnings of Black Protest Politics in South Africa to 1912.* Cape Town: David Philip.

Odendaal, A. (2013) *The Founders: The Origins of the ANC and the Struggle for Democracy in South Africa.* Johannesburg: Jacana Media.

Roux, E. (1967) *Time Longer than Rope.* Madison, WI: Wisconsin University Press. (Chapters 7, 8 and 10)

Walshe, Peter (1970) *The Rise of African Nationalism in South Africa: The African National Congress, 1912–1952.* Los Angeles: University of California Press.

Seven

The Natives Land Act of 1913

BACKGROUND

The 1913 Natives Land Act is one of the most notorious pieces of legislation in the history of South Africa. Although much land had already been taken away from Africans as a result of colonial conquest before 1913, a significant amount still remained available for them to farm, even if in many cases they did not actually own the land.

By the end of the nineteenth century, four and a half million Africans lived on the reserves, where land was communally owned and distributed for use among individuals or families by traditional leaders. Some of the Africans who lived outside the reserves farmed for themselves on state-owned or mission land. The majority, however, lived on white-owned farms, either as wage labourers or tenant farmers.

Tenants fell into three categories: cash tenants, labour tenants and sharecroppers. Cash tenants paid rent for farmland in cash. Labour tenants were normally families who had the use of a portion of farmland; in return they provided labour to the landowner for a certain period (usually three to six months) each year. Sharecroppers used the land of a white farmer and then shared the crop with him or (on rare occasions) her. Many prospered, farming efficiently and earning a good income even after sharing the crop with the landowner. Cash tenants, too, were able to profit from commercial farming.

After the mineral discoveries and the growth of towns, sharecropping became widespread, especially in areas with easy access to the burgeoning new markets of the Witwatersrand. Most sharecroppers and cash tenants worked the land of poorer white landowners who had insufficient capital to expand production to meet the growing demand for agricultural products. Wealthier landowners farmed commercially, employing wage labourers or labour tenants. They opposed sharecropping and rent tenancy because they believed that it deprived them of cheap labour, since Africans preferred to be sharecroppers or cash tenants. These commercial farmers called on the government to ban such activities.

By the late nineteenth and early twentieth centuries, African farmers had begun to buy back land that their ancestors had lost to colonial expansion. Most commonly this was done by people pooling their resources to form groups or syndicates. Although Africans had bought only a very small portion of commercial farmland by 1910, it gave rise to protests from white farmers who resented the competition they offered.

Main Provisions of the Land Act

Largely as a result of pressure from politically powerful capitalist farmers, the government passed the Natives Land Act of 1913. This Act set aside 7.5 per cent of South Africa's landmass as reserves where Africans (over 70 per cent of the population) could own land – mainly through communal ownership. No African was allowed to buy or rent land or be a sharecropper on land outside the reserves. This was to ensure that Africans could not compete with white farmers for land, and to force sharecroppers and tenants to become either labourers or labour tenants. Any African living on a white-owned farm had to work directly for the landowner for at least 90 days a year.

Some white farmers wanted to abolish the reserves altogether, so that Africans couldn't own land anywhere. However, this was opposed by the mine owners, who depended on migrant labour. As described in Chapter 4, the families of migrant labourers subsidised family incomes through their farming activities, either in the reserves or in neighbouring countries. This meant that wages for the mine workers could be lower. Therefore, the mining industry insisted on the necessity of the reserves.

The government realised that the reserves were too small to sustain the population that they were expected to accommodate. So the Act also established the Natives Land Commission (the Beaumont Commission) to identify land that could be added to the reserves. In 1916 the commission presented its report to the government. It proposed the addition of seven million hectares, which would increase the 'reserved' land to about 14 per cent of South Africa's total land area. However, owing to opposition from white farmers, this land was not released for addition to the reserves until the Native Trust and Land Act was passed in 1936. Even then, it was 0.8 million hectares less than the land area recommended by the Beaumont Commission.

Evictions and Resistance

The 1913 Act was left to the provinces to implement when they saw fit. The Orange Free State implemented it immediately. Thousands of sharecroppers and cash tenants were evicted from the land they farmed. Many were forced to become low-paid labourers or labour tenants. Many did not realise that the law had changed and thought that they had been evicted by the landowner's individual decision. Whole families wandered about with their livestock – often for months – looking for alternative land on which to farm. Of course, the new law ensured that such land was unavailable. Extreme suffering compelled many to sell or kill their starving livestock to keep themselves alive. Most were eventually

Dairy Farming in 1902: The Land Act provide for farmers like these to be evicted from any part of South Africa not designated as a "native reserve".

forced to move to the reserves or across the borders to neighbouring protectorates or colonies such as Bechuanaland, Basutoland, Swaziland or Rhodesia. In time, many of the men became migrant mine labourers. Others made their way to the new towns and cities, where they found jobs as low-paid workers or joined the ranks of the unemployed.

From the time the Squatters Bill (the initial version of the Land Act) was first published early in 1912, African organisations and communities expressed their outrage against the proposals in villages, towns and cities throughout the country. They held meetings to voice their protest and made representations to the authorities, but to no avail.

Sol Plaatje, the secretary general of the newly formed ANC, together with other ANC leaders, travelled through the rural areas of the Orange Free State to investigate the hardships caused by the Land Act. Subsequently, Plaatje wrote and published *Native Life in South Africa*, his famous exposé of the cruel consequences of the Act for Africans in South Africa's rural areas.

In February 1914, ANC president John Dube led a delegation to see Prime Minister Louis Botha to protest against the Act. When this failed, the Congress sent a delegation made up of five leading members to London to ask the British government to intervene on behalf of Africans. This, too, was unsuccessful and the Land Act remained in force in South Africa.

Aside from the immediate, calamitous consequences of the Natives Land Act, it also had appalling long-term consequences. It was one of the most important factors in shaping and maintaining the racial inequalities that continue to this day in South Africa. For more than a century it has made for a very skewed pattern of land distribution and has ensured that the ownership of commercial farming land in South Africa has remained overwhelmingly in white hands.

ANC delegation to London, 1914. Left to right: Thomas Mapikela, Rev. Walter Rubusana, Rev. John Dube, Saul Msane, Sol Plaatje. Source: Historical Papers Research Archive, University of the Witwatersrand, South Africa.

CHAPTER 7: DISCUSSION QUESTIONS

1. Land dispossession by European settlers began long before the 1913 Natives Land Act became law, and continued long afterwards. However, many scholars, politicians and informed laypeople consider the Act a defining moment in the process of land dispossession. This interpretation is even implied in current legislation on land restitution. Why do you think that this interpretation is so widely held? Do you agree with it?

2. Discuss how the provisions of the Natives Land Act benefited each of the following groups:
   a. White large-scale commercial farmers
   b. Mine owners

3. Discuss how the Natives Land Act affected each of the following groups:
   a. Wage labourers on white-owned farms
   b. Labour tenants

c. Sharecroppers

d. Cash tenants

Chapter 7: Additional Readings

Online readings

Bundy, C. (2013) *Casting a Long Shadow: The Natives Land Act of 1913 and its Legacy.* http://www.sahistory.org.za/sites/default/files/file%20uploads%20/casting_a_long_shadow_by_colin_bundy.pdf.

Industrialisation, Rural Change and Nationalism (2004) Turning Points in History Series, Book 4. Johannesburg: STE Publishers. (Chapter 1)

Modise, L. and N. Mtshiselwa (2013) *The Natives Land Act of 1913 Engineered the Poverty of Black South Africans: A Historico-ecclesiastical Perspective.* http://uir.unisa.ac.za/bitstream/handle/10500/13143/Modise-Mtshiselwa.pdf?sequence=1&isAllowed=y.

Pampallis, J. (1991) *Foundations of the New South Africa.* Cape Town: Maskew Miller Longman. (Chapter 5). https://www.sahistory.org.za/sites/default/files/file%20uploads%20/foundation_of_the_new_south_africa_original_final.pdf

South African Native National Congress (1916) *Resolution against the Natives Land Act 1913 and the Report of the Natives Land Commission.* http://www.anc.org.za/content/resolution-against-natives-land-act-1913-and-report-natives-land-commission-south-african.

Books

Meli, F. (1988) *A History of the ANC: South Africa Belongs to Us.* London: James Currey. (Especially Chapter 2, section on The Early Years)

Plaatje, Solomon (2016 [1915]) *Native Life in South Africa.* Johannesburg: Wits University Press.

Roux, E. (1967) *Time Longer than Rope.* Madison, WI: University of Wisconsin Press. (Chapter 7)

Thompson, L. (2014) *A History of South Africa.* Johannesburg: Jonathan Ball. (Chapter 5)

Worden, N. (2012) *The Making of Modern South Africa: Conquest, Apartheid, Democracy,* 5th edn. Hoboken, NJ: Wiley-Blackwell. (Especially Chapter 3)

Eight

World War I

World War I was fought between 1914 and 1918. Although it originated in and was fought mainly in Europe, fighting also took place in parts of Africa and Asia. It was essentially a war about the imperial interests and territorial ambitions of the large imperialist countries. On one side were Britain, France and Russia, joined later by Japan, Italy, the United States and several smaller countries. On the other side were Germany and the Austro-Hungarian Empire, later joined by Bulgaria and the Ottoman Empire. The war was a brutal conflict, the most destructive war that the world had yet seen. For the first time in history, tanks and aircraft were used in warfare. Over 16 million people lost their lives in the fighting, including approximately 7 million civilians. Over 20 million people were wounded.

ATTITUDES TO THE WAR

When Britain declared war on 4 August 1914, it did so on behalf of its empire, and so South Africa found itself at war. The South African government and its supporters, particularly the big mine owners and most English-speaking whites, supported the war effort enthusiastically. The attitude of other South Africans towards the war varied.

The African National Congress endorsed the war effort and called on African people to support the British Empire. This, in effect, meant the suspension of the campaign against the Natives Land Act and the introduction of passes for women in the Orange Free State. The ANC sent a delegation to Pretoria to assure the government of African support. Offers to help in the war effort were sent to the government from chiefs and others from across the country, including offers to recruit African troops.

The government, however, refused to allow Africans to serve in the armed forces in any combatant capacity and instead established the South African Native Labour

Corps. The Corps also included men recruited from neighbouring protectorates and colonies such as Basutoland, Bechuanaland, Swaziland and Rhodesia. Despite widespread resentment of the racist policy, about 71 000 Africans were recruited with the help of the ANC and some traditional leaders. One of the reasons for the support for the war effort given by African leaders was the hope that Britain would repay them for their loyalty, especially with regard to African grievances against the Natives Land Act and the discriminatory franchise laws. This hope would not, however, be realised; after the war Britain continued to refer all decisions regarding South Africa to the white government. In fact, the contribution of the African troops to the war effort was virtually ignored in the government's official history of the war.

Coloured people, through the African People's Organisation (APO), also supported the war effort. At first the government only allowed them to serve in non-combatant capacities. However, after the South West African campaign in late 1915, a separate coloured infantry corps was formed under white officers, and served in France and East Africa.

A significant section of Afrikaner nationalists took a very different view of the war. They still felt embittered by their defeat in the Anglo-Boer War and, as Britain turned its full attention to conducting the war, they saw an opportunity to shake off British control and re-establish Boer independence. In September 1914 a group of former Boer generals, supported by about 12 000 rebels, denounced Prime Minister Louis Botha and his deputy, Jan Smuts, as traitors and rose up in rebellion. Botha declared martial law, and within five months the rebels were crushed. Despite their defeat, the rebels became heroes of the Afrikaner nationalist cause and ultimately helped to strengthen it.

The National Party of General Hertzog did not formally join the rebellion but it strongly opposed South African participation in the war, labelling it 'England's war'. During the 1915 election campaign the National Party accused Botha of subordinating South Africa's interests to those of Britain. The party gained enough votes to become the official opposition, surpassing both the pro-British Unionist Party and the South African Labour Party.

The white labour movement, represented mainly by the South African Labour Party, was divided on the issue of supporting the war. The progressive wing of the party, which dominated the leadership positions, opposed the war. They called it an inter-imperialist conflict and said that the workers of the various countries had nothing to gain from killing each other. However, they were soon defeated by a conservative majority of party members who supported the government and the Empire. The anti-war grouping then split away and established the International Socialist League (ISL), which declared itself a Marxist organisation.

SOUTH AFRICA IN THE WAR

During World War I, South African troops served in two of Germany's African colonies – South West Africa (now Namibia) and German East Africa (now mainland Tanzania) – as well as in France, Belgium, Egypt and Palestine. Overall, more than 230 000 South

In this cemetery in Morogoro, Tanzania, the white soldiers were buried in individual graves, each with its own gravestone. The black soldiers – who had served as unarmed wagon drivers, labourers, stretcher bearers, porters and servants – were buried nearby in a mass grave. Seventy years later the ANC would establish a school for young South African exiles a few kilometres from this spot. Here a teacher inspects names on the headstone of the mass grave.

The SS Mendi *sank while carrying soldiers back home from Europe; 646 men died, including 616 black South Africans.*

Africans of all races fought in the war and over 12 000 lost their lives.

When the war broke out, Britain asked South Africa to invade South West Africa. Botha sent in the army in February 1915. The South Africans defeated the German armed forces, gaining control of the entire territory within five months.

In February 1916, Smuts led South African troops to the British colony of Kenya where they joined forces with other British imperial troops – especially Africans from Kenya, Uganda and Malawi under British officers. They then moved south into mainland Tanzania and spent most of the war chasing a small German army which employed hit-and-run tactics and kept retreating; by the end of the war they were found in Zambia. The imperial troops lost few men in combat, but thousands died from diseases such as malaria and dysentery. The biggest casualties occurred among the East African (Tanzanian and Kenyan) civilians, whose country was devastated. Almost a million of them were pressed into becoming porters for the military forces of both sides, and about 100 000 died from disease, exhaustion or malnutrition. Another 300 000 civilians died from the conflict and from famine caused by the loss of farm labour due to the mass conscription of men into the armies and by passing soldiers taking their food supplies and burning their homes and fields.

In France, South African troops were deployed against the German army. On orders from the South African government, soldiers of the South African Native Labour Corps were segregated from other troops, locked in closed compounds at night, and prohibited from drinking liquor or from forming friendships with Europeans. The African troops resented these restrictions and protested. During one protest against the compound system, thirteen men were shot and killed.

In one of the worst naval tragedies of the war, the ship SS *Mendi*, carrying mainly black South African troops, sank after being accidentally hit by a cargo ship in the English Channel while on its way to France. A total of 646 people were killed, of whom 616 were African members of the South African Native Labour Corps. The rest were white South African officers and members of the ship's crew. Their memory was subsequently kept alive by the ANC's Mendi Memorial Club. Since then, a number of monuments commemorating the *Mendi* dead have been erected in South Africa. Their names also appear on monuments in England and the Netherlands.

THE PARIS PEACE CONFERENCE

After the war, Louis Botha and Jan Smuts attended the Paris Peace Conference on behalf of the South African government. The ANC wanted the government to include a special 'native representative' in the South African delegation. When the government refused, the ANC decided to send its own delegation, made up of five senior members, to London to appeal to the British government.

At the end of the war the ANC had prepared a petition to King George V, expressing its loyalty to the Empire and its pride in the African contribution to the war. The petition also called for the enfranchisement of black people and urged that, contrary to the wishes of some white politicians, the territories of Bechuanaland, Basutoland and Swaziland should not be incorporated into the Union of South Africa. In addition, they requested that the future of the former German colony of South West Africa not be decided until its inhabitants were consulted. The ANC delegation presented the petition to the British Prime Minister, Lloyd George, who told them that he could not interfere in South Africa's internal affairs and referred the petition to the Governor General of South Africa. Predictably, there was no response to the demands.

The Peace Conference distributed Germany's colonies among the victors as mandate territories under the newly formed League of Nations. South Africa was given the mandate over South West Africa, with the responsibility to 'promote to the utmost the material and moral well-being of the inhabitants of the territory'. South Africa interpreted this to mean annexation and South West Africa became, in effect, a South African colony.

The ANC, disillusioned by the response to its appeals and requests for intervention on behalf of the African people, would never again send a delegation to plead to the imperial government.

SOCIO-ECONOMIC DEVELOPMENTS

The war years saw the continuation of the trends set in motion by the mineral discoveries: urbanisation, industrialisation, the expansion of transport infrastructure, the impoverishment of rural Africans, and the breakdown of traditional ways of life. The partial disruption of imports by the war led to the development of local manufacturing industries. Gold mining thrived because of an increase in the price of gold; agricultural exports increased because of the greater demand from Britain.

Attracted by jobs in industries or striving to escape the hardships of rural life, thousands of blacks moved to the towns, many settling there permanently. Most lived in congested African 'locations' established by municipalities on the outskirts of towns or in squalid and unhygienic inner-city 'slumyards' where they rented accommodation from private landlords. In some of the slumyards, Africans lived side by side with others from different parts of South Africa and with the poor of other groups: coloureds, Indians and whites. In this melting pot of influences, a new culture began to emerge, one that was uniquely South African and distinctly urban.

CHAPTER 8: DISCUSSION QUESTIONS

1. In the nineteenth and early twentieth centuries, the African National Congress usually looked to Britain for support against local whites. At the same time Britain rebuffed the African delegations that went to London to protest against the denial of political rights for black people and against the 1913 Natives Land Act. Against this background, what do you think would have been some of the arguments in the ANC both for and against support for Britain's war effort before a final decision was taken? Do you think the decision to support the war effort was the right one?

2. The Afrikaner rebels, the National Party and the left wing of the Labour Party all opposed South African participation in the war. Examine the contrasting reasons why each of these groups took the positions that they did. To what extent were they justified in taking these positions?

3. Discuss whether white and black South Africans gained anything from the war for which thousands of lives were sacrificed?

CHAPTER 8: ADDITIONAL READINGS

Online readings

Johnson, R. and N. Johnson (2016) Delville Wood: The First World War. http://www.delvillewood.com/premiereguerre2.htm.

Kleynhans, E. (2015) South African Invasion of German South West Africa (Union of South Africa). *International Encyclopaedia of the First World War.* https://encyclopedia.1914-1918-online.net/pdf/1914-1918-Online-south_african_invasion_of_german_south_west_africa_union_of_south_africa-2015-07-01.pdf.

Pampallis, J. (1991) *Foundations of the New South Africa.* Cape Town: Maskew

Miller Longman. (Chapter 8). https://www.sahistory.org.za/sites/default/files/file%20uploads%20/foundation_of_the_new_south_africa_original_final.pdf.

Paterson, H. (2004) First Allied Victory: The South African Campaign in German South-West Africa, 1914–1915. *Military History Journal*, 13 (2). http://samilitaryhistory.org/vol132hp.html.

Simons, Jack and Ray Simons (1983) *Class and Colour in South Africa, 1850–1950.* London: International Defence and Aid Fund. (Chapters 8 and 9) https://www.sahistory.org.za/sites/default/files/file%20uploads%20/class_and_colour_-_harold_jack_simons_r.e._simons.pdf.

South Africa in World War I. https://www.youtube.com/watch?v=bhYYqj-3swU.

Steinbach, D. (2015) Misremembered History: The First World War in East Africa. https://www.britishcouncil.org/voices-magazine/misremembered-history-first-world-war-east-africa.

Books and journal articles

Giliomee, H. and B. Mbenga (eds) (2007) *New History of South Africa.* Cape Town: Tafelberg. (Chapter 9)

Grundlingh, Albert (1987) *Fighting Their Own War: South African Blacks and the First World War.* Johannesburg: Ravan Press.

Meli, F. (1988) *A History of the ANC: South Africa Belongs to Us.* London: James Currey. (Chapter 2, especially pp. 48–50)

Morris, M. (2004) *Every Step of the Way: The Journey to Freedom in South Africa.* Cape Town: HSRC Press. (Chapter 8)

Nine

The Post-war Years, 1918–1929

Louis Botha died a few weeks after returning from the Paris Peace Conference, and Jan Smuts took over as Prime Minister of South Africa. Although he had fought against Britain as a Boer general, he had come to identify himself closely with British imperialist interests. During the war, he and Botha had been appointed to the British Imperial War Cabinet. After the war, in 1921, Smuts signed the Simonstown Agreement, guaranteeing the British Navy the use of the Simonstown naval base.

Industrial growth after the war led to the growth of the working class, both black and white. Inflation set in and prices rose sharply from 1917. The living standards of blacks, both urban and rural, declined rapidly while white workers, better organised in trade unions and with the influence that came with being voters, managed to maintain their wage levels in line with inflation for a few years.

THE SPANISH FLU

People's suffering, especially that of the poor, was greatly worsened by the influenza epidemic of 1918–19 (the so-called Spanish flu) that swept across much of the world. The Centers for Disease Control in the United States estimates that 50 million people died globally. It is likely that almost 500 000 South Africans out of a population of 7 million died of the disease, a far larger number than those who had died in the Anglo-Boer War, World Wars I and II, and the liberation struggle put together. The exact number of deaths can only be an estimate because the number of deaths among black people in rural areas was not recorded. Even among the urban population the crisis prevented the collection of accurate statistics. Factors contributing to the high death rate included the lack of a vaccine or other treatment for the disease and very poor observance of physical distancing or quarantine by infected people.

BLACK RESISTANCE

Strikes

The hard working and living conditions of black workers led to a marked increase in the number of strikes especially, but not only, on the mines. The reaction of employers and authorities was usually harsh. Strikers suffered severe punishments, including beatings, floggings and imprisonment.

In 1920 the largest strike yet to have taken place in South Africa occurred when 71 000 African miners closed down 21 mines for 12 days. They demanded the release of two arrested miners, a wage increase and better living conditions in the compounds. The strike was eventually broken by the use of brute force. In one incident at Village Deep, mine guards fired on workers, killing three and wounding forty.

Anti-pass campaigns

In 1913, municipalities in the Orange Free State were given the power to force black women (both African and coloured) to obtain passes that allowed them to live in municipal locations. This, unsurprisingly, met with strong opposition. In July, 600 women marched to the offices of the Bloemfontein municipality, handed over a bag of passes to the deputy mayor, and said they would not acquire any more. Resistance spread to other towns in the province. So many were arrested that in some towns such as Bloemfontein, Winburg and Jagersfontein prisoners had to be transferred to neighbouring town jails. While the ANC leadership supported the women with public criticism of government and petitions to the Prime Minister, it was the women themselves – at that time denied full membership of the Congress – who actually organised and sustained the resistance.

When war broke out in 1914, the anti-pass campaign was suspended in line with ANC policy (see Chapter 8). It resumed again in 1918 and led directly to the formation of the Bantu Women's League within the ANC. Charlotte Maxeke, its first president, led a deputation to make its views known to Prime Minister Louis Botha. In the Orange Free State, women once more refused to carry passes and were sent to prison until, in a rare victory for Africans at that time, the pass laws for women were suspended in 1920.

In the Transvaal, the ANC started an anti-pass campaign, meant partly to forestall the extension of the pass laws to women in the province, but also to show opposition to the pass laws in general. Protest marches and meetings were attacked by police and thousands were imprisoned. The extent of the casualties in the campaign is unclear, but the ANC president Sefako Makgatho later reported that 'some men and women are in their graves as a result of their refusal to buy passes'.

The Bulhoek and Bondelswarts Massacres

The government's violent reaction to anything it perceived as defiance was demonstrated by two events in 1921.

In Bulhoek in the Eastern Cape, armed police opened fire on a religious sect called the Israelites. They had occupied an open field, maintaining that God had ordered them not

1919: Anti-pass demonstrators rounded up by police. Source: UWC Robben Island Mayibuye Archive

to allow themselves to be forced to leave. They charged the police with spears and sticks. The police waited until they were only a few metres away and then opened fire, killing 163 people and wounding 129. Of the survivors, over a hundred were arrested, tried and imprisoned.

In the same year a dog tax was introduced in South West Africa (Namibia). The Bondelswarts, a Nama people, were particularly affected by this, as they used dogs for both hunting and herding, their main economic activities. Since most could not afford the tax, they would have to go to work as labourers on white-owned farms. When they refused to pay, soldiers were deployed against them and two aircraft dropped bombs over them. Over a hundred people were killed and the Bondelswarts were forced to submit.

THE COMMUNIST PARTY

In 1921, the International Socialist League joined together with some smaller left-wing organisations to establish the Communist Party of South Africa (CPSA). It consisted mainly of progressive white workers and became a member of the Communist International (Comintern). The Comintern had been established in the wake of the Russian Revolution and was made up of communist parties from all over the world. The CPSA's goal was to organise workers to overthrow capitalism and establish socialist states throughout the world. It opposed racial oppression and believed that workers of all races should unite to fight against the capitalist system. Once socialism had replaced capitalism, they believed, then racial oppression would be brought to an end. Initially the

CPSA saw no link between the class struggle of the workers and the national liberation struggle of black South Africans.

The White Miners' Strike, 1922

From the earliest days of the mining industry in Kimberley and the Witwatersrand, white workers had tried to ensure a privileged position for themselves at the expense of black workers. By using their right to vote and their relatively well-organised trade unions, they managed to force successive governments and their employers to accept their privileged status. By 1920, Africans had been excluded from nearly all skilled and semi-skilled jobs.

However, with the start of an economic depression in 1920, the gold price fell and the mine owners faced serious financial difficulties. After unsuccessful negotiations with white workers, the Chamber of Mines announced that gold and coal mines would cut the wages of many white workers and start replacing semi-skilled whites with black workers at lower rates of pay. On 2 January 1922, white coal miners went on strike, followed eight days later by gold miners. In all, about 25 000 workers went on strike; the event also became known as the Rand Revolt. After new talks failed to yield any agreement, the Chamber of Mines announced that it was stopping negotiations. The South African Industrial Federation, representing the miners, called a general strike of all workers in South Africa, though the call went largely unheeded.

Prime Minister Smuts then entered the dispute in strong support of the employers. He declared martial law, claiming that the country faced an insurrection. The government used devastating military force, including artillery, tanks and even aeroplanes, to bomb white working-class neighbourhoods on the eastern Witwatersrand. The strikers were pounded into submission and the strike came to an end. The result was that white semi-skilled miners were replaced by Africans, and the wages of the rest of the white workers were reduced by between 25 and 50 per cent. Though this led to more jobs for African workers, it did not result in an increase in their pay.

Towards the end of the strike, some 'commandos' created by striking workers attacked black workers, eliciting protests from the ANC and the Industrial and Commercial Workers' Union (ICU), as well as calls for restraint from white communist leaders.

An interesting aspect of the strike was the role of the Communist Party of South Africa, which had been formed just six months before the strike began. The CPSA's goal was to organise workers to overthrow capitalism. Although it advocated the unity of all workers, it decided to support the strike, whose aim was to maintain the industrial colour bar.

After the 1924 election of the Pact government, a coalition of the National Party and the Labour Party (see below), it became apparent that most white workers were willing to be junior partners of the capitalists as long as they were allowed to occupy a privileged position in relation to blacks. From the time of its 1924 congress, the CPSA started to focus its attention on recruiting blacks, who by the end of the decade made up the majority of the CPSA's membership (although not its leadership).

CHANGE IN GOVERNMENT

Although the white workers had been defeated in the 1922 strike, Smuts felt he needed to placate them before the 1924 election. The government passed legislation that further eroded the rights of black workers: the ability of blacks to become apprentices was restricted, although not yet altogether prohibited; urban municipalities were required to house blacks in segregated areas; and Africans and Indians were barred from becoming members of registered trade unions.

Though white workers may have welcomed such legislation, it was not enough to reconcile them to Smuts's government or to forgive his actions during the strike. Afrikaners, most of whom still lived in the rural areas, also expressed their unhappiness with what they saw as a pro-British government. The main opposition to Smuts's South African Party (SAP) came from a coalition between Hertzog's National Party – representing mainly Afrikaner farmers, workers and small business owners – and the largely English-speaking Labour Party. They negotiated an election pact, defeated the SAP, and formed a new administration that became known as the Pact government.

NEW RACIST LEGISLATION

J.B.M. Hertzog, the new Prime Minister, lost no time in passing further racist legislation. Tens of thousands of blacks in the state sector – the civil service, the railways and public utilities – lost their jobs and were replaced by 'poor whites' at 'civilised' rates of pay. These rates were meant to maintain a 'standard of living generally recognised as tolerable from a European point of view'. 'Uncivilised labour', on the other hand, was defined by the Department of Labour as 'persons whose aim is restricted to the bare requirements of the necessities of life as understood among barbarous and under-developed peoples'.

Racist legislation included the Wage Act of 1925, which enabled a new Wage Board to set minimum wages in industries where there was no collective bargaining. This was meant to remove the incentive for employers to replace white workers with black workers. The Mines and Works Amendment of 1926 (which came to be known as the Colour Bar Act) excluded Africans and Indians from most categories of skilled and semi-skilled labour.

The Native Administration Act of 1927 gave the government powers to take arbitrary action against Africans. The Governor General was made the Supreme Chief of all Africans outside the Cape Province.[14] He was given the authority (exercised on behalf of the government) to appoint and remove native commissioners, chiefs and headmen, alter the composition of 'tribes', and move individual Africans or even whole tribes 'from any place to any other place' in the country. The last-mentioned provision was used to banish militant politicians and trade unionists to remote parts of the country. The Act

---

14 Since Africans in the Cape Province could become voters because of the qualified franchise, to include them in this law would require a change to the constitution. This would have required a protracted process for which both opposition and British government support would be needed. The government preferred to avoid this.

also made it a punishable offence to 'promote hostility between Natives and Europeans'; in the absurd language of the racist state, this meant promoting racial equality.

This type of legislation emphasised the essentially colonial nature of South Africa, with local whites having replaced the British colonial government and acting themselves as colonisers. As noted in Chapter 5, the 'independence' of South Africa after 1910 had made very little difference to the rights of Africans and coloureds – or to the Indians who had been brought to South Africa from the British colony of India.

Afrikaner nationalist aspirations were appeased by several other developments. In 1925, Afrikaans replaced Dutch as an official language, and bilingualism (that is, knowledge of both English and Afrikaans) became compulsory in the civil service. In 1928 a new flag was adopted, displaying at its centre the flags of Britain and of both former Boer republics. At the 1926 Imperial Conference in London, South Africa joined with the other 'dominions' – that is, the settler colonies of Canada, Australia and New Zealand as well as Ireland – to successfully demand greater autonomy from Britain. The conference resulted in the Balfour Declaration, which stated that the dominions were 'autonomous and equal in stature' with each other and with Britain. A new association to which all belonged was established: the British Commonwealth of Nations. After this declaration was passed as law by the British Parliament in 1931, South Africa established its first Department of External Affairs and appointed diplomatic missions abroad.

The Industrial and Commercial Workers' Union

The most prominent liberation organisation at this time was the Industrial and Commercial Workers' Union. This was established in 1919 by Clements Kadalie, a forceful and skilful organiser who had come to South Africa from Malawi. It started as a small union in Cape Town which successfully fought a dock workers' strike and won wage increases for the workers. This success led to the rapid spread of the ICU throughout the Cape and then the whole country as well as to Lesotho, Mozambique, Namibia, Zimbabwe, Zambia and Malawi. The bulk of its membership was South African. It took up both trade union and political issues affecting black people.

The ICU was a general union that represented not only workers, but also peasants (poor, non-commercial farmers) and some small traders. At the height of its popularity in 1927, it claimed to have 120 000 members, and was thus probably the largest political organisation that Africa had yet seen. Most of the ICU's members were in the rural areas, but there were also many urban workers in industry and commerce. Members often had overlapping membership with the ANC or the CPSA or both.

In the rural areas the ICU fought against the eviction of tenant farmers and the mistreatment and meagre wages of farm workers. In many struggles, the ICU made successful use of the courts, although lawyers' fees did become a strain on the ICU's finances.

From its earliest days the ICU was the victim of government brutality. In one of the worst examples, in 1919 police in Port Elizabeth fired on a workers' march to demand the release of an arrested leader. They killed 21 people and wounded many more. The

1927. Clements Kadalie with British trade unionist in London. Kadalie founded and led the ICU from 1919 to 1928.

union's meetings were often disrupted and participants assaulted by police and white hooligans. Contact between ICU organisers and farm workers was made very difficult by white farmers, and many ICU members were evicted from farms and replaced with non-members from the reserves.

The ICU continued growing quickly up until 1927 but then it began a period of rapid decline; by 1930 it had virtually ceased to exist. The main reason for this was massive repression by the state and the ICU's inability to withstand this pressure due to organisational weaknesses, the emergence of sharp divisions among its leadership, and an attempt by Kadalie to turn it into a more traditional type of trade union that robbed it of much of its vibrancy. Some of its most dedicated and capable organisers were lost to the ICU when Kadalie led a move to expel communists from the organisation. After 1930 the ICU continued in name until the death of Kadalie in 1951, but it had long since ceased to function.

A Natal provincial breakaway, the ICU yase Natal, under A.W.G. Champion, broke away from the parent body in 1928. Under the onslaught of police repression, this had also effectively collapsed by 1930 although Champion continued to speak in its name.

African National Congress

After the anti-pass campaigns ended in the immediate post-war years, the ANC lapsed into a period of relative inactivity until about 1927. During this time African activists tended to channel their political activities through the ICU. In 1923, though, the ANC did take three decisions that were to strengthen its organisational identity for many years to come: it changed its name officially from the South African Native National Congress to the African National Congress, it approved 'Nkosi Sikelel' iAfrika' as its official anthem, and it adopted its black-, green- and-gold flag – the colours representing the people, the land and the mineral wealth beneath the soil.

The harsh measures against black people's rights taken by the Pact government, together with signs of the disintegration of the ICU, stirred the more militant sections of the ANC to revitalise the organisation. In 1927 Josiah Gumede was elected president and E.J. Khaile, a communist, became the secretary general. Gumede was keen to work with the CPSA and supported the use of more militant methods than those preferred by the ANC, including protest demonstrations and strikes. He developed a strong international perspective on the national liberation struggle. In 1927 he attended the International Congress of the League Against Imperialism in Brussels, Belgium, where he met with leaders of anti-imperialist movements from countries such as India, China, Cuba and Mexico. He also visited the Soviet Union; when he returned, he declared that he had seen the 'new Jerusalem'. His willingness to support the CPSA was reinforced by a 1929 resolution of the Comintern that instructed the CPSA to work for an 'independent native republic', thus placing the national liberation of Africans at the heart of the party's programme, alongside the class struggle of workers.

The older, more conservative leaders did not take kindly to Gumede's leadership. In 1930 they succeeded in removing him from office and replacing him with the much more conservative Pixley ka Isaka Seme.

CHAPTER 9: DISCUSSION QUESTIONS

1. The influenza (or flu) epidemic of 1919 killed five times more South Africans than all the wars since 1898. Why do you think that most of us know much more about the wars than about the flu epidemic? Do you think that history will treat the HIV/AIDS epidemic of the late-twentieth and the early twenty-first centuries or the Covid-19 pandemic of 2019–20 in the same way?

2. After the Union of South Africa was established, it was women, rather than the all-male ANC leadership, who were the first Africans to employ mass protest action when they conducted their anti-pass campaign. Why do you think this was so?

3. The Pact government was fundamentally an alliance between the white labour movement and Afrikaner nationalism. How did the government's policies and legislation benefit each of these groups?

4. Some historians argue that the Industrial and Commercial Workers' Union (ICU) was an integral part of the national liberation struggle and not a 'normal' trade union. Do you agree with this interpretation? Give reasons to back up your opinion.

CHAPTER 9: ADDITIONAL READINGS

Online readings

1918: South Africa's Death Toll. *Health24*. https://www.health24.com/Medical/Flu/The-1918-epidemic/1918-South-Africas-death-toll-20120721

Industrial and Commercial Workers Union (ICU). https://www.sahistory.org.za/article/industrial-and-commercial-workers-union-icu.

Jacobs, A. (2011) The Rise and Fall of the Industrial and Commercial Union of South Africa, 1919–1929. *International Journal of Humanities and Social Science,* 1 (1): 40–51. http://www.ijhssnet.com/journals/Vol._1_No._1;_January_2011/6.pdf.

Meli, F. (1989) *A History of the ANC: South Africa Belongs to Us.* London: James Currey. (Chapters 1 and 2)

Pampallis, J. (1991) *Foundations of the New South Africa.* Cape Town: Maskew Miller Longman. (Chapters 9 and 10). https://www.sahistory.org.za/sites/default/files/file%20uploads%20/foundation_of_the_new_south_africa_original_final.pdf.

Seekings, J. (2007) 'Not a Single White Person Should Be Allowed to Go Under': Swartgevaar and the Origins of South Africa's Welfare State, 1924–1929. *Journal of African History,* 48 (1): 575–94. https://open.uct.ac.za/bitstream/handle/11427/19492/not%20a%20single.pdf?sequence=6.

Segregation in Action. Johannesburg: The Apartheid Museum. https://www.apartheidmuseum.org/uploads/files/Resources/learners-Book/Learners-book-Chapter2.pdf.

Simons, Jack and Ray Simons (1983) *Class and Colour in South Africa, 1850–1950.* London: International Defence and Aid. (Chapters 8–13 and 16). https://www.sahistory.org.za/sites/default/files/file%20uploads%20/class_and_colour_-_harold_jack_simons_r.e._simons.pdf.

State Policies and Social Protest, 1924–1939. *South African History Online.* http://www.sahistory.org.za/article/state-policies-and-social-protest-1924-1939.

Books

Giliomee, H and B. Mbenga (eds) (2007) *New History of South Africa.* Cape Town: Tafelberg. (Chapter 10)

Meli, F. (1988) *A History of the ANC: South Africa Belongs to Us.* London: James Currey. (Chapter 3)

Morris, M. (2004) *Every Step of the Way: The Journey to Freedom in South Africa.* Cape Town: HSRC Press. (Chapter 8)

Roux, E. (1967) *Time Longer than Rope.* Madison, WI: Wisconsin University Press. (Chapters 14–16)

Thompson, L. (2014) *A History of South Africa.* Johannesburg: Jonathan Ball. (Chapter 5)

Ten

Slump and Recovery, 1929–1939

In the 1929 election, under the slogan 'Stem wit vir 'n witmansland' (Vote white for a white man's country), J.B.M. Hertzog's National Party won an outright majority, allowing it to rule without the support of the Labour Party. The following decade was characterised by a crisis in both the South African economy and in the liberation organisations, followed by a revival of both in the late 1930s.

ECONOMIC DEVELOPMENTS

The National Party took office on the eve of the Great Depression, which gripped the entire capitalist world. South Africa, like many other countries, entered a period of severe economic hardship. The quantity of exports fell, as did the prices of South Africa's main exports. This had a harmful effect on the mining, manufacturing and services industries. Production dropped sharply, thus increasing unemployment. The impact of the depression on white commercial farmers was somewhat allayed when the government introduced protective import tariffs and export subsidies.

The wages paid to farm labourers, however, were reduced. Farmers sought to increase the areas of land they themselves cultivated, and so labour tenants were increasingly forced to become full-time wage labourers or leave the farms altogether. In the cities and towns, thousands of black and white workers lost their jobs or had their wages cut. Many unemployed African workers were forced by circumstances to leave the urban areas and move to the reserves. White workers were partly protected by the 'civilised labour policy', which gave them preference over black workers in a shrinking job market.

The situation deteriorated further when South Africa's main trading partners – Britain and some other British Commonwealth nations – devalued their currencies in September 1931 so as to make their exports more competitive. In an attempt to assert

South Africa's economic independence from Britain, Hertzog refused to devalue the South African pound. This made exports more expensive, and so exports fell and wealthy individuals and foreign investors began withdrawing money from South Africa.

The South African government was eventually forced to devalue in December 1932. The result was an immediate increase in the price of exports, the most significant of which was gold. Manufacturing industry also grew strongly as mining capitalists and foreign investors invested in it. The living standards of almost all whites improved. South African industry benefited from growing state investment in state-owned enterprises such as the Iron and Steel Corporation (ISCOR), the Electricity Supply Commission (ESCOM) and the railways.

Social Conditions

The economic boom of the mid- and late 1930s led to rapid urbanisation as people of all races moved to squalid, overcrowded urban locations, often characterised by high rates of disease and crime. The proportion of African women in the Witwatersrand increased, but by 1936 they still constituted only about a third of the African urban population. Most urban men and women were migrants. In the rural areas, of course, women outnumbered men, and children generally lived with their mothers or grandmothers. Most women in the urban areas could get jobs only in domestic service. Others survived in precarious occupations such as hawking or the brewing and selling of home-made liquor.

While farming still provided an important source of income for rural families, agriculture became progressively less productive as the labour of young people was lost to the cities. The limited land available led to overstocking and impoverishment of the soil. An increasing share of rural incomes came from the remittances of urban relatives. Malnutrition and child mortality rose.

Government

Owing to fears of social disorder as a result of the economic crisis, the two largest white parties decided in 1933 to form a coalition government, with Hertzog (National Party) as Prime Minister and Smuts (South African Party) as his deputy. The following year the two parties merged to create the United Party. However, this merger was not supported by the radical nationalist section of the National Party, which accused Hertzog of betraying Afrikaner interests. Under the leadership of D.F. Malan, they formed the Purified National Party, which soon became known simply as the National Party.

In 1936, the United Party government passed two significant pieces of repressive legislation: the Representation of Natives Act and the Native Trust and Land Act. These became widely known as the Hertzog Bills before they were officially enacted. The former removed African men in the Cape Province from the common voters' roll. The value of their votes had already declined when, in 1930, voting rights had been given to white (but not black) women, thus decreasing the proportion of Africans on the voters' roll. African men were now placed on a separate roll and allowed to elect three white representatives

Prospect Township removals, Johannesburg, 1938. Source: UWC Robben Island Mayibuye Archive

to Parliament and two to the Cape Provincial Council. A Native Representative Council, which had only advisory powers, was established. One effect of removing Africans from the common voters' roll was that the 1913 Land Act also became applicable in the Cape Province.

The Native Trust and Land Act extended the land in the reserves from 8 per cent of South Africa's territory to 13 per cent. The intention was for the government to buy up additional land and add it to the reserves. This process proved to be very slow and fifty-five years later, in 1990, the additional land had still not all been transferred to the reserves (later known as bantustans or homelands). Farms owned by Africans outside the reserves – purchased before 1913 Land Act – and surrounded by white-owned land were labelled 'black spots'; the people who lived there could now be forced to move to areas adjacent to the reserves – land that was invariably of poorer quality than what they had left behind.

THE LIBERATION MOVEMENT

In early 1930s, the liberation movement was considerably weakened, partly because of government repression and partly as a result of internal divisions and conflict. Political meetings and other gatherings were frequently broken up by police, and militant activists were harassed, imprisoned or banished to remote rural areas. On 16 December 1930 Johannes Nkosi, a leading member of the African National Congress (ANC) and the Communist Party of South Africa (CPSA), was murdered at an anti-pass demonstration in Durban.

J.B.M. Hertzog and Jan Smuts dominated South African politics between the two World Wars.
Source (Jan Smuts): Yousuf Karsh

The anti-communism within the ANC that led to the removal of Gumede from the presidency in 1930 gained strength among the ANC leadership and other prominent Africans, including some church leaders. The more conservative also opposed all militant methods of struggle. The new president, Pixley ka Isaka Seme, ruled out any further cooperation between the ANC and the CPSA. The great militant leader of the previous decade, Clements Kadalie, now opposed pass-burning campaigns on the grounds that communists were supposedly leading them. However, a motion to expel communists, proposed at the ANC's 1931 conference, was defeated.

The CPSA fell into a crisis in the early 1930s as it moved into a period of sectarian factionalism under the new leadership of Douglas Wolton. He opposed cooperating with the ANC on the basis that it was reformist rather than revolutionary, and was not conducting a struggle for the working class. A number of the party's founders, including some leading trade unionists, were expelled. As the CPSA became enmeshed in internal conflicts, its membership declined drastically. It was not until 1934 that a strenuous reaction against such sectarianism was launched, led by Moses Kotane in particular.

The threat posed by the Hertzog Bills in the mid-1930s worried many black leaders of all political and religious persuasions. ANC president Seme and Professor D.D.T. Jabavu of the University of Fort Hare took the lead in convening the All African Convention (AAC) in December 1935. This attracted over 400 delegates from various organisations: the ANC, the African People's Organisation (APO), the South African Indian Congress (SAIC), the CPSA, and clergy of various denominations. Unusually for the time, the delegates also included a number of women. The meeting decided to constitute the AAC as a permanent organisation to oppose the Hertzog Bills and take up other relevant issues. An important decision was the adoption of a resolution submitted by Charlotte Maxeke to establish a National Council of African Women.

The All African Convention proved to be a turning point of sorts. The ANC rejected the idea, put forward by some, that it should dissolve itself in favour of the AAC. It decided instead to revive itself. It held a Silver Jubilee Conference in 1937 to celebrate the organisation's twenty-fifth anniversary, which generated considerable enthusiasm among African people. A number of ANC stalwarts were elected to the Native Representative Council and used their positions to travel around the country (at government expense) while helping to revive the ANC. Progress, however, was difficult and slow. The CPSA also began to rebuild itself and recruited new members. Communists again became active in the national movements: the ANC, the APO, and the Natal and Transvaal Indian Congresses. In the Western Cape, the National Liberation League (NLL) was established; its support came mainly from those sections of the coloured community opposed to the cautious approach of the APO. It was led by Zainunnisa 'Cissie' Gool, a prominent communist and daughter of the APO's founder, Dr Abdullah Abdurahman.

The late 1930s also saw the establishment of new trade unions organising African, coloured and Indian workers after the virtual collapse of their unions in the early years of the decade. Two trade union federations were established and they merged in 1941 to form the Council of Non-European Trade Unions (CNETU), which claimed 158 000 members in 119 unions, the largest of which was the African Mine Workers' Union. The Garment Workers' Union was a non-racial trade union made up mainly of women workers. It came under strong attack from white racist trade unionists and the Afrikaner nationalist movement in general, which opposed the participation of white workers in non-racial organisations.

AFRIKANER NATIONALISM

Dr Malan's National Party represented the interests of a range of Afrikaner groupings: farmers, business people, professionals, intellectuals, teachers and trade unionists. All of them aspired to overcome the 'second-class position' of Afrikaners in an environment where economic, intellectual and cultural life, and even the public service, were largely dominated by English-speakers. Achieving this was one of the main ambitions of the National Party. It promoted a narrowly nationalist ideology and was strongly supported by the Dutch Reformed churches. The poor white farmers and farm tenants who continued to migrate into the urban areas were mainly Afrikaners. The Afrikaner nationalist movement tried to organise them into all-white Afrikaner-dominated trade unions and other institutions such as youth, women's and cultural organisations.

The broad Afrikaner nationalist movement created a whole range of new institutions to help promote and develop Afrikaner culture. The most important of these was the Afrikaner Broederbond, a secret organisation of Afrikaner leaders in various fields including politics, business, religion, education and culture. The Broederbond created the Federasie van Afrikaanse Kultuurverenigings (FAK, or the Federation of Afrikaans

Charlotte Maxeke had a long and distinguished career as a
political and religious leader. She campaigned energetically
against the pass laws and for African education. She was the
first president of the Bantu Women's League (within the ANC)
and also became president of the Women's Missionary Society
of the African Methodist Episcopalian Church. Source: Historical
Papers Research Archive, University of the Witwatersrand,
South Africa.

Cultural Organisations), which grew to include over 300 affiliates: cultural bodies, youth
and student organisations, and church, charitable, scientific and educational groups.
Committees were established to strengthen and modernise the Afrikaans language.
Efforts were made to penetrate white trade unions and win Afrikaner workers from
'socialist' and 'foreign' influences.

Pro-Nazi ideology grew among certain sections of the Afrikaner community, who
saw an affinity between Nazism and their white supremacist ideology. A number of
paramilitary groups were established, including the relatively small but influential
Ossewa Brandwag.

Afrikaner-owned commercial concerns were established or extended, including the
insurance companies Santam and Sanlam (established in 1918), Volkskas Bank (1934), the
newspaper publisher Nasionale Pers (1914), and a number of agricultural cooperatives.
Many of these concerns were financed by mobilising the capital of farmers; they also
benefited from favourable government procurement policies. The Afrikaner nationalist
movement worked to mobilise Afrikaners to support Afrikaner-owned businesses of all
types, small and large, and was largely successful in this.

CHAPTER 10: DISCUSSION QUESTIONS

1. What developments in the 1930s showed that South Africa was an integral part of the world economy and partly dependent on it?

2. The Afrikaner nationalist movement was an alliance of various classes and interest groups in the Afrikaner community. Identify these groups and discuss how each expected to benefit from the movement.

3. The Hertzog Bills were an attack on two fundamental rights of African people, further diminishing their franchise rights and their right to land. These laws were not really necessary to maintain white supremacy; so why do you think the government adopted them despite strong protests from black organisations and even sections of the white population?

4. The liberation movement began to regroup and rebuild its strength in the late 1930s. Looking broadly at developments in South Africa, including the liberation movement itself, discuss what the reasons could have been for the turnaround in the fortunes of the liberation movement.

CHAPTER 10: ADDITIONAL READINGS

Online readings

Jabavu, D.D.T. (n.d.) *The Findings of the All African Convention* (Pamphlet written by the president of the All African Convention). http://uir.unisa.ac.za/bitstream/handle/10500/9760/JCP1_1_8_Part1.pdf?sequence=1&isAllowed=y.

McKenna, A. (2011) *The History of Southern Africa*. New York: Britannica and Rosen. (See Chapter 10). http://www.sahistory.org.za/sites/default/files/file%20uploads%20/amy_mckenna_editor_the_history_of_southern_afrbook4you.pdf.

Pampallis, J. (1991) *Foundations of the New South Africa*. Cape Town: Maskew Miller Longman. (Chapter 11). https://www.sahistory.org.za/sites/default/files/file%20uploads%20/foundation_of_the_new_south_africa_original_final.pdf

Simons, Jack and Ray Simons (1983) *Class and Colour in South Africa, 1850–1950*. London: International Defence and Aid Fund. (Chapters 17, 18, 20, 21 and 22). https://www.sahistory.org.za/sites/default/files/file%20uploads%20/class_and_colour_-_harold_jack_simons_r.e._simons.pdf.

South Africa Abandons the Gold Standard, Sparking a Period of Economic Expansion. *South African History Online*. https://www.sahistory.org.za/

dated-event/south-africa-abandons-gold-standard-sparking-period-economic-expansion.

Books

Davenport, T.R.H. (1991) *South Africa: A Modern History.* London: Macmillan. (Chapters 11 and 12)

Giliomee, H. and B. Mbenga (eds.) (2007) *New History of South Africa.* Cape Town: Tafelberg. (Chapters 11 and 12)

Meli, F. (1988) *A History of the ANC: South Africa Belongs to Us.* London: James Currey. (Chapter 4)

Roux, E. (1967) *Time Longer than Rope.* Madison, WI: Wisconsin University Press. (Chapters 19–23)

Thompson, L. (2014) *A History of South Africa.* Johannesburg: Jonathan Ball. (Chapter 5)

Eleven

World War II and After

World War II is commonly considered to have started when Nazi Germany, under the leadership of Adolf Hitler, invaded Poland on 1 September 1939. Two days later Britain and France ('the Allies') declared war on Germany. Within the next nine months, Germany invaded and occupied many European countries. It made an alliance with Italy and Japan (the three powers were collectively known as the Axis). In Asia, Japan had already in 1937 invaded China where it was facing stiff resistance. In September 1940, an Italian army based in Libya moved against British forces in Egypt, leading in a prolonged war in north Africa. In 1941, the Soviet Union and the United States were attacked by Germany and Japan respectively; they joined the war on the side of the Allies. Japan invaded and occupied countries in eastern and southern Asia, including the British colonies of Malaya and Burma and the French colony of Vietnam. The war lasted until 1945 when the Axis was defeated.

The Allies' struggle was ideological as well as military. Anti-fascist propaganda emphasised that the war was being fought to eliminate oppression and ensure freedom in the world. In August 1941 the leaders of the United States and Britain, Franklin D. Roosevelt and Winston Churchill, signed the Atlantic Charter which declared that all peoples should have the right to national self-determination, to choose their own form of government, and to be free from fear and want. These principles were endorsed by 26 governments, including South Africa. The United States and Britain (as well as South Africa and a number of others) saw the Charter as aimed at combating Germany and its allies, and inspiring resistance in the countries they had occupied. However, it inevitably had the effect of stirring up sentiment against oppression of all types in the colonies in Africa, Asia and elsewhere. South Africa was no exception, and black people were inspired to hope and strive for a future free from oppression.

WHITE POLITICAL REALIGNMENT

When the war broke out in 1939, Britain expected all countries in the British Commonwealth to support it. In South Africa, the government was divided on whether to enter the war. Smuts, the Deputy Prime Minister, favoured an immediate declaration of war in support of Britain. On the other hand, Prime Minister Hertzog and his followers, some of whom had Nazi sympathies, opposed South African participation in the war. Smuts managed to win majority support in Parliament, and South Africa entered the war.

Hertzog was forced to resign and Smuts became Prime Minister. Hertzog and his supporters merged with D.F. Malan's National Party to form the Reunited National Party (commonly referred to simply as the National Party). A year later Hertzog, believing the new party was too extreme, left it to form the Afrikaner Party.

SOUTH AFRICAN MILITARY INVOLVEMENT

In response to the Union Defence Force's call for volunteers, 330 000 men and women enlisted. Of these about 77 000 were Africans, who were enrolled into the South African Native Military Corps, and about 46 000 were coloureds and Indians, who joined the Cape Corps. Members of both corps mainly participated in a non-combatant capacity but when they moved into the arena of war they were sometimes armed and fought when their commanding officers thought that military circumstances required it. Their rates of pay were much lower than those for white soldiers. Over 11 000 South Africans, black and white, lost their lives during the war.

In 1940, South African troops, together with other armed forces from Britain and its colonies, invaded Ethiopia, which had been taken over by Italy in 1935. They successfully captured Addis Ababa and reinstated the Ethiopian emperor, Haile Selassie, who had been removed by the Italians. About 120 000 South African troops participated in the Allies' North African campaign against the Italian and German armies. They participated in several important encounters with the enemy, including the Battle of Tobruk (in Libya, 1941) and the Battle of El Alamein (in Egypt, 1942), where several thousands were taken prisoner by the German army. The Allies successfully drove the Italians and Germans out of North Africa. In 1943, the South African army joined the Anglo-American invasion of Italy and, by the end of the war in May 1945, they had reached northern Italy.

Earlier, in 1942, the South African army had joined British forces in invading Madagascar, a French colony that was controlled by Vichy France (the puppet, pro-Nazi regime that existed in parts of France). A few months later they handed it over to General de Gaulle's Free French Forces, which were fighting on the side of the Allies. The South African Air Force also made a contribution in the Madagascar operation; during the whole war it operated in a number of other locations including Ethiopia, North Africa, Italy, the Balkans, Romania and Poland.

ECONOMIC DEVELOPMENT

World War II had a substantial impact on the South African economy. Manufacturing

Members of the South African 6th Armoured Division in the Chianti Highlands as they approached the Italian city of Florence.

grew even faster than it had in the previous five years, although mining still remained by far the largest industry. South African factories began to produce military goods (arms, ammunition, military vehicles, soldiers' boots and uniforms) for South African and other Allied forces. They also began producing goods whose importation had been disrupted by the war. There was rapid growth in the construction, chemical, electronics, textile and other sectors. Mining also expanded, especially for coal and iron ore, products that were in demand by other industries. Steel manufacture expanded to keep military and other industries supplied, with the state-owned company ISCOR playing the major role. The government established trade missions in central and east Africa to promote the export of goods to countries whose supplies from Europe had been interrupted by the war.

With industrial expansion, it became necessary to recruit more workers. During the war the industrial labour force increased by 53 per cent; by far the most were African, and many were women. This resulted in a rapid expansion of the urban population, leading to an acute housing shortage and consequent overcrowding in African townships and informal settlements on the outskirts of cities such as Johannesburg, Cape Town and Durban. For the first time, blacks outnumbered whites in urban areas. By the end of the war almost a quarter of all Africans in South Africa lived in the urban areas, providing the social base that would invigorate the liberation movement in the years to come.

THE LIBERATION MOVEMENT

At the outbreak of the war, the National Executive Committee of the African National Congress (ANC) issued a statement. It would support the war effort only if Africans were armed and deployed as soldiers and not just as labourers, and were 'included in the South African body politic' – that is, allowed to vote for the government and have equal rights with whites. This position, however, was overturned by the ANC's annual conference, which endorsed the government's decision to declare war on the side of Britain. It also stated that the government 'should consider' giving full citizenship to 'African and other Non-European races' of South Africa. So while it had reservations, the ANC placed no absolute conditions on its support for the government's war efforts.

When the war began in 1939, the Communist Party of South Africa (CPSA) at first labelled it an inter-imperialist war, a power struggle between two sets of imperialist powers. It therefore urged South Africans not to support the war, either by joining the armed forces or by giving money. However, after Nazi Germany attacked the Soviet Union in June 1941, the CPSA took the view that the nature of the war had changed. It declared that the Soviet Union was the world's only socialist country where workers had taken over the factories, mines and the land, and ruled themselves; it had no colonies and stood for the national liberation of all oppressed people. The defeat of the Soviet Union would thus be a major blow for workers around the world. The party now changed its stance and gave full support to the war effort; it urged all South Africans to do likewise.

The revival of the liberation movement gained momentum during the war years. Within the ANC, the search for a more effective leadership led to the election of Dr A.B. Xuma as president in 1940. A new constitution was adopted to ensure greater centralisation and coordination of the provincial structures. For the first time, women were to be admitted as full members instead of as 'auxiliary members'. At its 1942 annual conference the ANC asked Xuma to establish a committee to study the Atlantic Charter and develop a Bill of Rights. A year later, this resulted in the ANC adopting the document 'African Claims in South Africa'. The document brought together most of the demands of the liberation movement: an end to racial discrimination; the right of all adults to vote and to be elected to Parliament; a fair redistribution of land; the abolition of discriminatory labour legislation; freedom of trade for Africans; the right to a good education for African children; and adequate medical and health facilities for all.

Despite the gradual revitalisation of the ANC, some young members were unhappy with its slow progress and the cautious approach of the leadership. They sought to turn the ANC into a dynamic and militant organisation. In response to pressure from the youth, the 1943 conference passed a resolution providing for the establishment of a Youth League and a Women's League. In April 1944, the ANC Youth League was formed in the Transvaal with Anton Lembede as its president. Other branches were later established in the Cape and Natal. Prominent members of the Youth League included Nelson Mandela, Oliver Tambo, Joe Matthews, Duma Nokwe, Robert Sobukwe and M.B. Yengwa. The Youth League called its philosophy 'African nationalism'. This involved an assertion of African identity, a rejection of 'foreign leadership of Africa', an emphasis on the unity

A wartime poster published in the progressive newspaper,
The Guardian. Source: UWC Robben Island Mayibuye
Archive

of Africans, and a belief that Africans must rely on their own efforts to free themselves. They rejected cooperation with the non-racial CPSA.

The ANC Women's League was established in 1943 to coincide with the admission of women into full membership of the ANC. It was not very active during the war years, but it did participate in the Women's Anti-Pass Conference in March 1944 and in the 1944–5 anti-pass campaign (see below).

The war years saw growing cooperation between the ANC and the CPSA. Together they campaigned for African soldiers to be allowed to carry arms. 'If you want the Non-Europeans to fight for democracy, why not give them democracy to fight for?' asked Moses Kotane, a leader of both the ANC and CPSA. In 1944–5, the two organisation also cooperated in a large anti-pass campaign which included a march of over 15 000 people in Johannesburg.

In 1943, a much-weakened All African Convention joined forces with a group known as the Anti-CAD[15] to form the Non-European Unity Movement (NEUM). Its membership was mainly in the Western Cape with some support in the Eastern Cape. It

---

15 CAD stood for the Coloured Affairs Department. The Anti-CAD was formed to oppose the government's establishment of that department.

adopted a Ten Point Programme, which called for universal franchise, redistribution of the land, revision of the tax and labour laws, and civil rights for all. The Unity Movement (as the NEUM would soon be called) would only cooperate with other organisations if the activities were 'principled' in terms of its programme. It condemned struggles for reforms as tantamount to accepting 'half a loaf' instead of total freedom. The result was to isolate the Unity Movement from the rest of the liberation movement and the overall resistance against oppression.

Community-level protests, provoked by particular grievances and not specifically organised by any national movement, took place in various areas. For example, from 1940 to 1944 the people of Alexandra township organised four separate bus boycotts to protest against a one-penny increase in the bus fare to central Johannesburg; they were successful on each occasion.

In the Aftermath of War

South Africa and the United Nations

World War II ended in 1945 with the defeat of the Axis powers. European and Asian countries that had been occupied by Germany and Japan were liberated. The end of the war also strengthened demands for independence and democracy by colonised countries around the world. However, the colonial powers refused to bow to these demands immediately. They did so gradually over the next three decades when compelled to do so by independence movements and international pressure.

In South Africa, the situation of black people became even worse after the war. During the war, Africans had been promised that passes would be abolished when the war was over, that rents would be lowered, and that veterans would receive benefits such as cash payments. They received few of these things: African war veterans received two pounds, a khaki suit and a small monetary gratuity depending on the length of their military service. White soldiers received government assistance to settle into civilian life, including scholarships for those who wanted to study further. Unlike blacks, they retained their military salaries until they found suitable jobs.

At the United Nations (UN), established at the end of the war, Smuts proposed that Namibia (then known as South West Africa) be incorporated into South Africa. Messages of protest were sent by Namibian chiefs as well as by the Botswana chiefs and the ANC. Smuts's proposal was rejected by the UN. Instead, it proposed that Namibia be made a Trust Territory under the UN Trusteeship Committee, and that it be led to independence. South Africa refused to accept this, and continued to administer Namibia illegally as though it were a fifth province of the country. In 1949 Namibian whites were given the right to elect six MPs to the South African Parliament.

Miners' strike

In August 1946, 75 000 African miners went on strike. They demanded a minimum wage of ten shillings a day (the average wage of African miners at the time was under two and a half shillings), adequate food, and the end of a War Measure that restricted gatherings of more than twenty people in mining areas. The strikers, led by the J.B. Marks, chairman of the African Mine Workers' Union and a prominent member of both the ANC and the CPSA, lasted only a week before police smashed it with the use of batons and firearms and the arrest of strike committee members. Despite such violence by the state, the number of trade unions in the mining and other industries continued to grow after 1946.

Indian passive resistance

In 1946, the South African Indian Congress (SAIC) protested against the Asiatic Land Tenure and Indian Representation Act of 1946 – popularly known as the Ghetto Act – which restricted Indian landownership to certain 'exempted areas'. The law was designed to force Indians to live and trade only in designated areas. It was passed in response to demands from white shopkeepers who resented competition from Indian businesses, and from white racists who wanted to prevent Indians living in 'white' neighbourhoods. The protests included a ten-day strike, the closure of Indian-owned businesses, and a passive resistance campaign in which thousands of Indian South Africans gathered and pitched tents on land reserved for whites. The campaign lasted for two years despite attacks by white hooligans and the arrest of 2 000 people – including 300 women – as well as fines and the imprisonment of many resisters.

During the campaign, solidarity was expressed by various organisations in the country, including the ANC and the CPSA. Zainunnisa 'Cissie' Gool, a communist member of the Cape Town City Council, led a group of volunteers who travelled to Durban to join the passive resistance campaign; a number were arrested, including Gool herself. The Reverend Michael Scott, an Anglican priest, and a number of other whites were also arrested for taking part in the campaign. A group of Africans in Germiston marched in solidarity with the passive resisters and were arrested.

The SAIC appealed to the United Nations, where it was supported by newly independent India and a majority of countries in the General Assembly. The Smuts government refused to change its policies, but the whole affair served to highlight its racist policies. This was the beginning of an international campaign to isolate South Africa that later included economic, sports and cultural sanctions. The campaign would grow steadily and last for fifty years until the abolition of racist rule in 1994. (For more information about the international campaign against apartheid, see Chapter 16 and Theme 9.)

An important development following the campaign against the Ghetto Act was the signing in March 1947 of a joint declaration by Dr A.B. Xuma, Dr G.M. Naicker and Dr Yusuf Dadoo, the presidents of the ANC, the Transvaal Indian Congress (TIC) and the Natal Indian Congress (NIC) respectively, which pledged 'the fullest cooperation between African and Indian peoples'. It called on 'all freedom-loving citizens' to cooperate in the struggle for full franchise rights, equal economic and industrial rights, recognition of African trade unions, the 'removal of all land restrictions against non-Europeans and the provision of adequate housing facilities for all non-Europeans'. It also demanded freedom of movement and the removal of all discriminatory and oppressive laws. This pact was

Dr G.M. Naicker addressing a passive resistance meeting in Durban, 1946. Source: UWC
Robben Island Mayibuye Archive

of major symbolic importance in the development of unity among oppressed people but,
as will be seen, it would be sorely tested just two years later when anti-Indian riots broke
out in Durban (see Chapter 12).

Community struggles

The immediate post-war years saw the growth of community struggles. One of the largest
of these occurred in Johannesburg where, in April 1944, James Mpanza established the
Sofasonke Party and led thousands of Africans onto open land near Orlando where they
built homes made of corrugated iron, scraps of wood and other material. The police
initially failed to move the settlers. Their example was soon followed by others, and
similar shanty towns were established near other townships on the Rand, both during
and after the war. In some areas people set up their own rudimentary system of local
government and taxation. In the late 1940s the authorities destroyed these settlements. In
the Johannesburg area, people were removed to large housing estates near Orlando called
the South Western Townships (now known by the acronym Soweto).

D.F. Malan's first government. The National Party won the 1948 election with a majority of seats but a minority of votes.

The 1948 elections

During the war, many sections of the Afrikaner nationalist movement sympathised with the Nazis and their allies. The most militant of these organisations was the Ossewa Brandwag (Ox-wagon Sentinel), which at its peak grew to about half a million members. Through its armed wing, it waged a campaign of sabotage against state infrastructure such as railway lines, post offices and electric pylons. When it became clear that Germany would be defeated, the Ossewa Brandwag lost members as they realised that their dreams of seizing power would not be realised by using sabotage tactics. Many joined (or rejoined) Malan's National Party, which now came to dominate the Afrikaner nationalist movement. What was left of the Ossewa Brandwag was absorbed by the Afrikaner Party, which made an electoral pact with the National Party. The entire Afrikaner nationalist movement thus came under the hegemony of the National Party, which absorbed the Afrikaner Party three years later.

The Nationalists fought the 1948 election under the slogan of apartheid. Apartheid policy was similar to the segregation policies of previous white governments but was harsher and went much further. Its main aim was to maintain and strengthen white supremacy. It called for the separation of blacks and whites in all spheres of life, with each 'race group' having its own designated areas; virtually all towns and cities and most of the rural areas were reserved for the white minority. Africans would have no political rights at all in the white areas but would exercise their rights only in their 'own' areas –

that is, the reserves. Coloureds and Indians would also have their rights further curtailed.

The National Party appealed to various sectors of the white population, especially the Afrikaners, who constituted about 60 per cent of voters. They promised that white workers would benefit from the extension of job reservation laws, greater employment of Afrikaners in the public service, increased skills training opportunities, and a wide-ranging social welfare programme for whites. Afrikaner businesses, both large and small, looked forward to state support for their businesses through state purchases of their products and services, tariff protection and subsidies. Farmers, who still constituted the majority of Afrikaner voters, were promised 'the special concern and protection of the state', including higher prices for farm products. The campaign was successful; the Nationalists won the 1948 election by five seats, although with a minority of the total votes. D.F. Malan became the new Prime Minister, and South Africa moved into a period where the oppression of the majority would be more intense and systematic than ever before.

CHAPTER 11: DISCUSSION QUESTIONS

1. How and why was D.F. Malan able to unite a previously divided Afrikaner nationalist movement in the late 1940s?

2. What were the most important social and economic developments in South Africa during World War II? In what way did these developments change the country and the lives of its people?

3. Look at the Bill of Rights section of the ANC's 'African Claims' document (1943). Compare it with the 'ANC Youth League Manifesto' (1944). Discuss the similarities and differences in the overall approach of the two documents. (See the additional readings list for links to the documents.)

4. The community struggles of the late 1940s are reminiscent of today's community protest actions. Why do you think that similar activities are still being undertaken by poor communities?

CHAPTER 11: ADDITIONAL READINGS

Online readings

African National Congress (ANC) (1943) Africans' Claims in South Africa. https://www.sahistory.org.za/archive/africans-claims-south-africa-adopted-anc-1943-annual-conference.

The Atlantic Charter (1941). https://larouchepub.com/eiw/public/2015/eirv42n10-20150306/25_4210.pdf.

Industrialisation, Rural Change and Nationalism (2004) Turning Points in History Series, Book 4. Johannesburg: STE Publishers. (Chapters 1, 2 and 3). http://www.sahistory.org.za/archive/book-4-industrialisation-rural-change-and-nationalism-commissioned-department-education.

Non-European Unity Movement (NEUM) (1943) The Ten-Point Programme. https://www.sahistory.org.za/archive/document-8-ten-point-programme-1943.

Pampallis, J. (1991) *Foundations of the New South Africa*. Cape Town: Maskew Miller Longman. (Chapters 12 and 13). https://www.sahistory.org.za/sites/default/files/file%20uploads%20/foundation_of_the_new_south_africa_original_final.pdf.

Simons, Jack and Ray Simons (1983) *Class and Colour in South Africa, 1850–1950*. London: International Defence and Aid Fund. (Chapters 23 and 24). https://www.sahistory.org.za/sites/default/files/file%20uploads%20/class_and_colour_-_harold_jack_simons_r.e._simons.pdf.

South Africa and WW2: The Forgotten Army. https://dirkdeklein.net/2016/09/18/south-africa-and-ww2-the-forgotten-army/comment-page-1/.

Books

Davenport, T.R.H. (1991) *South Africa: A Modern History*. London: Macmillan. (Chapter 13)

Giliomee, H and B. Mbenga (eds) (2007) *New History of South Africa*. Cape Town: Tafelberg. (Chapter 12)

Meli, F. (1988) *A History of the ANC: South Africa Belongs to Us*. London: James Currey. (Chapter 4)

Roux, E. (1967) *Time Longer than Rope*. Madison, WI: Wisconsin University Press. (Chapter 24)

Thompson, L. (2014) *A History of South Africa*. Johannesburg: Jonathan Ball. (Chapter 5)

Twelve

Apartheid Established, 1948–1960

The first priority of the National Party (NP) after winning the 1948 election was to consolidate its power. It did this by entrenching its parliamentary majority and ensuring Afrikaner nationalist control of the major organs of the state. The right of Indians to elect parliamentary representatives, granted in 1946 but never exercised, was now formally withdrawn. Coloureds were removed from the common voters' roll. Constituency boundaries were altered to favour the NP. D.F. Malan retired as Prime Minister in 1954. He was replaced by J.G. Strijdom, who died in 1958 and who was followed by Dr Hendrik Verwoerd. The United Party opposition in Parliament retained the support of most English-speakers and a small number of Afrikaners. However, it offered no clear alternative to the NP and hence was weak and became increasingly ineffective.

NP members (usually approved by the secret Afrikaner nationalist society, the Broederbond – see Chapter 10) were appointed to senior positions in the civil service, the education system, the armed forces, the police and state enterprises such as the South African Broadcasting Corporation (SABC), the South African Railways, the Electricity Supply Commission (ESCOM), and the Iron and Steel Corporation (ISCOR). Similarly, leading Afrikaner nationalists were appointed to top positions in the judiciary.

The end of World War II had changed Afrikaner nationalist perceptions of Britain, which they no longer considered a major obstacle to the achievement of Afrikaner power. The NP supported the United States and Britain in the Cold War against the Soviet Union that developed after World War II. In 1950 the government sent a military contingent to fight in the Korean War in support of the United States and its allies, the chief of which was Britain.

If life had been oppressive for blacks under colonialism before this time, it was about to become much worse. The main objective of the NP from the time of its election was to put in place its policy of apartheid, which it saw as essential to the continuation of white supremacy and Afrikaner power.

For a decade before the NP took power, the liberation movement had grown in size, organisation and militancy. Trade unions had been able to win higher wages in manufacturing and commerce. In the rural reserves, overcrowding and the consequent impoverishment of the land had led to increasingly greater hardships. This had driven migrant workers to be more vigorous in their demands for higher wages to supplement their families' diminishing incomes.

Such developments threatened South Africa's cheap labour system and white political and economic dominance. The government was determined to counter what it saw as threats to white supremacy. Its strategies included restrictions on political activity; the further exclusion of blacks from political representation; limitation of trade unions rights; stricter pass laws; further restrictions on landownership; and stricter racial segregation of residential areas, educational institutions, hospitals and even places of recreation. These developments naturally prompted strong opposition from democratically minded people and especially from the Congress Alliance. This opposition is dealt with in Chapter 13.

RESTRICTIONS ON POLITICAL ACTIVITY

The first major restriction on political activity was the Suppression of Communism Act of 1950. This outlawed the Communist Party of South Africa (CPSA) and made it an offence to 'propagate communism'. The Act was more than just an attack on the CPSA, though; it defined the term 'communism' so broadly that it could include virtually any form of non-parliamentary political opposition. It gave the minister the power to ban any person he considered to be engaged in 'communist activities'. Depending on the minister's order, a banned person could be confined to a particular district, prevented from doing certain types of work, or holding office in a trade union, a political party or other organisation. Over the years many communists and even more non-communists were banned under the provisions of this Act.

The Criminal Law Amendment Act of 1953 provided for long terms of imprisonment, floggings or fines for breaking any regulation 'in support of any campaign for the repeal or modification of any law'. The Public Safety Act of 1953 gave the government powers to declare a State of Emergency and to detain anyone without trial.

RACIAL SEGREGATION

The Population Registration Act of 1950 required that every person in South Africa be classified into one of four so-called racial groups: Native (later changed to Bantu), European (later white), coloured or Indian. Other laws prohibited marriages between whites and members of other groups. Extramarital sexual relations between whites and others were made punishable by up to seven years' imprisonment.

The Group Areas Act of 1950 designated specific parts of the urban areas for the occupation of particular 'racial groups'. Under the Natives Resettlement Act of 1954,

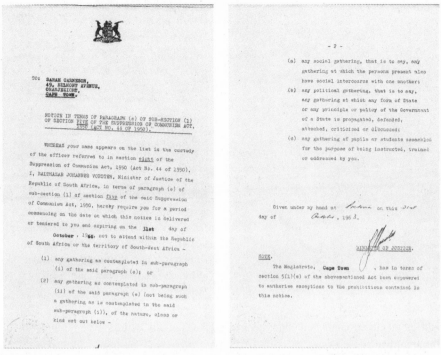

An early banning order restricting the trade union and political activity of Sarah Carneson, a former member of the CPSA. Later banning orders, such as those received by hundreds of people in the 1960s and later, were much more restrictive. They often included orders for the banned person to remain at home from 6 pm to 6 am, to report daily to the police, not to leave their magisterial district without permission, not to meet with more than one other person at a time, and not to communicate with another banned person. Source: Sarah Carneson.

hundreds of thousands of Africans were forcibly removed from their homes and businesses in 'white' areas to various townships or other places in their own 'group areas'. Many Indians and coloureds were similarly forced to move, especially in Durban, Cape Town and Johannesburg. Thousands of African families working on white-owned farms had to move to the reserves, and white farmers began to switch to a greater use of contract labour so that they hired workers only for short periods when the farm was busy and did not need to pay them during quiet times.

Only Africans who had lived in a particular urban area since birth or who had worked there for one employer for ten years or more had a right to live in that area. All others needed a permit to stay for longer than 72 hours. Labour bureaus were established to control the movement of workers into the cities to ensure that labourers did not leave white-owned farms unless farmers' labour needs were met.

Laws were passed requiring that whites and blacks were separated at all times except when blacks were providing labour for white businesses and in white homes. There were racially segregated parks, beaches, movie theatres, hotels, restaurants, railway carriages, buses, and a host of other facilities. There were even separate entrances to post offices

A sign in Durban that states the beach is for whites only. This kind of segregation was also applied to sports fields, cinemas, entrances of post offices and government offices, park benches and other public facilities.

and other government buildings. Invariably, facilities for whites were far superior to those for blacks.

Bantu Education

In the early 1950s most schools for Africans were run by missionaries of various denominations, with some financial assistance from the state. The rest were either state or community schools. The Bantu Education Act of 1953 provided for a separate, government-run school system for Africans. Separate state-run schools and education departments were also established for coloureds and Indians in 1963 and 1967 respectively. This restructuring of the school system brought it largely under the control of the government. From the beginning, a central purpose of the schools for Africans, coloureds and Indians was to train children to accept an inferior position in society and to promote an ethnic (as opposed to a national) consciousness. Mission schools were required to accept the state curriculum or they would lose their government subsidies. Many refused to accept these conditions and closed down or were taken over by the government.

White education also expanded in the 1950s, and parallel-medium schools were largely shut down in favour of separate Afrikaans-medium and English-medium schools in line with the policy to protect Afrikaner culture from being overwhelmed by that of English-speaking whites.

The Bantu Education system led to a large expansion of primary schools to help create an unskilled workforce with basic levels of literacy and numeracy to meet the demands of an expanding economy. Secondary schooling was also expanded rapidly, although enrolments were much lower there than in primary schools. African enrolments in primary schools expanded from 850 000 in 1953 to over 2.6 million in 1975, while secondary enrolments grew from 31 000 to 319 000 over the same period. To meet economic demands and in response to political pressures, enrolments continued to expand throughout the apartheid period. However, gross underfunding of black education compared with white education ensured that the quality of schooling for Africans remained well below that in white schools. In the 1975–6 financial year, for example, state spending on each white school student was R644; for Indians it was R189 per student; for coloureds R139; and for Africans only R42.

The Bantu Education concept was expanded to higher education in 1959 with the Extension of University Education Act. All except one of the existing universities would be reserved for whites; black students could only register at these institutions with special government permission. The only African university – the University of Fort Hare, established in 1916 – was designated for Xhosa students only.[16] Separate institutions were to be established for the other black ethnic groups, including coloureds and Indians.

Pass Laws

The pass laws were made stricter in order to ensure that workers were directed to where they were most needed by white business people, domestic employers and farmers.

The various passes previously required by Africans to be legally present in cities or particular parts of the country were consolidated into one document, officially called a 'reference book' but commonly known as a pass book. For the first time since 1920, women were required to carry passes. Pass books contained the name and photograph of the holder, his or her identity number, ethnic group, permission to be in a particular area, tax receipts, and an employer's signature every month. Africans had to carry their pass book at all times and show it to any policeman on demand. Those not carrying their pass book, or whose book was not in order, could be imprisoned or fined. The conviction of hundreds of thousands of Africans each year for pass offences became a feature of South African life.

Trade Union Rights

To avoid an upsurge of worker unrest as well as international condemnation, the government decided not to ban the black unions. Instead it tried to disable them through a number of incremental measures to restrict workers' rights. In the five years following the passing of the Suppression of Communism Act in 1950, 156 workers – both blacks and whites – were banned, thus depriving the unions of many of their most important leaders.

---

16 An anomaly was the Medical School of the University of Natal; it had been established in 1947 for black students and long remained the only institution in the country where blacks could train to be medical doctors.

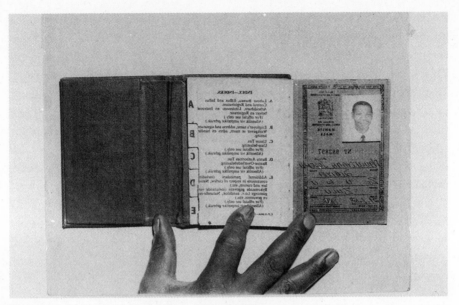

Passbook. Source: UWC Robben Island Mayibuye Archive.

Strikes by African workers were made illegal. African trade unions could no longer be registered and employers did not have to negotiate with them. If they did negotiate, any agreement was not enforceable by law, thus allowing employers to flout any agreement if it no longer suited them. The only legally binding negotiations were through the employer-dominated works and liaison committees. Further information on the assault on black trade unions by the NP and its allies is provided in Theme 7.

THE BANTUSTANS

In 1959, the Promotion of Bantu Self-Government Act provided for the establishment of eight (later, ten) 'bantustans' (later referred to as 'bantu homelands') – see Theme 2. These areas coincided roughly with the former reserves. Each bantustan was meant for members of a particular ethnic group. In time they were intended to become independent states. Every African was to become a citizen of a particular bantustan and would thus be deprived of his or her South African citizenship. According to apartheid propaganda, each African 'nation' was going to develop separately on its own, thus exercising its right to political self-determination. In fact, the bantustans were always completely dependent on the South African state.

The government saw the bantustans as one means of preserving white domination through a 'divide-and-rule' strategy. It also envisaged that white supremacy would be strengthened by the creation of a group of African collaborators (mainly chiefs) associated with the bantustan governments, who would in time become allies of the white regime. The bantustans were seen too as places to which the government could send unemployed Africans to keep them away from the white areas. At a time when the decolonisation movement in Africa and elsewhere was gaining momentum, the government hoped that the bantustans would give the impression internationally that South Africa was taking into account black people's aspirations to rule themselves.

THE APARTHEID ECONOMY

The repressive measures taken by the NP government resulted in a reduction of wages for black workers. This led to greater business profits and thus attracted large international and local investments, particularly from the big mining houses, which also started to invest in manufacturing and finance. The discovery of the rich Orange Free State goldfields boosted economic development with the opening of new mines and spin-off investment in manufacturing and construction.

The state intervened directly in the economy, establishing SASOL in 1950 to manufacture oil from coal, increasing the production of steel at ISCOR, expanding the railway network, and establishing financial institutions to provide capital for mining, manufacturing and agriculture. Tariff protection sheltered local industries from foreign competition. Afrikaner businesses especially benefited from government contracts and the accounts of many state institutions were transferred to Afrikaner-owned banks. Afrikaner businesses such as Sanlam, Rembrandt and Volkskas Bank grew into large corporations on par with those controlled by English-speakers.

White-owned commercial agriculture benefited from tariff protection, state-controlled prices and stricter pass laws; farms were provided with prison labour from 1954. White-owned small businesses were shielded from competition by the removal of Indian-owned businesses from the most desirable trading areas. White workers benefited from an expansion of the occupations reserved for whites, and many were promoted to supervisory, technical and clerical jobs with the necessary training provided.

As long as black resistance could be contained, there appeared to be few disadvantages to apartheid for the white population. Only a small number of left-wing whites supported the liberation movement's fundamental opposition to the system. For most, life went on as usual, with cheap black workers fuelling business profits and low-paid black domestic servants working in white homes. Living standards for whites improved as workers benefited from more stringent job reservation, and white businesses were protected from competition from blacks and from foreign imports. White lifestyles changed for the better with the spread of motor vehicle ownership and household appliances, the investment of resources in segregated public schools and hospitals, and a steady growth in incomes.

CHAPTER 12: DISCUSSION QUESTIONS

1. Do you think that apartheid was significantly different from the colonial and segregation periods that came before it? Discuss your reasons.

2. What do you think the apartheid government hoped to achieve with the pass laws? Consider the government's economic, political and social aims.

3. What do you think that the government wanted to achieve with the introduction of Bantu Education?

Chapter 12: Additional Readings

Online readings

Apartheid and Reactions to It. *South African History Online.* https://www.sahistory.org.za/article/apartheid-and-reactions-it.

Luthuli, A. (1964) Paper presented to the International Conference for Sanctions against South Africa, 1 April 1964, London. https://www.sahistory.org.za/archive/paper-presented-international-conference-sanctions-against-south-africa-1-april-1964-london.

McKenna, A. (2011) *The History of Southern Africa.* New York: Britannica and Rosen. (Chapter 10). http://www.sahistory.org.za/sites/default/files/file%20uploads%20/amy_mckenna_editor_the_history_of_southern_afrbook4you.pdf.

Pampallis, J. (1991) *Foundations of the New South Africa.* Cape Town: Maskew Miller Longman. (Chapter 14). https://www.sahistory.org.za/sites/default/files/file%20uploads%20/foundation_of_the_new_south_africa_original_final.pdf.

Pass Laws in South Africa, 1800–1994. https://www.sahistory.org.za/article/pass-laws-south-africa-1800-1994.

Books

Davenport, T.R.H. (1991) *South Africa: A Modern History.* London: Macmillan. (Chapters 14 and 15)

Giliomee, H. and B. Mbenga (eds) (2007) *New History of South Africa.* Cape Town: Tafelberg. (Chapter 13)

Meli, F. (1988) *A History of the ANC: South Africa Belongs to Us.* London: James Currey. (Chapter 5)

Morris, M. (2004) *Every Step of the Way: The Journey to Freedom in South Africa.* Cape Town: HSRC Press. (Chapter 9)

Thompson, L. (2014) *A History of South Africa.* Johannesburg: Jonathan Ball. (Chapter 6)

Thirteen

Initial Resistance to Apartheid, 1948–1960

The shock produced by the accession to power of D.F. Malan's apartheid government motivated the African National Congress (ANC) to shift to the more militant stance advocated by the Youth League and the Communist Party of South Africa (CPSA). This new attitude was reflected at the 1949 ANC conference, where the Programme of Action, drafted by the Youth League, was adopted. The Programme claimed the right to self-determination for the African people and rejected all forms of white domination. It also called for mass struggle through boycotts, strikes and civil disobedience, and stressed the need to issue propaganda material to 'raise the level of political and national consciousness'. At the same conference Dr J.S. Moroka replaced Dr Xuma as president and Walter Sisulu became secretary general. During the 1950s, the ANC grew into a mass movement, developed strong cross-racial alliances, and began to clarify its vision of what it believed a future democratic South Africa should be like. However, the decade did not start on a very promising note for the liberation movement.

AFRICAN–INDIAN CONFLICT

Despite the promise of cooperation between Africans and Indians following the Xuma–Naicker–Dadoo Pact, unity was threatened by events in Durban in early 1949. An incident involving the beating of an African boy by an Indian shopkeeper in central Durban quickly and explosively developed into an outburst of violence by Africans against Indians – and counter-violence by Indians defending themselves. The carnage lasted for two days and spread to many outlying areas like Cato Manor, leaving at least 140 people dead, over a 1 000 injured, 300 buildings destroyed and 40 000 Indian refugees without homes. The police made little effort to protect people who were under attack but, with the help of the Navy, did eventually intervene to suppress the violence with heavy-weapons fire that added dozens to the death toll.

The deeper causes of the violence lay in the oppressive poverty in the squalid shanty towns in which Africans and Indians lived and the overall system of racism that affected them both, although to a different extent. Many Africans, with some support from local ANC leaders, channelled their frustrations towards Indians with whom they were in close day-to-day contact rather than at the oppressive political and economic system.

When the violence broke out, ANC and Natal Indian Congress (NIC) leaders mounted a joint effort to end it and to give aid and medical attention to those who were injured and displaced. Both organisations saw the maintenance of unity as crucial in the face of apartheid oppression and managed to maintain solidarity in the face of threats. At the community level, however, the trauma could not be easily erased and inter-racial tensions remained for years to come.

COMMUNIST PARTY: DISSOLUTION AND RE-ESTABLISHMENT

When the government passed the Suppression of Communism Act in 1950, the CPSA leadership decided to dissolve the party. The decision of the Central Committee was not unanimous but most felt it was necessary to avoid the consequences of refusing to disband, including prison terms of up to ten years for being a member. Most rank-and-file members accepted the dissolution as a tactic to avoid repression and they remained active in other organisations, including the ANC, the Natal and Transvaal Indian Congresses, the trade unions and women's movements. In 1953 a number of former CPSA members met in a secret conference. They decided to reconstitute the party under a new name, the South African Communist Party (SACP). It operated secretly as an underground organisation and only announced its existence publicly seven years later, in 1960.

MASS ACTION

The first major manifestation of the ANC's militancy after the adoption of the Programme of Action was a general strike in Johannesburg and other Witwatersrand towns on 1 May 1950. Police fired on groups of strikers in Sophiatown, Orlando, Alexandra and Benoni. Eighteen people were killed and over thirty wounded. To express their outrage, the organisations called a National Day of Protest and Mourning on 26 June in cities thorough the country. Other demonstrations took place on 6 April 1952 to protest against the government's celebration of the 300th anniversary of the arrival of Jan van Riebeeck at the Cape.

In June 1952, the ANC and the South African Indian Congress (SAIC) launched a Campaign of Defiance against Unjust Laws, which became popularly known simply as the Defiance Campaign. Its purpose was to mobilise popular opposition to certain unjust laws, including the pass laws, the Bantu Authorities Act, the Group Areas Act and the Suppression of Communism Act. The campaign took the form of large numbers

Two of the leaders of Defiance Campaign, James Moroka and Yusuf Dadoo. Source: Jurgen Schadeberg

of volunteers publicly but peacefully breaking segregatory and other laws, thus inviting arrest and imprisonment. The aim was to arouse large numbers of people to action in support of the campaign's demands. The volunteers were to act in small groups in a disciplined, non-violent fashion. A national volunteer board was established to coordinate the campaign, and Nelson Mandela was appointed the 'Volunteer in Chief'.

After publicly announcing what they would do, thousands of people in different parts of the country walked through 'whites only' entrances at railway stations and other public places or demanded service at 'whites only' counters in post offices and civil service offices. Africans defied the pass laws while non-Africans entered African locations without a permit. People who had been banned defied their banning orders. Over 8 000 people were arrested across the country. They refused to pay fines, and in some places prisons were filled to capacity.

Nearly fifty members of the two Congresses were arrested and convicted for launching the campaign, and Chief Albert Luthuli was dismissed as a chief when he refused to resign as ANC provincial president in Natal.

The government passed laws that threatened harsh action against those who defied the law. Congress leaders then called off the campaign and sought other forms of struggle. The ANC formulated the M-Plan, so named because Mandela was put in charge of implementing it. Its aim was to organise the ANC membership into cells at grassroots level and link them to higher levels. The new structure was meant to connect the leadership with ordinary members, and allow it to communicate with members without the use of public meetings and press statements. At the ANC's December 1952 conference Luthuli was elected president general of the ANC.

The willingness of the Defiance Campaign to confront the government openly inspired many to join the organisation. The ANC's paid-up membership increased from about 7 000 to approximately 100 000. White ANC supporters, some of whom had participated in the campaign, established the Congress of Democrats (COD) in 1953. The influence of the African People's Organisation had waned considerably and pro-Congress coloureds established the South African Coloured People's Organisation (SACPO), renamed the Coloured People's Congress (CPC) in 1959. SACPO and COD joined with the ANC and the SAIC to form the Congress Alliance. The Alliance coordinated the work of the member organisations and was soon joined by the Federation of South African Women (FEDSAW) and the South African Congress of Trade Unions (SACTU).

LIBERAL RESISTANCE

In April 1953 a radical liberal grouping established the Liberal Party. They were mainly (but not only) whites who were anti-racist and who believed that all racist legislation ought to be abolished, but they were opposed to the influence of communists in the COD. Initially the Liberal Party supported a qualified franchise – that is, votes for all who qualified by having a certain level of education and income – but later changed its policy to support a universal franchise.

In 1959, a group of six liberal Members of Parliament (MPs), mainly associated with a section of big business, broke away from the United Party to form the Progressive Party. The Progressives espoused a formal non-racialism but believed in a qualified franchise, which, at the time, would still have left the whites as the majority of the electorate. At the next election in 1961, all the Progressive Party MPs except Helen Suzman lost their seats. She remained the party's only MP for 17 years and provided the only effective parliamentary opposition to National Party rule during this period. She used her relatively privileged position as an MP to expose apartheid's inherently cruel and oppressive nature, and to do what she could to improve the conditions of political prisoners. She remained in Parliament until 1989.

COMMUNITY RESISTANCE

Apartheid was opposed not only at the national level, but also around local issues. When the government decided to remove people from Sophiatown in Johannesburg to Meadowlands township, the community resisted. The ANC organised protest meetings in Sophiatown as well as elsewhere on the Rand, and residents declared that they would not move. However, the government sent in 2 000 troops and 80 trucks in February 1955 to remove people by force and Sophiatown was destroyed.

In Alexandra and other townships in the Johannesburg and Pretoria areas, as well as in Port Elizabeth and elsewhere, bus boycotts took place to protest against rises in bus fares. In the biggest of the bus boycotts, the people of Alexandra walked to work and back from January to June 1957, as they had done in the 1940s; they were ultimately successful in keeping the fares unchanged.

In the rural areas, too, there were conflicts between authorities and local people throughout the 1950s. Residents rose in revolt in many areas of the Transvaal and Natal as well as in Thembuland and Pondoland in the Eastern Cape. Grievances included forced removals of rural communities; the deposition of popular chiefs who refused to cooperate with the authorities; the collaboration of other chiefs with government officials; the issuing of passes for women; stock limitation laws; insecurity of tenure; and the introduction of Bantu Education.

The best-known case of rural resistance was the 1960 revolt in Pondoland, where rural people organised resistance to the imposition by the government of unpopular chiefs and Bantu Education and demanded parliamentary representation and lower taxes. On 6 June 1960, a peaceful outdoor meeting was attacked by both aircraft and ground-based police; 11 people were killed. People responded by organising secretly in mountainous areas; a committee known as Intaba (Mountain) directed the resistance and for a time exercised considerable authority, establishing people's courts for example. The government declared a local State of Emergency in November 1960 and the revolt was crushed by armed force. Thousands were detained and 30 people were later sentenced to death.

Bantu Education

The Bantu Education Act (see Chapter 12 and Theme 3) provoked strong protests from Africans, who were virtually unanimous in their condemnation of it. At its 1954 conference, the ANC called on African parents 'to withdraw their children from primary schools indefinitely from 1 April 1955'. Not all parents supported this call, as they believed it might lead to their children getting no education at all. The ANC decided to call off the nation-wide boycott of schools, but agreed that the boycott could continue in areas where there was support for it. Support for the boycott was strongest on the East Rand, in Bethlehem in the Free State, and in Port Elizabeth. Where boycotts did take place, communities established alternative schools, which they called 'cultural clubs' to avoid the prohibition on unauthorised schools. Police harassment, the prosecution of staff, and a shortage of funds, equipment and adequate premises made it very difficult to operate these schools. By 1960 all had been forced to close. The imposition of Bantu Education remained an abiding grievance.

Mission schools that refused to accept the discriminatory Bantu Education curriculum lost their government subsidies. Most could not afford to continue and were closed. Some were handed over to the government or continued as separate missionary schools without government subsidies.

When the Extension of University Education Act of 1959 was passed (see Chapter 12), most of the lecturers at the University of Fort Hare resigned in protest, including the vice principal and prominent ANC leader, Professor Z.K. Matthews.

The leaders of the 1956 Women's March to the Union Buildings: Sophie Williams-de Bruyn, Helen Joseph, Lilian Ngoyi and Rahima Moosa. Source: Jurgen Schadeberg

THE WOMEN'S MOVEMENT

The women's movement, particularly the ANC Women's League (ANCWL), grew significantly during the 1950s. Women participated in the major activities of the Congress Alliance including the Defiance Campaign, various community struggles and the campaign to organise the Congress of the People (see below).

The pass laws were one of the most deeply felt grievances for all Africans. A major focus of the women's movement in the 1950s was opposition to the extension of the pass laws to African women. The ANCWL participated in this campaign as part of the Federation of South African Women. Formed in April 1954, FEDSAW was a non-racial, national organisation, headed by Ida Mntwana, which became part of the Congress Alliance. Its most celebrated activity took place on 9 August 1956 when Lilian Ngoyi, Helen Joseph, Sophie Williams and Rahima Moosa led 20 000 women to the Union Buildings in Pretoria. As they marched, they famously sang the struggle song 'Wa thinta abafazi, wa thinta imbokodo'. Its words translate as 'Now you have touched the women/ you have struck a rock / You have dislodged a boulder / you will be crushed!' At the Union Buildings, Prime Minister J.G. Strijdom refused to see them and their petition was left at his office. August 9 is now observed in South Africa as a public holiday, National Women's Day.

Both before and after 9 August, there were many instances of resistance to the pass laws by women in both urban and rural areas. One notable example was in the small Free State Town of Winburg, where hundreds of women marched to the magistrate's office and burned their pass books. A number of them were arrested and imprisoned.

Women who operated shebeens in Cato Manor in Durban resented the fact that it was illegal for them to brew liquor at home while the municipality ran beer halls that sold beer to African men. In June 1959, a crowd of women attacked a beer hall, driving out customers, spilling sorghum beer and destroying equipment. This was followed by a series of clashes between the Cato Manor community and police over a period of six months.

TRADE UNION MOVEMENT

From the late 1940s white racists in the trade union movement had been agitating for separate unions for whites and blacks. In 1954 they established the Trade Union Council of South Africa (TUCSA). Its constitution did not allow the affiliation of trade unions with African members. In response the anti-racist unions joined together to establish the non-racial South African Congress of Trade Unions (SACTU) in May 1956. This new federation emphasised the organisation of unorganised workers. Its membership grew from 20 000 workers in 19 unions in 1956 to 53 000 in 51 unions in 1960. SACTU also undertook to participate in the political struggle against racism and exploitation, and became an active partner in the Congress Alliance.

CONGRESS OF THE PEOPLE

In December 1953, in response to a proposal from its Cape provincial president, Z.K. Matthews, the ANC suggested to its partners in the Congress Alliance the organisation of a 'Congress of the People'. The purpose of the gathering was to draw up a Freedom Charter, outlining the principles for a democratic South Africa of the future. A National Action Council was established to organise the congress. Local committees were established throughout South Africa; they held hundreds of meetings in urban and rural areas to gather people's grievances and demands. A drafting committee sorted through the material and then drafted the Freedom Charter.

The Charter was discussed and adopted at the Congress of People, which was held in Kliptown, Johannesburg, on 26 June 1955. It represented people's demands for a non-racial South Africa with political rights for all 'regardless of race, colour or sex', equality for all, a fairer distribution of wealth, the right to social security and education, and friendly relations with all other countries. The Charter was the most important document yet developed by the South African liberation movement, and offered a vision that inspired the struggle for freedom for four decades.

THE TREASON TRIAL

In early December 1956 police swooped on homes all over South Africa, arresting 156 people, including most of the leaders of the Congress Alliance, on charges of high treason. They were accused of 'a country-wide conspiracy' to overthrow the state, inspired by 'international communism'. Key to the prosecution's argument was that the accused

Congress of the People. Source: UWC Robben Island Mayibuye Archive.

had participated actively in the campaign to draw up the Freedom Charter, which, it claimed, was a communist document. To back this up, the prosecutors pointed out that the Charter called for the abolition of all racial discrimination and the granting of equal rights to all. This, they contended, would involve the violent overthrow of the state. The charges were flimsy and the defence lawyers systematically exposed their flaws. After a year charges were withdrawn against 61 of the accused and later against many of the others. The trial dragged on until 1961 when the last 30 accused were found not guilty.

A large campaign of solidarity grew up during the trial, with demonstrations outside court, and a Treason Trial Defence Fund was set up to collect money for legal fees. In Britain, Canon Collins established the International Defence and Aid Fund for the same purpose. This fund continued to collect money for the legal defence of South African political activists throughout the entire apartheid period and became associated with the anti-apartheid movement.

THE ESTABLISHMENT OF THE PAN AFRICANIST CONGRESS

A section of the ANC led by Robert Sobukwe was unhappy with its increasing cooperation with white, coloureds and Indians; they believed that Africans should 'go it alone'. They felt that the ANC had abandoned the true African nationalism of the Youth League that had prevailed during Anton Lembede's time, and adopted the slogan 'Africa for the Africans'. They also objected to what they saw as the growing influence of communists in the ANC and referred to Marxism as a foreign ideology.

The Africanists, as they called themselves, campaigned against the Freedom Charter and objected to the formulation that 'South Africa belongs to all who live in it'. When they failed to prevent the Charter's adoption, they continued to campaign against it. In April 1959, they left the ANC and formed a new organisation, the Pan Africanist Congress (PAC).

THE SHARPEVILLE CRISIS

On 21 March 1960 the police opened fire on a PAC-organised demonstration in Sharpeville, outside Vereeniging. They killed 69 people and wounded 180. Police also killed another five people at demonstrations in Langa and Nyanga in Cape Town. News of the killings evoked outrage throughout the country and abroad. A two-week general strike in Cape Town was met with violence from the police. Philip Kgosana of the PAC led a march of 30 000 people to protest against police violence and was himself arrested. ANC president Albert Luthuli called a one-day stay-away on 28 March to protest against the massacres in Sharpeville, Langa and Nyanga. Overseas, demonstrations were held in a number of countries. In Britain, activists established the Anti-Apartheid Movement to 'co-ordinate all the anti-apartheid work and keep South Africa's apartheid policy in the forefront of British politics'. This would be the first of many such movements around the world.

The South African government responded to the internal and external protests by banning the ANC and the PAC on 8 April 1960. It declared a State of Emergency and started to round up many of its opponents – over 2 000 people, mainly members of the Congress Alliance but also many PAC members.

CHAPTER 13: DISCUSSION QUESTIONS

1. The Defiance Campaign was the first formal campaign in which the ANC asked its members to consciously break the law – and they did so in large numbers. Try to identify some reasons why this form of mass, non-violent struggle was chosen. To what extent do you think it was effective?

2. What did the Congress Alliance represent that was new in South African history? What foundations did it lay for the future of the liberation struggle and for a democratic South Africa?

3. From what you know (or can find out), evaluate how important the Progressive Party was as an opposition to apartheid?

4. Examine the Freedom Charter and discuss to what extent it was implemented after 1994. For those parts that were not implemented, were there good reasons for this? (In discussing this question, it may also be useful to read the ANC's 1968 document 'Revolutionary Programme of the ANC', which was a detailed analysis of the Freedom Charter.)

CHAPTER 13: ADDITIONAL READINGS

Online readings

Levy, N. (2012) *The Final Prize*. Cape Town: South African History Online. (Chapters 8–12). https://www.sahistory.org.za/archive/final-prize-norman-levy

Liberation History Timeline, 1950–1959. *South African History Online*. https://www.sahistory.org.za/topic/liberation-history-timeline-1950-1959.

Liberation Struggle in South Africa, 1950s. *South African History Online*. https://www.sahistory.org.za/archive/liberation-struggle-south-africa-1950s.

Pampallis, J. (1991) *Foundations of the New South Africa*. Cape Town: Maskew Miller Longman. (Chapter 15). https://www.sahistory.org.za/sites/default/files/file%20uploads%20/foundation_of_the_new_south_africa_original_final.pdf.

South African Congress of Trade Unions (SACTU). *South African History Online*. http://www.sahistory.org.za/organisations/south-african-congress-trade-unions-sactu.

The Freedom Charter. http://www.anc.org.za/content/freedom-charter.

Books

Davenport, T.R.H. (1991) *South Africa: A Modern History*. London: Macmillan. (Chapters 14 and 15)

Giliomee, H. and B. Mbenga (eds) (2007) *New History of South Africa*. Cape Town: Tafelberg. (Chapter 13)

Lodge, T. (1983) *Black Politics in South Africa since 1945*. London: Longman. (Chapters 2–8)

Meli, F. (1988) *A History of the ANC: South Africa Belongs to Us*. London: James Currey. (Chapter 5)

Morris, M. (2004) *Every Step of the Way: The Journey to Freedom in South Africa*. Cape Town: HSRC Press. (Chapter 9)

Thompson, L. (2014) *A History of South Africa*. Johannesburg: Jonathan Ball. (Chapter 6)

Fourteen

Repression and Regrouping, 1960–1964

The massacres at Sharpeville and elsewhere, the State of Emergency, the banning of the African National Congress (ANC) and the Pan Africanist Congress (PAC), and the arrest and banning of political activists focused international attention on South Africa. The United Nations Security Council passed a resolution blaming the South African government for the recent killings and called on it to 'bring about racial harmony'. The many African countries that had or were about to achieve independence strengthened the international voice of condemnation against apartheid.

After the bannings, hundreds of political activists of various parties fled the country, especially those from the ANC, PAC and the South African Communist Party (SACP). The ANC sent Oliver Tambo out of the country to England, where he was soon joined by Yusuf Dadoo, who had been sent out by the SACP. Their task was initially to mobilise international support and build links with other African anti-colonial movements such as those in Zimbabwe, Mozambique, Angola and Algeria.

After the events at Sharpeville, an economic slowdown that had started the previous year gathered momentum. Foreign investors, fearing instability, disinvested from South Africa and new investment – both domestic and foreign – dried up. Gold and foreign exchange reserves fell by 51 per cent between January 1960 and May 1961. The recession lasted until 1964, by which time the regime had managed to suppress the liberation movement. An economic boom then followed, which lasted until 1972.

In September 1966, South Africa was stunned by the news that Prime Minister Hendrik Verwoerd had been stabbed to death in Parliament by a parliamentary messenger, Dimitri Tsafendas. He was succeeded by B.J. Vorster, who had previously been Minister of Justice and of Police and Prisons.

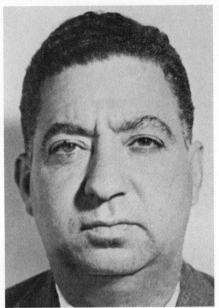

Prime Minister Hendrik Verwoerd and the man who assassinated him in Parliament, Dimitri Tsafendas.

The Republic of South Africa

In early 1960, Verwoerd organised a referendum of white voters to decide whether South Africa should become a republic, thus realising a decades-old Afrikaner nationalist dream. The majority of white South Africans – 52 per cent – voted in favour of a republic, which was officially established on 31 May 1961.

In March 1961, the All-In African Conference, held in Pietermaritzburg, called on the government to organise a national convention of elected representatives of all South Africans to draw up a non-racial, democratic constitution for the country. If the government did not call a national convention – and no one seriously expected that it would – then there would be 'country-wide demonstrations on the eve of the proclamation of the Republic'. A National Action Council, headed by Nelson Mandela, called for a three-day strike on 29–30 May, but it was not as successful and widespread as had been hoped.

Soon after the March conference, a warrant was issued for Mandela's arrest. However, he managed to evade the police as he toured the country organising people to carry out the conference's decisions. He wrote to Verwoerd to demand a national convention. He received no reply but Verwoerd did report to Parliament that he had received Mandela's 'arrogant letter'.

Underground Structures and a Turn to Arms

After it was banned, the ANC began to build an underground organisation. With most of

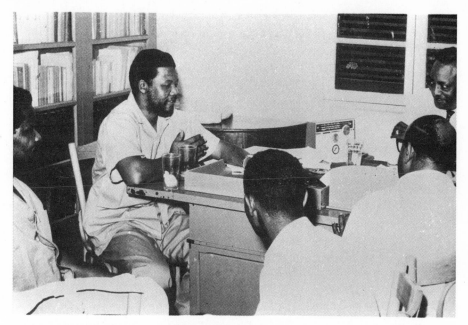

Nelson Mandela had the opportunity to meet with various leaders of Africa's newly independent countries when he addressed a conference of the Pan African Freedom Movement for East and Central Africa (PAFMECA) in Addis Abba, January 1962. Source: Photo by API/Gamma-Rapho via Getty Images

the leadership either in detention or in hiding, this was a daunting task. Nonetheless they did manage to build some structures based on the M-Plan (see Chapter 13), established means of communication, and made plans to boycott government celebrations of the fiftieth anniversary of the Union of South Africa on 31 May 1960. The SACP reorganised its underground work in line with the new conditions and coordinated with the ANC. The PAC, too, began to organise underground structures. After the lifting of the State of Emergency and the release of most political detainees, it became possible for members of the banned organisations to carry out some limited political work through other organisations, for example the African Students' Association.

After their organisations had been banned, many leaders of the liberation movements came to the conclusion that peaceful action alone could not succeed in ending apartheid oppression. A group of ANC and SACP leaders decided to establish Umkhonto we Sizwe (MK) to conduct an armed struggle. After much debate, this decision was endorsed by the leadership of the ANC and the SACP. MK was regarded as separate from the ANC but under the ANC's political guidance. Its members came from all the organisations of the Congress Alliance. MK announced its existence on 16 December 1961 with a number of sabotage explosions at government buildings and electrical power installations. Over the next eighteen months, MK operatives made over 200 such attacks in all major cities and some smaller towns. MK's policy was to avoid taking human life. In June 1962, the government passed the Sabotage Act, providing for the death penalty for sabotage.

Soon after the formation of MK, Mandela was sent out of the country to attend a Pan-African Freedom Conference in Addis Ababa. After the conference he toured Africa, meeting many of the leaders of the newly independent states to seek their support. He arrived back in South Africa secretly in July 1962 but was arrested a month later. He was charged with inciting workers to strike and leaving the country illegally, and was sentenced to five years' imprisonment with hard labour.

Another armed group, known as Poqo and associated with the PAC, was established at about the same time as MK. It killed a number of suspected informers and policemen in Langa and Paarl as well as a few whites, who were apparently selected at random.

Exiled PAC leaders in Maseru, headed by Potlako Leballo, planned a national uprising on 8 April 1963. However, the plan ran into trouble when Leballo stated at a press conference that a revolution would soon be launched in South Africa and that 155 000 PAC members were ready to strike when he gave the word. Soon afterwards, the Basutoland police raided the PAC office and seized a list of names, supposedly of PAC members. The list was apparently handed over to the South African Police and many PAC members were arrested. Although the crackdown was a devastating blow to the PAC, it did establish a presence in exile. In 1968, the PAC formed the Azanian People's Liberation Army (APLA), whose main military actions were a few attacks carried out on civilians after the PAC was unbanned in 1990.

A small number of mainly white radicals, also frustrated by the lack of success of non-violent forms of protest, established the National Committee of Liberation (later renamed the African Resistance Movement, or ARM). It was uncovered by the police in early 1964 and many of its activists were imprisoned. Later in the year, one of its members, John Harris, planted a bomb at a whites-only platform of Johannesburg's Park Station. The bomb killed one person and injured fourteen others. Harris was arrested and sentenced to death.

A New SACP Programme

In 1962 the SACP adopted a new programme, *The Road to South African Freedom*, which elaborated the theory of 'colonialism of a special type', which would later be adopted by the ANC and the broader liberation movement. It characterised South Africa as a colonial society but one in which the oppressor and oppressed shared the same territory. The establishment of the Union of South Africa in 1910, it said, did not represent a true form of decolonisation. The oppression of black people had continued as before, although power passed from Britain to South African whites. One implication of this concept was that the immediate aim for revolutionaries was 'a national democratic revolution' to overthrow the colonial white-supremacist state and establish a national democracy. This would, the SACP believed, lay the basis for the advance to socialism.

Oliver Tambo, president of the ANC. He led the organisation
for the entire period of its exile, from 1960 to 1990.

A Heavy Blow

On 1 May 1963, the government passed the General Law Amendment Act, which empowered the police to detain anyone for up to 90 days without trial – and to repeat the detention for as many times as the police wanted. Hundreds of detentions followed and the liberation movement, including both the ANC and PAC, lost many of its leaders and rank-and-file members. They were frequently kept in solitary confinement and many were cruelly tortured. Looksmart Ngudle was the first of a long line of detainees to die in detention because they refused to cooperate with the police.

The heaviest blow to the liberation movement occurred when the police raided the headquarters of Umkhonto we Sizwe in Rivonia, outside Johannesburg, capturing members of the High Command. Mandela was brought from prison to stand trial with his colleagues in what became known as the Rivonia Trial. Eight members of the High Command were sentenced to life imprisonment for sabotage and 'furthering the aims of communism'. They were Nelson Mandela, Walter Sisulu, Govan Mbeki, Ahmed Kathrada, Raymond Mhlaba, Elias Motsoaledi, Andrew Mlangeni and Denis Goldberg. In the following few years, a number of Congress Alliance leaders, including Wilton Mkwayi and Bram Fischer, as well as numerous other activists, were arrested and sentenced to long terms in prison.

Even before the Rivonia arrests, a number of key leaders had been instructed to leave the country to join Oliver Tambo and Yusuf Dadoo. They included Moses Kotane, J.B. Marks, Duma Nokwe and Joe Slovo. By 1966 the entire leadership were in prison, banned or in exile. Very little remained of the underground structures, and communication with the External Mission was minimal.

The trade unions suffered a similar fate. SACTU members and leaders were detained, banned or went into exile. In 1964, despite national and international protests, Vuyisile Mini, a prominent SACTU and ANC leader who had joined MK, was executed together with two fellow trade unionists, Wilson Khayinga and Zinakile Mkaba, on charges of sabotage and complicity in the murder of a police informer. By 1964, SACTU had lost so many people that it could no longer operate openly. SACTU members in exile formed an external mission to rally international support for workers' struggles and to give support to those operating inside South Africa.

INTERNATIONAL PRESSURE AGAINST APARTHEID

While the South African regime was asserting its dominance inside South Africa, the international situation was gradually becoming more hostile to white supremacy and apartheid. In a speech to the South African Parliament in February 1960, British Prime Minister Harold Macmillan, who was ending a tour of African countries, said that a 'wind of change' was blowing through Africa and that his government could no longer give support to 'some aspects of your policies'.

In December 1961, ANC president Albert Luthuli travelled to Norway to receive the 1960 Nobel Peace Prize, awarded for his important contribution to the non-violent struggle for freedom in South Africa. In his speech at the award ceremony, he called for economic sanctions against South Africa until apartheid was abolished.

His call and the growing anti-apartheid sentiment in the world – from the governments of socialist and former colonial countries as well as anti-racist movements in Western countries – were taken up by the United Nations. Both the General Assembly and the Security Council recommended economic and other sanctions against South Africa. The sanctions were not mandatory, and at first they were ignored by most Western countries, South Africa's main trading partners. However, the international campaign to isolate South Africa did ensure that most newly independent countries did not establish diplomatic relations with South Africa and that South Africa's economic contacts with the rest of the African continent remained much more restricted than they might have been.

International pressures on the government also grew closer to home. In the 1960s liberation movements in Rhodesia (Zimbabwe), the Portuguese colonies of Mozambique and Angola, and South West Africa (Namibia) took up arms against their colonial rulers. Although their ultimate success only came later, their struggles increased the vulnerability of the apartheid government, prompting it to give military and economic support to the Portuguese and to the white minority government in Rhodesia.

*Albert Luthuli, ANC president and winner of the
Nobel Peace Prize in 1961.*

The ANC in Exile

In view of the debilitating blows suffered by the ANC inside South Africa, the External Mission had to assume the leadership of the movement and take the main responsibility for leading the struggle. After the death of Albert Luthuli in 1967,[17] Oliver Tambo was appointed acting president, a position he retained until 1977 when he was appointed president by the National Executive Committee (NEC) after secret consultations with imprisoned leaders on Robben Island.

In exile, the ANC made contact with other southern African liberation movements that were also in exile, and began to cooperate with them. These movements included the Zimbabwe African People's Union (ZAPU), the Front for the Liberation of Mozambique (FRELIMO), the People's Movement for the Liberation of Angola (MPLA) and the South West Africa People's Organisation (SWAPO).

The ANC, SACP and MK insisted from the beginning that the armed struggle was an extension of the political struggle and that MK should always remain subordinate to the political structures. After leaving South Africa, young MK soldiers received training in friendly countries, including the Soviet Union, China and some Eastern European and North African countries. After being trained, they returned to military camps that had been set up in Tanzania (and, later, in Angola as well). Originally it had been planned to

---

17 The press reported that Luthuli had been struck by a train while crossing a railway bridge because he was 'deaf and near blind'. This version of events has been disputed by his family, who say that he walked the same way and knew when the train would pass, and that witnesses had reported the presence of security police in the area on the day of his death (http://www.iol.co.za/news/politics/family-seek-probe-into-albert-luthulis-death-237099).

send them back to South Africa to train others, but hostile governments in Rhodesia and the Portuguese colonies made this impossible.

The ANC formed a military alliance with ZAPU in 1967. Its aim was to establish routes back to South Africa through Rhodesian territory. Once inside Rhodesia, the small MK contingent, with some ZAPU members, fought a number of battles with Rhodesian forces. The South African government then sent police and military forces to assist the Rhodesians. This was the first time that the ANC had engaged enemy forces in guerrilla warfare. The campaign was ultimately unsuccessful in reaching its objectives, and in early 1969 surviving MK soldiers returned, via Botswana and Zambia, to their bases in Tanzania. Some of them spent months in prison in Botswana for entering that country illegally.

When they reached the Zambian capital, Lusaka, where the ANC then had its headquarters, they were bitterly disappointed that they were not officially welcomed or debriefed on their experiences and the lessons to be learned from them. One of the soldiers, Chris Hani, later stated to an internal commission of inquiry that they 'found the movement in a stalemate position. There was no longer any direction, there was general confusion or an unwillingness to discuss the lessons of the revolution.'

In April 1969, the ANC's NEC called a week-long consultative conference in Morogoro, Tanzania. The conference was held in response to the demands of rank-and-file cadres, especially soldiers. In what became known as the Hani Memorandum, they expressed the view that ordinary members of the movement were being excluded from decision-making, and sometimes not even informed about decisions. They stated that MK members had lost confidence in the ANC's leadership in exile and demanded a conference to take stock of the situation, make plans for the future and review the composition of the leadership. After strong initial opposition from some members of the leadership, the conference took place.

The Morogoro Conference took a number of important decisions that revitalised the ANC's External Mission. A new NEC of nine members (previously there had been 23) was elected, with Oliver Tambo reaffirmed in his position as acting president. Alfred Nzo was elected secretary general. The conference also established a high-level Revolutionary Council to take overall responsibility for military matters. In addition, it was decided that non-African revolutionaries who were members of other Congress Alliance organisations should be integrated into the ANC's External Mission, although they could not become members of the NEC. The conference adopted two important documents: *Strategy and Tactics of the ANC* and *Revolutionary Programme of the ANC*, the latter being a detailed analysis of the Freedom Charter.

After the Morogoro Conference, the ANC started to infiltrate cadres into South Africa and slowly began to rebuild the underground there. They produced pamphlets and on a number of occasions distributed them by means of 'pamphlet bombs', which after explosion propelled multiple copies of pamphlets into the air in crowded places. Other ANC literature began to circulate secretly inside the country. Between 1971 and 1973, six trained guerrillas who had infiltrated the country were arrested and each sentenced to fifteen years in prison.

BANTUSTANS AND COUNCILS

Inside South Africa, the government pressed on with its bantustan programme. In 1963 the Transkei was given 'self-government' with Kaiser Matanzima as its 'chief minister'. Some members of the Bhunga (the Transkeian parliament) were to be elected while the majority were appointed by the South African government. The Transkei's status was officially described as that of a 'self-governing territory within the Republic of South Africa' until it gained nominal independence in 1976. Its budget was heavily dependent on grants from the South African government, and its political freedom was highly circumscribed. It was never recognised by any country other than South Africa.

Of course, the government realised that millions of Africans would always reside in the urban areas and not in the areas where they had 'citizenship'. In order to create a semblance of representation, Urban Bantu Councils (UBCs) were introduced in 1961. These bodies had limited administrative powers; but they were widely rejected and gained no popular legitimacy.

The government also established self-governance structures for the coloured and Indian populations. The Coloured People's Representative Council (CPRC) had a limited capacity to make laws affecting coloured people. It was established in 1969, with half of its members elected and half appointed by the South African government. The South African Indian Council was also created in 1969 to make recommendations to the government about matters affecting Indians. All its members were at first appointed by the government; then, from 1974, half the members were elected. Both the CPRC and the Indian Council were widely rejected in the communities they were meant to serve.

ECONOMIC RECOVERY

After the government had managed to inflict serious damage on the liberation movement in the early 1960s, foreign investors lost their fear of an impending revolution. American, British and other Western corporations started once more to invest in South Africa, especially in the mining industry. By 1965 overseas capital was again flowing into South Africa, where cheap labour and capital-friendly laws assured businesses of handsome profits. The economy enjoyed a boom in mining and industrial production as well as in commercial activity that lasted until 1973. Blacks, of course, benefited very little.

As the country became more militarised in response to the challenges posed by the liberation movement, the government promoted the development of a military-industrial complex, including both private and state-owned enterprises. ARMSCOR, for instance, developed and manufactured arms and also procured military equipment for South Africa. Private companies benefited from the increased demand for military vehicles, uniforms, electronic equipment and other products for use by the South African Defence Force. South Africa also developed nuclear and biological weapons at this time, allowing it to intimidate neighbouring states even though they were never actually used.

CHAPTER 14: DISCUSSION QUESTIONS

1. Did the murder of Dr Hendrik Verwoerd by Dimitri Tsafendas play any role in weakening apartheid? To what extent can any individual make a significant difference to the course of history?

2. There was an economic crisis after Sharpeville and an economic boom after 1965. How can political events affect the economy (specifically investment)? Do you know of any other such events or processes either before or since the 1960s?

3. Do you think the decisions of the ANC and the PAC to embark on an armed struggle were useful in attaining their aims? Why or why not?

4. What did the government hope to achieve by establishing bantustans for black people and Representative Councils for coloured people and Indians? To what extent were these structures accepted by the people that they were supposed to represent?

5. Do you agree with the concept of 'colonialism of a special type'? What did this concept add to the SACP's (and, later, the ANC's) understanding of South African society?

CHAPTER 14: ADDITIONAL READINGS

Online readings

1960–1966: The Genesis of the Armed Struggle. *South African History Online.* http://www.sahistory.org.za/article/1960-1966-genesis-armed-struggle.

Lerumo, A. (1987) *Fifty Fighting Years.* London: Inkululeko Publications. (Chapter 5). http://www.sacp.org.za/main.php?ID=3945.

Levy, N. (2012) *The Final Prize.* Cape Town: South African History Online. (Chapters 13 and 14). https://www.sahistory.org.za/archive/final-prize-norman-levy.

Mandela, N. (1963) Statement from the Dock at the Opening of the Defence Case in the Rivonia Trial. http://www.anc.org.za/content/nelson-mandelas-statement-dock-rivonia-trial.

Pampallis, J. (1991) *Foundations of the New South Africa.* Cape Town: Maskew Miller Longman. (Chapters 16 and 17). https://www.sahistory.org.za/sites/default/files/file%20uploads%20/foundation_of_the_new_south_africa_original_final.pdf.

Resistance to Apartheid. The Apartheid Museum. https://www.apartheidmuseum.org/sites/default/files/files/downloads/Learners%20book%20Chapter4.pdf.

South African Communist Party (SACP) (1962) *The Road to South African Freedom.* https://www.sahistory.org.za/sites/default/files/Programme%20of%20the%20South%20African%20Communist%20Party%201962-%20The%20Road%20to%20South%20Africa%20Freedom.pdf.

Books

Davenport, T.R.H. (1991) *South Africa: A Modern History.* London: Macmillan. (Chapter 15)

Giliomee, H. and B. Mbenga (eds) (2007) *New History of South Africa.* Cape Town: Tafelberg. (Chapter 13)

Lodge, T. (1983) *Black Politics in South Africa since 1945.* London: Longman. (Chapters 8, 9, 10 and 11)

Meli, F. (1988) *A History of the ANC: South Africa Belongs to Us.* London: James Currey. (Chapter 6)

Fifteen

Revival of the Mass Movement, 1964–1979

Apartheid had been at its strongest during the economic boom from 1964 to 1972. The liberation movement had been significantly weakened and the South African economy had grown more robustly than at any time since the mineral revolution in the late nineteenth century. From 1973, however, the economy slowed markedly as the entire capitalist world went into a recession.

The economic boom of the 1960s and early 1970s had given rise to new economic problems. Industries needed larger markets to keep on expanding, but the poverty of most South Africans, due to racial oppression and low wages, meant that the home market was small. South Africa's natural export market in Africa could not be developed appreciably owing to independent Africa's hostility to apartheid. The international economic recession of the early 1970s further reduced exports and decreased foreign investment. The massive rise in the price of imported oil in 1973 and the drop in gold and other commodity prices further deepened the economic problems. The lack of skills training for black workers and the weakness of the internal market that resulted from apartheid-induced poverty played an important role in entrenching structural weaknesses in the economy.

THE STUDENT MOVEMENT AND BLACK CONSCIOUSNESS IN THE UNIVERSITIES

The devastation suffered by the liberation movement in the early 1960s left radical resistance to apartheid severely weakened. Students – especially those in the new ethnically segregated universities for Africans, coloureds and Indians and at the all-black medical campus of the University of Natal – were the first to begin filling this vacuum. This was the first sign of a gradual revival of organised opposition to apartheid, which would grow until it exploded in the Soweto Uprising in 1976 (see below).

Steve Biko, the most prominent leader of the Black Conscious
Movement who died in police detention in 1977, aged 30.

In 1968, black university students formed the all-black South African Students' Organisation (SASO), whose most prominent leader was Stephen (Steve) Bantu Biko. The SASO leadership developed an ideology that became known as Black Consciousness. They stressed the need for psychological liberation, believing that years of subjugation had caused black people to lose confidence in themselves and to develop feelings of inferiority. They insisted that blacks should not work in the same political, social and cultural organisations as whites; liberal whites, they said, tended to dominate multiracial organisations. SASO garnered support at all the black universities as well as at some teacher training colleges and seminaries.

SASO rejected the terms 'non-European' and 'non-white' that had long been used in South Africa and took to using the word 'black'. The organisation stressed the importance of unity among all black people – Africans, coloureds and Indians – in the struggle against white domination. SASO also rejected the bantustan system as a means of dividing black people and strongly criticised those black leaders who participated in the bantustan governments and other state-created institutions. It also gave voice to student grievances on individual campuses.

Although the authorities at first mistakenly saw SASO as an example of 'separate development' in action, the organisation's increasing hostility towards the government and its policies soon changed that. In 1972, there were mass expulsions of black students at some universities, followed by prolonged student strikes. Solidarity demonstrations by the white National Union of South African Students (NUSAS) were violently dispersed by the police.

A strike meeting at Coronation Brick and Tile Company, Durban, 10 January 1973. Source: UWC Robben Island Mayibuye Archive.

In 1972, SASO called a meeting of various educational, cultural and religious organisations to form the Black People's Convention (BPC), the political arm of what became known as the Black Consciousness Movement. The BPC set up clinics, crèches and literacy programmes in rural communities, and in 1972 established a trade union, the Black Allied Workers' Union (BAWU).

RE-EMERGENCE OF WORKER RESISTANCE

The economic boom from 1964 to 1972 had done little to benefit black, and particularly African, workers whose wages had remained low despite rising prices. At the beginning of 1973, a spontaneous outbreak of strikes in the Durban area marked the beginning of a revival of the workers' movement. The strikes started at the Coronation Brick and Tile Company, where almost 2 000 workers managed to win a small wage increase. This minor success encouraged workers in other factories, and further strikes broke out, especially in the textile industry, a major employer in the area. In the first three months of 1973, 61 000 workers were involved in strikes in and around Durban. Police tried to intimidate workers with shows of force and used tear gas to break up meetings. Workers invariably refused to put forward representatives to negotiate on their behalf, suspecting that they would be victimised as 'ringleaders'. Having no trade unions or strike funds, the workers could not stay on strike for long without pay.

The strikes spread to other parts of the country throughout 1973 and 1974, particularly to the Witwatersrand. Although the increases in wages achieved were small, the strikes represented the first large-scale resistance by African workers since the early 1960s. The experiences gained led to the formation of new, independent, unregistered trade unions for black workers; by 1977 there were 27 such unions. It was becoming obvious to the government that the existing labour laws, which prohibited Africans from belonging to registered trade unions, no longer prevented effective worker organisation. Facing labour shortages, business was increasingly calling on the government to scrap job reservation so that it could employ black workers in jobs previously reserved for higher-paid white workers. The government appointed the Commission of Inquiry into Labour Legislation (known as the Wiehahn Commission) to examine the existing law and make recommendations for change. The commission's report is dealt with in Chapter 16.

INDEPENDENCE FOR MOZAMBIQUE AND ANGOLA

In 1975, the Portuguese colonies of Mozambique and Angola gained their independence. This followed long armed struggles by liberation movements in those colonies and an anti-fascist revolution in Portugal that was precipitated to a large extent by the burden of fighting the colonial wars. The struggle in Mozambique was led by the Front for the Liberation of Mozambique (FRELIMO), and in Angola by the People's Movement for the Liberation of Angola (MPLA). The new governments of the two countries were strong supporters of the liberation movements of South Africa, Namibia and Zimbabwe, which set up operations in both countries. Fighters of the South West Africa People's Organisation (SWAPO) could now extend their military operations into Namibia from Angola; the Zimbabwe African National Union (ZANU) could operate from Mozambique; while the Zimbabwe African People's Union (ZAPU) continued to operate from Zambia.

The African National Congress (ANC) received considerable moral, material and diplomatic support from both Angola and Mozambique. Mozambique's border with South Africa enabled the ANC's External Mission to establish closer links with its internal structures and to infiltrate fighters into South Africa. Swaziland's (eSwatini) territory also became more accessible for use by the ANC.

Shortly before the date set for Angolan independence, 11 November 1975, the South African army entered Angola. Their mission was to support two organisations – the National Union for the Total Independence of Angola (UNITA) and the National Front for the Liberation of Angola (FNLA). Both of them were backed by South Africa and the United States, and were fighting to prevent the MPLA from taking power. South African forces got to within 120 kilometres of Luanda, the capital city, before being repulsed by the MPLA with the support of Cuban soldiers who had come in response to calls from the MPLA's pre-independence administration in Angola.

The defeat of the South African army was a huge morale-booster for black South Africans, as indeed was the independence of both former Portuguese colonies.

SCHOOL STUDENTS ORGANISE

From the early 1970s, black secondary school students, young workers and unemployed youth in various parts of the country began to organise themselves into cultural, religious and sporting bodies. Many built links with each other on a provincial basis. The organisations often had a political content, using their activities as a cover for political discussions. Most of them were influenced to some extent by Black Consciousness ideology.

The various youth organisations began to see a need to organise themselves on a wider, regional or national basis. The South African Students' Movement (SASM) was established in 1973 and it grew rapidly. Its main base of support was in the Witwatersrand townships, but it also received backing in townships and rural areas throughout much of the country. Unsurprisingly, SASM met with state repression. Each year more and more SASM activists were arrested and imprisoned for offences ranging from organising and participating in political activities to writing articles and poetry critical of the government.

As they became increasingly militant, some of the youth began to discuss the issue of armed struggle. They sought out older ANC members for political advice, developed contacts with the ANC's underground structures, and made arrangements to recruit youth and send them out of the country for military training. In this way the ANC began to influence sections of the youth and student movement. In time this merger between youth and experience would grow to be extremely important. For the time being, though, Black Consciousness remained the dominant ideology of the student movement. At the same time, SASM and other groups continued working to raise political consciousness in schools and communities.

BANTU EDUCATION AND THE JUNE 16 UPRISING

As described in Chapter 12, Bantu Education was established in the 1950s to provide a separate, inferior system of schooling for Africans. In an effort to meet the demand for skilled and especially semi-skilled labour in the economy and in the growing bantustan bureaucracies, the number of Bantu Education schools grew rapidly – at first in the primary school system and, from the late 1960s, in the secondary school system. However, state expenditure on school facilities did not keep pace with the increase in student numbers, causing severe overcrowding in schools. The problem was made worse when the government decided to do away with Standard 6 (Grade 8), then the highest grade in primary school. This led, in 1975, to the simultaneous promotion of Standard 5 (Grade 7) and Standard 6 (Grade 8) students to the first year of secondary school (Form 1). As a result, many classes had to be held on a shift basis; some classes were overcrowded, with up to a hundred students or more in a single class. Dissatisfaction among students, teachers and parents ran high.

In this volatile situation, the government introduced its new language policy for secondary schools in the South Transvaal region in 1975. Until then, vernacular languages were the languages of learning in primary schools and students then changed to English when they reached secondary school. Now the schools were told that they had to teach some classes in English, some (including mathematics, history and geography) in Afrikaans, and others in the students' mother tongue. The principals and teachers as well as the students (who were generally not proficient in either English or Afrikaans when they left primary school) protested. When the government refused to change its policy, the students started to take a more active role in the dispute.

From early 1976 students in some Soweto schools refused to attend classes taught in Afrikaans. In May, students at a number of schools stopped attending classes altogether. The Soweto regional committee of SASM and two members from each school formed the Soweto Students Representative Council (SSRC) to support the school boycotts. The SSRC called for a demonstration on 16 June. On this day police opened fire on the demonstration, killing 13-year-old Hector Pieterson and at least three others. Students retaliated by throwing stones, bottles and other projectiles. Thus began an uprising that spread throughout the country, lasting until 1978. African and coloured students and youth in other parts of the country boycotted classes in schools and universities; they also organised demonstrations, most notably in the Cape Town townships of Langa, Nyanga and Gugulethu.

Government buildings were attacked and often burned – including administrative buildings, school and university buildings, and municipal halls. Suspected police informers were attacked, and the Soweto Urban Bantu Council was forced to resign. Thousands of students and others were detained and many were tortured by police seeking information. Dozens of students were banned. In 1977 hundreds of black teachers resigned in solidarity with the students.

When the government finally backed down on the Afrikaans language issue in mid-July 1976, this had little impact in quelling the uprising. By that time, it had turned into a movement opposing Bantu Education and the apartheid system as a whole. The exiled wings of the ANC and the Pan Africanist Congress (PAC) welcomed the uprising and used the situation to spread their ideas. The ANC was particularly active in recruiting student activists to its underground structures. Those students who left the country to avoid police persecution or to get military training were met by and recruited by the liberation movements. Most joined the ANC, whose exile structures were better prepared and more organised than those of the PAC.

Parents together with community and church organisations in Soweto established the Black Parents' Association. It organised funerals for victims of police violence, spoke on behalf of parents, and strove to build unity between students and the adult community. Workers responded to a number of calls by students for strikes in support of democratic demands.

The state acted with increasing brutality as the school boycotts, demonstrations and strikes continued and spread to rural as well as other urban areas. The murder in detention of Black Consciousness leader Steve Biko in September 1977 led to country-wide – and indeed world-wide – outrage and helped fuel the uprising. In October 1977 the government announced the banning of 18 organisations, including SASM, SASO, BPC, SSRC and the Christian Institute. Three newspapers – *The World, Weekend World* and a church paper *Pro Veritate* – were also banned.

On 16 June 1976 highschool students in Soweto, South Africa, protested for better education. Police fired teargas and live bullets into the marching crowd killing innocent people and ignited what is known as The Soweto Uprising.

School boycotts continued until early 1978 and then began to subside. The Soweto Students League, which had replaced the SSRC, decided to call for a return to classes. The uprising that had started on 16 June 1976 came to an end. However, the renewed spirit of resistance it had helped spark would ensure that respite for the government would be short-lived.

DEVELOPMENTS IN THE BANTUSTANS

In October 1976, the Transkei bantustan became 'independent' with Chief Kaiser Matanzima as 'prime minister'. South African law now considered all black South Africans of Transkeian origin – whether they lived there or not – citizens of the Transkei; they were no longer South African citizens. The government saw Transkei's independence as a first step in creating ten separate, ethnically defined bantustans and depriving all Africans of their South African citizenship. It was widely regarded, both in South Africa and abroad, as a 'divide-and-rule' tactic aimed at undermining the legitimacy of African demands for political rights in a united South Africa. Most bantustans were led by traditional leaders trusted by the government.

Transkei's 'independent' government remained completely dependent on South Africa, both economically and politically. The phoney independence was strongly condemned by the United Nations, and South Africa was the only country in the world that recognised the Transkei – or any bantustan that would later be declared independent. Three more (Bophuthatswana, Venda and Ciskei) were proclaimed to be independent in 1977, 1979 and 1981 respectively. Another six (KwaZulu, KaNgwane, Lebowa, Gazankulu, QwaQwa and

KwaNdebele) were given 'self-governing' status in preparation for 'independence' before the shift to democracy in 1994 resulted in the dissolution of the entire bantustan system.

The most prominent of the bantustan leaders was Chief Mangosuthu Buthelezi. In 1970 the government appointed him leader of the KwaZulu Territorial Authority and in 1975 he became chief minister of the KwaZulu bantustan. Buthelezi was a former member of the ANC. He established Inkatha Yenkululeko Yesizwe (usually known simply as Inkatha) as a cultural and political movement. It used ANC colours and other symbols, taking advantage of the ANC's reputation and popular support. Inkatha grew into a large movement with thousands of members; the traditional leadership in KwaZulu was its main pillar of support. Although Buthelezi led the bantustan administration and cooperated with the South African government, he remained opposed to KwaZulu becoming independent.

The Black Consciousness Movement had, from its earliest days, dismissed all the bantustan leaders as collaborators and stooges of the government. The leadership of the ANC, on the other hand, had initially supported the establishment of Inkatha, seeing it as a possible way to remobilise people inside the country. However, differences between the two organisations surfaced in about 1979, particularly around two key strategic issues. Buthelezi was opposed to the armed struggle and to the ANC's calls for international economic, sports and cultural sanctions against South Africa as a means to weaken the apartheid state. The division between the ANC and Inkatha became deeper over the years and turned into a brutal conflict in which thousands lost their lives. The government supported Inkatha against the ANC and its allies, especially the United Democratic Front (UDF) and the Congress of South African Trade Unions (COSATU). This conflict is considered in the next chapter.

CHAPTER 15: DISCUSSION QUESTIONS

1. Discuss the background and the reasons for the birth and development of the Black Consciousness Movement. Why do you think that it first developed among university students?

2. The wave of strikes that started in Durban in 1973 and the student uprising that began in 1976 marked important events in the opposition to apartheid. Discuss their significance in South African history. Do you see any relationship between these two outbreaks of resistance?

3. How did anti-colonial movements in other African countries affect South Africa between 1960 and 1990?

4. What could be some of the reasons that the Inkatha movement in the KwaZulu bantustan enjoyed stronger popular support than other bantustan-based political parties?

CHAPTER 15: ADDITIONAL READINGS

Online readings

Bonner, P. (2004) The Soweto Uprising of June 1976: A Turning Points Event. *People, Places and Apartheid.* Turning Points in History Series, Book 5. Johannesburg: STE Publishers. https://www.sahistory.org.za/archive/book-5-people-places-and-apartheid-chapter-2-soweto-uprising-june-1976-turning-points-event.

Pampallis, J. (1991) *Foundations of the New South Africa.* Cape Town: Maskew Miller Longman. (Chapters 17 and 18). https://www.sahistory.org.za/sites/default/files/file%20uploads%20/foundation_of_the_new_south_africa_original_final.pdf.

Phillips, L. (2017) *History of South Africa's Bantustans.* http://africanhistory.oxfordre.com/view/10.1093/acrefore/9780190277734.001.0001/acrefore-9780190277734-e-80.

South African Students' Organisation (SASO) (n.d.) The Ideology and Politics of Black Consciousness. https://www.sahistory.org.za/archive/chapter-3-saso-ideology-and-politics-black-consciousness.

The Durban Strikes and the Resurgence of the Trade Union Movement in 1973. *South African History Online.* http://www.sahistory.org.za/article/durban-strikes-and-resurgence-trade-union-movement-1973.

Books

Badat, S. (1999) *Black Student Politics, Higher Education and Apartheid: From SASO to SANSCO, 1968–1990.* Pretoria: HSRC Press. (Chapters 2–6)

Biko, S. (1987) *I Write What I Like.* Johannesburg: Heinemann. [Also available as a YouTube audio book with the same name: https://www.youtube.com/watch?v=bukvj3y1rGc.]

Giliomee, H. and B. Mbenga (eds) (2007) *New History of South Africa.* Cape Town: Tafelberg. (Chapter 14)

Lodge, T. (1983) *Black Politics in South Africa since 1945.* London: Longman. (Chapter 13)

Magubane, B. (2006) Introduction to the 1970s: The Social and Political Context (Chapter 1). In *The Road to Democracy in South Africa*, Volume 2, 1970–1980, edited by the South African Democracy Education Trust. Pretoria: Unisa Press.

Meli, F. (1988) *A History of the ANC: South Africa Belongs to Us.* London: James Currey. (Chapters 6 and 7)

Sixteen

Apartheid under Pressure, 1976–1989

The Soweto Uprising proved to be a watershed event, marking intensified resistance to apartheid which continued throughout the 1980s. It also marked a turnaround in the fortunes of the African National Congress (ANC), which had found it difficult to resume its struggle inside South Africa since its banning and the heavy repression that followed. However, it had prepared itself sufficiently to provide the guidance, direction and support that many young revolutionaries were looking for in the wake of the Soweto Uprising.

Although Umkhonto we Sizwe (MK) remained a relatively small organisation, it had developed its basic structures and secured opportunities for military training in various African and socialist countries such as the Soviet Union and the German Democratic Republic. The ANC developed friendly ties with independent southern African countries (known as the front-line states[18]) and created small organisational centres there to facilitate its military and political efforts inside South Africa. These countries all paid dearly for their solidarity with the ANC and several were attacked by South African military forces.

Internationally the ANC built links with sympathetic governments and supported the establishment of the anti-apartheid movements in many countries. Despite support for the apartheid regime from some prominent Western leaders, anti-apartheid movements campaigned, increasingly successfully, for economic, diplomatic and other sanctions against South Africa. Many countries in Africa and elsewhere provided higher education

---

18 The front-line states were Angola, Botswana, Lesotho, Mozambique, Swaziland (eSwatini), Tanzania, Zambia and Zimbabwe.

and vocational scholarships for ANC students. The international anti-apartheid movement grew to become one of the largest solidarity movements ever to have existed in the world.

The international profile of the liberation struggle was boosted when Archbishop Desmond Tutu, who had become a prominent leader of the mass movement in South Africa, was awarded the Nobel Peace Prize in 1984. A campaign demanding that the government release Nelson Mandela from prison was initiated by the ANC and taken up by progressive groupings inside South Africa and abroad. Mandela became the most prominent symbol of South Africa's struggle for freedom.

Inside South Africa, the ANC had worked to create underground structures and communications systems. Leaflets and official ANC statements as well as the journals of the ANC and the South African Communist Party (SACP) were secretly distributed throughout the country. The ANC's Radio Freedom, broadcasting from various African countries, became an important medium of communication.

While the ANC and SACP continued as allied but independent organisations, their activities often merged. Communists worked as an integral part of ANC and MK structures at both leadership and rank-and-file levels. Some prominent leaders held leading positions in both the ANC and SACP, including Moses Mabhida, Dan Tloome, Yusuf Dadoo, Joe Slovo, Chris Hani and John Nkadimeng.

After the events of 1976–8, the ANC quickly asserted itself as the leading force of the liberation struggle. The Pan Africanist Congress (PAC) and various Black Consciousness bodies maintained an organisational presence but it was the ANC to which most South Africans looked for leadership. It assisted students and other young people who wanted to leave the country, and provided them with the opportunity to receive military training in MK or to continue their studies abroad. The ANC established a school for young exiles, the Solomon Mahlangu Freedom College in Morogoro, Tanzania, and a vocational training centre at nearby Dakawa. Crucially, links were strengthened between the External Mission and the underground structures in South Africa, and between the ANC and the rapidly growing mass organisations that are discussed below.

In Zimbabwe the liberation struggle had forced the white minority regime of Ian Smith to the negotiating table. The talks resulted in a democratic constitution and the country became independent on 18 April 1980, with Robert Mugabe as the new Prime Minister.

The White Elite Feels the Pressure

Following the 1976 Uprising, tensions appeared within the National Party on how to deal with the pressure for change. Prime Minister B.J. Vorster represented an intransigent faction that saw no need to change but thought that the situation could be controlled by force alone. The opposing faction, led by P.W. Botha, felt that alongside the iron fist of repression there was a need for reforms to stabilise the system. In 1978, Vorster was weakened by a corruption scandal involving the Department of Information. The

Botha faction took advantage of the situation to oust Vorster, and Botha became Prime Minister.

As the 1980s unfolded, the political crisis deepened. Resistance from black South Africans kept growing and became widespread. The government and leaders of the big business corporations were particularly concerned about the economic crisis caused by international sanctions. Many foreign companies withdrew their investments and financial sanctions made it difficult to get loans from abroad. Inflation rose rapidly, reaching a high point of over 20 per cent in 1986.

Business leaders began to look for ways to ease political tensions. Many of them recognised the overwhelming popularity of the ANC among black South Africans. In September 1985, a delegation of businessmen led by Gavin Relly of the Anglo American Corporation visited the ANC's headquarters in Lusaka for discussions. This was followed over the next five years by other white delegations, including business people, religious leaders and intellectuals. Discussions with ANC leaders largely consisted of sharing views on the nature of a post-apartheid South Africa. Contacts between black leaders in South Africa and the ANC also increased during this time, both openly and in secret.

Resistance Spreads

The trade union movement

From the time of the 1973 Durban strikes, the trade union movement had gained momentum. New unions were formed, and membership increased. In 1979, 12 of the new unions joined together to form the Federation of South African Trade Unions (FOSATU). The new federation was open to all workers regardless of colour and promoted shop-floor democracy and worker control of the unions. In 1980 another group of unions formed a separate federation, the Council of Unions of South Africa (CUSA), which was more oriented to Black Consciousness ideology.

In November 1985, after a three-year-long process of discussions – urged on and aided by the South African Congress of Trade Unions (SACTU) and the ANC – a new federation, the Congress of South African Trade Unions (COSATU), was formed with about 450 000 paid-up members. It included FOSATU and a number of smaller federations and individual unions. It committed itself to non-racialism, worker control and militant trade unionism. Elijah Barayi was elected its first president. COSATU was committed to participating in the struggle for national liberation and in 1987 formally adopted the Freedom Charter, thus openly indicating its sympathies with the ANC and the United Democratic Front (UDF). In the first six months of its existence, COSATU organised two national general strikes, a prelude to many similar actions.

CUSA, which had been part of the unity discussions from the beginning, decided not to join COSATU, objecting to its non-racialism. In 1986, it joined a new, smaller federation, the Azanian Confederation of Trade Unions (AZACTU), to form the National Council of Trade Unions (NACTU). One result of CUSA's decision not to join COSATU was that its largest affiliate, the National Union of Mineworkers (NUM), left to become a founding member of COSATU.

Durban,1985: the Congress Of South African Trade Unions launch. Source: Paul Weinberg/ South/Gallo images

Education and students

After the return of students to school in 1978, grievances against Bantu Education continued. The education system remained a major focus of activism in the struggle against apartheid. In 1979 two new national student organisations were established: the Congress of South African Students (COSAS) for students in secondary schools and in technical and teacher training colleges, and the Azanian Students' Organisation (AZASO) – later renamed the South African National Students' Congress (SANSCO) – for university students.

Both were initially oriented to Black Consciousness ideology but by 1981 they had changed their thinking and declared their support for the Freedom Charter. They also developed links with the white students' organisation, the National Union of South African Students (NUSAS), which was becoming increasingly more radical in its support for a non-racial, democratic society.

During much of the 1980s African education was in a state of turmoil. While this resulted from opposition to inferior education, it also threatened to deprive young people of an education altogether. Concern with this state of affairs led parents and political, community and student organisations to establish the National Education Crisis Committee (NECC) in December 1985 to coordinate education struggles and strategies. It called on students to return to school but also initiated a national stay-away on 16 June 1986 to mark the tenth anniversary of the Soweto Uprising. It further proposed that teachers and students should unite to create an alternative system of education, referred to as People's Education.

Political funerals of police victims became common in the 1980s. Source: Kevin Carter/Sygma/ Sygma via Getty Images

The United Democratic Front

From the late 1970s, numerous community or civic organisations emerged in South Africa. Many were linked to specific local struggles such as campaigns against rent or bus fare increases and consumer boycotts. Community militancy extended to both urban and rural areas as many took up ANC president Oliver Tambo's call to make South Africa ungovernable. From the mid-1980s the government-organised Community Councils began to collapse in the face of strong opposition from located communities, which started to replace them with street and area committees – often referred to as 'organs of people's power' – to undertake dispute resolution and basic local administration.

In 1983, approximately 400 national, regional and local organisations came together to form the United Democratic Front. The affiliates included community, trade union, women's, student, cultural, sporting and religious organisations opposed to apartheid; most were committed to the principles of the Freedom Charter. Members of the affiliates numbered about one and a half million people of all classes and colours, including a small but growing number of whites. The End Conscription Campaign, made up of progressive white youth, resisted the conscription of young white men into the apartheid armed forces. In its first major campaign, the UDF led opposition to the new national constitution introduced by P.W. Botha, which created a three-chamber parliament – one each for whites, coloureds and Indians (see below). The UDF also initiated a successful boycott of the first elections to the coloured and Indian chambers; less than 18 per cent of the potential electorate actually voted.

In 1987, leaders of various regional youth organisations came together to establish the South African Youth Congress (SAYCO). With half a million members, SAYCO became the UDF's largest affiliate.

At about the same time that the UDF was formed, the National Forum (NF) was established by groups from Black Consciousness and Unity Movement traditions. The NF rejected non-racialism, arguing that blacks could not work with progressive whites for the overthrow of apartheid. Its largest affiliates were the Azanian People's Organisation (AZAPO) and NACTU. By 1986 the NF had 53 affiliates but it could not rival the widespread influence of the UDF.

THE ARMED STRUGGLE

With the influx of young people after the 1976 Uprising, Umkhonto we Sizwe grew rapidly, providing training for the new recruits in camps in Angola. In Lesotho, Swaziland, Botswana and Mozambique, MK worked to facilitate military and underground activities inside South Africa. These included the spectacular attack on the SASOL plant in Sasolburg in June 1980, in which several storage tanks were blown up, an attack on the Koeberg Nuclear Power Station in December 1981, and the explosion of a large bomb near the Air Force offices in central Pretoria in May 1983. The number of MK actions increased after 1976 to about 200 a year by the late 1980s, including acts of sabotage and engagements with both the police and the armed forces. MK also fought alongside the Angolan army against South African military incursions into Angola.

Despite all this, it is true to say that MK was never a military threat to the apartheid regime's existence. It did, however, play two important roles in the liberation struggle. First, it had the effect of raising the hopes of the oppressed people, as they saw that the government was vulnerable; it inspired many to join the struggle and thus contributed to the growth of mass resistance. Second, the armed attacks forced the government to increase both military and police spending, thus adding significantly to its economic crisis.

THE REGIME'S POLICY RESPONSE

As mentioned above, the Botha government's response to the growth of resistance was two-pronged: to reform apartheid on the one hand, and to enforce its position by heavy suppression on the other. Some of the reforms (particularly those relating to labour) were substantive and met a number of long-standing popular demands. Most were merely cosmetic. None of the reforms came close to meeting the liberation movement's demands for a democratic, unitary, non-racial and non-sexist South Africa.

Reforms

Ideological shifts emerged within the National Party as it tried to find ways to dampen opposition from blacks and to maintain white supremacy. For the first time since the beginning of colonialism, a white government was in retreat, being reactive instead of proactive in setting the country's agenda. P.W. Botha told whites that they would need to 'adapt or die' and that there would have to be 'healthy power-sharing' with blacks. In propaganda aimed at an international audience, the government de-emphasised racial issues. It began to claim that its main purpose was to defend free enterprise capitalism and Western civilisation from the forces of 'international communism', which it identified with the ANC and the SACP.

In 1983 the government passed legislation to change the country's constitution. The new constitution created a parliament with three separate chambers – one each for whites, coloureds and Indians. Each chamber was to deal with legislation of concern to its 'own' group – for example, education or housing. Matters of common concern would need to be addressed by all three chambers. If they could not agree, the matter would be referred to a President's Council, whose majority was appointed by the white chamber and the President. The post of prime minister was abolished and a president was effectively appointed by the majority party in the white chamber – that is, the National Party. P.W. Botha became the country's first President. The constitution was designed to give coloureds and Indians some stake in the apartheid system and to co-opt them by offering them a subordinate role in government. The scheme was unable to achieve this objective, as shown by the boycott of the first election to the coloured and Indian chambers.

Under the new constitution the government's plans for Africans were unchanged: political rights for Africans would be exercised through the bantustans, mainly led by traditional leaders, and to a lesser extent by local Community Councils in urban townships. The government saw the leaders of these structures as allies with an interest in the apartheid system.

The government changed the name of the Department of Bantu Education to the Department of Education and Training in a futile attempt to improve its image. Enrolments in secondary schools for Africans tripled between 1975 and 1986 as the government tried to produce a more skilled workforce. Quality remained low, however, and probably fell; in 1986 government expenditure per African student was only 14 per cent of that spent on each white student.

The better organisation of workers and their increased militancy prompted the government to review labour legislation. In addition, big business was pressing the government to scrap job reservation laws and allow black workers to perform jobs that were being carried out by higher-paid white workers. After a review of labour legislation by the Wiehahn Commission in 1979, the labour laws were amended. Unions with African members could now be registered and were thus recognised in law; this meant that they also had the right to strike. Even though these were important victories for the workers, there were serious limitations. For example, domestic workers, farm workers and public servants were excluded from the new provisions and were denied the right to strike.

Among the most important developments around this time was the abolition in 1986 of the pass laws, which had contributed so much to the oppression of Africans for more than a century. The importance of this change is underlined by the fact that in 1984 almost 240 000 Africans had been arrested under the pass laws.

The government also attempted to find allies in the urban areas through the development of a black middle class. It aimed to create a stratum of urban blacks with a stake in the system, to draw them away from revolutionary activity, and encourage them to have a moderating influence on the liberation movement. Racially discriminatory pay for professionals in the public service was abolished. As a result, the incomes of black teachers, doctors, nurses and others increased. Large corporations, with government approval, began to promote blacks into certain middle-management positions. Some forms of 'petty apartheid' were abolished, allowing certain restaurants, hotels and recreational facilities to be used by all.

The reforms did little to stem opposition to the apartheid system. If anything, they increased it because people saw the defensive nature of the regime's actions as a sign of weakness.

Increased repression

At the same time as it was trying to make apartheid more palatable to some sections of the black community, the government increased its repression. In July 1985 it announced a State of Emergency in 36 of the country's 260 magisterial districts, including most major urban areas. The emergency was lifted in March 1986, but three months later a new State of Emergency was imposed on the entire country and it lasted until 1990.

During the two States of Emergency the powers of the police were greatly expanded. They arrested thousands of people, in most cases without bringing them before the courts. Those arrested included national and local leaders and activists of political, trade union, community, women's and youth organisations. Many of them, including children and old people, were kept in solitary confinement for long periods of time and were cruelly tortured. Others were tried by apartheid courts; most were sent to prison while some were sentenced to death.

The media were prevented from reporting on what the government called 'unrest situations' and from publishing any information about detainees. The army was sent into the townships to support the police in asserting control.

Attacks on black protesters and activists were carried out not only by the police and the military but by vigilante groups linked to bantustan governments, including members of the KwaZulu-based Inkatha movement and Mbokodo, an organisation aligned to Simon Skosana of the KwaNdebele bantustan. Others were associated with the Community Councils. Secret death squads were established by the police to kill prominent opponents of the government, both inside South Africa and abroad. Their victims included Griffiths and Victoria Mxenge, Cassius Maake, Ruth First, Joe Gqabi, Dulcie September and, in Namibia, Anton Lubowski.

The 1980s saw ultimate power in the state pass to the military and security establishment. The State Security Council – chaired by the President and including the Ministers of Defence, Police, Justice and Foreign Affairs as well as a few top military and police officers – took all the major strategic decisions, becoming more powerful than the Cabinet itself. In the decade from 1976 to 1986, military expenditure increased almost five-fold and the police budget eight-fold. Compulsory military service for white youth was extended. Separate military forces were established in the four 'independent' bantustans, headed or advised by South African or ex-Rhodesian officers.

Military attacks were made against front-line states to destabilise them and prevent them from giving assistance to the ANC. ANC personnel were targeted and many were killed in Mozambique, Angola, Lesotho, Swaziland, Botswana, Zimbabwe and Zambia; in most raids local people also lost their lives. In Mozambique and Angola, South Africa supported counter-revolutionary rebel organisations – the Mozambican National Resistance (RENAMO) and the National Union for the Total Independence of Angola (UNITA). As a result, large areas of the two countries were devastated in brutal wars against the newly established governments there.

War in Angola and Independence in Namibia

From 1980 to 1985, the South African Defence Force (SADF) occupied large areas of southern Angola. Approximately 100 000 South African troops were deployed against the Angolan army and the People's Liberation Army of Namibia (PLAN), the military wing of the South West Africa People's Organisation (SWAPO). In addition, they confronted PLAN fighters inside Namibia. At the same time, South Africa established a puppet administration in that country, with limited powers, made up mainly of Namibian bantustan leaders and other allies of Pretoria. However, South Africa won support neither from the Namibian people nor from any section of the international community. As a result, it was forced to rely on military force to prevent a democratic government from gaining power.

In 1987 South Africa launched a major attack into south-eastern Angola. They met unexpectedly strong resistance from Angolan and Cuban forces around the town of Cuito Cuanavale. While the Battle of Cuito Cuanavale raged, other Angolan and Cuban troops moved south towards the Namibian border, cutting off the South Africans' line of retreat. In order to extricate its troops, the South African government began talks with Angola and Cuba, which insisted that any agreement on the SADF's withdrawal from Angola be linked to independence for Namibia. In December 1988 an agreement was reached: South Africa would withdraw from Angola and end its occupation of Namibia, and Namibia would become independent. In addition, it was agreed that all Cuban forces would be withdrawn from Angola over a period of 27 months. The Angolan government also agreed that MK military bases in Angola would be closed; the ANC withdrew its soldiers and moved them to Uganda and Tanzania.

On 21 March 1990, SWAPO won Namibia's first democratic elections and its leader, Sam Nujoma, became the first President of the newly independent nation.

SPEAKING TO THE ENEMY

By the end of the 1980s it was clear that the South African state was losing control and the economy was deteriorating rapidly. As a result, some leading members of the regime realised that apartheid was unsustainable. They began to consider new options for the future and made tentative moves to establish contact with the ANC in exile. At the same time, sections of the ANC leadership were coming to the conclusion that the broad liberation movement was not in a position to take power by force and establish a non-racial democracy in the foreseeable future. Unless steps were taken by both sides to break the stalemate, a long and destructive struggle lay ahead. Some leaders, including the imprisoned Nelson Mandela, saw the possibility of a peaceful transformation to a non-racial democracy and took some cautious steps in this direction.

These views were not shared by all leaders or members on either side. Progress in opening communication between the two sides was therefore initially slow and hesitant.

CHAPTER 16: DISCUSSION QUESTIONS

1. How did various sections of the white political and military elite respond to the increasing pressures from internal and external opposition to apartheid, including international sanctions?

2. The international anti-apartheid movement was one of the most widespread and effective solidarity movements in world history. Discuss the main ways in which it contributed to the defeat of apartheid.

3. Evaluate the importance of Umkhonto we Sizwe as an instrument of the liberation struggle.

4. Discuss how and to what extent the various strands of resistance – for example, the mass movements (including the UDF), the ANC underground, the armed struggle by MK, the trade unions, the international anti-apartheid movement – complemented one another to defeat the apartheid regime.

CHAPTER 16: ADDITIONAL READINGS

Online readings

Congress of South African Trade Unions (COSATU). *South African History Online.* https://www.sahistory.org.za/topic/congress-south-african-trade-unions-cosatu.

Multimedia: South Africa, the United Nations and Apartheid. https://www.brandsouthafrica.com/people-culture/history-heritage/multimedia-south-africa-the-united-nations-and-apartheid

National Education Coordinating Committee (NECC). https://omalley. nelsonmandela.org/omalley/index.php/site/q/03lv02424/04lv02730/05lv0 3188/06lv03208.htm.

Pampallis, J. (1991) *Foundations of the New South Africa.* Cape Town: Maskew Miller Longman. (Chapters 19–20) https://www.sahistory.org.za/sites/ default/files/file%20uploads%20/foundation_of_the_new_south_africa_ original_final.pdf.

The People Armed, 1984–1990. *South African History Online.* https://www. sahistory.org.za/article/people-armed-1984-1990.

United Democratic Front (UDF). *South African History Online.* http://www. sahistory.org.za/organisations/united-democratic-front-udf.

Books

Badat, S. (1999) *Black Student Politics, Higher Education and Apartheid: From SASO to SANSCO, 1968–1990.* Pretoria: HSRC Press. (Chapters 7–10)

Giliomee, H. and B. Mbenga (eds) (2007) *New History of South Africa.* Cape Town: Tafelberg (Chapter 14)

Houston, G. (1999) *The National Liberation Struggle in South Africa: A Case Study of the United Democratic Front, 1983–1987.* Cape Town: HSRC Press.

Houston, G. (2008) Introduction (Chapter 1). In *The Road to Democracy in South Africa*, Volume 3, edited by South African Democracy Education Trust. Pretoria: Unisa Press. http://www.sadet.co.za/docs/RTD/vol3/vol3_ chapter%201.pdf.

Magubane, B. (2010) The Crisis of the Garrison State (Chapter1). In *The Road to Democracy in South Africa*, Volume 4, Part 1, 1980–1990, edited by South African Democracy Education Trust. Pretoria: Unisa Press.

Thompson, L. (2014) *A History of South Africa.* Johannesburg: Jonathan Ball. (Chapter 7)

Seventeen

Tentative Talks and an Escalation of Violence

As noted in Chapter 16, the unfolding situation in South Africa in the 1980s caused some prominent figures in both the National Party (NP) and the African National Congress (ANC) to start thinking about alternative ways of moving forward. It began to dawn on the government that it would not be able to destroy the liberation movement. At the same time, leading ANC figures, including Oliver Tambo and the still-imprisoned Nelson Mandela, realised that although the regime had been weakened, it was not going to collapse in the near future and that further conflict would probably result in a lengthy and destructive civil war that would benefit no one. Some initial secret meetings between senior members of the government and the ANC began to take place from the mid-1980s. These followed earlier formal meetings between the ANC and representatives of various white groups, including the Afrikaner Broederbond.

The government had made several offers to Mandela to release him conditionally – that is, on condition that he move to the Transkei and that he renounce violence – but he had refused. Then in 1986 an informal meeting took place between Mandela and the Minister of Justice and Prisons, Kobie Coetsee. Mandela held more than forty meetings with Coetsee and senior government officials over the next three years. In 1989 he had a short meeting with P.W. Botha. The talks were exploratory, with each side getting to know the other and trying to find out what they hoped to achieve. One should keep in mind, though, that during this period there was very little peace-making taking place. Throughout the entire period, the state used brutal repression while the black population and the liberation movement were struggling to weaken – and ultimately to overthrow – the apartheid state.

The new developments took place in a changing international context. In view of the rising levels of turbulence in South Africa, the main backers of the apartheid regime, particularly Britain and the United States, began to pressure it to release Mandela and other imprisoned leaders of the liberation movement. This was partly because of their concern that Western interests in southern Africa could be damaged, but also in response to the growing influence of the anti-apartheid movements internationally, including in their own countries. In October 1989, the government agreed to release five of the men sent to prison with Mandela in 1964: Walter Sisulu, Ahmed Kathrada, Raymond Mhlaba, Andrew Mlangeni and Elias Motsoaledi. Two others, Denis Goldberg and Govan Mbeki, had been released in 1985 and 1987 respectively.

By 1989, with the beginning of the collapse of the socialist systems in the Soviet Union and its Eastern European allies, the argument of the South African government that it was protecting capitalism from the forces of 'international communism' could no longer be taken seriously. The ANC was also forced to reconsider its position in the light of the collapse of its strongest international allies, which were no longer in a position to provide the same support as before.

New Leadership in Government

Despite approving the talks between his government and the ANC, P.W. Botha was not himself prepared to consider any solutions that would result in an end to white rule. He was not alone in this among Cabinet members and the NP leadership, but a group of 'reformists' within the party were gaining strength.

When Botha suffered a stroke in early 1989, he resigned as leader of the National Party but remained as President; F.W. de Klerk became the new NP leader. However, in August that year the Cabinet revolted against Botha; he was forced to resign as President and was replaced by De Klerk, a more reform-minded – or at least a more realistic – leader. In the all-white election of September 1989, the National Party remained the strongest political party, but almost a third of the electorate voted for the right-wing Conservative Party, which opposed any significant political change at all.

While willing to end apartheid, the NP leadership under De Klerk rejected a 'pure one-person-one-vote system' and insisted on 'group rights' so that people would be represented in a future parliament on the basis of their ethnic or racial group rather that just as individual voters. In their view a new constitution should be based on consensus between such groups rather than embodying majority rule based on the wishes of individual voters. Whites would thus have a veto to ward off any threat to their interests.

February 1990

On 2 February 1990, almost six months after De Klerk replaced Botha, he announced in Parliament the unbanning of the ANC, the South African Communist Party (SACP), the Pan Africanist Congress (PAC), and 58 other organisations. He also announced the easing (though not the ending) of the State of Emergency regulations, including a

Nelson Mandela's release from prison, 11 February 1990.

partial lifting of restrictions on the press. The police, however, still retained draconian powers and many political prisoners still remained behind bars. De Klerk also said that he intended releasing Nelson Mandela in the near future. Nine days later Mandela walked out of Victor Verster Prison a hero, being watched on television by millions in South Africa and around the world. He joined the leadership of the liberation struggle as it moved into a new phase. While the structure of apartheid society still remained in place, the new balance of forces would ensure fundamental change and the creation of a new political dispensation.

PREPARING FOR NEGOTIATIONS

In the months after the unbanning of the liberation organisations, most exiled leaders returned to the country and a round of 'talks about talks' began. The aim of this process, which lasted almost two years, was to decide how negotiations about the future of South Africa should take place. The most important things to be agreed on were the questions of who would participate in the negotiations, what form they should take and what their agenda would be.

The government's violence against ANC supporters and other black civilians continued after February 1990, and a great deal of time was spent discussing this. The ANC and its allies also insisted that they could not negotiate until the government lifted the State of Emergency, released all political prisoners, allowed all exiles to return to South Africa without fear of prosecution, and repealed the remaining apartheid laws. The government complied with most of these demands although, for example, many political prisoners were not immediately released. Within the ANC there were sharp debates about whether to abandon the armed struggle. Eventually, the ANC declared that it would suspend the armed struggle though it would not disband Umkhonto we Sizwe.

With the ANC legalised and generally accepted as the leading force in the liberation struggle, the United Democratic Front (UDF) decided to dissolve itself in March 1991. Its affiliates at national, regional and community level around the country continued to exist and to mobilise people for mass action in support of the ANC. They accepted the ANC's leadership role but, perhaps as a consequence, surrendered their own; their contribution to national policy-making and leadership gradually began to decline. The ANC and the SACP established a formal alliance with the Congress of South African Trade Unions (COSATU), the most significant organisation in civil society that was not a political party. This became known as the Tripartite Alliance.

The ANC's first conference after becoming legal was held in Durban in July 1991. The conference declaration stated that the possibility of eradicating apartheid by peaceful means had 'emerged through our struggles'. But it also noted 'with alarm' the continuation of state violence against black communities, which endangered the negotiations process. It resolved to intensify peaceful mass organisation and mobilisation. Finally, it restated its adherence to the principles of a united, non-racial, non-sexist and democratic South Africa as enshrined in the Freedom Charter. Oliver Tambo, who had suffered a stroke in 1989, declined to stand for a leadership position; he was then elected to the largely honorary position of national chairman. The conference elected Nelson Mandela as ANC president and Cyril Ramaphosa as secretary general.

ESCALATION OF VIOLENCE

The entire period starting from February 1990, and continuing through the preliminary talks and the formal negotiations, was marked by violence. This was carried out by the government's security forces and their allies and aimed primarily at weakening the ANC and its supporters. The violence inevitably resulted in counter-violence. The number of violent deaths actually increased after February 1990, averaging over 3 300 per year between February 1990 and April 1994.

In the province of Natal, a violent conflict had been going on throughout the 1980s between ANC supporters resisting the authority of the bantustan authorities and Inkatha, which controlled the KwaZulu bantustan. The police provided both funding and training to Inkatha and other counter-revolutionary groups. The conflict in Natal escalated after February 1990 and resulted in thousands of deaths. It soon spread to other parts of South Africa, especially the Witwatersrand townships, where Inkatha-supporting hostel dwellers attacked members of surrounding communities, killing many residents and destroying their homes and property.

Inkatha was renamed the Inkatha Freedom Party (IFP) in July 1990. Its leader, Mangosuthu Buthelezi, had long believed himself to be one of the most important black political leaders in South Africa, and he resented the government's recognition of the ANC and its decision to open negotiations with it. In this he and his party were in agreement with elements in the government's police and military forces and with the Conservative

F.W. de Klerk and Nelson Mandela shake hands at the Annual Meeting of the World Economic Forum held in Davos, Switzerland, January 1992.

Party and other right-wing forces. They strongly opposed the establishment of a unitary South African state, preferring instead either an independent state in the KwaZulu-Natal area or a very loose federation.

Much of the anti-liberation violence was carried out by a 'third force' – that is, neither the government nor the liberation movement. This third force consisted of members or former members of the security forces with links to white right-wing political forces who orchestrated anti-ANC activities. These included attacks on communities, murders, torture, kidnappings, and the shooting or stabbing of commuters on trains. In these activities they collaborated with the IFP and bantustans like Ciskei or Bophuthatswana, whose leaders were resisting the establishment of a unitary, democratic South Africa. In some parts of the country, 'vigilante' groups were clandestinely trained to carry out violence.

One of the worst of the hundreds of violent incidents was a massacre by Inkatha-aligned hostel dwellers of 80 people in the Phola Park informal settlement on the East Rand in two days of indiscriminate attacks in September 1990. On 17 June 1992, at least 49 people, including 23 women and children, were murdered in their sleep in Boipatong in the Vaal Triangle area by hostel dwellers. Mandela accused the government of complicity in the Boipatong attack as part of a strategy to destabilise and weaken the ANC. He and the ANC then withdrew temporarily from the negotiations (see Chapter 18).

Violent conflict was often described by the government and parts of the media as 'black-on-black violence', a formulation that was aimed at deflecting attention from the involvement of the security forces. De Klerk always denied any connection with or knowledge of police or military involvement in the killings, but the ANC disputed this. In fact, a number of later inquiries, both official and unofficial, did find evidence of direct police involvement in the violence.

On April 1993, Chris Hani, the popular general secretary of the SACP and a leading member of the ANC's National Executive Committee, was shot and killed by Janusz Waluś with the assistance of Clive Derby-Lewis, both extreme right-wing racists. The ensuing popular anger, especially among blacks, threatened to plunge the country into a bloodbath and to collapse the entire process of negotiations.

The crisis was calmed by a televised appeal from the ANC president Nelson Mandela. For the first time ever, he was given airtime to address the nation. He called for restraint and appealed to people, and particularly the youth, not to 'destroy what Chris dedicated his life for ... freedom for all of us'. He also appealed to people not to interpret the assassination racially, pointing out that although it had been carried out by 'a white man, full of prejudice and hate', it was an Afrikaner woman who witnessed the crime and who assisted in bringing the killers to justice. All South Africans, he said, should stand together. Mandela was possibly the only person who had the authority to appeal successfully to the entire country in this way. His address, a year before the first democratic election, was symbolic of the passing of power from the old government to a new democratic order even though the negotiations to achieve this were not yet complete.

CHAPTER 17: DISCUSSION QUESTIONS

1. In the late 1980s and early 1990s various actors came to the conclusion that a negotiated settlement – especially between the South African government and the ANC – was both desirable and possible. All had previously either opposed negotiations or did not believe that they could achieve anything. What were the reasons that each of the following changed their approach to resolving the conflict in South Africa:
   a. The government;
   b. The leadership of the ANC;
   c. The Western powers, particularly the United States and Britain.

2. Why do you think that violence in South Africa escalated just as the governing National Party and the African National Congress were beginning to look for peaceful ways to resolve their differences?

CHAPTER 17: ADDITIONAL READINGS

Online readings

Anon. (2017) *Negotiations and the Transition.* https://www.sahistory.org.za/

topic/negotiations-and-transition.

African National Congress (1992) *Negotiations: A Strategic Perspective.* http://disa.
ukzn.ac.za/sites/default/files/pdf_files/pre19921125.026.021.000.pdf.

Lane, C. (1994) *South Africa's Violent Road to Real Democracy.* https://newrepublic.
com/article/120502/violence-south-africa-after-end-apartheid.

Maharaj, M. (2008) *The ANC and South Africa's Negotiated Transition to Democracy
and Peace.* Berlin: Berghof Research Center for Constructive Conflict
Management. https://www.berghof-foundation.org/fileadmin/redaktion/
Publications/Papers/Transitions_Series/transitions_anc.pdf.

Truth and Reconciliation Commission (TRC) (1998) *Report of the Truth and
Reconciliation Commission,* Volume 2. Chapter 7: Political Violence in the Era
of Negotiations and Transition, 1990–1994. https://www.justice.gov.za/trc/
report/finalreport/Volume%202.pdf.

Books

De Klerk, F.W. (1998) *The Last Trek – A New Beginning: The Autobiography.*
Johannesburg: Macmillan. (Chapters 13 to 18)

Giliomee, H. and B. Mbenga (eds) (2007) *New History of South Africa.* Cape
Town: Tafelberg. (Chapter 15)

Mandela, N. (1994) *Long Walk to Freedom: The Autobiography of Nelson Mandela.*
Johannesburg: Macdonald Purnell. (Part 10)

Ndlovu, S.M. (2013) The ANC, CODESA, Substantive Negotiations and
the Road to the First Democratic Elections (Chapter 17). In *The Road to
Democracy in South* Africa, Volume 6, edited by South African Democracy
Education Trust. Pretoria: Unisa Press.

Sparks, A. (1995) *Tomorrow Is Another Country.* Johannesburg: Struik.

Thompson, L. (2014) *A History of South Africa.* Johannesburg: Jonathan
Ball. (Chapter 8). https://www.sahistory.org.za/sites/default/files/
file%20uploads%20/leonard_monteath_thompson_a_history_of_south_
afrbook4me.org_.pdf.

Eighteen

Negotiations and the Coming of Democracy

On 20 December 1991, the Convention for a Democratic South Africa (CODESA) met in Kempton Park. It was a broad gathering to which all political parties and the leaders of the ten bantustans were invited. Nineteen parties actually attended. Those who refused to attend included the Pan Africanist Congress (PAC) and the Azanian People's Organisation (AZAPO) as well as white right-wing parties such as the Conservative Party and other even more extreme racist parties such as the Afrikaner Weerstandsbeweging (AWB). Mangosuthu Buthelezi insisted that the Inkatha Freedom Party (IFP) and the Zulu king should have separate delegations. When this was rejected, he himself stayed away but allowed an IFP delegation to attend.

This first meeting of CODESA was relatively brief. It adopted a Declaration of Intent that set out some basic principles for the new constitution, including one person one vote, a bill of rights, an independent judiciary and the abolition of the bantustans. It also created five working groups to investigate a new constitution, the setting up of an interim government, the future of the homelands, a time period for the implementation of the changes, and the electoral system.

Meanwhile, De Klerk was coming under increasing pressure from the more right-wing sections of the white community who opposed the talks. He decided to hold a referendum among the white electorate on 17 March 1992 – the last such racially exclusive poll in South Africa's history. The results showed that 69 per cent of the voters endorsed the 'reform process' that was 'aimed at a new constitution through negotiations'.

The negotiations resumed (as CODESA 2) in March 1992. The National Party (NP) feared that whites would be sidelined and lose all influence over government, and sought ways in which they could exercise a veto over all legislation. The African

Joe Slovo, Chris Hani and Raymond Mhlaba, leaders of the South African Communist Party.
Source: Africa Media Online.

National Congress (ANC) would not even consider such arrangements, which it believed would hamper any efforts by a new government to bring about meaningful change. The differences could not be resolved and the talks broke down on 26 May. Three weeks later, with the country enraged by the Boipatong massacre (see Chapter 17), Mandela announced that the ANC was suspending all further talks with the government. It began a campaign of 'rolling mass action', consisting of large demonstrations, strikes and consumer boycotts throughout the country. At one of the largest demonstrations, Ciskei police fired on a crowd of tens of thousands in Bisho, killing 29 people.

Without the negotiations, there appeared to be no clear way forward, and the ANC and NP began to communicate about the possibility of reconvening the formal negotiations process. In August and September 1992, a series of meetings took place between the chief negotiators for the government and the ANC, Roelf Meyer and Cyril Ramaphosa respectively. The outcome of their talks, known as the Record of Understanding, was signed by Mandela and De Klerk on 26 September. They agreed to resume the official negotiations.

TOWARDS AN AGREEMENT

The government and the ANC agreed that the negotiations should aim to establish a democratically elected constitutional assembly. They also agreed that 'problematic hostels' would be identified and that further measures would be taken, 'including fencing and policing to prevent criminality by hostel dwellers and to protect hostel dwellers against external aggression'. Furthermore, they agreed that 'the public display and carrying of

1993: Roelf Meyer (National Party) and Cyril Ramaphosa (ANC) during the Codesa talks on November 21, 1993. Source: Gallo Images/Tiso Blackstar Group

dangerous weapons ... should be prohibited'. Organisations would, however, be able to apply for an exemption for particular events; this was an attempt to appease the IFP, which insisted that its supporters had the right to carry 'traditional weapons'. The IFP, however, was not satisfied and Buthelezi was angered that he had not been consulted in the informal discussions.

In August 1992, Joe Slovo, chairman of the South African Communist Party (SACP), published an article in the party's journal, the *African Communist*, pointing out that South Africa's civil service, police and army had the potential to destabilise a new, young democracy. He proposed the inclusion of 'sunset clauses' in the interim constitution that would provide some guarantees for the jobs and pensions of the hundreds of thousands of South African civil servants, judges, police and military personnel. He also suggested a temporary power-sharing arrangement in government after the first election, with all major parties having seats in the Cabinet in proportion to their share of the popular vote. After frank and heated debate within the Tripartite Alliance, these principles were accepted by the ANC. It believed that both the sunset clauses and a government of national unity would decrease the possibility of destabilisation and lay the basis for national reconciliation.

The formal negotiations – now known as the Multi-party Negotiating Process (MPNP) – resumed on 1 April 1993. All major political parties participated except for the IFP and the Conservative Party, which both remained opposed to the process. By November, after months of painstaking negotiations amid the continuing violence, a consensus on an interim constitution was reached. A date for the first democratic elections was set for 27 April 1994.

Among the provisions of the interim constitution was the incorporation of the ten bantustans and the four existing provinces into nine new provinces with their own legislatures. One of the most contentious issues in the negotiations was whether the country should be a unitary or a federal state. The NP wanted a federal state with most powers devolved to the provinces. The ANC, on the other hand, preferred a strong central state where power was concentrated in the national government. Eventually it was agreed that the provinces would have considerable powers, the most important of which were the administration of basic education and public health services. However, the bulk of state power would be located with the national government. Elections would be organised and overseen by an Independent Electoral Commission. A Constitutional Court was to be established as the highest court of the land in all matters relating to the constitution.

In order to give effect to power-sharing for the first years of democratic government, a government of national unity would be established. The president of the country would be appointed from the majority party, and all parties that received at least 20 per cent of the vote would be entitled to choose a deputy president. A party that won at least 5 per cent of the vote would be entitled to positions in the Cabinet. The larger and more powerful of two parliamentary chambers, the National Assembly, would be elected by proportional representation. Voters would vote only for a party and not for individual representatives. The second house would be known as the Senate and would consist of ten members nominated from each province. Public sector employees would keep their jobs until they retired. There would be 11 official languages.

The interim constitution guaranteed fundamental human rights for individuals, including the right to life, the right of all adults to vote, freedom from unfair discrimination, freedom of movement, freedom of expression, freedom of religion, belief and opinion, freedom of assembly, the right to basic education, and a range of other rights. The legislature to be established after the first elections would act as a constitutional assembly to adopt a new constitution, which would incorporate the principles agreed upon in the negotiations. Unlike the interim constitution, the new constitution would have legitimacy derived from being adopted by representatives of a government elected by all the people of South Africa.

THE APRIL 1994 ELECTIONS

The period just before the first democratic elections was marked by violence in many parts of the country, especially in the KwaZulu bantustan, Natal and the Witwatersrand. The white right-wing organisations, including the Conservative Party, joined together to form a new party, the Volksfront. It was headed by General Constand Viljoen, a former head of the South African Defence Force. Although numerically small and not representing most Afrikaners, the organisation included a number of senior police and military officers and senior government officials as well as many rank-and-file members with military training.

Neither the Volksfront nor the leaders of KwaZulu, Bophuthatswana and the Ciskei wanted to be part of the agreement reached by all other parties, and refused to

Voters standing in long queues during the 1994 general elections. Source: Gallo Images / *Rapport* Archives

register for the elections. The Volksfront sought to establish a *volkstaat* as a homeland for Afrikaners. Together, the three bantustans and the Volksfront established a formal alliance (the Freedom Alliance), which sought a loose federation in which they could remain virtually independent. This was not to be. Viljoen was eventually persuaded to participate in the elections by Mandela, who promised measures to protect the rights of cultural communities, including Afrikaners, and to set up a council to investigate the prospect of a *volkstaat*. Viljoen formed a new party, the Freedom Front, which included most of the white right-wing organisations. The governments of Bophuthatswana and the Ciskei, which faced rebellion from their people as well as pressure from the South African government, were forced to submit and were reincorporated into the rest of South Africa.

By the beginning of April 1994, only Buthelezi's IFP still refused to participate in the elections, a dangerous prospect given its potential for continuing violence in the post-election period. However, pressure from Inkatha's local and foreign financial supporters, and an assurance that the position of the Zulu monarchy would be recognised in the new constitution, persuaded Buthelezi to change his mind at the last minute.

The elections were held on 27 April 1994. All residents of South Africa as well as citizens living abroad were eligible to vote for both national and provincial legislatures. Despite the violent run-up to the elections, they went off remarkably peacefully and the Independent Electoral Commission described the few violent incidents as 'negligible'. After the elections, the political violence that had long disrupted life in the country came to an abrupt end in most parts. In the new province of KwaZulu-Natal, however, a reduced level of violence between supporters of the IFP and the ANC did continue for at least five years.

The elections for 400 seats in the National Assembly were won by the ANC with 63 per cent of the vote, while the National Party won 20 per cent and the IFP 11 per cent. In addition, the Freedom Front won 2.17 per cent, the Democratic Party 1.7 per cent, the PAC 1.3 per cent and the African Christian Democratic Party 0.5 per cent. Twelve other parties all received less than the 0.25 per cent required for representation in Parliament. In the provincial polls, the NP won a majority in the Western Cape and the IFP took KwaZulu-Natal. The other seven provinces were all won by the ANC.

The 1994 election marked the end of a long struggle for a non-racial, democratic state with a government elected by all the people, formal equality of all before the law, and the other liberal-democratic freedoms contained in the Bill of Rights. Ahead lay the mammoth challenges of eradicating poverty and radically reducing inequality, overcoming racism, sexism, homophobia and other forms of bigotry, and creating a common national identity out of the fragmentation and inequality left by centuries of colonialism and apartheid. Despite the challenges, it was clear that a whole new era had dawned, and there was widespread optimism that there was now a constitutional basis for tackling these challenges.

CHAPTER 18: DISCUSSION QUESTIONS

1. In April 1993 both the Conservative Party and the Inkatha Freedom Party refused to join in the negotiations that led to the adoption of the interim constitution. Six months later, a new alignment of the Afrikaner right-wing parties, the Volksfront, established the Freedom Alliance in association with the leaders of three bantustans. Why do you think that the right-wing Afrikaners in the Conservative Party and Volksfront made an alliance with the bantustan leaders? What do you think they had in common?

2. In the light of experience after April 1994, do you think that the solution agreed to at the constitutional negotiations regarding the distribution of powers between the national government and the provinces was the best one? If so, why do you think this? If not, how do you think it should have been different? In both cases, give your reasons for thinking this way.

CHAPTER 18: ADDITIONAL READINGS

Online readings

Maharaj, M. (2008) *The ANC and South Africa's Negotiated Transition to Democracy and Peace.* Berlin: Berghof Research Center for Constructive Conflict Management. https://www.berghof-foundation.org/fileadmin/redaktion/ Publications/Papers/Transitions_Series/transitions_anc.pdf.

Negotiation, Transition and Freedom. Turning Points in History Series, Book 6. Johannesburg: STE Publishers. (Chapters 1 and 2). http://sahistory.org. za/archive/book-6-negotiation-transition-and-freedom-commissioned- department-education.

Negotiating the Transition. South African History Online. https://www.sahistory. org.za/archive/chapter-9-negotiating-transition.

Republic of South Africa (1993) *Constitution of the Republic of South Africa* (The Interim Constitution). https://en.wikisource.org/wiki/Constitution_of_ the_Republic_of_South_Africa,_1993.

Slovo, J. (1992) Negotiations: What Room for Compromise? In *The African Communist,* no. 130, Third Quarter 1992. https://omalley.nelsonmandela. org/omalley/index.php/site/q/03lv02424/04lv02730/05lv03005/06lv0300 6/07lv03030/08lv03038.htm.

Books

De Klerk, F.W. (1998) *The Last Trek – A New Beginning: The Autobiography.* Johannesburg: Macmillan. (Chapters 32–35)

Giliomee, H. and B. Mbenga (eds) (2007) *New History of South Africa.* Cape Town: Tafelberg. (Chapter 15)

Mbatha, K. (2017) *Unmasked: Why the ANC Failed to Govern.* Johannesburg: KMM Review Publishing. (Chapter 2).

Morris, M. (2004) *Every Step of the Way: The Journey to Freedom in South Africa.* Cape Town: HSRC Press. (Chapter 13)

Sparks, A. (1995) *Tomorrow Is Another Country.* Johannesburg: Struik.

Thompson, L. (2014) *A History of South Africa.* Johannesburg: Jonathan Ball. (Chapter 8). https://www.sahistory.org.za/sites/default/files/file%20up- loads%20/leonard_monteath_thompson_a_history_of_south_afrbook4me. org_.pdf.

Nineteen

The Mandela Presidency, 1994–1999

A New Government

On 10 May 1994, Nelson Mandela was inaugurated as the first president of a democratic South Africa. Thabo Mbeki became the first deputy president and F.W. de Klerk the second deputy president. The Inkatha Freedom Party (IFP), having obtained more than the necessary 5 per cent of the vote, was entitled to seats in the Cabinet alongside the two largest parties. Mandela appointed a Cabinet made up of 18 members from the African National Congress (ANC), six from the National Party (NP) and three from the IFP, including Mangosuthu Buthelezi as Minister of Home Affairs.

In the provinces, premiers were elected by the legislatures and set about establishing provincial administrations, initially relying on the structures and personnel from the old 'white' provincial administrations or the bureaucracies of the now-dissolved bantustans. At the local level, interim structures were established involving power-sharing between the previously existing local governments, the liberation movements, other political parties and local civic organisations. The first democratically elected local government elections took place only in 2000.

A New Constitution

In line with the negotiations leading to the establishment of democratic government, the two chambers of Parliament, sitting together, acted as a constitutional assembly charged with drafting a new constitution. The process was bound by the principles negotiated before the elections (see Chapter 18). But within these parameters, there was another round of tough negotiations before the new constitution was eventually adopted almost

President Nelson Mandela at his inauguration on May 10, 1994 in Pretoria. Source: Gallo Images / Sunday Times / David Sandison

unanimously in October 1996; it went into effect in February 1997.

This permanent constitution replaced the Senate with a National Council of Provinces (NCOP) made up of representatives from the provinces. Its main function is to ensure that provincial interests are taken into account at the national level of government and to provide a forum for public debate on issues affecting the provinces.

In addition to the rights guaranteed in the interim constitution (see Chapter 18), the Bill of Rights added other citizens' rights including economic and social rights such as the right of access to housing, health care and social security as well as to sufficient food and water. In addition to the right of individuals to basic education, the state was obliged to make further (post-school) education progressively available. Everyone has the right to receive education in the language of their choice in public institutions 'where that education is reasonably practicable'. This last right was the outcome of intense negotiation, with the NP and the Freedom Front demanding that Afrikaans single-medium public schools should be allowed, while the ANC, the Pan Africanist Congress (PAC) and others sought to ensure that formerly whites-only schools did not use language as a means to exclude learners on the basis of race.

The constitution established seven state institutions to support constitutional democracy – the so-called Chapter Nine institutions. These included the South African Human Rights Commission, the Public Protector and the Independent Electoral Commission.

An important difference between the interim constitution and the final one was that the provision for 'power-sharing' – that is, the need for minority parties to be represented in the Cabinet – was dropped.

THE LEGACY

When the new government took office in May 1994, it faced many important challenges, including the building of a democratic and stable state. The legacy of colonialism and apartheid was still entrenched in South African society: appalling levels of poverty alongside great wealth; sharp racial and gender inequalities in every sphere of social and economic life; and deep-rooted ideologies and practices of racism and sexism.

The new government – and especially the majority party, the ANC – had been elected explicitly to overcome this legacy. The resources at its disposal were in short supply and had to be spread over a wide range of priorities. Most leaders of government and its important institutions had very little relevant experience and had to learn on the job. People with technical and professional skills were in short supply, partly because apartheid had restricted education for blacks. The shortages of skilled personnel were much worse in the rural municipalities and most rural provinces than they were in the cities or the predominantly urban provinces such as Gauteng and the Western Cape.

Almost all state institutions were dominated by white men. The most important of these included the administration of the national government and the municipalities, the police, the military, the state-owned enterprises, and most education and health institutions. A similar situation prevailed in the private sector, where all the large commercial and industrial corporations and even most small businesses were mainly owned and managed by whites.

Against this reality stood the elevated hopes and expectations of the black population for an end to poverty, improved living standards, increased public and social services, democratic participation, an end to racism, and the opportunity to participate fully in the economy and in all political, social and cultural institutions. The new government's challenge was to create the conditions to meet these needs.

NEW INSTITUTIONS OF DEMOCRACY

Public servants from the previous era kept their jobs as agreed in the 'sunset clauses' (see Chapter 18). Many did not want to serve under the new government and left during the first few years after the 1994 elections. In order to meet popular expectations and transform South Africa into a successful democracy, serving the needs of the people as a whole, the new ANC-led government had to develop a more efficient administration, led and staffed by people with sympathy for the government's goals and willing to pursue them vigorously. The challenges facing provincial government administrations – some of which had to be established from scratch – were even more difficult than those of the national government.

But there was an inherent contradiction: there were few Africans – or, for that matter, progressive whites – with the skills and experience needed to run large government bureaucracies. The old public service had been mainly geared to servicing the apartheid system. While most of its public servants had managerial and administrative skills, many were not sympathetic to the wishes of the democratic government or to popular expectations.

In general, the government did identify and appoint enough well-educated, senior civil servants, mainly blacks, who were in sympathy with the new dispensation. However, most middle- and lower-level posts continued to be held by whites, and this only changed gradually in the following few years as more blacks were recruited and promoted. A sizeable number of existing white public servants at all levels accepted the priorities of the new era and continued to use their skills and experience in the changed circumstances. In many provincial and especially municipal administrations, skills even at the top levels continued to be in short supply.

A new Constitutional Court was established as the highest court in the land in all matters relating to the constitution. The court's judgments were binding on all individuals and organisations, including the government. In its first judgment on 6 June 1995 the court declared the death penalty to be unconstitutional.

The South African National Defence Force (SANDF) was created by a merger of the old South African Defence Force (SADF), the military forces of the bantustans, Umkhonto we Sizwe (MK) and the Azanian People's Liberation Army (APLA), the PAC's military wing. This was a challenging task given their different backgrounds. Initially there was some conflict and a refusal by the former liberation forces to accept the subordinate role that the old apartheid military expected them to adopt. Some members from both groupings left and moved to civilian life, but by the end of Mandela's term of office a united force had been established although racial tensions persisted.

The new South African Police Service (SAPS) came about as a result of the merger of the South African Police and the ten bantustan police forces. None of them enjoyed popular legitimacy nor had they been trained to function in a democratic environment. Most members were black but the overwhelming number of senior officers were white. Clearly this situation needed to be transformed and the change process was soon started.

PARTY POLITICS

Relations between the parties in the Government of National Unity were tense, especially between the ANC and the NP, with each distrusting the other. During the negotiations in the constitutional assembly, the NP had argued strongly, but unsuccessfully, for 'power-sharing'. Their lack of success led to bitter disappointment within the NP, and De Klerk was accused of betraying Afrikaner interests. In truth, he did what he could, but the idea of obligatory power-sharing between the majority party and much smaller parties was simply not acceptable to the ANC.

The NP decided to withdraw from the Government of National Unity at the end of 1996. In August 1997, De Klerk resigned as leader of the NP and retired from politics. The NP rapidly lost membership and soon disappeared as a political force. Seven years later, what little was left of the party dissolved itself and its leaders joined the ANC – surely the ultimate humiliation. Most of its supporters transferred their allegiance to the Democratic Party (DP), which thereafter changed its name to the Democratic Alliance (DA). It was effectively a white party with considerable support from coloured voters in the Western Cape. The DA combined liberals and former NP supporters, and gradually grew to become the largest opposition party.

The new Constitutional Court in session. Source: Gallo Images / Beeld / Felix Dlangamandla

Social Infrastructure

One priority for the new government was expanding and transforming the social infrastructure. Schooling was made compulsory for all children up to Grade 9. The former whites-only public schools were no longer allowed to exclude black students, and parents who could afford it increasingly sent their children there in search of better-quality education. Schools elected governing bodies made up of parent, teacher and (in secondary schools) learner representatives. They were allowed to charge school fees, and wealthier (mainly white) communities were able to use their private resources to subsidise their schools so as to maintain the quality of education. The government shifted funding towards poorer schools, but it was not enough to upgrade most poor schools adequately.

Racial discrimination with regard to social grants was abolished and the grants, though small, were expanded to include millions more people. For example, a child support grant was introduced in 1998 with the goal of reaching 3 million children within five years. This was the beginning of a welfare system that would grow over the following decades. Old age pensions and disability grants were also expanded. These social grants made a significant impact in reducing extreme poverty.

Between 1994 and 1999 the number of households with piped water increased by 37 per cent. From 1994 to 2001, 3.5 million new households received electricity. In the first eight years of democratic government, 1.4 million housing units were completed.

Despite these achievements, the challenges remained large, partly due to population growth and migration from rural to urban areas, which required more infrastructure. There were early signs of a growing black middle class as more blacks were employed in mid-level and senior positions in the public service and the state-owned enterprises. Reluctantly and slowly, and under pressure from the government, the private corporate sector also began to recruit black people in senior positions. Nonetheless, the level of people's income and wealth in South Africa as a whole was still largely determined by their race.

The government's biggest failure in the first five years of democracy was its scandalous response to the HIV/AIDS pandemic, which was then spreading rapidly and, at that time, resulted in death for nearly all its victims. The South African government failed to put in place a large-scale and effective campaign to fight the disease. The result was the growth of tension between the government and organisations of AIDS sufferers, AIDS organisations and medical researchers. In 2001 the Medical Research Council declared that AIDS was the leading cause of death in South Africa.[19]

TRUTH AND RECONCILIATION COMMISSION

One of the new government's highest priorities was to promote reconciliation among former enemies – that is, between blacks and whites as well as among blacks who had fought on different sides. Mandela believed that this was essential to stabilise the country, to avoid further conflict, and to promote the growth of a single national loyalty among South Africans.

The most important of the reconciliation initiatives was the Truth and Reconciliation Commission (TRC), established in 1995. Its aims were to investigate gross human rights abuses from 1 March 1960 (just prior to the Sharpeville massacre) to 1994. It was also empowered to grant amnesty to those who confessed to such abuses provided that they revealed the whole truth and that their actions had been undertaken for a political purpose. The commission was also required to draft a policy for reparation to victims. Archbishop Desmond Tutu was appointed to chair the commission with Dr Alex Boraine (a former Methodist minister and Progressive Party MP) as his deputy.

The TRC held public hearings at which both victims and perpetrators of human rights abuses appeared. Accounts of murder, abduction and torture by the state and its associates were told by the victims and their families and by perpetrators seeking amnesty. The TRC held 150 hearings over two years and recorded 38 000 gross violations of human rights. The hearings were public and the media covered them comprehensively so that South Africans from all walks of life became aware of the many crimes committed during the apartheid period. The TRC received over 7 000 applications for amnesty and granted 1 500 amnesties for crimes committed.

F.W. de Klerk appeared before the commission and apologised for apartheid, but claimed that he had not authorised or been aware of the atrocities committed by the police; however, this was contradicted by two former Cabinet ministers. The ANC

---

19 During the second post-liberation administration, government responses to HIV/AIDS became even less effective when President Mbeki refused to recognise prevailing scientific views regarding HIV/AIDS and its causes. This meant that freely available treatment was not introduced until 2008.

The Truth and Reconciliation Commission in session. Source: Gallo Images/Oryx Media Archive

admitted that violations of human rights, including killings and torture in MK camps, had been committed by itself and its allies during the course of the struggle. It demanded a blanket amnesty for its members on the grounds that they had been waging a just war and that their actions should not be judged in the same way as those of a repressive and unjust regime. The commission, however, rejected this argument and drew a distinction between the concept of a 'just war' and 'just means'. The ANC relented and 37 ANC politicians applied for and were granted amnesty. Mangosuthu Buthelezi appeared before the commission but accepted no blame, claiming that the ANC was responsible for all the violence. In its report the TRC was critical of the ANC and the United Democratic Front (UDF) but laid most of the blame for human rights violations on the apartheid government and its allies.

The TRC's report was criticised to some extent by all the major political parties because it did not accept all their arguments. Archbishop Tutu himself later pointed to some of the TRC's failings. He wrote:

A key weakness of the Commission was that it did not focus sufficiently on the policies or political economy of apartheid. The failure to examine the effect and impact of apartheid's policies resulted in the need for ... the 'trigger-pullers' to bear the collective shame ... and let those who benefited from apartheid to escape responsibility.

The TRC's legacy was compromised by the fact that there were few prosecutions of those who did not apply for amnesty or who were refused amnesty. The government was also criticised for being slow in its payment of reparations to victims.

Despite these problems, the TRC was largely considered, both in South Africa and abroad, as having been successful because of the wide public participation in its processes. Unlike many cases of similar post-conflict (or post-dictatorship) processes elsewhere, the South African TRC's hearings took place in public and heard detailed evidence from both perpetrators and victims. The evidence from both groups, shown at length on television, had an unsettling impact on the nation's psyche; it forced whites in particular to come face to face with the harsh realities that lay behind the system that they had lived under and benefited from. It also gave thousands of victims the opportunity to speak openly about their experiences and to have them officially recognised.

THE ECONOMY

The new government inherited a severely damaged economy. Economic growth had declined steadily from the mid-1970s. In 1994, the unemployment rate for the entire population was 35 per cent but for Africans it was 43 per cent. The government struggled to overcome these challenges but with limited success. Despite achievements in providing infrastructure and social services, levels of extreme poverty, inequality and unemployment proved to be stubborn and showed little sign of diminishing.

Unemployment increased as a result of a process of deindustrialisation which had started from around 1990 as South Africa became further integrated into a global economy increasingly dominated by neo-liberal policies. The government gave in to pressure to rapidly lower import barriers and remove other forms of protection such as subsidies for certain local industries. The rationale was to make South African industries more efficient by exposing them to international competition. However, the effect was that many local industries were severely harmed by cheap imports, especially from Asia. Particularly affected were various industries in rural locations and small towns; many of them ceased production. Women workers, usually in low-paid work, tended to be the worst affected by industrial closures.

The economy did have a number of strengths and benefited from the lifting of international sanctions. There was a modern economic sector with strong financial institutions, a strong mining sector and manufacturing base, some sound and respected educational institutions, and a number of large, reasonably effective state-owned enterprises. These institutions – both private and public – had been largely geared to serving the white population and the apartheid system. With sufficient investment and skills development, the government believed that they could be expanded to benefit the whole population.

Before the 1990s, the ANC had supported the establishment of a system in which the state would play an interventionist role to bring about a redistribution of the country's wealth. In 1993 it adopted the Reconstruction and Development Programme (RDP), which envisioned development *through* redistribution. The belief was that both these imperatives – development and redistribution – had to be addressed, and that government investment in infrastructure and social benefits would kick-start development and increase employment. However, international financial institutions and foreign governments and corporations, as well as South African big business, were pressing the ANC leadership to take a market-oriented approach. This included eliminating protections for local industry, privatising state-owned enterprises, and allowing local corporations to move their money freely and invest it abroad. Both these opposing views had support within the ANC.

After the 1994 elections, the RDP was adopted by government. However, in 1996 the RDP was replaced by the Growth, Employment and Redistribution (GEAR) programme. Unlike the RDP, GEAR advocated a reduced role for government and placed more emphasis on the free market as an engine of economic growth, claiming that this would also lead to redistribution and increased employment. The introduction of GEAR led to sharp differences within the ANC. The more left-wing sections, including those associated with the South African Communist Party (SACP) and the Congress of South African Trade Unions (COSATU), strongly opposed the new direction. This rift in the ANC's ranks would endure for over two decades, taking different forms at different times.

CONCLUSION

By the end of the twentieth century, South Africa had entered a new era. It had made a successful transition to a democracy. It had a new constitution, newly elected legislatures, a renewed judicial system, and a government administration preparing itself to meet a new set of challenges. Public debate on government policies flourished as never before. Official racism had been abolished, but racist attitudes remained and continued to affect people's lives. The country was once more a respected member of the international community. It joined the Organisation of African Unity and the Southern African Development Community, from which it had been excluded.

Serious challenges remained, and attempts to rectify or reduce structural injustices and inequalities remained works in progress. Many of these issues have been mentioned in this chapter; they would define the agenda for the government and the country in the years that followed.

CHAPTER 19: DISCUSSION QUESTIONS

1. Do you think that the agreement to implement a Government of National Unity after the 1994 election was a wise one? Did it help to calm tensions or reduce the level of conflict after the election?

2. What do you think were the five most important tasks facing South Africa's democratic government during its first term (1994–9)?

3. What do you think were the major strengths and weaknesses of the Truth and Reconciliation Commission (TRC)?

Chapter 19: Additional Readings

Online Readings

African National Congress (1994) *The Reconstruction and Development Programme.* https://www.sahistory.org.za/sites/default/files/the_reconstruction_and_development_programm_1994.pdf.

Cornish-Jenkins, H. (n.d.) *Despite the 1994 Political Victory against Apartheid, Its Economic Legacy Persists.* https://www.sahistory.org.za/article/despite-1994-political-victory-against-apartheid-its-economic-legacy-persists-haydn-cornish.

Department of Finance (1994) *Growth, Employment and Redistribution: A Macroeconomic Strategy.* Pretoria: Department of Finance. http://www.treasury.gov.za/publications/other/gear/default.aspx.

A History of Official Government HIV/AIDS Policy in South Africa. *South African History Online.* https://www.sahistory.org.za/topic/history-official-government-hivaids-policy-south-africa.

Negotiation, Transition and Freedom (2004) Turning Points in History Series, Book 6. Johannesburg: STE Publishers. (Chapters 3 and 4) http://sahistory.org.za/archive/book-6-negotiation-transition-and-freedom-commissioned-department-education.

Republic of South Africa (1996) *The Constitution of the Republic of South Africa.* http://www.justice.gov.za/legislation/constitution/SAConstitution-web-eng.pdf.

Truth and Reconciliation Commission (TRC) (1998) *Report of the Truth and Reconciliation Commission.* https://www.justice.gov.za/trc/report/index.htm.

Books

De Klerk, F.W. (1998) *The Last Trek – A New Beginning: The Autobiography.* Johannesburg: Macmillan. (Chapters 14–31)

Giliomee, H. and B. Mbenga (eds) (2007) *New History of South Africa.* Cape Town: Tafelberg. (Chapter 15)

Morris, M. (2004). *Every Step of the Way: The Journey to Freedom in South Africa.* Cape Town: HSRC Press. (Chapter 12)

Muthien, Y., M. Khosa and B. Magubane (eds) *Democracy and Governance Review: Mandela's Legacy 1994–1999.* Pretoria: HSRC Press.

Thompson, L. (2014) *A History of South Africa.* Johannesburg: Jonathan Ball. (Chapter 9). https://www.sahistory.org.za/sites/default/files/file%20uploads%20/leonard_monteath_thompson_a_history_of_south_afrbook4me.org_.pdf.

Part B
Themes in South African History

Theme One

The South African Economy

Various economic sectors played important roles in South Africa at different times. Furthermore, economic changes played a major part in bringing about changes in South Africa's politics and society. Therefore, any full understanding of South African history should include an understanding of the economy.

For hundreds of years South Africa's main economic activity was subsistence agriculture. Then, diamonds were discovered in the late 1860s and gold in the mid-1880s. These discoveries introduced a period of rapid change, which became known as the mineral revolution. Mining and commercial farming became the two dominant economic sectors in South Africa. In the mid-1900s, manufacturing became prominent, and competed with the mines and farms for labour. By the 1970s, South Africa experienced another economic shift with the rise of the financial and services sectors.

Although South Africa's economy changed and developed throughout the twentieth century, gold mining played a defining role throughout this period. South Africa was the world's main source of gold for many years. State taxes on gold mines provided the government with money to support and develop other sectors like agriculture and industry. South Africa produced other minerals such as platinum, coal and iron ore, which also made important economic contributions, especially from the mid-twentieth century. Gold, however, was a unique export item. Unlike other products, there was unlimited demand for it because the world's money supply was based on gold until the 1970s.

In this chapter we will trace the development of South Africa's economy from the mineral revolution until the early 1990s. The mineral revolution transformed South Africa's economy, society and politics. Some of its legacies are still felt today.

Gold miners: Mining was the bedrock of the South African economy throughout the twentieth century.

THE MINERAL REVOLUTION: THE RISE OF GOLD MINING

Before the mineral revolution, the economy of southern Africa was based on agriculture. There were a few commercial centres with some basic financial services but no factories. Most African and Boer societies consisted mainly of self-sufficient subsistence farmers. Commercial farming had developed in some areas such as the Cape and Natal, but agricultural exports were insignificant.

The mineral revolution integrated South Africa into the global economy. Foreign money flowed into South Africa through investments and mineral exports. Immigrants from Europe were attracted to the country by new work opportunities. Mining stimulated other sectors as well. New towns and transport systems, especially railways, developed. Increased urbanisation stimulated businesses and some basic manufacturing. Commercial farming increased to meet the demands of the urban and mine populations. More labour was needed on the farms, and farmers began to compete with the mines for workers.

Economic changes brought social and political changes to South Africa. Farmers and mine owners desperately needed labour, but they were determined to keep black wages low. By restricting access to land and imposing taxes, white authorities forced black workers to work in the mines and on the farms for low wages.[20]

Gold mining in South Africa was difficult and expensive. The ore – that is, the gold-

---

20 Racial discrimination played a central role in South Africa's economic history. Some of these racist practices will be mentioned, but for a deeper understanding of racist legislation and practices such as the migrant labour system, the 1913 Natives Land Act, the colour bar and the 'civilised labour' policy, refer to Chapters 4, 7 and 9.

bearing rock – was located very deep underground, and expensive machinery was needed to mine it. There was a lot of gold ore, but it was of low grade and contained a lot of impurities. Individuals could not undertake the mining, since expensive machines and large numbers of workers were needed to extract the gold. Mining companies with foreign shareholders were set up to raise the money to cover these costs. These companies recruited labour from across southern Africa including Zimbabwe, Mozambique and Malawi.

Mining companies maintained attractive profits by keeping black wages very low. A racist system of low-wage migrant labour developed that remained virtually unchanged until the 1970s.[21] By the early 1900s, white workers had established trade unions and negotiated a relatively privileged position for themselves on the mines. Most semi-skilled and skilled positions were reserved for whites, who also received significantly higher wages than black workers.

Gold mining increased British interest in the Boer republic of the Transvaal, which led to the Anglo–Boer War (1899–1902). In 1910 the Union of South Africa was established and the South African Party (SAP) came to power. Union brought some economic coherence to South Africa with a uniform system of laws, taxes and import duties. It also meant that the economic benefits of gold mining could be used to advantage the white population in all four provinces, rather than just the Transvaal.

UNION AND THE SAP: GOVERNMENT PRIORITISES COMMERCIAL FARMING AND MINING

Commercial farming had increased throughout the period of the mineral revolution, but not all white farmers prospered. By the early 1900s there was a growing number of impoverished white farmers, including sharecroppers known as *bywoners*. Most impoverished whites were Afrikaners. Many abandoned farming and migrated to the new towns in search of work. Other poor white farmers relied on African sharecroppers and tenants for their income. The 1913 Natives Land Act banned Africans from being sharecroppers, and as a result many poor white farmers lost this income and also abandoned farming.

The Land Act played an important role in destroying African commercial agriculture and increasing the reliance of Africans on wage labour. It was a deliberate attempt by the SAP government to make more workers available to white employers, including successful commercial farmers. The SAP also supported white farmers through financial measures. Agriculture was still the largest economic sector, although it was not as profitable as mining. The National Land and Agricultural Bank was established in 1912 to support white farmers who struggled to get credit from other banks. Commercial agriculture grew slowly during this period, partly because farmers continued to use outdated farming methods. In 1918, for example, there were only 231 tractors in South Africa.

The SAP was sympathetic to mining interests. White farmers might have wanted

---

21 For more on the migrant labour system, see Chapter 4.

Africans' land, but the mines insisted that African reserves be protected, as these areas supported the migrant labour system. This allowed the mine owners to pay lower wages to African miners because their incomes were subsidised by their families who were farming in the rural reserves. Yet, gold mining continued to be expensive and production costs increased throughout the 1910s. By the early 1920s, half the mining companies in Johannesburg were operating at a loss. To increase profits, the mines wanted to cut white wages and employ more lower-paid black (African and coloured) workers in semi-skilled positions. White workers refused and went on strike.

The resulting conflict led to the Rand Revolt of 1922. White miners in Johannesburg went on strike, but Prime Minister Jan Smuts called in the military to crush the revolt. The failed rebellion was a victory for the mine owners, who cut white workers' wages by 25 per cent. More black workers were employed at the expense of white workers, and they also filled certain semi-skilled positions such as drill sharpening.

Smuts's handling of the Rand Revolt helped to make gold mining profitable again, but it caused the SAP to lose the 1924 elections. The National Party (NP), under J.B.M. Hertzog, formed a coalition with the Labour Party and created the Pact government. The SAP had catered to the interests of the mine owners. The Pact government's priorities were very different.

Pact and Fusion: The Rise of Manufacturing

The Pact government came to power on the promise that it would improve the economic conditions of white workers, farmers and Afrikaner small-business people. The NP won the 1929 elections, but it lost significant support during the Great Depression, which began in 1929. In 1933 the NP and SAP 'fused' to form the United Party (UP). The UP government, also known as the Fusion government, ruled South Africa from 1933 until 1948. Many of the economic policies introduced under the Pact government continued under the Fusion government.

Throughout the years of the Pact and Fusion governments, gold sustained the economy, especially during the Great Depression. South Africa went off the gold standard in 1933, as a result of which the South African pound (the currency at the time) was devalued. This made South African products cheaper on the international market, and exports expanded accordingly. This had a particularly positive influence on the gold-mining sector. The United States significantly increased the fixed dollar price of gold in 1934, and gold prices soared because of the devalued currency.[22] The Pact government taxed the mines more heavily than the SAP had. Revenue from the mines funded the development of white agriculture and manufacturing.

The Pact government introduced a number of supportive measures for white farmers such as farm subsidies, cheaper railway rates for agricultural products, capital works, loans and drought grants. More farmers mechanised, and by 1946 there were over 20 000 tractors in South Africa. This support for white farmers did not immediately increase

---

22 See Chapter 10 for more detail about the economy during and after the Great Depression.

their agricultural output significantly. However, it did lay the foundations for the improvement of commercial farming in the 1950s under the post-1948 National Party.

The Pact government focused on improving the situation of the poor whites, who were mainly Afrikaans-speaking. Although the colour bar protected white workers from black competition, such protection was not thought to be enough. The Pact government was determined to create more employment for white workers in the state sector, particularly in the Iron and Steel Corporation (ISCOR), founded in 1928, and on the railways and in the harbours. Apart from state-driven employment, the government also aimed to increase white employment by expanding private manufacturing.

The SAP had not focused on developing secondary industry, but a successful manufacturing sector was vital for the Pact government. Since agriculture was still weak, Hertzog's government believed a strong manufacturing sector could boost the economy. Mining was obviously important but it was still unclear for how long it would be sustainable. In addition, the government was keen to diversify the economy so that it would be less dependent on mining. The fact that the mining industry was controlled to a large extent by British capital also strengthened Hertzog's determination to lessen the country's dependence on this sector.

The development of secondary industry also provided an opportunity to create jobs for poor whites. The government ensured that 40 per cent of the manufacturing labour force was reserved for whites (as opposed to 10 per cent in mining). By 1949 whites made up only 34 per cent of the industrial labour force, but this was because there were more jobs available than white people to fill them.

The Pact and Fusion governments stimulated local industry through an import-substitution policy that aimed to replace imports with local goods by imposing tariffs on foreign products. In addition, the South African pound was devalued, thus making South African goods cheaper overseas and so stimulating exports. Under these protected conditions, manufacturing expanded rapidly. Between 1933 and 1939, industrial employment grew by 60 per cent. It rose by another 50 per cent during World War II. South Africa expanded its military production to help equip the Allied forces in Europe, Asia and North Africa. Consumer goods industries also grew, and their products were exported to fill the gap caused by industrial disruption in the war zones abroad. By 1950 there were almost as many people employed in manufacturing as in mining. This economic shift was accompanied by social changes, such as rapid urbanisation.

The deterioration of the reserves caused greater numbers of African people to migrate to the urban areas in search of jobs. Industry was more attractive to them than mining and agriculture since it paid higher wages. Segregationist legislation had increased in the 1930s, but the laws were relaxed during World War II. As whites joined the military, more blacks could take up semi-skilled and skilled positions previously denied to them under the colour bar. Employers also preferred black employees since they could pay them less. Urbanisation increased dramatically as the black population responded to the new opportunities. In 1921 about 14 per cent of the African population lived in cities and towns. This increased to about 19 per cent in 1936, and then to 24 per cent in 1946.

After World War II, Smuts accepted that an urbanised African population was economically necessary for the growing industrial sector. The National Party, under D.F. Malan, disagreed. They wanted to reverse African urbanisation. Furthermore, the NP wanted to provide stronger support for white workers and small businesses, assist the growth of large Afrikaner-owned businesses, increase the number of Afrikaners in senior positions in the state, and, above all, entrench white domination. The NP gained increasing support for its views. In 1948 the United Party lost the election, and the National Party came to power. It would rule South Africa until 1994.

EARLY APARTHEID: THE GROWTH OF AFRIKANER CAPITAL

Many countries experienced a 'golden age' or economic boom after World War II, which lasted until the early 1970s. South Africa was no exception. The country's economy was also buoyed by the growth of the mining sector during this period, after new gold seams were discovered in the Orange Free State and Transvaal.

The National Party, led by D.F. Malan[23] and espousing the policy of 'apartheid', defeated Smuts's United Party in the 1948 elections. The NP was determined to tighten segregationist measures that had been relaxed during the war. Under NP rule the movement and labour of Africans became highly regulated. NP leaders like J.G. Strijdom believed that if the system of unskilled migrant labour worked for mining, it would work also for manufacturing. The colour bar, restrictions on black trade unions, the extension of passes to women, forced removals to the bantustans and Bantu Education – all policies enforced or extended by the NP government – contributed to creating a rural, unskilled labour force. Urbanisation slowed and more black people were forced to look for work as labourers on white farms. Just as this was happening, though, white farmers' labour needs were decreasing owing to mechanisation.

Under Pact and Fusion rule, agricultural output had increased at an average rate of about 2.1 per cent per year. Under the NP, white commercial agriculture thrived, with agricultural production increasing at an average of 3.9 per cent a year between 1948 and 1980. With state aid, more farmers mechanised. The number of tractors on farms increased from 20 000 in 1946 to 120 000 in 1960. Maize yields improved dramatically. However, white farmers continued to rely heavily on state aid and protection.

South Africa's expanding manufacturing industry attracted substantial foreign investment in the late 1950s, and this contributed to its boom in the 1960s. State industry also expanded with the establishment of SASOL in 1950 and ARMSCOR in 1968. On average, manufacturing's real output increased at a rate of 7.3 per cent a year between 1948 and 1974. Employment in private manufacturing grew from 439 000 workers in 1949 to 1 166 000 in 1972.

Some argue that apartheid and its exploitative policies assisted the growth of the South African economy during these years. Yet, it is important to note that the country's

---

23 Malan's National Party had been formed in 1934 by a group of ultra-right-wing Afrikaners who opposed the fusion of the NP and SAP. They called themselves the Purified National Party, but soon became known simply as the National Party. These processes are described in Chapter 10.

growth rate was actually lower than that of many similar economies which grew in the post-war boom. White-owned businesses benefited enormously from apartheid's exploitative policies, but it is questionable whether apartheid boosted and strengthened the economy as a whole. However, what is certain is that apartheid promoted the growth of white capital at the expense of the black population. In the reserves (later known as bantustans), the migrant labour system took (mainly) men away from home for most of the year, disrupting family life and stability. Poverty was rife in these rural areas, and farming became increasingly difficult there as the population grew and land became increasingly scarce.

Afrikaners had long dominated commercial farming, but between 1949 and the mid-1970s Afrikaners managed to increase their share of ownership in other sectors. Afrikaners' stakes in mining rose from 1 per cent to 30 per cent, in manufacturing and construction from 6 per cent to 25 per cent, and in finance from 6 per cent to 15 per cent. Government policies played a significant role in this shift. The NP government made use of Afrikaner financial institutions such as Volkskas Bank, and it did more business with Afrikaans companies. The state bureaucracy grew and was filled with Afrikaners. A focus on providing universal white education of quality created a new generation of skilled whites. The white middle class expanded.

By the early 1970s, South Africa had experienced a century of economic growth. This growth hid some of the structural weaknesses in the economy that became apparent in the late 1980s.

Late Apartheid: Economic Decline

The world experienced a general economic downturn in the 1970s. South Africa's economy began to fall on hard times in the 1980s. Between 1973 and 1994 South Africa's gross domestic product (GDP) per capita declined at an average rate of 0.6 per cent a year. Gold had sustained the economy in previous times of economic trouble, but it became more difficult and expensive to mine the ore as the seams were becoming exhausted.

In the 1970s, gold lost its unique place in the world financial system. The United States abolished the fixed price of gold, allowing market forces to determine the price. Furthermore, countries no longer relied primarily on gold to back their currencies. Initially this worked in South Africa's favour. Gold prices soared in the 1970s from a fixed price of $35 per ounce to peak at $850 in 1980. This helped cover the increased production costs. However, the gold price plummeted in 1982 to $380 per ounce.

The higher prices had made it possible to mine lower-grade ore at a profit. But as gold became more difficult to mine, less gold was produced and exported. Gold's contribution to total exports fell from 45 per cent in the early 1980s to less than 24 per cent in the mid-1990s. The gold mines had employed over 500 000 workers in 1986. By the end of the 1990s there were less than 200 000 people employed on the gold mines. Gold's decline became obvious in the late 1980s, and it reduced confidence in South Africa's economy.

The state had hoped that manufacturing would take the place of gold in the economy. Unfortunately, manufacturing's output and productivity had slowed by

Ford workers at a factory in Port Elizabeth (Gqeberha), 1970s

the 1980s because South Africa's industry was not as efficient as that of other global manufacturers. The NP had actively limited the growth of a skilled black labour force, but modern industrial economies need skilled workers to improve output and efficiency. In 1960, most urban African workers filled unskilled positions. By 1980, unskilled workers made up less than half of the African workforce in Johannesburg. The NP could not ignore these economic realities.

By the 1970s the NP was forced to recognise that strict segregationist policies held back economic growth. It tried to deal with this by introducing limited reforms. The colour bar was relaxed. The state increased its spending on black education. Pass laws were gradually relaxed throughout the 1970s and were abolished in 1986. The state also loosened its tight grip on organised labour. By 1979 the increasingly militant black trade unions were recognised officially and were allowed to take part in collective bargaining. The wages of black workers had also increased across all sectors since the mid-1970s. In mining, the migrant labour system began to be dismantled in the 1970s.

However, these limited reforms could not save the economy. South Africa had seemed a stable investment environment in the 1960s. But the surge in strikes and political resistance during the 1970s and 1980s, together with international trade and financial sanctions by the mid-1980s, led to a weakening economic performance. Sanctions came at a time when South Africa desperately needed access to loans and direct investments. In 1985, because of a complete lack of confidence in South Africa's economic situation, foreign lenders recalled their loans and the state was plunged into a debt crisis. Government finances were further damaged by the accumulating strain of having to support ever-increasing police and military spending as resistance to apartheid grew.

It became obvious to some senior figures in the NP and in private business that apartheid was preventing economic growth. Their voices joined the domestic and international forces calling for an end to apartheid and they played a role in persuading the NP to agree to negotiations with the liberation movement. When the ANC took power in 1994, it inherited a structurally weak economy with the majority of the population living in poverty. In 1996, South Africa's expanded unemployment rate[24] was about 40 per cent. While the years immediately after apartheid ended did see some economic growth, the economy remained fragile and vulnerable. However, South Africa has enormous potential for economic growth. It is one of the most developed African economies, and is the most industrialised country on the continent. The mining of a variety of minerals continues to be important, with 70 per cent of the world's platinum coming from South Africa. South African universities are globally competitive and include the leading institutions in Africa.

South Africa today faces severe economic challenges, while holding great potential for economic growth. People hold different views on how to harness this economic potential. Throughout the 1990s and the early 2000s the ANC's economic policies generated much debate. The direction, nature and control of South Africa's economy continue to be a central theme in South Africa's political debates in the 2020s.

THEME 1: DISCUSSION QUESTIONS

1. What was your understanding of South Africa's economic history before you read this chapter? Did it change or confirm any of your thoughts about the economy? What was the most interesting information you learned?

2. What role did gold mining play in South Africa's history? List and explain the different ways gold mining shaped, maintained and developed South Africa's economy and society. Begin with the mineral revolution and end in the 1990s.

3. Segregationist policies like the colour bar, pass laws, forced removals and Bantu Education all worked together to oppress black people and maintain white supremacy. How did each of these policies prevent the majority of black people from improving their economic situation? How did these policies affect the South African economy in the long term? In your discussion, make sure you refer to the economy during late apartheid.

---

24 Official unemployment statistics usually omit discouraged workers who are not actively looking for work. The expanded rate includes those workers, and it is thus a better indication of how many people are actually unemployed.

4. What role did white Afrikaner nationalism play in South Africa's economic policies?

5. White commercial farming in South Africa in the twentieth century relied heavily on state protection and support. How should we respond to this information in the context of land redistribution discussions in the late 2010s and early 2020s?

6. What are the greatest challenges facing South Africa's current economy? Make a list and discuss which challenges are the result of pre-1994 policies. Consider realistic ways in which the state can address these challenges. Are any of the challenges the result of post-1994 policies? If so, also consider realistic ways in which to address these new challenges.

THEME 1: ADDITIONAL READINGS

Online readings

Freund, Bill (2011) South Africa: The Union Years, 1910–1948; Political and Economic Foundations. In *The Cambridge History of South Africa*, Volume 2, *1885–1994*. Cambridge: Cambridge University Press. (Chapter 5, pp. 211–53). http://www.sahistory.org.za/sites/default/files/file%20uploads%20/robert_ross_anne_kelk_mager_bill_nasson_the_cabook4me.org_.pdf.

Industrialisation, Rural Change and Nationalism (2004) Turning Points in History Series, Volume 4. Johannesburg: STE Publishers. http://www.sahistory.org.za/archive/turning-points-books-1-6.

Keegan, Timothy (2004) Imperialism and the Union in South Africa. In *Migration, Land and Minerals in the Making of South Africa*. Turning Points in History Series, Volume 3. Johannesburg: STE Publishers. http://www.sahistory.org.za/archive/turning-points-books-1-6.

Nattrass, Nicoli and Jeremy Seekings (2011) The Economy and Poverty in the Twentieth Century. In *The Cambridge History of South Africa*, Volume 2, *1885–1994*. (Chapter 11, pp. 518–72) http://www.sahistory.org.za/sites/default/files/file%20uploads%20/robert_ross_anne_kelk_mager_bill_nasson_the_cabook4me.org_.pdf.

Seekings, Jeremy and Nicoli Nattrass (2005) *Class, Race and Inequality in South Africa*. New Haven, CT: Yale University Press. http://www.sahistory.org.za/sites/default/files/file%20uploads%20/professor_jeremy_seekings_nicoli_nattrass_classbookos.org_.pdf.

Yekela, Drusela Numvuso (2004) The Socio-economic Impact of the Mineral Revolution on South African Society. In *Migration, Land and Minerals in the Making of South Africa*. Turning Points in History Series, Volume 3.

Johannesburg: STE Publishers. http://www.sahistory.org.za/archive/turning-points-books-1-6.

Online visual sources

A graph showing South Africa's credit rating history since 1994: 'One Graph Showing South Africa's Credit Rating History: 1994–2017', *Business Tech*, 29 November 2017. https://businesstech.co.za/news/finance/213641/one-graph-showing-south-africas-credit-rating-history-1994-2017/.

A graph showing the South African government's spending on agriculture from 1910 to 2010: 'South Africa's Government Spending on Agriculture between 1910 and 2010', *Agricultural Economics Today*, 10 March 2018. https://wandilesihlobo.com/2018/03/10/south-africas-government-spending-on-agriculture-between-1910-and-2010/.

A PowerPoint presentation showing various graphs concerning South Africa's economy: 'South Africa's Next Ten Years: The Time-Traveller Scenarios', Centre for Risk Analysis, published 29 July 2014 on *SlideShare.* https://www.slideshare.net/SABPP/dr-frans-cronje-of-the-south-african-institute-of-race-relations-south-africas-next-ten-years-sabpp.

Books

Feinstein, Charles (2005) *An Economic History of South Africa: Conquest, Discrimination and Development.* Cambridge: Cambridge University Press.

Theme Two
South Africa's Bantustans

GENERAL OVERVIEW

Bantustans were areas of land in South Africa, mostly rural, that the apartheid government set aside for Africans. The National Party (NP) argued that Africans could gain some form of self-determination in these areas which was denied to them in the rest of South Africa. Before 1949, dozens of rural reserves were scattered across South Africa. The NP then grouped together areas where most people spoke the same language into one bantustan or 'homeland'.[25] Ten bantustans were established. They were Bophuthatswana, Ciskei, Gazankulu, KaNgwane, KwaNdebele, KwaZulu, Lebowa, QwaQwa, Transkei and Venda.

The initial legislation was intended to establish the bantustans as self-governing areas, where more administrative powers were granted to selected African traditional leaders. However, in response to increasing domestic and international pressure, the government passed legislation in the early 1970s to enable them to attain what it referred to as 'independence'. This was more an attempt to create a greater legitimacy for the bantustans than to grant them any real independent existence. Some bantustan leaders, for example in KwaZulu, refused to take independence, but four bantustans were declared independent states between 1976 and 1981: Transkei, Ciskei, Bophuthatswana and Venda. Their independence, however, was not recognised by any other country because it was always clear that they were entirely under the control of the South African government.

The bantustans helped the apartheid government to extend its control over the movement and labour of the African population. By assigning all Africans to a particular

---

25 The apartheid government coined the term 'bantustan'. However, because its opponents criticised the entire concept so harshly, the word came to be used as almost a swear word. The government then started to use the word 'homeland' in an attempt to create legitimacy for the system by implying that these areas were the natural and authentic homes of the African population. The word 'bantustan', however, continued to be used by apartheid's opponents.

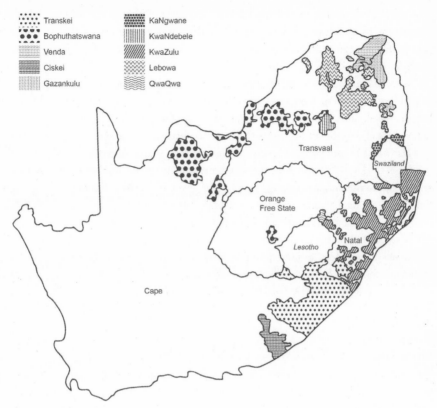

Map of the bantustans

bantustan, the government effectively stripped them of their South African citizenship. It used this to justify forcibly removing 'surplus' Africans whose labour was not required by employers in what was called 'white South Africa'. At the same time the ethnically based bantustans sought to divide Africans on the basis of ethnicity and thus weaken the growth of a national consciousness and undermine any national liberation movement.

By portraying the bantustans as independent states, the government hoped to convince the world that the African population in South Africa was gaining self-determination in the same way that other former European colonies were gaining their independence at the time. No other country recognised the independence of any bantustan. After the 1994 elections, the bantustan governments were dissolved and their areas and administrations integrated into South Africa's new provinces.

Reserves: The Basis of the Bantustans

The bantustans developed out of the reserves, which were set up in the late 1800s and early 1900s. The 1913 Natives Land Act finalised the reserve boundaries, setting aside about 7.5 per cent of South Africa's land for Africans, who made up 67 per cent of the population. The government did recognise that this was insufficient and appointed the

Beaumont Commission to identify further land for addition to the reserves. However, opposition from white farmers prevented the implementation of the commission's proposals until the 1936 Native Trust and Land Act – and even then the additions fell short of the area identified by the commission.

Reserve land was often inferior to white-controlled land in terms of access to water, availability of grazing land and suitability for agriculture. The reserves soon became overcrowded. This strained the natural resources further, causing the environment to deteriorate. The poor conditions in the reserves entrenched the system of migrant labour and also caused more people to move to the towns in search of work.

From the late 1930s the white government implemented rural betterment schemes in an attempt to rehabilitate the reserve land. 'Betterment' included forced cattle culling and fencing off fields. Later it involved resettling scattered homesteads into denser villages. The scheme was bitterly resented by the populations of the reserves.

Reserves fell under the authority of the Department of Native Affairs, but various scheduled areas were administered in different ways under the successive Union governments. The NP established one system of rule for all the reserves by means of the Bantu Authorities Act of 1951, and thus laid the foundation for the bantustan administrations.

ESTABLISHING THE BANTUSTANS: 1950S AND 1960S

The NP claimed that different races needed separate political systems. The Bantu Authorities Act laid out the political structures that would operate in the reserves. These would be the only recognised political structures for Africans in the country.

'Bantu Authorities' was a broad name for the various councils that would run the reserves: Tribal Authorities, Regional Authorities and Territorial Authorities. Tribal Authorities formed the foundation for the entire structure and were responsible for running local affairs. Each consisted of a council made up of a government-appointed chief and his advisors. A Regional Authority was a council made up of members from two or more Tribal Authorities. Two or more Regional Authorities combined to make up a Territorial Authority. It was the areas administered by Territorial Authorities that came to be known as bantustans or homelands. A white government official supervised all the Bantu Authorities; he could veto decisions and remove or appoint chiefs and councillors. Territorial Authorities often ruled over scattered pieces of land; Bophuthatswana and KwaZulu were the most fragmented.

The Promotion of Bantu Self-Government Act of 1959 insisted that Africans were not a homogeneous group but were divided into different 'national units'. Regional and Territorial Authorities were therefore usually created along ethnic lines. The Act stated that the Department of Bantu Affairs would gradually release more administrative responsibilities to the Territorial Authorities, thereby guiding the national units towards greater self-governance.

It took the government nearly twenty years to establish Bantu Authorities across all the reserves. Most Territorial Authorities were established by the late 1960s. The project was strengthened by the Bantu Homeland Citizenship Act of 1970. In terms of the Act, all Africans were assigned to a bantustan, whether or not they identified with the area, language or culture. They were still under South African law, but when their bantustan became 'independent' they were immediately considered by the government as foreigners, thus depriving them of their South African citizenship.

The Bantu Authorities Act abolished the Native Representative Council, and the Promotion of Bantu Self-Government Act removed the African population's elected white representatives in Parliament and the Cape Provincial Council.[26] This meant that Africans were completely excluded from national politics, and that the public African voice became ethnically divided. Only the Bantu Authorities could approach the government to present African grievances. Furthermore, the Bantu Authorities Act extended the power of the chiefs, who became accountable to the government rather than to their people. The Bantu Authorities were also soon associated with betterment schemes, since they had to implement them.

The Defiance Campaign of 1952 protested against the Bantu Authorities Act as well as other racially based legislation. Resistance to the Bantu Authorities and betterment schemes was widespread in the rural areas. Significant protests took place in Witzieshoek, Zeerust and Sekhukhuneland in the 1950s and in Pondoland in 1960. While the protests slowed the implementation of the Bantu Authorities, they were unable to prevent it.

CONSOLIDATING THE BANTUSTANS: 1970S TO EARLY 1980S

By the 1970s Pretoria was determined to grant the bantustans self-government, followed by nominal independence. Transkei had already gained self-government in 1963. Ciskei, Lebowa, Venda, Gazankulu, Bophuthatswana and QwaQwa gained self-government between 1972 and 1975. KwaZulu eventually accepted self-government in 1977, and KaNgwane and KwaNdebele in 1981.

Self-governing bantustans were led by chief ministers. Chief ministers could only appoint cabinet ministers for some departments such as Education, Agriculture, Public Works and Finance. Pretoria still maintained control over National Security, Postal and Telegraph Services and Foreign Affairs. The Tribal and Regional Authorities remained in place in the self-governing territories, but a legislative assembly replaced the Territorial Authority. All laws passed by self-governing bantustan parliaments had to be approved by Pretoria.

The apartheid state was determined to maintain the authority of the chiefs and to limit the power of elected representatives in bantustan governments. In Transkei, the legislative assembly was made up of 64 chiefs (representing the 64 different Tribal

---

26 Before 1951 some African men in the Cape Province could elect three white Members of Parliament and two white Members of the Provincial Council. From 1936 African men could also elect six Africans to the 12-member Native Representative Council (NRC). The other six were white government officials. The NRC was, in fact, a toothless body; it was dismissed by one of its members, Paul Mosaka, as a 'toy telephone' because no one was listening to what was being said.

Authorities) and 45 elected representatives. In 1975, Lebowa tried to separate the chiefs from a fully elected parliament by setting up a separate House of Chiefs. Pretoria refused. This meant that many leaders occupied positions not because of merit or competence, and this often led to mismanagement and corruption. Bantustan residents could do very little in these cases since their leaders were not elected.

The limited form of democracy meant that many bantustans developed into one-party states that were supported by the apartheid security forces. Opponents were intimidated, arrested and detained. Corruption was widespread, as the apartheid state and many bantustan government officials channelled resources to their supporters and sometimes actively withheld resources from opponents. In the Ciskei, for instance, people have recounted how they needed a membership card for the Ciskei National Independence Party (CNIP) to gain access to services like housing or pensions.

Transkei was granted 'independence' in 1976, Bophuthatswana in 1977, Venda in 1979 and Ciskei in 1981. So-called independent bantustans technically gained full control over all government departments. With their own military, government, president and courts, these bantustans might have appeared independent, but their relationship with the apartheid state made it impossible for them to exercise any real independence.

RELATIONS BETWEEN THE APARTHEID STATE AND BANTUSTANS

The bantustans faced numerous economic challenges that made it difficult for them to act as independent countries. They inherited the underdeveloped state of the reserves – poor agricultural conditions, little infrastructure, very few shops and businesses, and no industrial centres. Most families relied on migrant or commuter labour. Bophuthatswana had platinum mines, but during the 1970s it could not tax the mining companies. Most bantustans were made up of scattered pieces of land, and some were so small that they could never be economically viable. With only restricted education available for Africans, the bantustans also faced skills shortages.

The apartheid government promoted economic dependence by actively preventing independent economic growth. In the 1950s and 1960s the state did not want any industrial development in the bantustans, but this policy changed in the 1970s. However, when industries were established, they were allowed to pay workers very low wages, which made them attractive to businesses, some of which set up factories in or near the bantustans. In 1982 the KwaZulu Bata Shoe Company paid workers between R14 and R28 a week. The starting wage in the rest of South Africa for the footwear industry was R46.55 per week.

Pretoria also blocked the bantustans from taking their own political and economic initiatives. All foreign aid had to be approved by Pretoria. It once refused to issue a visa for a British aid worker who was to direct a development project in KwaZulu. Furthermore, bantustans that were situated on the coast, such as the Ciskei, Transkei and KwaZulu, had no established ports.

Bantustan governments prioritised the development of education, public works and agriculture. Over 50 per cent of their budgets were spent on these areas. However, with an underdeveloped economy, and with the majority of citizens living in poverty, they could not raise enough money through taxes to develop the bantustans adequately. They relied heavily on grants from the apartheid state, but these often fell short of what was needed, and the bantustans were thus kept in a state of dependence.

Some bantustan leaders initially attempted to speak out against the NP, but their defiance rarely translated into any concrete actions. Economic dependence meant that the bantustans could never take any truly independent political stances because Pretoria could simply refuse to provide funds, including leaders' salaries.

The bantustans and the apartheid government had a relationship of mutual dependence. The bantustans needed the central government's funding and their populations relied on work outside the bantustans. Pretoria needed the bantustans for social control and political justification for its racist policies. However, it was never an equal relationship, and power clearly resided in the central government.

CONDITIONS IN THE BANTUSTANS

The harsh conditions faced by black workers on many white-owned farms caused some Africans to move voluntarily to the bantustans. Others were attracted by the prospect of secure housing or plots of lands and greater access to high schools. However, that some people moved voluntarily to the bantustans should be seen as an indication of the difficult conditions Africans experienced in the rest of rural South Africa, rather than a sign of attractive conditions in the 'homelands'.

The bantustans also became hopelessly overcrowded as the NP forcibly removed many African people to them. QwaQwa's population increased from 24 000 in 1970 to 100 000 in 1975, and then to 200 000 in 1980. Of the 3.5 million people who were forcibly removed between 1960 and 1983 throughout South Africa, about 2.5 million were relocated to the bantustans. People were often dumped in camps where there were atrocious living conditions. At one stage, 25 per cent of babies died before their first birthday as a result of malnutrition and disease in these camps.

Public services in the bantustans were far inferior to those in other parts of South Africa. For example, while there were 10 hospital beds for every 1 000 whites in 1973, and 5.6 beds per 1 000 for African urban populations, there were only 3.5 beds per 1 000 people in the bantustans.

The bantustans enjoyed very little political support from the majority of the African population in both the rural and urban areas. Most of their political support (and this was largely ambivalent) came from the chiefs, whose powers were extended through the Tribal Authorities, and from a small African elite whose prosperity and wealth were tied to the bantustan structures. The lack of mass political support became particularly evident in the democratic era when some of the strongest support for the African National Congress (ANC) in the first democratic election in 1994 came from areas that were once part of the bantustans.

Many African people may have justifiably appreciated the fact that their culture was promoted through the bantustan system, particularly by radio stations associated with the bantustans that broadcast in African languages. On the other hand, the apartheid government's plan was to use these radio stations to promote an ethnic – as opposed to a national – consciousness in order to fragment the national liberation movements and strengthen the bantustans. These stations, which were renamed by the South African Broadcasting Corporation (SABC) after 1994, included Ukhozi FM, Lesedi FM and Motsweding FM.

Bantustan schools and universities provided fertile ground for the growth of the national resistance movement. Black Consciousness took root and developed in all the black universities. Students at these universities established the South African Students' Organisation (SASO) in the 1970s, and from the 1980s they became centres of strong support for the United Democratic Front (UDF) and the ANC. People therefore made use of the opportunities available in the bantustans, but this rarely translated into political support for bantustan structures themselves.

THE BANTUSTANS AND THE NATIONAL LIBERATION MOVEMENTS

The bantustans and their governments were harshly criticised by all the liberation organisations. Open opposition initially came from the Black Consciousness Movement. Steve Biko of SASO referred to the bantustans as 'tribal cocoons' and 'sophisticated concentration camps'. All the Black Consciousness organisations believed that the bantustans weakened the struggle against apartheid: by promoting various ethnicities, this 'divide and rule' strategy prevented the growth of a united opposition to apartheid. SASO and others, including some left-wing academics and the largely white National Union of South African Students (NUSAS), pointed to the inferior conditions and poor opportunities of the bantustans, and described them as little more than migrant labour reservoirs or dumping grounds for surplus labour.

The Black Consciousness Movement saw the bantustan leaders as apartheid collaborators. At Robert Sobukwe's funeral in 1978, black youth demanded that Chief Mangosuthu Buthelezi and Professor Mlahleni Njisane (the Transkei 'ambassador' to South Africa) leave the event. These two bantustan representatives were stoned by some members of the crowd as they left. Hatred of bantustan leaders was also fuelled by the fact that some bantustan governments worked closely with the apartheid security forces to intimidate, arrest and detain liberation struggle activists, and also suppressed trade unions.

The division between 'collaborators' and 'resisters' was not always clear. Some political activists accepted jobs in the bantustan administrations but continued to work for the underground liberation movements. Bantustan leaders and liberation movement activists were often part of interrelated networks based on family ties, and they shared social, political and educational experiences. Some of the leading figures in the ANC were drawn from the rural elites, which included chiefly and royal families. This contributed to a sometimes complex relationship between the ANC and the bantustan administrations.

The ANC completely rejected the legitimacy of the bantustans, but until the late 1970s it did think that bantustan structures could be used to advance the interests of the national liberation movement. Oliver Tambo of the ANC met formally with Inkatha

A herder taking his cattle out to graze, Ledig, Bophuthatswana (1985). Source: Photograph by David Goldblatt

leader Mangosuthu Buthelezi in London in 1979 to discuss relations between the two organisations. However, they failed to find any common ground and the meeting was followed by an increasingly hostile relationship over the next decade and a half. This included violent conflict between Inkatha, supported by the government, on the one hand, and the ANC, the United Democratic Front and progressive trade unions, on the other. In general, most bantustans had an antagonistic relationship with the national liberation movement.

However, there were exceptions. For example, in 1986 the Inyandza National Movement led by KaNgwane's chief minister, Enos Mabuza, met with the ANC and agreed on a common aim of 'a system of majority rule in a united, democratic and non-racial South Africa' and undertook to cooperate to achieve this. After 1987, when Bantu Holomisa became the leader of the Transkei, the ANC and the Pan Africanist Congress (PAC) were allowed to operate from there.

The clashes between Inkatha and UDF–ANC-aligned supporters continued throughout the 1980s and early 1990s. About 11 000 people in KwaZulu and Natal and about 14 000 nationally died in this conflict. The violence presented a real threat to the negotiations of the early 1990s, by which time the bantustans were beginning to crumble.

DECLINE OF THE BANTUSTANS: LATE 1980s TO 1994

By the 1980s, the apartheid project, including the bantustans, was beginning to unravel. Internal differences between factions in the bantustans became more prominent. Military coups d'état took place in Ciskei and Transkei. The Transkei officially unbanned the ANC and PAC in 1989. Student protests and boycotts were widespread in a number of bantustans.

In order to attract more chiefs to the liberation struggle, the ANC and the UDF backed the creation of the Congress of Traditional Leaders of South Africa (CONTRALESA). CONTRALESA took part in the constitutional negotiations and ensured an official role for the chieftaincy in the new South African democracy after 1994.

Most bantustans were willing to participate in the elections and to reintegrate into South Africa. However, Ciskei, Bophuthatswana and KwaZulu initially refused to do so. When popular protests against these bantustan leaders took place in the early 1990s, the leaders drew on apartheid's security forces, their own military, vigilante groups and right-wing Afrikaner groups to try to crush the revolts.

Popular protest against the Ciskei's military government resulted in the Bisho Massacre in 1992. In 1994 Lucas Mangope called on militant right-wing Afrikaner groups for support after Bophuthatswana's army refused to suppress a protest. Armed right-wing white groups actually intervened but were defeated by a popular uprising and by the Bophuthatswana police and army, which turned against Mangope. The conflict between Inkatha and UDF–ANC supporters in KwaZulu intensified.

Ciskei and Bophuthatswana eventually gave in to popular demand and agreed to take part in the 1994 elections. On the eve of the elections, only KwaZulu still refused to participate. Buthelezi finally conceded, but only after the government and the ANC agreed that the institution of the Zulu monarchy would be safeguarded by the new constitution.

After the first democratic elections in 1994, all the bantustans were dismantled and were absorbed into South Africa's new provinces. However, their complex legacies persisted, and most former bantustan areas remained among the poorest and least developed parts of South Africa.

THEME 2: DISCUSSION QUESTIONS

1. What did you know and understand about South Africa's bantustans before you read this theme? Did it challenge or confirm any of your ideas? What was the most interesting part of the reading for you? Provide reasons or examples for your answers.

2. How have the bantustans played a role in shaping modern South Africa? What were some of their effects and how should we react to these legacies?

3. Why do you think Steve Biko referred to the bantustans as 'sophisticated concentration camps'? Do you think this is an accurate description? What was the relationship between the bantustans and the apartheid state's labour policy?

4. Do South African chieftaincies and monarchies contradict or uphold the values of South Africa's current constitution? What role and power should chiefs and monarchs hold in South African society? Should we view traditional institutions as protectors of patriarchy, or are they preservers of cultures that colonialism tried to destroy?

5. In 1970 Mangosuthu Buthelezi said, 'Homeland leaders who have accepted separate development have done so because it is the only way in which blacks in South Africa can express themselves politically.' Lucas Mangope stated in 1977, 'We would rather face the difficulties of administering a fragmented territory, the wrath of the outside world and accusations of ill-informed people. It is the price we are prepared to pay for being masters of our own destiny.' What is your response to these statements? Should we see bantustan leaders as collaborators with the apartheid state, or should we analyse their actions as pragmatic responses to a difficult political situation?

THEME 2: ADDITIONAL READINGS

Online readings

Biko, Stephen Bantu (1984) Let's Talk about Bantustans. *Frank Talk*, 1 (4): 22–4. http://disa.ukzn.ac.za/ftsep8416837118001004sep198413.

Bonner, Philip (2011) South African Society and Culture, 1919–1948. In *Cambridge History of South Africa*, Volume 2, *1885–1994*. Cambridge: Cambridge University Press, pp. 275–83. http://www.sahistory.org.za/sites/default/files/file%20uploads%20/robert_ross_anne_kelk_mager_bill_nasson_the_cabook4me.org_.pdf.

Butler, Jeffrey, Robert I. Rotberg and John Adams (1978) *The Black Homelands of South Africa: The Political and Economic Development of Bophuthatswana and KwaZulu*. Berkeley, CA: University of California Press. http://ark.cdlib.org/ark:/13030/ft0489n6d5/.

Delius, Peter (2018) Mistaking Form for Substance: Reflections on the Key Dynamics of Pre-colonial Polities and Their Implications for the Role of Chiefs in Contemporary South Africa. Mapungubwe Institute for Strategic Reflection. http://www.mistra.org.za/Library/ConferencePaper/Pages/Mistaking-Form-for-Substance-Peter-Delius-MISTRA-Working-Paper.aspx (with an introductory video clip found at https://www.youtube.com/watch?v=DTYRVHdniqc).

Du Pisani, André (n.d.) State and Society under South African Rule. Konrad-Adenauer-Stiftung. http://www.kas.de/upload/auslandshomepages/namibia/State_Society_Democracy/chapter2.pdf.

Former Black Homelands (Bantustans). *World Statesmen* (n.d.). http://www.worldstatesmen.org/South_African_homelands.html.

Ntsebeza, Lungisile (2005) *Democracy Compromised: Chiefs and the Politics of Land in South Africa.* Leiden: Brill. https://openaccess.leidenuniv.nl/bitstream/handle/1887/20609/ASC-075287668-173-01.pdf?sequence=2.

Phillips, Laura (2017) History of South Africa's Bantustans. *Oxford Research Encyclopedia of African History.* http://africanhistory.oxfordre.com/view/10.1093/acrefore/9780190277734.001.0001/acrefore-9780190277734-e-80.

The Homelands. (2017) *South African History Online*, 17 April 2011, updated 10 August 2017. http://www.sahistory.org.za/article/homelands.

Truth and Reconciliation Commission (TRC) (1998) *The Report of the Truth and Reconciliation Commission*, Volume 2. Chapter 5: The Homelands from 1960 to 1990. The O'Malley Archives, hosted by the Nelson Mandela Centre of Memory. https://www.nelsonmandela.org/omalley/index.php/site/q/03lv02167/04lv02264/05lv02335/06lv02357/07lv02372/08lv02377.htm#.

Werner, Wolfgang (1993) A Brief History of Land Dispossession in Namibia. *Journal of Southern African Studies*, 19 (1): 135–46. http://the-eis.com/elibrary/sites/default/files/downloads/literature/Werner%20land%20disposition%20in%20Namibia%201.pdf.

Online visual resources

A propaganda pamphlet issued by the apartheid government explaining bantustan administrations: *Bantu Authorities and Tribal Administration.* Pretoria: Department of Home Affairs, 1958. http://www.historicalpapers.wits.ac.za/inventories/inv_pdfo/AD1715/AD1715-1-2-5-001-jpeg.pdf.

A webpage containing video clips, maps and links to primary sources about South Africa's bantustans: Bantustans, *South Africa: Overcoming Apartheid* (n.d.). http://overcomingapartheid.msu.edu/multimedia.php?id=65-259-7.

Books

Ally, Shireen and Arianna Lissoni (eds) (2017) *New Histories of South Africa's Apartheid-Era Bantustans.* London: Routledge.

Delius, Peter (1996) *A Lion amongst the Cattle: Reconstruction and Resistance in the Northern Transvaal, 1930–94.* Portsmouth and Johannesburg: Heinemann and Ravan Press.

Fairbairn, Jean (2018) *Flashes in Her Soul: The Life of Jabu Ndlovu.* Hidden Voices Series, Book 2. Johannesburg: Jacana Media.

Gibbs, Timothy (2014) *Mandela's Kinsmen: Nationalist Elites and Apartheid's First Bantustans.* Johannesburg: Jacana Media.

Giliomee, H. and B. Mbenga (eds) (2007) *A New History of South Africa.* Cape Town: Tafelberg. (See pp. 323–5, The NP's Homelands Obsession; and pp. 350–3, Homelands or Dumping Grounds?)

Theme Three

The History of Schooling in South Africa

The South African education system is full of inequalities, which are based largely on racial and class lines. These inequalities are worse in the rural areas. In global ratings South African children consistently perform poorly and there is a high dropout rate. While some of today's problems may result from weak policies and poor implementation, most policies are necessarily aimed at overcoming historical challenges. In order to overcome these challenges, we need to understand how they have come about. Knowing the history of schooling in South Africa will give us a better understanding of how the challenges we face today have developed over the last two hundred years.

In modern South Africa, education has generally come to mean European-style schooling. This is very different from the education systems African societies used before colonisation. Here we will often refer to school learning and education as the same concept, but it is important to realise that modern schools only represent one type of education system. Societies throughout history have had different education systems based on the type of knowledge that each community valued and needed to function.

Schooling in the 1800s

As European-style schools arrived with the first colonisers, it might be tempting to believe that all white children have always had access to schooling. The reality is more complicated. The history of the 1800s helps to explain why the state prioritised white schooling so much in the twentieth century.

In the late 1800s, for people of European descent, the quality of education, access to schooling and ideas about schooling were different across South Africa. Schooling was not compulsory. Many white children, particularly in the rural areas, did not go to school at all. Children in urban areas generally had better access to schools. Wealthier white settlers sent their children to the few secondary schools in the Cape or to Europe for a better education.

The Boers believed schooling was a private matter and ultimately the responsibility of the church and parents, not the state. Yet the British believed that the state should provide or at least support schools. This was partly because schools were considered an effective way of instilling British values and the English language in the diverse populations in their colonies around the world. They also believed that schooling for coloured and African people was a way to exert control over these populations. There was more support for African and coloured education in the British colonies than in the Boer republics, although the Orange Free State (OFS) provided some aid for mission schools.

The majority of children did not have any access to school in the nineteenth century. For those who did, mission schools provided the only education available. Mission education played an important role in the spread and growth of schooling in the 1800s. By 1865, 70 per cent of all students[27] in the Cape's state-aided schools were in mission schools. The British mainly gained control over education by offering financial assistance to the various mission schools, which were generally under-resourced and in need of funds. This financial aid came with certain conditions. English had to be the language of instruction. Furthermore, African children had to spend time every day learning a manual skill in order to prepare them for a life of manual labour.

Most mission schools were village primary schools where children were taught basic literacy and numeracy. Resources were limited, attendance was irregular, and the quality of schooling was generally very low. A few of the mission schools, including some secondary schools and teacher training facilities, had a high status and provided good-quality education.

African and white children sometimes attended the same school, but unequal treatment and segregation existed all the same. For example, African and white children ate at separate tables, and slept in different dormitories.

For much of the 1800s, African parents were not enthusiastic about enrolling their children in mission schools. They believed that the schools undermined African culture and heritage, and did not offer the type of education needed for their own farming societies. It was not until the late 1800s, when most independent African kingdoms had come under white control, that enrolment increased. As the self-sufficient farming societies were destroyed through colonisation and more African people were forced to take up wage labour, parents hoped that some schooling would allow their children to obtain work in colonial society and to earn better wages.

Quality education, particularly post-primary education, was very difficult to access, for both black and white children. In 1892 only 1 per cent of school-going white children

---

27 We use the word 'student' to refer to anybody attending an educational institution. as explained in the section 'A Word on Terminology' on pages 12–13.

in the Transvaal had an education higher than Standard 6 (Grade 8).[28] This was partly because secondary education was not really needed in farming societies at that time, but also because it was expensive for most people. A minority of black children received some secondary education from the few mission schools that had secondary departments.

Schooling in the nineteenth century was not only unequal across racial lines, but also across class lines, with the poor receiving little or no basic schooling and higher education being reserved for the wealthy. Government attitudes to white education changed in the 1900s, but many of the early practices and policies regarding black education continued throughout the twentieth century.

SCHOOLING FROM 1900 TO 1953

After the Anglo-Boer War, the British gained complete control over the former Boer republics, the South African Republic (Transvaal) and the Orange Free State. After the Union of South Africa was established in 1910, each province became responsible for its own school systems and policies, including 'native' education. Compulsory schooling for white children between 7 and 14 years was introduced in all the provinces by 1918, together with free access to state schools. Schooling was not compulsory for black children. By 1940 less than a quarter of African children of school-going age were in school.

The provinces were generally happy to leave African education in the hands of the missionaries while providing some state financing. This helped the provinces maintain control over the important aspects of education, such as curricula. The Transvaal drew up a separate curriculum for African primary schools, although all students wrote the same Senior Certificate (matric) exam.

State funding for African education was set at a specific limit. When the state made additional money available, this came from African people's taxes, even though most African children were not in school. Spending per child was grossly unequal throughout this period. The state spent about a tenth or less on each African child compared with white children. For example, in 1940 annual expenditure on white pupils was about £26 per child, compared to £2 for each African child. State and mission schools continued to be under-funded and under-resourced. Primary schooling was even worse off in the rural areas. Rural primary schools catered to about 54 per cent of the African school-going population but resources were scarce. Schools had few teachers, less than half the children had access to books or desks, and two classes often had to share a loose-standing blackboard.

Secondary schooling expanded during this time, but at very unequal rates for white and black students. In 1925, white children enrolled in secondary school made up 10 per cent of total school enrolments. This increased by 1945 to 17 per cent. In contrast, secondary enrolments in 1925 only made up 0.5 per cent of the African school population,

---

28 Today we refer to each year of schooling as a 'grade'. In the past, Grades 1 and 2 were known as Sub A and Sub B or Class 1 and Class 2. Grade 3 was Standard 1, Grade 4 was Standard 2, and so on.

and this increased slightly to 2 per cent by 1945.

The commercial and manufacturing sectors of the economy grew in the mid-1900s. They saw some value to themselves in having a settled African urban middle class. As a result, by the late 1930s, more state attention was given to expanding African secondary schooling. Mission institutions received more money to set up secondary boarding schools, and the state also built some high schools in African townships. Although more children had access to secondary school, the schools still lacked adequate resources and qualified teachers. The pass rates remained low under these conditions.

Owing to a shortage of resources and qualified teachers, African children received a very inferior education compared to white children throughout this period. Relatively few progressed beyond Standard 3. Most African children in school were concentrated in the first four years of schooling and were usually two years older than white children in the same grade.

In the Union of South Africa, English and Afrikaans were recognised as the only official languages, but these were not the home languages of African children. The provinces had different language policies for black schools, but after 1935 it was accepted practice that the first four years of schooling took place in the mother tongue in all schools. In Standard 3, either English or Afrikaans was introduced as the medium of instruction. Most African schools used English.

Resistance to poor school conditions took place throughout this period. There were many grievances against the schools, which were often to do with the quality of food at the boarding schools, authoritarian teachers, and the compulsory manual labour that was part of the school day for African children. Boycotts and sometimes more violent forms of resistance, such as damaging school property or intimidating teachers, took place at several schools. However, these actions were sporadic and isolated.

We tend to focus on Bantu Education as the root of many of our educational issues, but the inequalities that riddle our system were in place long before Bantu Education became official policy in 1953.

SCHOOLING UNDER APARTHEID: 1950S AND 1960S

The National Party (NP) gained power in the 1948 elections and made the restructuring of black schooling a priority. Segregated education was an important part of the policy of apartheid. In 1949 the Eiselen Commission was set up to investigate black education. The commission's recommendations laid the foundation for the Bantu Education Act of 1953.

Under the NP black education was brought firmly under central state control. African schooling in all the provinces became the responsibility of the Department of Bantu Education. All black schools had to follow the curriculum set out by the Education Department, which was separate from the curriculum for white schools. All African schools had to be registered with the department, and in order to do so they had to meet the conditions imposed by the government. Private and mission schools could only operate with the permission of the government and only in designated African areas and using the government curriculum. Schools on private white-owned farms were taken out of missionary hands and given to the farmers, who sometimes made use of the children's labour during harvest time. The Bantu Education Act withdrew government subsidies from mission schools: some closed down altogether while others handed control over to the state, arguing that Bantu Education was better than no education at all. The Catholic Church, which could raise other sources of funding, decided to continue to run its own schools independently, but they too were forced to switch to the Bantu Education curriculum. In 1953 there were over 5 000 state-aided mission schools. By 1965 only 509 out of 7 222 African schools were mission schools.

Mother-tongue instruction was emphasised under apartheid in the primary schools. African children's mother-tongue instruction was extended from the first four years of school to the first eight years – that is, until the end of primary school. By 1959 the Standard 6 (Grade 8) school-leaving certificate examination was written in an African language. The state applied a dual-medium policy in African secondary schools. Previously, African secondary schools mainly used English as a language of instruction. Bantu Education expected all African secondary schools to teach certain subjects in Afrikaans. However, this policy was not always followed or strictly applied and English remained the main language of learning for most African secondary schools.

The NP's belief that vernacular languages should be used in the schools of the various ethnic groups extended even to white education. Some dual-medium schools (English and Afrikaans) had been set up in the 1940s for white children. These were now abolished, and English- and Afrikaans-speaking children were segregated. Unlike their African counterparts, white English and Afrikaans children were schooled from primary school to university in their mother-tongue. At no point were white children required to learn an African language.

African primary school enrolments increased throughout the apartheid period as the economy grew and employers demanded a more literate and skilled workforce. More primary schools were built in some places to accommodate the increased numbers. Another way that the government dealt with the increased primary intake was by introducing the platoon system in Sub A and Sub B. Half the children were taught in the morning and the other half in the afternoon. The government insisted that only women teach the lower grades, since they could pay them less. Not only were the African primary teachers not compensated for their extra work in teaching two shifts, but African children received significantly less school time per day than what was necessary in the most critical learning phase.

Unlike previous governments, the NP did not want a settled African urban middle class in 'white' South Africa. It aimed to push African secondary education into the bantustans. It was very difficult to register an African secondary school in the urban areas. Ultimately the state wanted the bantustans to be responsible for all African education. In 1965 over 50 per cent of the African school population was studying in schools in the reserves (the areas which the government intended to turn into bantustans). By 1985 this had risen to 70 per cent. Some of the policies adopted in the bantustans appeared to reflect what many African people felt about language use in schools. For example, in

Schoolchildren crowded in classroom. Source: Africa Media Online, Photograph by Drum Photographer BAHA

1963 the Transkei decided that mother-tongue instruction would only be given until the end of Standard 2, after which English would be the language of instruction. By 1974 all the bantustans except QwaQwa followed a similar language policy in their schools. Yet, while bantustans had more flexibility in terms of policy, the quality of the education in most schools remained poor owing to a lack of funds.

In 1963 and 1965, the Coloured Persons Education Act and the Indian Education Act were passed respectively. Education for these two groups became the responsibility of the Department of Coloured Affairs and the Department of Indian Affairs. Schooling was made compulsory for coloured and Indian children, but they were only allowed to attend schools in coloured and Indian areas. In addition, they could only be taught by teachers from their own 'population group'.

Apartheid ensured that there were education departments for different races, each with a separate curriculum. This meant that there were different matric exams, different expectations and different aims of schooling.

Most African parents, teachers and students were unhappy about the introduction of Bantu Education. African teacher organisations protested against the new system as early as 1952, but the government either dismissed politically active teachers or refused to recognise organisations like the Cape African Teachers' Association. Parents and children also took part in protests. The African National Congress (ANC) called for school boycotts, which started in April 1955, mostly on the East Rand of Johannesburg and in areas of the Eastern Cape. Over 12 000 children took part. During the boycotts the ANC organised alternative education for the affected children through 'cultural clubs' set up by the African Education Movement. They purposely used the term 'cultural clubs' to get around the law regarding schools. Some of these 'clubs' were very effective but the government used repression to crush the protests and the clubs.

The government issued an ultimatum to boycotting children that if they did not return to school by 25 April 1955 they would be expelled. The ANC was divided over whether to continue the boycott or to call it off, and did not reach a final decision. Many children returned to school, but thousands did not and were expelled. Owing to a lack of money, facilities and teachers, as well as government harassment, the cultural clubs were all closed by 1960. School-based resistance continued throughout the 1960s, but this was not organised on the grand scale of the 1950s boycott. Popular, widespread resistance to Bantu Education did not emerge again until the 1970s.

SCHOOLING IN THE 1970S: A TURNING POINT IN STUDENT RESISTANCE

The late 1960s and early 1970s saw a renewed period of resistance in education. The South African Students' Organisation (SASO) was formed in 1968, and promoted the spread of Black Consciousness (BC) in the 1970s. BC organisations like the South African Students' Movement (SASM) and the Black Community Project (BCP) were established in 1972. Many people were inspired by Angola and Mozambique gaining independence from the Portuguese. In this atmosphere of anticipation, challenge and protest, the government decided to change some of its education policies. These changes provided the spark for the black youth to revolt in 1976, and introduced a period of more intense, overt and large-scale resistance to the entire apartheid regime.

By the late 1960s the NP recognised the need for more skilled African labour in urban areas, and it began to establish African secondary schools in towns. African secondary enrolment increased by about 14 per cent each year between 1967 and 1974. Between 1974 and 1975 it increased by 52 per cent.

Previously, African children had to have 13 years of schooling before matriculating: eight years of primary school (Sub A to Standard 6) and five years of secondary school (Form 1 to Form 5). In 1975 the state changed this to 12 years. Under the new system, primary school ended with Standard 5. This doubled the number of children who moved to secondary school in 1976, as both Standard 5 and Standard 6 students were promoted to Form 1 simultaneously. This caused great stress in already overcrowded classrooms, and frustration among parents, teachers and students ran high.

In 1974, in an attempt to promote the Afrikaans language, the government began to enforce the Bantu Education dual-language policy more strictly in secondary schools in the Southern Transvaal region which included Soweto. It insisted that social studies and mathematics be taught in Afrikaans, and that science and practical subjects (for example, art, needlework or woodwork) be taught in English. Most students had a poor grasp of both these languages. The same language policy was also introduced in Standard 5 in primary schools from 1975. Primary schoolchildren were thus expected to write their school-leaving examinations in English and Afrikaans, even though this was the first year they were taught in either of these languages.

By extending the dual-medium policy to the primary schools, the state created a greater number of students who were dissatisfied with the system. There were many more African children in primary school than in high school. This helps to explain why so many primary schoolchildren took part in the 1976 protests.

In response to these policies, as well as to broader community issues, about 20 000 Soweto youth staged a coordinated protest on 16 June 1976. The police responded violently and the situation escalated over the next few weeks. The protests quickly spread to many other areas in South Africa, and by July the Cape Town coloured schools had joined the demonstrations. These commonly involved marches, boycotts, calls for stay-aways, damage to institutions and confrontations with the police. The state responded with brutal suppression. They reacted violently to protests, and arrested and detained leaders. About 1 000 people were killed in this period. Black Consciousness organisations were banned. The uprisings continued throughout 1977 and only abated in 1978.

The student uprisings brought international attention to apartheid's injustices and oppression, and it caused many young people to become activists in South Africa. In 1979 the Congress of South African Students (COSAS) was formed. Many young people also left the country to join the ANC or the Pan Africanist Congress (PAC). Education remained important for the liberation organisations. In 1978, the ANC set up the Solomon Mahlangu Freedom College (SOMAFCO) in Tanzania where exiled students could receive an education. The institution eventually included a crèche, nursery school, primary school and high school. The ANC also organised higher and technical education opportunities for students in various countries.

Education and the Broad Liberation Struggle: From 1978 to 1990

In response to the student uprising between 1976 and 1978, the government made some limited reforms that it hoped would pacify the people. Afrikaans was no longer a compulsory medium of instruction and English could be introduced as a language of instruction from Standard 3. The Bantu Education Act was replaced by the Education and Training Act in 1979. The Department of Bantu Education was renamed the Department of Education and Training (DET). More money was made available and more schools were built in the 1980s. African secondary school enrolment increased rapidly but conditions remained difficult. The government still maintained its segregated policies but, under political pressure, it set up a commission of inquiry, which resulted in the De Lange report of 1981. The report recommended one department providing equal education of quality for all. The government rejected this.

The government's limited attempts at reform were ineffectual and by the 1980s conditions in African schools had become intolerable. Teachers were working under stressful conditions, and struggled with the large classes, few resources and their own lack of adequate training in an inferior and rapidly expanding teacher education system. To cope, many teachers taught in authoritarian ways, used excessive corporal punishment (which was then legal), and required of their pupils rote learning. Critical thinking, skills development and class discussions were not prioritised or were even avoided. Students were frustrated. A 1983 survey of Transvaal youth showed that most students believed that their teachers hindered their success in the classroom; only a third were satisfied with their school's efforts. The difficult learning conditions played a large role in the school boycotts of the 1980s.

Urban secondary schooling was severely disrupted by the protests and unrest of the late 1970s and 1980s. Students lost faith in schooling. Many children attended school irregularly or not at all. When they did attend, many did not do their homework or came late for class. Some students physically prevented others from attending schools, sometimes through violent intimidation. Learning time was also lost to police raids and school closures.

Many of the school youth became politicised, and identified with the broader anti-apartheid struggle. In the 1970s, student demands had focused on language policies and better resources. By the 1980s there was a growing awareness of the larger systemic issues of a racist, capitalist society. COSAS was active and helped to coordinate protests and demands, and affiliated to the United Democratic Front (UDF). School resistance also crossed racial lines. The 1980 school boycott started in Cape Town's African schools and then spread to the coloured and Indian schools. The growing resistance created a sense of optimism in many young people. They believed that the end of apartheid was near, and consequently they often prioritised protest activities over schooling. A popular slogan of the time was 'Liberation first, education later'.

The poor learning conditions in most African schools in the 1980s affected children's lives and their future job prospects. About 150 000 students dropped out of high school every year at that time. The quality of matriculation passes deteriorated. From the late 1960s up to 1975, about 33 per cent of matriculants passed with a university entrance qualification. After 1980, more African students were writing matriculation exams than ever before, but only about 13 per cent qualified for university entrance. About 50 per cent of those who wrote the examination failed altogether. White schooling, on the other hand, was not disrupted and whites had much higher pass rates. For example, in 1986, 45 per cent of white matric candidates attained university entrance and only 8 per cent failed. Most of the African students who failed during the 1980s did not rewrite their exams and many joined the ranks of the unemployed.

By 1985 the African secondary schooling system had virtually disintegrated in the urban areas. The Soweto Parents' Crisis Committee, concerned that the frequent school boycotts were seriously harming the education of the youth, called for national action to combat the crisis. In response, the National Education Crisis Committee (NECC – later 'Crisis' was changed to 'Coordinating') was established in December 1985. After consultation with the ANC and student structures, the NECC called on the youth to replace the call for 'Liberation before Education' with 'People's Education for People's Power'. Teachers and students were encouraged to return to school and undermine the system from within by developing People's Education in place of Bantu Education.

'People's Education' was a broad concept. It included an alternative education programme that was meaningful, relevant and empowering. Some teaching material was created, most notably for history, for which a textbook was developed. It was planned that the alternative curriculum would initially be taught in schools two afternoons a week. However, the difficult conditions that existed at the time made this all but impossible. People's Education also envisaged setting up alternative, democratic, community-based school structures to counter the authoritarian education structures of the DET, and Parent-Teacher-Student Associations were established where there was enough support for them.

Disrupted schooling and school closures, together with the banning of COSAS in 1985, weakened student organisational structures. From a political point of view, it was better for students to return to school so that they could organise collectively in order to strengthen resistance against apartheid.

The government reacted to the protests with characteristic brutality. The police and the army were deployed to schools. They raided schools, and intimidated and arrested students and teachers. COSAS and the NECC were banned, as was People's Education material. The government tried to force students to attend school by expelling those who missed a certain number of days.

There were also attempts, once again, at limited reform. In 1986 private schools were allowed to enrol children of all colours. The government also began spending more money per capita on black education. In 1978, for every R1 spent on an African child, the government spent about R3 on a coloured child, R5 on an Indian child and R12 on a white children. By 1989 these ratios had changed. For every R1 spent on an African child, the state now spent about R2 on coloureds, R3 on Indians and R4 on whites. Unequal spending was reduced but not eradicated.

The student uprisings had a number of effects. By prioritising political liberation, schooling was severely disrupted in black urban areas. Together with appalling school conditions, the unrest contributed to the poor matric passes and the high number of dropouts in African and coloured schools. From a different point of view, it played an important role in the broader resistance movement against apartheid. The protests helped to create political awareness among the youth. More young people became involved in politics, and the membership of political organisations grew. The crisis in education caused traditional methods of teaching and learning to be re-evaluated. Alternative forms of education were imagined and attempts were made, through People's Education, to develop these alternative programmes. But the disruption of the educational process undoubtedly also had a negative impact on the education of young people.

SCHOOLING IN THE 1990S AND BEYOND

COSAS and the NECC effectively 'unbanned' themselves in 1989 and started to campaign openly once again. By 1990 South Africa had entered a period of negotiations and transition. The ANC was unbanned, political prisoners were released and exiles returned home. Violence continued but policy changes started to take place in education. In 1990 the government allowed children of all colours to be enrolled in government schools, thus marking the end of legal state segregation. However, this change was still largely superficial since it was very difficult for most children to access these schools – 90 per cent of the (white) parents had to agree to declare the school 'open'.

When the new democratic government came into power, education was recognised as a constitutional right in the 1996 constitution. It is now compulsory for all children to attend school, whether state or private, and all state schools follow the same curriculum and write the same matric exams. Racial discrimination of any sort is illegal. Unfortunately, while formal policies have changed, many of the actual school realities experienced in the twentieth century still persist, such as an unequal distribution of resources and lack of competent teachers in township and rural schools. Government has been criticised for its ineffective implementation of policies, particularly in rural areas. Recent school protests have also highlighted more subtle forms of racism in the former white schools. For example, school dress codes and hair-style regulations often conform to the traditions of the colonial and racially segregated past, and racist attitudes continue among some staff members. Schooling and education thus remain contentious and emotional topics in today's society.

THEME 3: DISCUSSION QUESTIONS

1. What was your impression of the history of schooling in South Africa before you read this theme? Did the information change any of your impressions? What was the most interesting part of the reading? Provide reasons for your answers.

2. Based on your own experience and knowledge of South Africa's current education system, write a list of challenges that our schools, teachers and learners face today. Some people blame the ANC government for weak policy implementation. Others point out that the government has had to overcome significant historical challenges that cannot be fixed quickly. What do you think? Which challenges are a result of weak policy implementation and which challenges are inherited from the past? What can we do to overcome these challenges?

3. African, coloured and Indian resistance to racist state education policies faced a dilemma. Should children boycott school in an effort to change discriminatory policies and lose their chance of getting a formal school education? Or should children attend school and be exposed to an inferior education but get some formal schooling? Do you agree with the idea in the mid-1980s to replace 'Liberation before Education' with 'People's Education for People's Power'? If you had children during this time, what would you want them to do?

4. Schooling as we know it today was introduced as a result of colonialism. In an attempt to break away from our colonial past, should we reject the school system and the knowledge it teaches? Provide reasons for your answers. Also, if you think the current school system should be replaced with a different type of education system, explain what you think needs to replace it.

5. Can we compare the school boycotts of the 1980s with the Fees Must Fall movement of the mid-2010s? If so, what are the similarities and what are the differences?

THEME 3: ADDITIONAL READINGS

Online readings

Adler, N., S. Leydesdorff, M. Chamberlain and L. Neyzi (eds.) (2009) *Memories of Mass Repression: Narrating Life Stories in the Aftermath of Atrocity.* London: Routledge. https://books.google.co.za/books?id=hTYrDwAAQBAJ&pg=PR7&lpg=PR7&dq=memories+of+mass+repression&source=bl&ots=gBQh4eCqz7&sig=wQzuy-UT-5SLWou_ifS1vKpe6dA&hl=en&sa=X-&ved=0ahUKEwiimfrNpPrXAhUJ2hoKHRUXAk8Q6AEIPjAE#v=onepage&q=memories%20of%20mass%20repression&f=false.

Baard, Frances and Barbie Schreiner (1986) *My Spirit is Not Banned* (extract on the Bantu Education boycott). http://www.sahistory.org.za/archive/bantu-education-boycott.

Christie, Pam (1991) *The Right to Learn: The Struggle for Education in South Africa,* 2nd edn. Johannesburg: SACHED and Ravan Press. (Chapters 1 and 2). https://www.researchgate.net/publication/263756900_Right_to_Learn_the_struggle_for_education_in_South_Africa.

Fiske, Edward and Helen Ladd (2005) *Elusive Equity: Education Reform in Post-apartheid South Africa.* Cape Town: HSRC Press. (Chapter 3: Education and Apartheid). http://www.hsrcpress.ac.za/product.php?productid=2090&freedownload=1.

Jansen, Jonathan D. (1990) Curriculum as a Political Phenomenon: Historical Reflections on Black South African Education. *Journal of Negro Education,* 59 (2): 195–206. https://repository.up.ac.za/dspace/bitstream/handle/2263/1384/Jansen%20(1990)c.pdf?sequence=2.

Lessons from the Student Protests of the 1980s. (2015) *GroundUp,* 23 October 2015. https://www.groundup.org.za/article/lessons-student-protests-1980s_3431/.

Moloantoa, Daluxolo (2016) The Contested but Pivotal Legacy of Missionary Education in South Africa. *The Heritage Portal,* 15 September 2016. http://

www.theheritageportal.co.za/article/contested-pivotal-legacy-missionary-education-south-africa.

Morrow, Sean, Brown Maaba and Loyiso Pulumani (2004) *Education in Exile: SOMAFCO, the ANC School in Tanzania, 1978 to 1992.* Cape Town: HSRC Press. http://www.hsrcpress.ac.za/product.php?cat=33&freedownload=1&productid=1960.

School Boycotts Relived (2010) *Joburg*, 21 September 2010. https://joburg.org.za/index.php?option=com_content&view=article&id=5708&catid=122&Itemid=203.

Van Eeden, E.S. and L.M. Vermeulen (2005) Christian National Education (CNE) and People's Education (PE): Historical Perspectives and Some Broad Common Grounds. *New Contree*, no. 50. https://dspace.nwu.ac.za/bitstream/handle/10394/5320/No_50%282005%29_Van_Eeden_ES_%26_Vermeulen_LM.pdf?sequence=1&isAllowed=y.

Online visual resources

Today Marks the 60th Anniversary of the Bantu Education Act (2013) *SABC Digital News*, 3 October 2013. https://www.youtube.com/watch?v=kn1ITFpAVDI.

National Electronic Media Institute of South Africa (2016) The Role of Mission Schools in SA Education. https://gatewaystoanewworld.wordpress.com/2016/10/28/the-role-of-mission-schools-in-sa-education/.

Books

Hartshorne, Ken (1992) *Crisis and Challenge: Black Education, 1910–1990.* Cape Town: Oxford University Press.

Kallaway, Peter (ed.) (1984) *Apartheid and Education: The Education of Black South Africans.* Johannesburg: Ravan Press.

Kallaway, Peter (ed.) (2002) *The History of Education under Apartheid, 1948–1994: 'The Doors of Learning and Culture Shall Be Opened'.* Cape Town: Pearson Education South Africa.

Unterhalter, E., H. Wolpe, T. Botha, S. Badat, T. Dlamini and B. Kgotseng (eds) (1991) *Apartheid Education and Popular Struggles.* Johannesburg, Ravan Press.

Theme Four

Poverty and Inequality

INTRODUCTION

South Africa is one of the most unequal societies in the world. In 2016, the wealthiest 10 per cent of the population earned between 55 per cent and 60 per cent of the total income in the country. The inequality is also reflected in racial terms. In 2016, nearly half of the African population lived in poverty, while less than 1 per cent of the white population was considered poor. This inequality was not inevitable; it did not *have* to happen.

There are different definitions of poverty. In this theme, poverty is defined as the inability to meet basic needs such as enough nutrition, shelter and clothing, as well as access to education and health facilities. Poverty also affects people's living conditions in the form of unhealthy surroundings, high crime rates and limited access to infrastructure like piped water, electricity or public transport.

Free market capitalism naturally results in inequality. In some countries, such as the social democracies in Western Europe or some developmental states in Asia, governments have intervened to protect workers against the excesses of the market. In South Africa (before 1994) the government also intervened, but mainly to protect white workers and white privilege, while oppressing and exploiting the coloured, Indian and African populations. When we consider what South African society looked like in the late 1800s and early 1900s, and what it looks like today, we can trace a number of important political decisions that played a major role in creating this unequal society.

FROM SELF-SUFFICIENCY TO RELIANCE ON WAGE LABOUR

In the late 1800s, most of the country's rural communities were self-sufficient; that is, they produced what they needed to survive. They did not, for the most part, need money. As the gold mining industry developed after 1886, it required large numbers of

Aerial view of the stark difference between township and middle-class houses in Cape Town.

workers but struggled to attract them from societies that were mostly self-supporting. In British-controlled territories, colonial governments imposed taxes on conquered African societies, and these taxes had to be paid in cash. This forced many African men to take up wage labour in order to earn money for taxes. Most of these workers were migrants, although in time many began to settle permanently in the towns and cities.

The British set aside some rural land, known as reserves, for conquered indigenous populations. Mine owners supported the existence of the reserves because they did not want an urbanised African working class. They preferred the migrant labour system, which helped them to keep tight control over their African workers, who lived in dingy, overcrowded compounds during the period of their employment contracts. Mine owners paid lower wages to African men because they argued that the workers' incomes were supplemented by their families' farming activities in the reserves.

Despite the loss of land to white conquest, in the early 1900s most African societies were still self-sufficient in food and were able to meet most of their needs through agriculture. Farming by Africans was not limited to the reserves in the early 1900s. Individually or in groups, a small number of Africans bought farms on land that had been taken over by white settlers, and became commercial farmers. Most farmed profitably and sold their produce in the towns. Although Africans had bought only a very small portion of commercial farmland, many white commercial farmers resented the competition and protested loudly.

Many poorer white farmers did not have the technology, wealth or labour available to cultivate all their land. They entered into contracts with African sharecroppers or labour tenants. These agreements allowed many African families to farm on white-controlled land without becoming wage labourers.

The 1913 Natives Land Act was a turning point for African people's access to land, and negatively affected their self-sufficiency. The Act limited landownership by Africans to the reserves. They could no longer buy or rent land outside the reserves. Furthermore, the Act banned sharecropping and cash tenancy, also known as 'squatting',[29] by Africans on white-owned farms. Families that had successfully farmed on white-owned land were no longer allowed to do so.

The Land Act was applied unevenly. Many white landowners immediately evicted African families, especially in the Orange Free State. Thousands were not aware that the law had changed and thought that they had been evicted by their landlords' individual decision. They wandered about with their families and their livestock in the winter of 1913, looking for other farms on which to stay. Of course, no white farmers would take on tenants and many Africans were forced to kill their animals in order to survive. They eventually ended up in the reserves, or crossed the borders into Lesotho and Botswana, or moved to the cities to become unskilled labourers.

Although the number of sharecroppers on white-controlled land fell sharply, the practice continued to some extent until the 1950s when the apartheid government began to clamp down hard on it. Under apartheid the remaining 'squatters' either became wage labourers or labour tenants, or they were evicted and settled in the bantustans.

As the reserves became overcrowded after 1913, a strain was put on the natural resources. When agricultural conditions deteriorated, families became less self-sufficient and poverty intensified. As noted above, in the early 1900s most households could still rely on subsistence agriculture for most of their needs. By the 1940s, however, most African people were unable to produce enough food to meet their basic needs, and malnutrition was widespread. Most households relied on migrant labour remittances in order to survive. A late 1940s survey in a Ciskei district found that the local population would have starved without the remittances.

Partly as a result of the worsening conditions in the reserves, urbanisation increased dramatically in the 1930s and 1940s. After the apartheid government came to power in 1948, it tightened the pass laws. Black urbanisation then slowed in the 1960s as people could not easily move to the urban areas. The apartheid state also forcibly relocated about 2.5 million people to the bantustans between 1960 and 1983. The bantustans became so overcrowded that successful smallholding agriculture was completely destroyed for the majority of households. Some studies showed that, in the 1960s, only 10 per cent of Africans could feed themselves entirely by means of agriculture. Wage labour was now necessary for survival, not only to pay taxes. As there were few jobs available in the bantustans, most households relied heavily on the meagre remittances of migrant workers.

Migrant workers travelled to the mines and cities for work. However, black and white workers did not compete on an even playing field. Racist policies ensured that white

---

29 In later years the word 'squatting' was used differently. From the 1940s it came to refer to the unlawful occupation of an uninhabited building or piece of land.

workers were privileged and black workers were largely limited to the lowest-paid jobs. Coloured and Indian workers earned more than African workers, but less than whites.

A Racialised Labour Market

By the early 1900s the South African working class was divided along racial lines. White, African, coloured and Indian workers were not equal in the eyes of the law. Racist labour practices developed throughout the twentieth century and played a major role in creating South Africa's unequal society.

Black workers did not operate in a free labour market. White workers were free to travel and work where they wanted. African labour was highly regulated through the migrant labour system, the pass laws and other legislation. While white, Indian and coloured workers relied on trade unions to promote their welfare, African trade unions were not officially recognised until 1979. Before this, employers did not have to negotiate with African employees and it was illegal for Africans to strike. They could thus not use collective bargaining to negotiate higher wages or safer working conditions.

Coloureds and Indians could generally take up wage labour anywhere (except the Orange Free State in the case of Indians), but segregationist laws prevented them from setting up businesses in 'white' areas. Many coloureds and Indians who had long lived in areas later declared white were evicted with little compensation for their properties or businesses. They were forced to move to new townships. Indians could not even enter the Orange Free State and needed special permission just to pass through.

From the early days of mining and manufacturing, white workers demanded higher wages than blacks, even if they did the same work. Because black labour was cheaper, employers preferred to hire blacks where they could. White workers felt threatened and resented black competition, particularly for unskilled and semi-skilled jobs. They pressured the government to intervene and protect white jobs. Two important racist policies, introduced in the early twentieth century, concerned 'job reservation' and 'civilised labour'.

Job reservation, also known as the colour bar, reserved certain semi-skilled and skilled jobs for whites, and sometimes for coloureds and Indians. African workers were almost entirely limited to unskilled labour. At first the colour bar legally applied only to mining, but by 1956 it could be applied to almost all industries. Other jobs were not formally reserved under the colour bar but were reserved for people with certain qualifications, which most blacks could not achieve given their limited education and training opportunities.

The 'civilised labour' policy was implemented by the Pact government elected in 1924. According to the policy, whites were 'civilised' and Africans people were 'undeveloped', and therefore whites needed a higher salary to meet their 'civilised' needs. The policy also promoted the practice of increasing white employment. The government and white society in general pressured employers to take on impoverished whites as workers rather than blacks.

A racial wage gap remained throughout the twentieth century. By 1936, whites earned on average thirteen times more than Africans and six times more than coloureds and

Indians. In 1970 the ratio of wages for whites and Africans was approximately six to one in the manufacturing sector and twenty to one in mining. Even though the wage differential decreased in the 1980s when Africans could belong to legal trade unions, there remained a marked difference between their wages and those of whites. Wages for coloureds and Indians tended to fall somewhere in-between. Even middle-class jobs like nursing and teaching saw intense discrimination throughout the twentieth century. For example, in 1979 an African nurse's starting salary was two-thirds that of a white nurse with the same qualifications. Racial differences continued into the twenty-first century, unsupported by the law but reflecting the inequalities inherited from earlier years.

ACTIVE PROMOTION OF WHITE WELFARE

The early 1900s saw the growth of the 'poor white problem'. A number of factors contributed to a growing number of poor white farmers leaving their farms to look for work in the towns. These included the destruction caused by the Anglo–Boer War, and the lack of skill and capital among many. Many *bywoners* also left the farms. *Bywoners* were whites, often family members, who lived on a farm but did not own it. Sometimes they were sharecroppers, but their roles were not always clearly defined. Many were evicted by less wealthy white farmers, who preferred to employ African sharecroppers or labour tenants, since they were able to pay them less even if they were more productive. Other *bywoners* left farms that could no longer support them.

In the early 1900s thousands of impoverished white farmers and *bywoners* moved to the cities. Lacking skills, they could only do unskilled labour, but they competed with black workers, who could be paid less and who were often more experienced and efficient. By 1920 there were about 100 000 poor whites in the cities, most of them Afrikaans-speaking. By 1930 this number increased to 300 000, or about a third of the white Afrikaner population. The poor whites had two big advantages over blacks. First, they had the right to vote, and so the government had an incentive to help improve their living standards. Second, the racism that pervaded white society won them sympathy from the government and many white employers, and thus worked in their favour.

The Union governments under Louis Botha (1910–19) and Jan Smuts (1919–24; 1939–48) tended to act in the interest of British and local big business interests, especially mining, rather than the interests of poorer Afrikaners and small business. When General J.B.M. Hertzog came to power in 1924, he prioritised white Afrikaner interests, a tendency that was further strengthened when the National Party (NP) under D.F. Malan came to power in 1948.

Hertzog introduced a system of welfare grants. In 1928 the first state pensions were provided to needy whites and coloureds, although coloureds received less than whites. In the 1930s the state began to provide child support and disability grants to whites and coloureds. It also established the Unemployment Insurance Fund (UIF), which paid a grant to contributing workers who were temporarily unemployed. However, UIF was only available to higher earners, thereby excluding most black people. The welfare system thus existed for the benefit of whites and, to a lesser extent, of coloureds.

Smuts extended the state welfare system in the mid-1940s. Africans and Indians could apply for pensions and disability grants. Africans, Indians, coloureds and whites received different amounts, thus aggravating already existing inequalities. In the late 1960s, the highest state pension for Africans was one-seventh of that for whites. In the late 1940s, Smuts also extended UIF to include more African urban workers. The NP resented this; they claimed the grants discouraged Africans from looking for work. When the NP took power in 1948, it quickly reversed the UIF law to exclude most African workers again.

Under Hertzog in the 1920s and 1930s, the state actively created work for unskilled and unemployed whites, especially on the railways, harbours and other state-owned enterprises. Thousands of black workers lost their jobs and were replaced by whites. During the Great Depression in the 1930s, 22 000 black workers lost their jobs, compared to 4 000 white workers. Public works were set up to provide jobs for poor white workers. Hertzog also enforced a quota of 40 per cent white workers in the growing manufacturing sector, further protecting them from competition.

White access to education improved throughout the 1900s, and became a central focus of the apartheid government after 1948. In the 1940s, only 50 per cent of white children in Grade 8 (Standard 6) reached Grade 10 (Standard 8). By 1970 most white children completed Grade 10, with the majority finishing matric. More whites gained access to universities and entered various professions. Apprenticeship programmes, especially in the state-owned enterprises, the police and armed forces, provided technical and artisan training to young whites. The white state bureaucracy expanded and provided more white-collar work for newly qualified whites. White semi-skilled and skilled workers also moved into the expanding manufacturing, commercial and services sectors.

The government also intervened heavily to improve white farming. White farmers obtained substantial financial and technical support, especially after 1924. They had access to low-interest loans, tax rebates, drought grants and export subsidies. State support allowed more white farmers to mechanise, which improved efficiency and increased agricultural output.

State support for the white population, especially Afrikaners, caused the white middle class to expand significantly, while the white working class declined. In 1946 white Afrikaners made up 29 per cent of white-collar workers; by 1977 this had increased to 65 per cent. Successive governments were largely successful in lifting the majority of whites out of poverty, and apartheid played an important role in expanding the white middle class.

APARTHEID ENTRENCHES RACIAL DISCRIMINATION

While the segregationist policies privileged white workers, the growth of secondary industry in the 1930s, and the wartime conditions of World War II, meant that these policies were not always applied strictly. For example, the colour bar and pass laws were relaxed during World War II. Smuts accepted that the economy needed an urbanised skilled African labour force. Some African high schools were set up by the state during the 1940s in major urban areas.

However, the NP was opposed to the creation of an urbanised African skilled labour force. It wanted to create and maintain a rurally based, unskilled labour force that depended on low-wage migrant labour. White farmers and urban employers would call on rural African workers as needed, but when their work contracts were finished, they had to return to the reserves (later known as the bantustans or homelands). The NP hoped that this would finally satisfy the labour needs of white farmers. After it came to power in 1948, the NP tried to reverse the movement of Africans to urban areas, and extended the colour bar to more occupations. It tightened the pass laws, which slowed African urbanisation and limited African people to the farms or bantustans. Forced removals also moved 'surplus' people to the bantustans, where there were very few job opportunities.

Importantly, the government purposely limited access to quality education for blacks at a time when it emphasised this for white Afrikaners. The Bantu Education Act of 1953 was a systematic attempt to undermine the academic aspirations of the African population.[30] While schools for Africans had struggled under previous governments, a few elite mission schools had provided a quality education to a minority of African children. Bantu Education expanded primary school opportunities, mainly the early grades, but it offered a vastly inferior education. Until the 1970s, most African children did not progress past Grade 4. The NP also continued the discriminatory policies of earlier governments. In 1968 government spending per African child was 6 per cent of that spent on each white child. This amount gradually increased in the 1970s and 1980s, but spending on education for African, coloured and Indian children only became equal to white spending after the 1994 democratic elections.

Coloured and Indian schooling also expanded, particularly in the 1960s and 1970s. The state spent more money per child on coloured and Indian students than on African students, but this was still less than the spend on whites. As a result, there were higher numbers of coloureds and Indians employed in semi-skilled, skilled and white-collar work. The Indian middle class grew substantially. The coloured middle class also expanded, but many coloured workers remained in unskilled labour.

The various state policies helped to entrench racial inequality. In 1975 rural African households made up nearly 90 per cent of the poorest South Africans. Whites made up only 2 per cent of people in the lowest income bracket. In contrast, 95 per cent of people in the highest income bracket were white, and only 2 per cent were African. Most coloured and Indian households earned less than whites but more than unskilled and semi-skilled urban African workers.

By the early 1970s the African rural population could no longer rely on agriculture to meet their basic needs. Malnutrition was common in the bantustans, which also had high infant mortality rates. People needed wage labour to survive. The NP had successfully created a pool of unskilled labour desperate for work. This happened just as the economy's labour needs were changing. The growing manufacturing, financial, commercial and services sectors needed less unskilled and more skilled labour. Farm mechanisation also

---

30 Refer to Theme 3 – The History of Schooling in South Africa – for more information about education in South Africa.

resulted in white farmers requiring fewer unskilled workers, and as a result many African and coloured farm workers lost their jobs. South Africa's economic growth also began to slow and decline from the mid-1970s and throughout the 1980s. The NP had created a surplus unskilled labour force, and by the 1980s the struggling economy could not absorb these extra workers. Unemployment and poverty increased as a result.[31]

LIMITED REFORMS: TOO LITTLE, TOO LATE

During the 1970s and 1980s the apartheid government tried to implement some reforms to address the skills shortages and to meet the political demands of the resistance movements. Some of the labour regulations were relaxed. Trade unions with African members were finally recognised in 1979. New unions were born and some older ones grew their membership; they began to win better wages for their members. The colour bar and pass laws were applied less strictly and, in 1986, were finally abolished. A small number of black people started to move into lower- and middle-management positions in the larger corporations.

The state tried to meet the need for skilled labour by expanding African urban education during the 1970s and 1980s. For example, in 1972 there were only eight secondary schools in Soweto, but by 1976 there were twenty. Black schooling expanded further in the 1980s. More black children reached high school than ever before, but dropout rates remained high and the quality of matric passes for African children was very low.

The changes largely benefited the urban blacks who were skilled and employed. They did not help the masses of unskilled and unemployed people. Intra-racial inequality – that is, inequality within the black or white group – intensified. The African middle class expanded very gradually, but poverty continued to be a way of life for most people in urban areas. It was even worse in rural areas where there were few job opportunities for unskilled workers. By the 1980s most households in the bantustans relied almost completely on migrant labour remittances.

The state's limited reforms were unsuccessful in addressing the poverty and inequality experienced by the black population. It was also not able to address the shortage of skilled labour or to suppress the growing mass resistance to apartheid. Schooling, particularly for Africans, remained woefully inferior. South Africa's economic growth declined in the 1980s. Mining, agriculture and manufacturing shed jobs throughout the 1980s and 1990s. Black unemployment increased steadily throughout the 1980s as the demand for unskilled labour decreased and as economic growth declined.

When the African National Congress (ANC) came to power in 1994, it inherited a deeply unequal society divided along racial and class lines. In 1993, the richest 10 per cent of South Africans earned about a hundred times more that the poorest 10 per cent. Legally, white privileges were removed, but most whites were now part of the middle class and no longer relied on the state for welfare or economic protection.

---

31 Refer to Theme 1 – The South African Economy – for more information about South Africa's economy.

Poverty is still rife in South Africa, as seen in this photograph from 2018, showing a blind man begging for donations from pedestrians.

Poverty and Inequality after 1994

Inter-racial inequality – that is, inequality between whites and blacks – has declined since 1994, while intra-racial inequality has continued to grow. In 2015 there were about 21 000 white millionaires, while the number of black millionaires had increased to about 17 000. However, in 2016, more than 30 million South Africans (55 per cent of the population) lived on less than R779 per person a month.

Poverty in South Africa remained racialised long after the coming of democracy in 1994. About 47 per cent of the African population and 32 per cent of the coloured population lived in poverty in 2016. Less than 5 per cent of Indians and less than 1 per cent of whites lived in poverty in the same year. The white population's economic privileges were no longer legally protected, but most whites were able to enjoy the economic advantages of the middle and upper classes. This included access to quality education, private pension funds and inherited wealth. This helps the white population to maintain its position of relative privilege. Although it is difficult to define precisely what the middle class is, it is generally accepted that it has expanded as many hundreds of thousands of Africans, coloureds and Indians moved into positions in the public service, private business and the professions that were previously inaccessible to them. By 2015 many black households that considered themselves middle class remained economically vulnerable. Few black people had inherited wealth from their parents, and so, while a black and a white person might earn the same salary, the latter would generally be wealthier because of his or her accumulated wealth. Moreover, many black earners found themselves having to provide for poorer family members outside their immediate household because they were more likely than whites to have poorer relatives.

The white governments of the twentieth century purposely promoted white people's welfare and actively hindered the economic development of all other groups, especially Africans. A long history of discriminatory policies has entrenched poverty and inequality in post-apartheid South Africa. Addressing these injustices remains one of the biggest challenges faced by post-1994 governments.

THEME 4: DISCUSSION QUESTIONS

1. What was the most significant or interesting information you learned from the reading? Share this with your discussion group and explain why you found it interesting.

2. South Africa is one of the most unequal societies in the world. How did white domination and policies of the last 150 years contribute to creating this unequal society?

3. If you had to choose, which three actions do you think had the largest impact on South Africa's inequality and poverty? Why did you choose these three? Feel free to refer to the table from Activity 2.2 to help you devise an answer.

4. Consider your own family's wealth or poverty. How did some of the actions of previous governments contribute to your family's current situation? Do you know any specific examples from your own family history that illustrate how segregation and apartheid affected your family? How should we deal with this legacy left by apartheid in our families? How should we react to this legacy in other families?

5. South Africa spends a large part of its national budget on social development and welfare – for example, on education, health and social grants. However, inequality and poverty are not being significantly reduced. Why do you think this is so? To what extent are historical obstacles preventing us from reducing inequality in our country? To what extent should we hold the post-1994 government accountable for South Africa's continued inequality and poverty?

6. What do you think about the role of land expropriation in reducing poverty? To what extent would land expropriation help to lessen poverty and inequality in South Africa? If you were in government today, how would you tackle this issue? Provide reasons for your answers.

THEME 4: ADDITIONAL READINGS

Online readings

Black Sash Advice Office (1978) Interim Report, February to August 1978 (section on Unemployment and Apartheid). *South African History Online.* http://www.sahistory.org.za/archive/unemployment-and-apartheid.

Nattrass, Nicoli and Jeremy Seekings (2011) The Economy and Poverty in the Twentieth Century. In *The Cambridge History of South Africa*, Volume 2, *1885–1994.* (Chapter 11, pp. 518–72). http://www.sahistory.org.za/sites/default/files/file%20uploads%20/robert_ross_anne_kelk_mager_bill_nasson_the_cabook4me.org_.pdf.

Plaatje, Solomon Tshekisho (1916) *Native Life in South Africa, Before And Since the European Rebellion*, 4th edn. https://www.sahistory.org.za/sites/default/files/Native%20Life%20in%20South%20Africa_0.pdf.

Seekings, Jeremy and Nicoli Nattrass (2005) *Class, Race and Inequality in South Africa.* New Haven, CT: Yale University Press. http://www.sahistory.org.za/sites/default/files/file%20uploads%20/professor_jeremy_seekings_nicoli_nattrass_classbookos.org_.pdf.

White Workers and the Colour Bar (2012) *South African History Online*, 3 April 2012, updated 15 November 2012. http://www.sahistory.org.za/luli-35.

Books

Feinstein, Charles (2005) *An Economic History of South Africa: Conquest, Discrimination and Development.* Cambridge: Cambridge University Press.

Giliomee, H. and B. Mbenga (ed). (2007) *A New History of South Africa.* Cape Town: Tafelberg. (Chapter 11: Diverse Communities, pp. 254–82; and Afrikaner Economic Mobilisation, pp. 291–3)

Theme Five

Life under Apartheid: Urban and Rural Experiences

Racial categorisation and discrimination have played defining roles in South Africa's history. Legal racial discrimination existed long before the National Party (NP) came to power in 1948 and implemented its policy of apartheid. Well-known apartheid laws often built on existing laws and practices in order to take racial segregation even further.

The Population Registration Act of 1950 meant that every person in South Africa had to be registered as a member of a specific so-called racial group: Native (later changed to Bantu), European (later white), coloured, or Indian (later Asian). A person's classification directly affected how they experienced life under apartheid. An unskilled black worker had very different experiences from those of an unskilled white worker. People within the same group also had very different experiences of apartheid, depending on where they lived and what work they did. An African farm worker led a very different life from an African teacher in a city. Theme 5 explores some of these different experiences as we examine what life was like under apartheid.

Rural and urban experiences are discussed separately in this theme, but in reality the relationship between black rural and urban residents was complex. During the early apartheid years (1950s and 1960s), most Africans living in urban areas were first-generation immigrants from the reserves or the farms. Many were migrant workers who sent remittances home to their families, and many saw their time in the towns as temporary. Unjust laws that affected rural populations also affected people in the urban areas.

By the late 1960s and 1970s many African people were second-generation immigrants. They had been born in the urban areas, and saw themselves as permanent urban residents. This meant that their ties to their rural families weakened. However, migrant labour continued throughout apartheid, and remittances became more and more important to families in the bantustans (or homelands). Therefore, there was still a deep connection between many urban and rural people throughout the apartheid years.

RURAL LIFE

Betterment planning in the reserves and bantustans

In the early 1900s, African society was largely centred around agriculture and cattle. The 1913 Natives Land Act prevented Africans from owning or renting land outside the reserves. The natural resources of the reserves deteriorated quickly as more and more people were forced to farm on a limited amount of land. From as early as 1918, the average reserve family produced less than half of their basic food requirements from agriculture. Malnutrition was widespread by the 1940s. Many people were forced to leave the reserves and become migrant workers so that they could feed their families.

The government was forced to recognise the poor agricultural conditions in the reserves. The United Party under Jan Smuts implemented 'betterment planning' in the 1940s. These schemes tried to rehabilitate the natural resources of the reserves. The NP continued betterment planning when it came to power in 1948.

Betterment included various measures. Betterment planners believed that overgrazing by cattle was a major cause of the land's deterioration. They ignored the central role that cattle played in African culture, and forced families to reduce their cattle herds, thereby directly affecting their wealth. People were forced to cull or to sell off their cattle at very low prices, often to white commercial farmers. The apartheid state intensified this practice when it passed stock limitation laws in the 1950s, which limited the number of cattle Africans could own. Betterment planning also included compulsory cattle dipping and vaccination, but people were so suspicious of the state's motives that they often refused to participate in these schemes.

Land was reorganised and redistributed under betterment schemes. Areas were fenced, forests were planted, and dams were built. People lost access to land without sufficient compensation. In Witzieshoek (today known as Phuthaditjhaba) families normally ploughed between 17 and 26 hectares of land. Betterment planning limited families to plots of 1 to 3 hectares. The chief and headmen allocated the new strips of land and were accused of choosing areas with the best soil or largest areas for themselves and their supporters.

Betterment planning also included 'villagisation'; planners believed this allowed for a more efficient layout and use of land. The state forcibly removed people from their scattered homesteads and resettled them in denser villages, often far away from their fields. Villagisation broke up established communities and social structures, as people were often settled next to strangers. This created social insecurity. In places like Nzongisa in the Transkei, crimes like theft and trespassing increased. The number of people forced to move as a result of betterment was incredibly high. One study suggests that over a million people were moved forcibly in Natal alone as a result of betterment planning.

The betterment policy was bitterly resented by rural populations. Communities protested in different ways. Some merely ignored the new plans, and cut through fences and chopped down trees for firewood. Others openly protested, and the state had to call in the military and the police. Communities were also angered by the state working with chiefs who took the side of government instead of their own people. The Bantu Authorities Act of 1951 formalised this process. Many people saw the Act as a way for the apartheid state to use the chiefs and headmen to force through betterment. Fierce and violent protests and rebellions against the Bantu Authorities Act took place throughout the 1950s and early 1960s in areas such as Zululand, Zeerust, Sekhukhuneland and Pondoland. Part of the hatred directed at the new Act was its close link in many people's minds to betterment planning.

In places like the Transkei, betterment planning slowed in the 1960s. By the 1970s it was replaced to a large extent with government showcase projects such as irrigation schemes and tea plantations. Most of these failed and did not bring the desired development to the bantustans. In fact, by the 1970s agriculture had virtually collapsed in the bantustans and most households relied almost completely on migrant labour remittances for their basic needs.

Poverty and hardship in the bantustans

Although it had been growing before, the population density of the bantustans doubled between 1970 and 1980. This was partly due to natural population growth, but also to influx controls that prevented people from leaving the bantustans to move to the cities. But the over-populated bantustans experienced even more overcrowding as thousands of people were forcibly moved there from the mid-1960s until the 1980s. The bantustans became dumping grounds on which the government settled the 'surplus' African population (those whose labour was not required by employers outside the bantustans) in special relocation camps.

Conditions in these relocation camps varied, but were generally terrible. Some consisted of small, poorly constructed huts or houses, while others had only tents. Services like adequate sewerage and piped water were either very basic or non-existent. Most had no educational or recreational facilities. Camps like Sada in the Ciskei, which housed 40 000 people, had a clinic but no permanent doctor. Others lacked even more basic needs such as access to water, firewood and shelter.

Many families in the camps had no income beyond a state pension, which was lower for Africans than for other black groups and much lower than for whites. Families had no land to farm. In these camps, one out of every four children died of malnutrition or disease before their first birthday. One of these camps, Dimbaza in the Ciskei, became known and condemned by the international community through the work of the anti-apartheid movements, which produced a widely distributed movie named *Last Grave in Dimbaza*. As a result, a few more resources were funnelled to some of these camps by the state, but others remained in desperate poverty.

While the conditions in the relocation camps were horrendous, even in established areas life in the bantustans fell far below the standard of living experienced by the white minority and even by the urban African population in South Africa. By the mid-1970s there were only 54 doctors in all of the ten bantustans. Malnutrition was not limited to the resettlement camps. One 1973 study estimated that about 40 per cent of children under the age of ten died of malnutrition or malnutrition-related causes in some Transkei districts.

A very small African elite benefited from the creation of the bantustans. For the majority of African people, though, life in the bantustans was characterised by hardship and poverty. Life on the white-owned farms outside the bantustans was also difficult, particularly after the apartheid state came to power.

Life on white-owned farms

In the early years of apartheid, between 2.2 and 3 million Africans lived on white-owned farms outside the bantustans. Of these, about 800 000 were employed by white farmers on a permanent basis. Except in the Western Cape where coloured workers predominated, the overwhelming majority of farm workers were African. In 1950, nation-wide, about 100 000 permanent workers and another 100 000 casual labourers on farms were coloureds or Indians.

Conditions for farm workers on white-owned farms were notoriously bad. Farm wages were much lower than mining or urban wages. The workers were frequently verbally and physically abused by their employers. Many farmers used black children as labourers, keeping them out of school for extended periods. The difference between the living conditions of most white owners and those of black workers was stark by the late 1960s. Whites had access to electricity, piped water and sewerage, large and sturdy farmhouses, and good education for their children. Most farm workers lived in huts and shacks with no electricity and had little or no access to piped water or modern toilets. Some African families experienced such harsh conditions that they voluntarily left white-owned farms to settle in the bantustan relocation camps.

Most black people living on white-owned farms were wage labourers, but some also had direct access to land. Many white farmers struggled to attract labour to their farms in the first half of the twentieth century. Unable to compete with urban wages, white farmers often entered into relations where they provided black families with access to land in return for their labour (labour tenants), or for cash (cash tenants), or for a share of the harvest (sharecroppers). Cash tenancy and sharecropping by Africans were outlawed by the 1913 Natives Land Act, but still continued in many areas into the 1950s. Some families moved from farm to farm looking for better contracts, while others lived on a specific farm for generations. A few sharecroppers became successful farmers. One such farmer, Kas Maine, whose life has been described in a well-known book,[32] made a profit from sharecropping in 1948 that was equal to a teacher's yearly salary.

The apartheid state clamped down on the practices of sharecropping and cash tenancy. It also made labour tenancy illegal. Many African farmers thus became wage

---

32 Charles van Onselen, *The Seed is Mine: The Life of Kas Maine, a South African Sharecropper, 1894–1985,* New York, Hill and Wang, 1996.

Kite flying near Phuthaditjhaba, Qwa Qwa. 1 May 1989. Source: Courtesy The David Goldblatt Legacy Trust and Goodman Gallery

labourers. The apartheid state also focused on mechanising white farms. As a result, white farmers no longer needed as many unskilled workers. All these developments caused great numbers of black families to be evicted from the white-owned farms. Over a million Africans were evicted in this way and resettled in the bantustans.

About 100 000 coloured farm workers lost their jobs owing to mechanisation during apartheid. Unlike Africans, they were not moved to the bantustans, and could travel freely to the towns and cities. Here, however, they competed with African unskilled workers, who were usually paid less, and so many ended up as unemployed. Coloured workers on wine farms also faced the legacy of the 'dop system'. Under this system workers received a certain amount of wine as part of their wages. In a context of hardship and poverty, this contributed to widespread alcoholism in both adults and children. As late as 2020, South Africa had one of the highest rates of foetal alcohol syndrome[33] in the world; it is particularly prevalent in the Western Cape and Northern Cape.

The apartheid state forcibly removed African families living on mission land, tenants on white-owned farms or tenants on land owned by Africans outside the bantustans. The

---

33 Physical and mental damage in a child caused by alcohol exposure while in the womb. The symptoms include learning disabilities, bone and joint deformities, heart defects and hyperactivity.

patches of land occupied by these groups of people were referred to by the government as 'black spots'. Rural removals affected even more than those in urban areas. Most of the African-owned land had been bought before the 1913 Land Act came into effect. Only people whom the government recognised as legal landowners before they were forcibly moved were eligible for any compensation. Tenants and farm workers received no compensation when they were moved to bantustans, and they were often unable to take all their personal possessions with them. Between 1960 to 1983, about 3.5 million people were relocated as the result of forced removals from the towns and the countryside.

INFLUX CONTROL: PASSES AND LABOUR BUREAUS

Although the apartheid state did not create the pass laws, the National Party organised them into a unified system, extended them and enforced them much more strictly. Before apartheid, only African men needed to carry passes, but from the 1950s the government forced women to carry passes. A pass book was an identity document that stated whether a person was present legally in a 'white' area. An African person without the necessary permission could stay legally in an urban area only for 72 hours.

People in the bantustans could not travel freely to the cities to look for work. They had to apply to the local labour bureau (which issued passes) for a job and had to accept the first job offered, if any jobs were available. Africans had to carry their passes at all times and had to present them on demand. Hundreds of thousands of people were arrested and imprisoned for pass offences each year.

Some Africans had the right to be permanent residents in towns if they met certain conditions. These were set out in section 10 of the Native Laws Amendment Act of 1952. Only a person born in an urban area and who had lived there continuously for at least ten years or who had lived and worked continuously in an urban area for fifteen years was eligible for section 10 rights. Their dependants had the same rights.

Regardless of the strict policing, many people, desperate for work, continued to migrate to the towns and cities during the apartheid era. However, African urbanisation slowed during the 1960s and 1970s largely because of the strict enforcement of the pass laws. As apartheid began to weaken in the face of people's resistance, urbanisation once again increased during the 1980s. The pass laws were finally abolished in 1986.

URBAN LIFE

The housing shortage in the cities

Before the 1940s most African workers in urban areas lived in single-sex hostels or in servants' quarters on white people's properties. A minority lived in houses in segregated locations such as Alexandra or in multiracial neighbourhoods like Sophiatown in Johannesburg, Cato Manor in Durban or District Six in Cape Town. The rapid urbanisation of the 1940s caused many of these areas to become rapidly overcrowded. Living standard were poor; there were few services or amenities; landlords charged

Black men lining up for pass books, Johannesburg, 1960. Source: AP Photo

exorbitant rents; and there were high levels of violence.

Africans were not allowed to buy property and were limited as to where they could live. Neither private employers nor the white government built new accommodation during this period. In response to the housing shortage, squatter movements became prominent in the mid-1940s. The most well-known movement was led by James 'Sofasonke' Mpanza in Soweto. By 1950, over 100 000 people lived in shacks on the Witwatersrand, about 50 000 in Durban and about 150 000 in Cape Town.

Cities like Johannesburg tried to counter the growing squatter movements by making more land available for occupation by black people. However, the apartheid state of the 1950s demolished the large informal settlements as it pursued its policy of strict residential segregation. Africans were to be settled in new townships like Soweto, which were located on the outskirts of cities. By 1958 about 100 000 new houses had been built.

The new townships were carefully planned so that they were clearly separate from the white urban areas, and could be easily patrolled and isolated in the event of a rebellion. While many new houses were built, they were still not enough to meet the accommodation needs of the urban black population. Accommodation continued to be overcrowded, and areas continued to be poorly serviced and lacking in amenities such as schools, libraries and parks. Symptoms of social despair, such as alcoholism, domestic abuse of women and children, and violent crime, featured prominently in the townships.

Lack of adequate housing and services for blacks in urban areas remained an issue throughout the apartheid period. By the end of the 1970s informal settlements, housing up to 500 000 people, had grown on the edges of the cities. Homes continued to be destroyed by the government and people forcibly relocated into the 1980s.

While many black people struggled to find decent accommodation throughout the apartheid period, the general living conditions of the white population improved between the 1950s and the 1980s. Apartheid saw many more whites move into the middle class, but the benefits were not shared equally. Inequality within the white population increased, particularly in the 1980s. Despite this, by the 1980s most whites lived in houses or flats in low-density, well-serviced suburbs marked by low levels of violent crime. Many houses had gardens and even swimming pools. It was the norm for a white family to employ at least one African or coloured domestic worker.

Forced removals

Most suburbs were officially racially segregated before apartheid, but by 1950 almost every town had an area where both black and white lived together. The NP government passed the Group Areas Act in 1950. It insisted on strict residential segregation throughout all urban areas. From the mid-1950s the apartheid state began to break up multiracial neighbourhoods and forcibly remove people to racially segregated townships. Sophiatown in Johannesburg is a well-known case from the mid-1950s. The area was declared a white suburb and callously renamed Triomf (Triumph). In Johannesburg Africans were forcibly moved to the new township of Soweto while coloureds were moved to locations such as Eldorado Park, and Indians to Lenasia.

The forced removals in terms of the Group Areas Act began to take place on a massive scale in the 1960s and continued until the 1980s. Between 1960 and 1983, over 850 000 people were forcibly removed as a result of the Group Areas policy. Most of those affected were coloured and Indian people. One out of every four coloured people, and one out of every six Indian people, were affected by these removals. On the other hand, only one out of 666 whites were forced to move as a result of the Group Areas Act. The forced removals included the 65 000 coloured people compelled to leave District Six in Cape Town in the late 1960s. In Durban, at around the same time, African residents of Cato Manor were forcibly resettled in KwaMashu, Lamontville and Umlazi, while Indian people were moved to Chatsworth.

Forced removals saw neighbourhoods, and sometimes even families, broken up and settled in new areas, often without much infrastructure. Furthermore, the new townships were usually far away from the urban areas where people worked, and they lacked adequate transport facilities to get residents to their places of work. The lack of established social ties played a large role in the high crime rates of the new townships.

From the mid-1970s the apartheid state tried to gain the support of coloured and Indian people as resistance to apartheid grew. It focused on providing better housing and amenities for them, including education and health care. This contributed to the upward mobility and generally better living conditions experienced by the coloured and Indian population compared with Africans. The Indian middle class expanded significantly. While many coloured workers remained in manual labour, the number of coloureds employed in semi-professional and white-collar jobs tripled between 1965 and 1985. However, many working-class coloureds and Indians remained poor as they lived in dilapidated neighbourhoods with high levels of crime.

THE CHANGING NATURE OF LIFE UNDER APARTHEID

The African, coloured and Indian youth of the 1970s and 1980s had very different childhood experiences from those of their parents. Their expectations and demands differed from those of the generation of the 1950s and 1960s. By the 1980s many urban townships violently challenged the apartheid regime and its representatives.

The late 1970s and 1980s townships witnessed many stay-aways, boycotts, strikes and marches organised by trade unions, civic organisations and youth groups against the apartheid state. Schooling for Africans in many parts of the country, especially in urban areas, virtually collapsed as students demanded an end to apartheid education. The protests also spread to the rural areas, including many bantustan schools and universities (see also Theme 3).

A partial and then a national State of Emergency was declared during the 1980s. The military and police tried to suppress the protest action and patrolled the townships, often raiding schools and homes. Protesters attacked and burned symbols of the apartheid state, such as the homes of black town councillors and police officers, as well as government buildings. The violence between the United Democratic Front (UDF) and the African National Congress (ANC), on the one side, and the Inkatha Freedom Party (IFP) and various vigilante groups (both secretly backed by the apartheid state), on the other, increased throughout the 1980s and 1990s, resulting in the deaths of thousands of people on both sides.

The police arrested and tortured thousands of people, including school-aged students during this politically turbulent time. The country-wide activism continued into the 1990s, until the fall of apartheid.

CONCLUSION

The 1980s and early 1990s saw many of the early apartheid laws changed or scrapped. Petty apartheid laws like the banning of racially mixed marriages, the use of separate amenities, and the pass laws were scrapped in the mid-1980s. The 1913 Natives Land Act and the Group Areas Act were finally abolished in 1991. By 1994 all racially discriminatory laws had been abolished.

After 1994, when all racial discrimination had been eliminated in the eyes of the law, the legacies of past injustices continued to be felt in the everyday lives of the many ordinary black South Africans who still did not have access to adequate housing, education and health services, jobs and land. Despite the efforts and successes of the new democratic government – as well as of political and civil organisations and individuals – poverty, unemployment and inequality persisted well into the post-apartheid era. Efforts to overcome these challenges remain central to creating a free, fair and equitable society.

THEME 5: DISCUSSION QUESTIONS

1. What was the most interesting information you learned from the reading? Did you learn anything significant that you did not know about before? Share your thoughts with your group.

2. Do you, or anybody you know (parents, grandparents, teachers), have any memories of what life was like under apartheid? Do your memories confirm or contradict any of the information presented in the chapter? Share your thoughts, memories and stories with your group.

3. Although apartheid discriminated against all people of colour, we can see that various people had different experiences of apartheid based on their location, time period and 'racial' categorisation. What are some of the main differences between the experiences of the following groups:
    a. of the people in the bantustans compared with those on white-owned farms?
    b. of the rural population compared with the urban population?
    c. of apartheid in the 1960s compared with the 1980s?
    d. of the African, coloured, Indian and white populations?

4. The aim of betterment planning was to rehabilitate the strained natural resources of the reserves. Why did people resist betterment? What were the major problems with betterment? Why was betterment doomed to fail under apartheid?

5. What strategies were used by the government to create divisions among the black population under apartheid?

6. Sophiatown, District Six and Cato Manor are well-known examples of forced removals. Do you think the farm and 'black spot' evictions are as well known? Are many people aware of the bantustan relocation camps? Why or why not? How does this reflect on our society's historical knowledge and memory?

THEME 5: ADDITIONAL READINGS

Online readings

Badat, Saleem (2012) Resistance and Banishment in Witzieshoek. In *The Forgotten People: Political Banishment under Apartheid* (extract published on *South African History Online*). https://www.sahistory.org.za/topic/resistance-and-banishment-witzieshoek.

Butler, Jeffrey, Robert I. Rotberg and John Adams (1977) *The Black Homelands of South Africa: The Political and Economic Development of Bophuthatswana and*

KwaZulu. Perspectives on Southern Africa 21. Berkeley, CA: University of California Press. https://publishing.cdlib.org/ucpressebooks/view?docId=ft0489n6d5;brand=eschol.

History of Cato Manor (2011) *South African History Online* (blog), 16 March 2011. https://www.sahistory.org.za/places/cato-manor.

Mbeki, Govan (1984 [1964]) *The Peasants' Revolt.* London: International Defence and Aid Fund. (Chapter 9: Resistance and Rebellion). https://www.sahistory.org.za/topic/james-sofasonke-mpanza-and-johannesburg%E2%80%99s-squatter-movement-1938-1947.

James Sofasonke Mpanza and Johannesburg's Squatter Movement, 1938 to 1947. *South African History Online* (blog), 21 January 2013. https://www.sahistory.org.za/topic/james-sofasonke-mpanza-and-johannesburg%E2%80%99s-squatter-movement-1938-1947.

Platzky, Laurine and Cherryl Walker (1985) *The Surplus People: Forced Removals in South Africa.* Johannesburg: Ravan Press. https://www.datafirst.uct.ac.za/dataportal/index.php/catalog/581.

Posel, Deborah (2011) The Apartheid Project, 1948–1970. In *The Cambridge History of South Africa*, Volume 2: *1885–1994.* Cambridge: Cambridge University Press. http://www.sahistory.org.za/sites/default/files/file%20uploads%20/robert_ross_anne_kelk_mager_bill_nasson_the_cabook4me.org_.pdf.

Ross, Robert, Anne Kelk Mager and Bill Nasson (eds.) (2011) *The Cambridge History of South Africa*, Volume 2: *1885–1994.* Cambridge: Cambridge University Press. http://www.sahistory.org.za/sites/default/files/file%20uploads%20/robert_ross_anne_kelk_mager_bill_nasson_the_cabook4me.org_.pdf.

Seekings, Jeremy and Nicoli Nattrass (2005) *Class, Race and Inequality in South Africa.* New Haven, CT: Yale University Press. (Chapters 2 and 3). http://www.sahistory.org.za/sites/default/files/file%20uploads%20/professor_jeremy_seekings_nicoli_nattrass_classbookos.org_.pdf.

Online visual sources

Curling, Chris and Pascoe Macfarlane (1974) *Last Grave at Dimbaza.* Film produced by Nana Mahomo, Antonia Caccia and Andrew Tsehiana, 1974. https://youtu.be/aHH5sA-GB20.

Forced Removals in South Africa (n.d.). http://overcomingapartheid.msu.edu/multimedia.php?id=65-259-6.

Books

Desmond, Cosmas (1971) *The Discarded People: An Account of African Resettlement in South Africa.* Harmondsworth: Penguin Books.

Gibbs, Timothy (2014) *Mandela's Kinsmen: Nationalist Elites and Apartheid's First Bantustans.* Johannesburg: Jacana Media.

Giliomee, H. and B. Mbenga (eds) (2007) *New History of South Africa.* Cape Town: Tafelberg. (Chapters 4 and 14)

Theme Six

Women's Struggles

Throughout the twentieth century, women across the world faced social, political, legal and economic discrimination, and even more so before that. For black women in South Africa this discrimination overlapped with racial and class discrimination. There are a number of ways to approach the study of women's struggles.

This theme sets out to introduce readers to a better understanding of the role women played in South Africa's political history in the twentieth and early twenty-first centuries. It will highlight some important events and movements, but readers are encouraged to further explore women's roles, struggles and victories in South Africa by consulting the Additional Readings list.

WOMEN'S STRUGGLES BEFORE APARTHEID, 1910–1948

Women's participation in political organisations

Most national organisations set up to challenge racial discrimination in South Africa in the late nineteenth and early twentieth centuries were established and led exclusively by men. The South African Native National Congress (SANNC), the forerunner of the African National Congress (ANC), did not allow women to become full voting members. When Dr Kesaveloo Goonam (the first Indian female doctor in South Africa) requested that women be represented in the Natal Indian Congress (NIC), she was told that Indian women were not advanced enough.

The Communist Party of South Africa (CPSA) differed from organisations like the ANC and NIC in this sense. From its establishment in 1921 it was, theoretically at least, committed to gender equality. Women could, and did, become full members from the start. The CPSA did not place a major focus on women's emancipation, especially in the 1920s when patriarchal attitudes were very strong in the organisation, which was dominated by men. Yet, since gender equality was important in the class struggle, it was one of the few parties that did commit to this as a basic principle. The CPSA provided an opportunity for women to take up leadership positions. Women such as Josie Mpama (also spelled Palmer), Ray Alexander and Hilda Watts gained prominence in the CPSA in the 1930s and 1940s.

Attitudes towards women's roles in the formal political sphere changed as the twentieth century progressed. In 1930 white women gained the right to vote. However, this happened largely because Prime Minister Hertzog wanted to add more white voters to the voters' roll, thereby decreasing the voting strength of male black voters. But it was not only white women who gained recognition in public politics. Charlotte Maxeke, head of the Bantu Women's League (BWL), was invited to be a speaker at the All African Convention of 1935. In 1943 the ANC allowed women to become full voting members, and in the same year the ANC Women's League (ANCWL) was established. In 1956 Lilian Ngoyi became the first woman elected to the National Executive Committee (NEC) of the ANC. Women were now seen as an important sector of society from which to recruit and mobilise members. Furthermore, one of the ANC's new aims from the 1940s was to improve the status of African women.

Changes were not limited to the ANC. In 1946 Dr Goonam was elected vice-president of the NIC. As time passed, more women assumed leadership responsibilities, although they remained a clear minority in leadership positions. However, this did not mean that women excluded themselves from the political sphere, particularly when political decisions affected their economic welfare.

During the Indian passive resistance campaign of 1913, inspired by Mohandas Gandhi, who was living in South Africa at the time, Indian women joined Indian men in defying discriminatory laws; many were arrested. African women participated in the anti-pass campaigns of the Orange Free State in 1913 (see below) as well as in later anti-pass campaigns, such as on the Witwatersrand in 1919 and in Potchefstroom in December 1929, when police fired on demonstrators and killed 100 people. Some examples of women's political involvement in the 1940s include the squatter movements, the 1943 Alexandra bus boycott and the 1946 Indian passive resistance campaign. Women did not dominate the leadership in these campaigns, but they were part of the grassroots mobilisation that often determined their success.

Women strike out on their own

Women were not only limited to supportive roles in political activities or in political forums run by men, especially when political decisions impacted on women's economic position. One of the most significant examples here is the 1913 anti-pass campaigns in the Orange Free State. Inspired by the Indian passive resistance campaign that took place in the same year, African and coloured women in Bloemfontein mobilised across ethnic and class lines and conducted an anti-pass campaign, long before the ANC looked to mass mobilisation as a weapon of struggle.

Like African men, African women in the Orange Free State were required to carry permits that had to be renewed monthly. Passes had long been required and, in fact, women's organised resistance to carrying them dated back to the 1890s. Matters came

African and coloured women protesting against pass laws in Bloemfontein, 1913. Source: South African History Online

to a head on 29 May 1913. After a series of letters, petitions and deputations (including to the National government), which were all ignored, a group of Bloemfontein women marched to the police station where they tore up and burned their passes. Eighty women were arrested. On the day they were due to appear in court, 600 women marched from Waaihoek, the township outside Bloemfontein, to show their solidarity with the arrested women. Some brandished sticks and a number of them were promptly arrested and found guilty, but they refused to pay the fines and chose to serve jail sentences instead.

The incident sparked similar protests in other major Orange Free State towns. The jails became so full that women had to take turns serving their sentences. Dr Abdurahman of the African People's Organisation (APO) applauded the women for their action and pointed out that it reflected poorly on men: 'We, the men who are supposed to be made of sterner stuff than the weaker sex, might well hide our faces in shame, and ponder in some secluded spot over the heroic stand made by the daughters of Africa ...'[34]

The Bantu Women's League, headed by Charlotte Maxeke (who supported the campaign), was formed in response to these protests and continued to agitate against passes for African women. Maxeke met with Prime Minister Louis Botha in 1918. Although the law was not changed, Botha pressured the Orange Free State provincial government to relax the enforcement of passes. Some argue that this campaign played a significant role in causing provincial and national authorities to treat passes for women with greater caution in the following decades.

---

34 Nomboniso Gasa (ed.), *Women in South African History: Basus'iimbokodo, Bawel'imilambo / They Remove Boulders and Cross Rivers*, Cape Town: HSRC Press, 2007, p. 140.

Women and the trade union movement before apartheid

In the 1910s and 1920s most women were occupied with duties in the home. Less than a quarter of white, coloured and Indian women were involved in wage employment and only ten per cent of African women worked for wages. Most women workers were in domestic service. Only 7 per cent of women workers were involved in manufacturing by the mid-1920s, and most of these were white. Women only made up 12 per cent of the industrial labour force in 1925. Many were not unionised and the concerns of women workers were largely ignored. Some changes began to take place in the 1930s and 1940s.

Women in industry were mainly white in the 1930s, but by the 1940s more coloured women entered this sphere of employment, together with some African women. Very few Indian women took up formal employment at this time. Women were still channelled into work traditionally associated with their domestic roles. For this reason, while women made up just over a tenth of the industrial labour force overall, they did begin to dominate certain industries, such as the textile and food industries. Industry-based unions in these areas were largely made up of women.

The Garment Workers' Union (GWU) in the Transvaal and the Food and Canning Workers' Union (FCWU) in the Cape were two important unions during this period. They played a significant role in empowering women by providing a platform for them to voice their grievances, and also helped them to develop their organisational and leadership skills through union activities. Furthermore, together with support from the Communist Party, the unions enabled more women to understand the links between the oppression they faced at work and in their homes. Lilian Ngoyi (from the GWU) and Frances Baard (from FCWU) were both active in the ANC Women's League. Lucy Mvelase, who was elected vice-president of South African Congress of Trade Unions (SACTU) in 1955, came from the GWU.

The greater involvement of women in trade unions, together with the extension of full membership to women in national political organisations, helped increase women's awareness and formal participation around issues of gender, class and race. With both black and white members, unions like the FCWU and GWU assisted the growth of class and gender solidarity across racial lines. The links created between female trade union members, the CPSA and the ANCWL helped lay the foundations for the development of the Federation of South African Women (FEDSAW), a national women's movement, in the 1950s.

WOMEN RESIST APARTHEID, 1948–1990

Women during early apartheid

When FEDSAW was established in 1954, it adopted the Women's Charter. The preamble to the Women's Charter states: 'We, the women of South Africa, wives and mothers, working women and housewives, African, Indian, European and Coloured, hereby declare our aim of striving for the removal of all laws, regulations, conventions and customs that discriminate against us as women, and that deprive us in any way of

June 1959. Police attacking the large women's demonstration in Cato Manor, Durban. Source: UWC Robben Island Mayibuye Archive.

our inherent right to the advantages, responsibilities and opportunities that society offers to any one section of the population.'[35] FEDSAW was the first successful independent national women's body that aimed to unite women across classes and races in their fight against gender, racial and class discrimination. While political movements like the ANC recognised women's oppression, they did not see women's emancipation as important as national liberation.

Probably the most well-known event in South African history involving women was the Women's March to the Union Buildings, which took place on 9 August 1956. Nowadays August 9 is commemorated every year as National Women's Day. The Women's March stands out for its scale, its organisational success, the multiracial character of its leadership, and the role it played (and continues to play) in South African women's political consciousness. The march was of great significance, and will be dealt with shortly below. However, this was not the only contribution of women to resistance to apartheid during the 1950s and 1960s.

Women were active in the Defiance Campaign,[36] which was launched in 1952.

35 Cherryl Walker, *Women and Resistance in South Africa*, London: Onyx Press, 1982, p. 279.

36 The Defiance Campaign was a campaign of non-violent resistance against apartheid conducted

Women like Florence Matomela, a leader in the ANC Women's League, participated on the day the Defiance Campaign began, and she was arrested later that year. When Bantu Education was introduced and many African parents kept their children out of school, women helped provide education in the alternative schools and clubs set up in the late 1950s. Women were involved in the 1959 Cato Manor riots, the 1960 anti-pass campaigns that resulted in the Sharpeville Massacre, and the 1962 rural women's revolt.

FEDSAW was active in preparing for the Congress of the People, held in 1955, which adopted the Freedom Charter. Its members helped collect demands from people across South Africa that would later be consolidated into the Freedom Charter. On the day of the congress, representatives of FEDSAW also read out the women's demands, based on the Women's Charter, that were included in the Freedom Charter. In 1956 women such as Ida Mntwana, Helen Joseph, Ruth First and Lilian Ngoyi were among the 156 Treason Trialists[37] arrested for their participation in the Congress of the People.

The 1956 Women's March was organised by FEDSAW. It brought together women from all the constituencies in the Congress Alliance – the ANC, South African Indian Congress, Coloured People's Congress, Congress of Democrats and SACTU. The 1956 march was not the first FEDSAW march. In fact, it was not the first women's march on the Union Buildings. The Black Sash, then a newly formed white women's anti-apartheid organisation, had marched to the Union Buildings in 1955 to protest against the government's attempts to remove coloured people from the common voters' roll. The Black Sash march inspired FEDSAW to use a similar tactic. In October 1955 FEDSAW organised about 2 000 women, deliberately chosen to represent South Africa's multiracial population, to fill the amphitheatre of the Union Buildings and present their petition against the government's plans to extend passes to women. The petition was ignored. This encouraged FEDSAW to organise a bigger march the following year, in which 20 000 women marched to Pretoria on 9 August 1956. They invited the Black Sash to join them, and some members of the Sash participated.

The march was the culmination of months of organisation, and the spirit and atmosphere of unity and determination among the women is often recalled. However, the march failed in its immediate aim. The government did not abolish passes for African women. But this was not the end of women's anti-pass campaigning, which continued throughout the 1950s and into the 1960s. After the 1956 march leaders of the ANC Women's League and FEDSAW were targeted and arrested by the police, and petitions from the march were used as evidence in the Treason Trial.

The banning of the ANC, and therefore the Women's League, in 1960 was accompanied by intense political suppression and caused FEDSAW to collapse by the early 1960s. Heavy state repression that targeted FEDSAW's leaders made it difficult for the organisation to regain its momentum.

The Black Sash was formed by a relatively small but active group of white women

---

by the ANC and allied organisations. See Chapter 13.

37 This was a major trial of 156 leaders of the Congress Alliance. All defendants were eventually acquitted of charges of treason against the state. See Chapter 13.

The Women's march, 9 August 1956. Marchers gather outside the Union Buildings in Pretoria.
Source: Jurgen Schadeberg

in 1955, initially to protest against the removal of the rights of coloureds to vote in parliamentary elections. It then changed its focus and continued to be active during the entire apartheid period, providing legal assistance to people, mainly women, affected by apartheid pass laws and raising public awareness of the forced removals of the 1970s and 1980s. It later broadened its membership to include black women. The Black Sash continues to be active in civil society today. It was one of the organisations that took the Department of Social Development to court in 2017 on behalf of social grant beneficiaries to ensure that they received their grants on time.

The mass resistance of the 1950s gave way to the underground and armed struggle of the 1960s. Resistance to apartheid continued during the 1960s but it was not coordinated on the same national scale of the 1950s and was quickly repressed. A group of Indian women marched to the Union Buildings in 1963 but they were met with violence; the police released dogs to attack the women, and beat them with batons. But there was a resurgence of political consciousness when the Black Consciousness Movement arose in the late 1960s and early 1970s. Internal political resistance grew throughout the 1970s and 1980s. While leadership positions in the resistance movements were still dominated by men, women continued to play an important role in challenging the state during the late apartheid period.

Women and late apartheid

New organisations were established in the 1970s that were aligned with the new Black Consciousness (BC) Movement. The Black Women's Federation was formed in 1975 with Fatima Meer as its president and Winnie Mandela as an executive member. Winnie Mandela also set up the Black Parents' Association in 1976. Both were banned in 1977 together with all other BC organisations. While neither of these two bodies had time to mature, they marked the revival of organised resistance politics at the time, in which women played a role.

Labour and student unrest became more prominent in the 1970s than in the earlier years, and women were not absent from these activities. Young women and girls took part in the student uprisings of 1976 and the school boycotts of the 1980s. The 1976 student uprising resulted in many young people, men and women, leaving South Africa to join the ANC and the Pan Africanist Congress (PAC) in exile. The ranks of Umkhonto we Sizwe (MK) grew. Although they formed a minority in MK, there were female soldiers and some, like Jackie Sedibe and Dipuo Mvelase, became senior commanders. However, women working for the ANC in exile often fulfilled traditional roles associated with their gender, such as typing and clerical work, or organising child care and welfare programmes. The ANC Women's Section (which replaced the Women's League in exile) was tasked with supporting the teenagers who left South Africa after the 1976 student protests as well as the children born to ANC members in exile.

Within South Africa, women participated in the labour unrest of the 1970s. Significant numbers of women workers went on strike throughout that decade, at times before their male counterparts. While women's strike activity was largely limited to immediate worker concerns, this began to change in 1979 with the formation of the Federation of South African Trade Unions (FOSATU). Women's participation in manufacturing increased during apartheid. In 1951 women made up 14 per cent of the industrial workforce but by 1980 this had grown to 25 per cent. By 1980 most women workers in industry were African.

When independent trade unions came to be recognised, and more African women began working in the industrial sector, women joined unions in the 1980s in greater numbers. Women such as Emma Mashinini participated in the creation of the Congress of South African Trade Unions (COSATU), which committed itself to gender equality as a founding principle. Unions in industries dominated by female workers brought large numbers of new members to COSATU. For example, the Commercial, Catering and Allied Workers' Union of South Africa (CCAWUSA) was the second-largest affiliate with 50 000 members, and FCWU the fourth-largest with 26 000 members.

COSATU helped to politicise workers through education on issues such as the relations between workers and broader community struggles, as well as grievance handling and disciplinary procedures. As in earlier decades, the unions succeeded in politicising and mobilising women, often creating a base from which women workers' struggles spread to their communities and homes. The Federation of Transvaal Women noted that a growing political consciousness among women in communities was often directly linked to the presence of women with union experience.

The unions were not the only organisations through which women mobilised to protect their interests or to challenge the apartheid state. Local grassroots organisations sprang up. Examples include the Phoenix Women's Circle, formed to address concerns around child care and nurseries. Another example was the Hambanathi Women's Action Group, which was set up to campaign for adequate burial facilities. Such grassroots organisations helped create networks of women who later supported the boycotts and stay-aways called by the trade unions and the United Democratic Front (UDF).

Various women's grassroots organisations also formed alliances among themselves and created regional bodies such as the United Women's Organisation (UWO) in the Cape and the Natal Organisation of Women (NOW). The UWO and NOW were formally aligned with the United Democratic Front in opposition to apartheid. Women also actively participated in the street and area committees that promoted residents' safety and helped undermine the apartheid authorities in the townships.

It is important to recognise that the popular mobilisation of the 1980s included women, many of whom took part in grassroots campaigns while others assumed leadership positions in various organisations and movements. The mass mobilisation contributed to the fall of apartheid. As apartheid crumbled in the early 1990s, women had to work together to ensure that gender equality would be guaranteed in the new South Africa.

WOMEN DURING THE MULTI-PARTY TALKS

Women unite for constitutional rights

The unbanning of the ANC in 1990 saw the ANC Women's League re-established in South Africa. It absorbed various women's organisations formed during the 1980s such as NOW and UWO. The Women's League took a leading role in creating the Women's National Coalition (WNC), which acted as a women's movement during the transition period. This body incorporated women from across the political spectrum, including the Inkatha Freedom Party and the National Party.

The WNC were determined to represent women's interests in the multi-party talks about the future of South Africa. The WNC lobbied for women to be part of the negotiating teams during the talks, for non-sexism to be a basic constitutional principle, and for women's right to equality to take precedence over traditional and customary law. This last aim was particularly important as the Congress of Traditional Leaders of South Africa (CONTRALESA) sought the protection of all aspects of customary law.

While the ANC was already committed to the principle of non-sexism, the WNC helped to ensure that this was translated into concrete action, such as lobbying for more female representatives during the negotiation process. The WNC faced obstacles in asserting its aims, but in the end the 1996 constitution committed the country to non-sexism and stated that women's right to equality supersedes the right of customary law. Furthermore, the constitution provides for a Commission for Gender Equality, which exists to 'promote, protect, monitor and evaluate gender equality'[38] in democratic South Africa.

---

38 Official website of the Commission for Gender Equality: http://www.cge.org.za.

CONCLUSION

Women's role and involvement in South African political history goes far beyond the 1956 Women's March to the Union Buildings. Women have played various roles as time and circumstance demanded. Some were heavily politicised and participated in activities that were part of broader race and class struggles; others organised and participated in events to meet more immediate needs. While women supported and worked with men, they also took independent initiatives, whether it was to start a burial society or to march against unjust laws.

Women successfully agitated to ensure that the 1996 constitution protected their rights as women. They continued to struggle for a better life, and many organisations and individuals still play a role in fighting for women's rights. Women have remained active in the formal political sphere. By 2019 they made up 45 per cent of members of Parliament, one of the highest percentages in the world.

Despite these victories, the aim of gender equality has still remained unfulfilled. Patriarchal attitudes persist at all levels of society. Women, particularly rural African women, continue to be one of the most oppressed and vulnerable groups, whether considered in terms of poverty, education, health or safety. Women have made significant strides, but the triple oppression of race, class and gender, although officially illegal, remains a fact of life for most of them. Eliminating it remains one of the big challenges of a democratic South Africa.

THEME 6: DISCUSSION QUESTIONS

1. What was your impression of women's role in South Africa's political history before you read this theme? How did reading this material change or confirm any knowledge or belief you had regarding women's participation in South African politics?

2. Non-sexism is an entrenched right in our constitution. Do you believe that women's right to equality should take precedence over the right of customary and traditional law?

3. The theme does not discuss the discrimination and sexual harassment that women faced in political organisations and trade unions. How should organisations deal with their own history of gender discrimination? Does this discrimination still exist in these bodies today? If so, what do you think would be the best way to tackle it?

4. Bodies like the ANC Women's League and certain trade unions played important roles in South Africa's history with regard to women's empowerment and organised mobilisation. Do you think these bodies are

still relevant today? If so, how? If not, why?

5. Because of South Africa's context, the national liberation struggle was seen as more important than the struggle for gender equality. Do you agree with this? Was this decision the result of patriarchal attitudes or was it the most practical decision at the time?

6. To what extent should programmes and policies that aim to emancipate women also include men in their solutions? For example, would four months' paid paternity leave (where fathers take leave on the birth of their child) help to address some of the child-care challenges that women face today? What role should men play in women's emancipation?

THEME 6: ADDITIONAL READINGS

Online readings

Gasa, Nomboniso (ed.) (2007) *Women in South African History: Basus'iimbokodo, Bawel'imilambo / They Remove Boulders and Cross Rivers.* Cape Town: HSRC Press. *http://www.hsrc.ac.za/en/research-data/view/2913* (register with your email address and you can download the book for free).

Joseph, Helen (1986) *Side by Side: The Autobiography of Helen Joseph.* London: Zed Books. http://www.sahistory.org.za/archive/side-side-helen-joseph.

History of Women's Struggle in South Africa (2018) *South African History Online.* https://www.sahistory.org.za/article/history-womens-struggle-south-africa.

Schmidt, Elizabeth S. (n.d.) Now You Have Touched the Women: African Women's Resistance to the Pass Laws in South Africa, 1950–1960. *South African History Online.* http://www.sahistory.org.za/archive/now-you-have-touched-women-african-womens-resistance-pass-laws-south-africa-1950-1960.

Walker, Cherryl (1991) *Women and Resistance in South Africa.* Cape Town: David Philip. https://books.google.co.za/books?id=xX-vhZQ1QpIC&printsec=-frontcover&dq=cheryl+walker,+women+and+resistance+in+south+africa&hl=en&sa=X&ved=0ahUKEwiWtpj8y_DpAhXQSBUIHQMLD2c-Q6AEIKDAA#v=onepage&q&f=false.

Books

Hassim, Shireen (2006) *Women's Organizations and Democracy in South Africa: Contesting Authority.* Pietermaritzburg: University of KwaZulu-Natal Press.

Mashinini, Emma (1989) *Strikes Have Followed Me All My Life: A South African Autobiography.* London: The Women's Press.

Visual resources

Community Video Education Trust has various interviews of women discussing their experiences under apartheid. Visit their website, http://www.cvet.org.za/index.php, and click on 'Browse Genres' and then click on 'Interviews'.

Black Sash: video interviews. *Overcoming Apartheid, Building Democracy.* http://overcomingapartheid.msu.edu/multimedia.php?id=65-259-B.

Theme Seven

The Trade Union Movement

INTRODUCTION

The working class in South Africa, as elsewhere, is exploited – that is, workers are paid wages below the value of their labour.[39] Because of this, many workers find it difficult to survive when wages do not keep up with the cost of living. A trade union is primarily an organisation of workers that fights to improve the wages and working conditions of its members and to protect workers from discrimination and unfair labour practices.

For black workers in South Africa and other colonised countries, their exploitation was made worse by another kind of oppression. As indigenous people whose country had been colonised, their land stolen and their social and political rights taken away, their very freedom had ceased to exist. They suffered racial discrimination from a colonial system that considered them inferior to whites. White workers could exercise some political influence through their right to vote for the government and try to get laws passed that protected their interests. There was a small section of progressive white workers who wanted to join with blacks to fight for their common interests, but most of them saw their interests as opposed to those of blacks and tried to win for themselves a privileged position within the working class. They fought to get higher wages than blacks and to have the better-paid jobs reserved for themselves.

Since the beginning of trade unionism in South Africa, black workers have faced a central dilemma. Should they focus on getting better wages and conditions, or should they play a role in the political struggle against black oppression? Or could they do both? These questions dominated the trade union movement from its infancy.

---

39 A first draft of this chapter was written by Michelle Friedman.

A meeting of white workers in Johannesburg disperses as troops appear at the far end of the street during the 1922 miners strike. Source: UWC Robben Island Mayibuye Archive.

THE BEGINNINGS OF TRADE UNIONISM IN SOUTH AFRICA

Trade unionism in South Africa has its roots in the gold mining industry. Most of the gold in South Africa is deep underground. So when gold was discovered on the Witwatersrand in 1885, mine owners needed large amounts of capital to buy machinery and equipment to open up the mines. As a result, the mines were operated by big companies from the start. The industry needed both skilled and unskilled workers.

Unskilled workers were mainly recruited from the rural areas of South Africa and from neighbouring countries. Taxes imposed by governments and the loss of much of their land pressured African men to look for wage work on the mines, in factories and in cities. Most were migrant workers who had contracts of three to twelve months; when the contract expired, workers returned to their rural homes. The wages of these migrant workers were low and they were housed in unhygienic and overcrowded compounds for the period of their contracts. Over time they learned various mining skills but this seldom resulted in higher wages.

Initially, most of the skilled workers were experienced miners who came from the tin, coal and gold mines of England and Australia. Some of them came to South Africa with trade union experience and established unions, mainly on the mines but also in some manufacturing industries. In addition to fighting for better wages and working conditions for themselves, they tried to prevent black workers from obtaining skilled work. They also pressured the government to pass legislation favourable to themselves.

For example, in 1911 the government introduced the Mines and Works Act, which reserved skilled and semi-skilled work for white workers. This led to a conflict of interest between the government and the mine owners. The Chamber of Mines preferred to use black workers in a greater variety of jobs because they could pay them less, while the government protected white workers because they had the right to vote and could help the government stay in power.

Although trade unions for white miners had existed since the 1890s, it was only during World War I that the Chamber of Mines, representing the mine owners, agreed to recognise them. In 1920 the price of gold fell sharply and the gold mining companies wanted to reduce costs by cutting the wages of white workers and replacing them with black workers at lower rates of pay. In January 1922, about 25 000 white miners in the Transvaal coal and gold mines went on strike, demanding to keep their privileged positions. The strike, known as the 1922 Rand Revolt, lasted for eight weeks and soon turned violent. Prime Minister Jan Smuts sent in the army and the strike was brutally crushed. Thousands of men lost their jobs while those who remained were forced to accept a huge drop in wages. The strike increased the divisions that already existed between black and white workers, especially as many whites were replaced by black workers.

THE INDUSTRIAL AND COMMERCIAL WORKERS' UNION

One of the earliest trade unions with a large black membership was the Industrial and Commercial Workers' Union (ICU). It was founded in 1919 by Clements Kadalie, an immigrant from Malawi, to represent dock workers in Cape Town. After it won wage increases in a successful strike, it expanded in the Western Cape and then spread further. In a very short time, it became a popular mass movement in both the rural and urban areas of South Africa and even extended its influence into neighbouring countries, especially Southern Rhodesia (now Zimbabwe).

It was at the time the largest mass-based organisation ever to have existed in South Africa and soon took on political dimensions; many saw it as an organisation fighting for the social and political rights of Africans. Its followers and leaders included members of political organisations such as the African National Congress (ANC) and the Communist Party of South Africa (CPSA). Many people were attracted by the ICU's militancy and its willingness to confront white employers and farmers, and it grew rapidly. At its height, it claimed 160 000 members, mainly Africans but also a few thousand coloureds and some whites.

Although it did not gain much influence among mine workers, the ICU drew a wide membership from industrial and commercial workers, small traders, and especially farm workers, sharecroppers and tenants on white-owned farms. The union used strikes and other forms of protest, including legal action, to protest against the harsh conditions, low wages and, in the case of sharecroppers and tenants, eviction from the farms. These activities often met with a brutal response from the authorities. During one protest march in Port Elizabeth in 1919, for example, police fired on the demonstrators, killing 22 people.

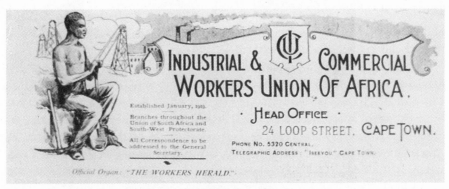

ICU Letterhead. Source: UWC Robben Island Mayibuye Archive.

By the late 1920s, serious weaknesses had become apparent in the organisation. Because its membership was scattered geographically and in many different occupations, it could not focus its energies or develop expertise in particular economic sectors. Well-organised workplace action supported by knowledgeable union officials was often difficult – and thus the ICU was less effective than it could have been.

From the mid-1920s the outlook of leaders like Kadalie and A.W.G. Champion of Natal began to change. Under the influence of the British Trades Union Congress, they wanted to make the ICU a more traditional, 'respectable' union. This was opposed by more radical leaders, leading to serious divisions in the organisation. At the 1926 conference, a resolution was passed excluding members of the CPSA from holding office in the ICU. The result was that the ICU lost some of its most capable and dedicated organisers. The organisation's new direction brought about a loss of the militancy that had attracted so many people to its ranks. From about 1927, the ICU began to lose membership. Personal rivalries and accusations of corruption among the remaining leaders led to a deepening crisis, and by 1930 it had almost entirely collapsed.

Despite its weaknesses, the ICU cannot be considered a complete failure. Later trade unions were able to learn from its mistakes. It was also important because it tried to organise farm workers, a group which was often ignored by other trade unions and political organisations. It provided hope, if only for a short time, to many of the dispossessed people of South Africa.

Trade Unions in the 1930s and 1940s

After the collapse of the ICU, some of its former members, including CPSA activists, established a new trade union federation called the Federation of Non-European Trade Unions (FNETU). Initially, it consisted of five unions and about 10 000 workers, mainly Africans. It called for a 48-hour week and equal pay for equal work. However, African trade unions were not recognised by law, and they found it difficult to organise. Migrant labourers presented a particular difficulty as they were forced to return to the reserves (or their home countries) when their contracts ended. When they returned to the city, they often found work in a different place. When severe economic depression hit South Africa in the early 1930s, many black unions almost collapsed. FNETU's influence declined as the bargaining power of workers weakened.

In the late 1930s the depression lifted, leading to a resurgence in new black and multiracial trade unions. In 1941 a new federation, the Council of Non-European Trade Unions (CNETU), was established. It grew throughout the period of World War II and by 1945 claimed a membership of 158 000 workers in 119 affiliated trade unions. Its president was Gana Makabeni until he was replaced by J.B. Marks, the chairman of the African Mineworkers' Union (AMWU); Marks was also a leading member of the CPSA and the ANC. Most of CNETU's membership was on the Witwatersrand though it also had solid support in the Cape, especially in Port Elizabeth.

When South Africa entered World War II in 1939, CNETU labelled it a war between imperialist powers and called on South Africans not to join the armed forces or donate money to the war effort. However, after Nazi Germany attacked the Soviet Union in June 1941, the CPSA changed its views and discouraged trade unions from striking, leading to some tensions with non-communists within the CNETU leadership. The CPSA believed that the fight against fascism should take priority over everything else, since the consequence of a Nazi victory would be devastating for the whole world and particularly for the working class. Strikes, however, did continue with some success. From 1940 industry had expanded enormously to meet the demand for military goods and to produce goods locally that could no longer be imported. The increased need for labour made it somewhat easier for most workers to demand higher wages, and they took advantage of this.

On the mines, however, conditions deteriorated during the war period. African mine workers were not given a cost-of-living increase, as the Wage Board[40] had decided that migrant labourers did not need a rise in wages. The workers demanded a substantial increase in their pay and food rations, a demand the mine owners refused to even consider. In August 1946, 76 000 mine workers from AMWU went on strike, closing 12 mines and partially closing nine others.

The response by the police and the mining companies was swift and ruthless. Police surrounded mine compounds and workers were forced down the shafts at gunpoint. The AMWU offices were raided and union leaders were arrested. During the strike, 12 workers were killed and over 1 200 were injured. The brutal crushing of the strike effectively destroyed the AMWU and marked a general weakening of the African trade union movement on the Witwatersrand. By 1949 a number of African trade unions had ceased to function, and CNETU was weakened as a result. Despite its failure, the 1946 strike was an important landmark because it was the first time that organised black mine workers had gone on strike.

---

40 Wage Boards were set up by the state to establish minimum wages in industries.

FORMATION OF SACTU

When the National Party (NP), with its policy of apartheid, came to power in 1948, the position of black workers weakened even further:

- African trade unions were not recognised and therefore were not allowed to strike.
- They were not allowed to take part in the Industrial Councils, which is where most important decisions were taken about workers. (White unions actively participated in the councils.)
- They were no longer allowed to attend Wage Board determinations.
- The Minister of Labour had the right to reserve any job for a particular race group.

These factors made it difficult for trade unions to organise effectively, especially when the new apartheid government banned over fifty progressive trade union leaders, both black and white, under the 1950 Suppression of Communism Act.

In October 1954, a conference of the mainly white trade union federation, the Trades and Labour Council (TLC), dissolved itself and formed the Trade Union Council of South Africa (TUCSA), which barred black unions and 'mixed' unions from being members. Some of the TLC unions opposed this racist move and in the following year they joined with CNETU to form a new trade union federation – the South African Congress of Trade Unions (SACTU). It elected Piet Beyleveld of the Textile Workers' Union as its president and Leslie Massina, former CNETU leader, as general secretary. At its founding, SACTU had 20 000 members from 19 affiliated unions. It focused its activities on growing and strengthening its member unions and establishing new ones. In a time of increasing repression, SACTU unions were militant; they organised a number of strikes demanding wage increases, especially in the Cape and Natal. By the early 1960s SACTU's membership had grown to 51 unions with a membership of 55 000.

SACTU organised workers on a non-racial basis, believing that politics and economics could not be separated in the struggle against exploitation and oppression. Therefore, it not only organised workers in the workplace, but it also took up broader political issues as part of the struggle against apartheid.

SACTU became part of the Congress Alliance, which was led by the ANC. Many of SACTU's leaders were among the accused in the Treason Trial of 1956–61; many were arrested and imprisoned after the ANC was banned in 1960. Some joined Umkhonto we Sizwe (MK) and shifted their focus to the armed struggle. A prominent SACTU leader, Vuyisile Mini, and fellow trade unionists, Wilson Khayinga and Zinakile Mkaba, were sentenced to death in 1964 for their role in MK activities. SACTU was not officially banned but the repressive conditions made it impossible to continue its normal activities. After 1961, some SACTU activists went into exile, where they worked closely with the ANC in mobilising support for the liberation movement among international trade unions.

TRADE UNIONS IN THE 1960s AND 1970s

During the 1960s manufacturing industry developed rapidly in South Africa. This led to a growth of the industrial working class, based in factories. However, because of government repression, little trade union activity took place.

This all began to change in the 1970s. The economic boom came to an end and workers faced uncertainty in the workplace. Rapid inflation led to rising costs, but the wages of black workers were not increased. In 1973 a number of spontaneous strikes broke out in Durban. This was a key moment in the black workers' movement. It inspired workers around the country and led to the rapid growth of membership in new black trade unions. These unions began to call for official recognition and for rights for all workers.

As a result of the increasing militancy and strength of trade unions, in 1977 the government appointed the Commission of Inquiry into Labour Legislation (the Wiehahn Commission). As a result of its report in 1979, the law was changed so that African workers were allowed to belong to registered trade unions and participate in the Industrial Council system; in addition, workers, whether white or black, could belong to the same unions. Unions now had a legal right to organise black workers and to strike. Another important change in the law abolished job reservation,[41] something that the unions and the entire liberation struggle had been fighting for since the late nineteenth century. However, despite the victories for the working class secured in the new legislation, the changes did not apply to public service workers, farm workers or domestic workers.

The government hoped that, as a result of these changes, trade union leaders would focus on complex industry-level negotiations in the Industrial Councils and would become less militant and less politically active, and lose touch with grassroots members. In this, the government would be disappointed; unions became increasingly militant, and both leaders and ordinary members became increasingly drawn into the growing political struggles of the 1980s.

THE FEDERATION OF SOUTH AFRICAN TRADE UNIONS

In 1979, the Federation of South African Trade Unions (FOSATU) was formed, with 45 000 members. By 1984 it had grown to over 120 000 members in eight affiliated trade unions. FOSATU believed that workers would have more bargaining power if they were organised into a tight trade union federation. It strongly upheld the principles of non-racialism, workers' control and workers' democracy. It promoted strong shop-floor structures led by elected shop stewards. FOSATU also believed that its trade unions should concentrate on improving the working and living conditions of workers, and should not be involved in national politics.

COUNCIL OF UNIONS OF SOUTH AFRICA

The 1970s also saw the emergence of new political thinking based on the ideas of Steve Biko and Black Consciousness. The Black Consciousness Movement began to cooperate with workers to develop trade unions based on its philosophy. This led to the formation

---

41 Job reservation laws reserved various jobs for whites only.

in 1980 of a separate federation of black trade unions called the Council of Unions of South Africa (CUSA). CUSA rejected the non-racialism of FOSATU, although it also supported workers' democracy and aimed to develop effective black leadership. Its most militant affiliate was the National Union of Mineworkers (NUM).

By the 1980s, the position of workers had strengthened. There had been many strikes, and the working class had made gains in improving working and living conditions. The trade union movement benefited from the growing strength of the political and community mass movements of the time, with which the unions cooperated. Most of these organisations supported the ANC, and many adopted the Freedom Charter as a vision for a democratic South Africa.

CONSOLIDATION OF THE TRADE UNION MOVEMENT

Despite common aims, the trade union movement was weakened by divisions. It was split into two different groups. The 'workerists' like FOSATU believed in focusing on strengthening workers' rights within the factories. The 'populists' argued that workers must be part of the wider national liberation struggle. These divisions played into the government's strategy, which was in effect to divide and rule.

As political struggles intensified in the 1980s, FOSATU realised that its position was no longer tenable. Their workers might be committed to strengthening workers' rights in the factories, but outside the workplace they were all victims of apartheid discrimination and repression. It began to see a space for worker action within communities. This shift allowed for the various trade union groupings to start thinking about uniting into a larger, coordinated federation.

In May 1984, FOSATU and the independent trade unions worked together to organise May Day rallies. At these rallies, there was a call for May Day (the internationally recognised Workers' Day) to be recognised as a public holiday in South Africa.

In November 1984, the Congress of South African Students (COSAS), FOSATU, the General and Allied Workers' Union (GAWU) and the United Democratic Front (UDF) collaborated in organising a successful stay-away to protest against the newly established Tricameral Parliament[42] – 800 000 workers stayed away from work and 400 000 students boycotted classes. In 1985 a range of trade union organisations worked together to launch a national consumer boycott of white shops and businesses. These actions helped to pave the way for unity. There were still a number of stumbling blocks, however:

- CUSA, following a Black Consciousness philosophy, was hostile towards the role played by white union officials in FOSATU.
- FOSATU was not prepared to form a new federation with unions that would not adopt its democratic style, with its focus on strengthening workers' rights in the workplace.

---

42 The Tricameral Parliament was the result of the 1983 constitution. The constitution established a parliament composed of three houses, one each for whites, coloureds and Indians. The intention was to maintain white supremacy but to co-opt coloureds and Indians as 'junior partners' and thus to split the growing unity among blacks. For more information, see Theme 8: South Africa's Constitutions.

• There were many clashes of personality, which led to tensions.

CUSA withdrew from the talks about unity, although the NUM, its largest affiliate, remained committed to unity and eventually broke away from CUSA.

In November 1985, the Congress of South African Trade Unions (COSATU) was launched, with 760 delegates from 33 trade unions, including the NUM. COSATU claimed a membership of 460 000 workers, the largest trade union federation in the history of South Africa – and it continued to grow. COSATU committed itself to both non-racialism and worker control. Under the slogan of 'one industry, one union', COSATU aimed to create one strong union in every industry, by uniting smaller unions. It also planned to organise black workers in areas where no unions existed: on farms, in domestic service and in the public sector.

While the trade union movement saw as its major task the creation of strong democratic shop-floor structures, COSATU also believed that it should play a political role in the struggle against apartheid. Increasingly, COSATU began to build links with wider community, youth, student and women's organisations, most of them under the umbrella of the UDF. COSATU and the UDF leaders also consulted closely, though secretly, with the exiled ANC.

In 1986, CUSA and some smaller trade unions with Black Consciousness sympathies also decided to merge. They formed the National Council of Trade Unions (NACTU) with a membership of almost 150 000 workers.

Repression was important in determining the political role played by the trade union movement. In 1988 the government banned the UDF and other civic and youth organisations. However, the trade unions were not banned at that time, although their activities were strictly curtailed by the state. Many trade union officials moved into positions of political leadership, and COSATU acted as a coordinating body to mobilise protests and to organise a strong alliance of anti-apartheid forces.

It was thus the trade union movement that kept the momentum of struggle going at this point. The period after 1986 was one of intense contestation between the mass democratic movement – an informal coalition of pro-liberation forces that included the trade union federations, UDF affiliates and others – and the apartheid state. The forms of struggle in various parts of the country, involving both urban and rural areas, included strikes, worker stay-at-homes, rent boycotts in state-owned housing, class boycotts by students, consumer boycotts, and attacks on government buildings in the townships. One of the most momentous events during this time was a strike in August 1987 by over 300 000 mine workers, led by the general secretary of the NUM, Cyril Ramaphosa. The strike ultimately failed to win wage increases or improvements in working or living conditions. But the fact that so many workers could conduct a three-week strike was an indication of the growing challenge posed to the entire apartheid system by the trade unions.

The authorities responded to popular resistance by declaring two States of Emergency (in 1985 and again from 1986 to 2000). Hundreds of activists, including many trade unionists, were arrested and imprisoned without trial; many were cruelly tortured and some were murdered by the authorities. Democratic organisations were banned and restrictions were placed on the media. In August 1989 the mass democratic movement, including the trade unions, embarked on a large-scale defiance campaign against segregated facilities and restrictions on meetings.

In the face of strong resistance to the entire apartheid system from trade unions and many other forces inside and outside South Africa, that white supremacy in South Africa began to crumble.

Conclusion

There can be no doubt that workers played a significant role in bringing about the end of apartheid. In the late 1980s, COSATU emerged as a driving force in the mass struggles to end white supremacy. The trade union movement had come a long way in the twentieth century – in fighting for workers' rights, in forging unity between the different trade union groupings, and in challenging the apartheid regime.

In 1990, after the ANC and the South African Communist Party (SACP) were legalised, they joined with COSATU to form the Tripartite Alliance. Together with its two partners, COSATU played a role in negotiating a transition to democracy. After the 1994 elections COSATU was able to influence the new democratic government, particularly to ensure the introduction of laws governing the labour movement and workers' rights. The new democratic system guaranteed important advances in the rights of workers. It outlawed unfair workplace practices and arbitrary dismissals, and gave workers the right to organise, to strike and to participate in national decision-making processes.

Workers, however, continued to face other challenges. Large numbers of them still worked for very low wages and in poor working conditions. As South Africa moved towards democracy, many union leaders took up positions in government, thus weakening trade union leadership. Differences that emerged in the trade union movement paved the way for fractures, breakaways and the formation of competing unions.

Trade unions were also affected by international developments and by changes in South Africa's national economy. International pressure resulted in the lowering of import duties and other trade barriers. This led to the increasing availability of cheaply produced goods from abroad, which severely harmed South Africa's manufacturing industries. Goods that had been made in South Africa now started to be imported. Many factories closed and workers lost their jobs, thus weakening the unions and increasing unemployment.

From the early 1990s the structure of the labour force began to change with the growth of the informal sector. This sector – day labourers, street traders, hawkers, car guards, beggars, waste recyclers and others – was made up of millions of poor workers earning very little in wages or benefits. Finding ways to improve the lives of these workers remains a challenge facing both the trade unions and the government.

Trade unions have played a central role in raising the living standards of their members as well as in bringing about democracy in South Africa. Their achievements were hard won, costing much sacrifice and bloodshed. Their challenges in a changed society would call for new strategies and renewed energy to help improve the lives of poor and exploited South Africans.

THEME 7: DISCUSSION QUESTIONS

1. The third paragraph of the Introduction says, 'Since the beginning of trade unionism in South Africa, black workers have faced a central dilemma. Should they focus on getting better wages and conditions, or should they play a role in the political struggle against black oppression? Or could they do both?' What is your view on this question?

2. Through most of the twentieth century the trade union movement was divided along racial lines. What do you think were the reasons for this? Did this benefit (a) the black workers and (b) the white workers?

3. The largest strikes in twentieth-century South Africa were the strikes by mine workers in 1922, 1946 and 1987. What does this tell us about the nature of the South African economy and the trade union movement? South Africa has seen both general workers' unions (e.g. the ICU) and federations of a number of industrial unions (e.g. COSATU or NACTU). Which option do you think is best for the workers? Give reasons for your opinion.

4. Since its earliest days, the black trade union movement has had a relationship with the Communist Party. Why do you think this was so?

5. What role did the trade unions play in the political struggles of the 1980s? How significant was this?

THEME 7: ADDITIONAL READINGS

Online readings

1946 African Mineworkers Strike. South African History Online. https://www. sahistory.org.za/article/1946-african-mineworkers-strike.

Alexander, R. and Simons, H.J. (1959) *Job Reservation and the Trade Unions.* Cape Town: Enterprise. http://www.historicalpapers.wits.ac.za/inventories/ inv_pdfo/AD1137/AD1137-G1-001-jpeg.pdf.

Battersby, J. (1987) Miners' Strike in South Africa Raises the Spirit of Resistance. https://www.nytimes.com/1987/08/16/weekinreview/miners-strike-in-south-africa-raises-the-spirit-of-resistance.html.

Congress of South African Trade Unions (COSATU). *South African History Online.* https://www.sahistory.org.za/article/congress-south-african-trade-unions-cosatu

Davenport, J. 2013. The 1987 Mine Strike. https://www.miningweekly.com/article/the-1987-mineworkers-strike-2013-09-27

Davenport, J. 2013. The Lead-Up to the 1922 Rand Revolt. https://www.miningweekly.com/article/the-lead-up-to-the-1922-rand-revolt-2013-08-16.

Industrial and Commercial Workers' Union (ICU). South African History Online. https://www.sahistory.org.za/article/industrial-and-commercial-workers-union-icu.

Pampallis, J. (1991) *Foundations of the New South Africa.* Cape Town: Maskew Miller Longman. https://www.sahistory.org.za/sites/default/files/file%20uploads%20/foundation_of_the_new_south_africa_original_final.pdf.

Simons, Jack and Ray Simons (1983) *Class and Colour in South Africa, 1850–1950.* London: International Defence and Aid Fund. https://www.sahistory.org.za/sites/default/files/file%20uploads%20/class_and_colour_-_harold_jack_simons_r.e._simons.pdf.

Sithole, J. and S. Ndlovu. (2006) The Revival of the Labour Movement, 1970–1980 (Chapter 5). In *The Road to Democracy in South* Africa, Volume 2, edited by South African Democracy Education Trust. Pretoria: Unisa Press. http://www.sadet.co.za/docs/RTD/vol2/volume%202%20-%20chapter%205.pdf.

Online visual resources

Hlanganani: History of Cosatu. LabourShow. https://www.youtube.com/watch?v=mkd_JM1PEo8.

Leading the Way: Black Trade Unions in South Africa (1985). https://www.youtube.com/results?search_query=south+african+trade+union+history.

Poster Book Collective (1991) *Images of Defiance: South African Resistance Posters of the 1980s.* Johannesburg: Ravan Press.

Trade Unions in South Africa (n.d.) https://www.youtube.com/watch?v=ua6mi-ISIZeU.

Books

Buhlungu, S. (2010) *A Paradox of Victory: COSATU and the Democratic Transformation in South Africa.* Pietermaritzburg: University of KwaZulu-Natal Press.

Friedman, M. (2011) *'The Future Is in the Hands of the Workers': A History of FOSATU.* Johannesburg: Mutloatse Arts Heritage Trust.

Forrest, K. (2011) *Metal That Will Not Bend: National Union of Metalworkers of South Africa.* Johannesburg: Wits University Press.

Kraak, G. (1993) *Breaking the Chains: Labour in South Africa in the 1970s and 1980s.* London: Pluto Press.

Ndlovu, S.M. and J. Sithole (2010). Trade Union Unity Summits and the Formation of COSATU, 1980–1990 (Chapter 17). In *The Road to Democracy in South* Africa, Volume 4, Part 1, edited by South African Democracy Education Trust. Pretoria: Unisa Press.

Seidman, J. (2007) *Red on Black: The Story of the South African Poster Movement.* Johannesburg: STE Publishers.

South African Committee for Higher Education (SACHED) (1989) *Freedom from Below: The Struggle for Trade Unions in South Africa.* Johannesburg: Skotaville Publishers.

Theme Eight

South Africa's Constitutions

INTRODUCTION

There are various ways in which societies can organise themselves politically. Examples include democracies, monarchies and dictatorships. Countries often use a constitution to define their political system. A country's constitution is a document that sets out the basic principles about how the government should be structured. It can also set out the fundamental rights of citizens and the responsibilities of different parts of the government. Post-apartheid South Africa chose to structure itself as a constitutional democracy. This means that its constitution forms the basis of the entire political system.

There are various types of parliamentary government. Some countries allow for parliamentary sovereignty. This means that parliament holds the most power and can make any law, as long as it is supported by a majority of members of the legislature (parliament). For most of the twentieth century, South Africa's racist constitutions allowed for parliamentary sovereignty. This changed in the 1990s when South Africa's interim and its final constitution created a constitutional democracy. In a constitutional democracy parliament can only create laws that are consistent with the rights protected by the constitution. This is also known as constitutional supremacy.

Democratic South Africa's constitution is widely regarded as one of the most progressive constitutions in the world. It forms the basis of our democracy, safeguards basic human rights, and puts in place many checks and balances in the system of the government to prevent abuse of power. The 1996 constitution was not South Africa's first constitution. South Africa had four constitutions before it finally adopted the current one. Studying the events surrounding the creation and adoption of the various constitutions, as well as their actual contents, provides a deeper understanding of the significance and implications of the entire political system.

THE SOUTH AFRICA ACT: THE 1910 CONSTITUTION

In 1910 the four separate, self-governing British colonies of the Cape, Natal, Transvaal and Orange River Colony united under one government to form a new country: the Union of South Africa. The Union was established by the South Africa Act, which was passed by the British Parliament in 1909. The South Africa Act functioned as the constitution of the Union of South Africa from 31 May 1910; it focused on the structure, powers and functions of the new government.

The 1910 constitution reflected the political situation of its time. The Anglo–Boer War (1899–1902) had intensified existing divisions between the Boer and British populations in southern Africa. The British victory further heightened the bitterness and resentment that many Boers felt towards the British. In recognition of this, the 1910 constitution showed the desire of white leaders to heal the divisions and create a united white population. As a dominion of Britain, South Africa recognised the British monarch as the head of government and its foreign policy was determined by Britain, but it had full control over all internal affairs. English and Dutch became the official languages of the country.

The constitution was not without controversy. During the Anglo–Boer War many blacks had sided with the British because they were promised 'equal laws, equal liberty' after the war. Many understood this to mean that the Cape franchise, which provided voting rights to some blacks, would be extended to the other three colonies. In the Cape, any man (though not woman), regardless of race, could vote provided he had a certain amount of wealth or property. During the peace negotiations with the Boers, the British failed to keep their promise. The Treaty of Vereeniging stated that a decision about the franchise for blacks would only be made once the colonies had gained self-government. However, when the Transvaal and the Orange River Colony became self-governing in 1906 and 1907 respectively, black people were denied the vote. The new constitution of 1910 provided an opportunity for Britain to keep its promise. It did not do so.

In 1908 a National Convention was called at which white, male leaders from the four colonies met to draft the new constitution. The question of extending the Cape franchise was the main point of contention. African organisations petitioned the National Convention to extend the rights enjoyed by the white population to African people. Their pleas were ignored. The South African Native Convention, which was called to oppose the constitutional proposals, sent a delegation to the British Parliament to plead that the racist clauses in the constitution be removed before Britain accepted it. They were unsuccessful, and the British Parliament signed the constitution into law.

In the interest of creating unity between English- and Afrikaans-speakers, the British had betrayed the black population. The South Africa Act only allowed for men of 'European descent' to be elected as representatives in the Union's government and only in the Cape could qualified blacks vote in general elections. The general structure and powers of government as laid out in the 1910 constitution would dictate South Africa's political system for over seventy years.

The monarch of Britain was recognised as the head of the executive, with a

Governor-General representing the king (or queen) in South Africa. The four colonies became provinces of the Union of South Africa. The national legislature was made up of two houses, the House of Assembly (the lower house) and the Senate (the upper house). Members of the lower house were directly elected by voters, who in all provinces besides the Cape were white men. The Governor-General nominated eight senators, and the four Provincial Councils chose the rest.

The constitution of 1910 created in the main two different political structures for black and white people. White men (and later women) could participate in a 'democratic' parliamentary government elected by white voters and by some qualified coloured and African voters in the Cape. The mass of African people, coloured people and 'Asiatics' were placed under the control and administration of the Governor-General – in effect, the white government.

The South Africa Act promoted parliamentary sovereignty. Section 59 stated: 'Parliament shall have full power to make laws for the peace, order and good government of the Union.' Parliament could make any laws dealing with the country's internal affairs, and could effect a change to most clauses in the constitution with a simple majority.

There were, however, a few limits on Parliament's power. The most important were that the Cape's franchise rights and the equal status of English and Dutch (later amended to English and Afrikaans) could only be changed with a two-thirds majority of both houses of Parliament.

The implications of parliamentary sovereignty directly impacted on the majority of people in South Africa. When the minority government passed any discriminatory laws, such as the 1913 Natives Land Act, the black majority had virtually no official channels through which to voice their objections. Apart from the small number of qualified coloured and African voters in the Cape, they were not directly represented in Parliament and they could not turn to the courts for protection because the courts could not force Parliament to review a law.

The 1910 constitution was amended several times before it was replaced in 1961. Amendments generally strengthened the power of the whites and the degree of South Africa's independence from Britain. The British Parliament's Statute of Westminster of 1931 recognised South Africa and three other British dominions – Canada, Australia and New Zealand – as being of equal status to Britain. This meant that South Africa could make its own foreign policy and appoint diplomatic representatives abroad.

Despite strong objections from many black organisations, in 1936 the Representation of Natives Act removed 'qualified' Africans from the common voters' roll in the Cape. In supposed compensation, an ineffective Native Representative Council was set up with advisory powers only and Africans could elect three white MPs.

In 1956, coloureds were also removed from the common voters' roll. There was widespread opposition to this from all black communities and from left-wing and liberal whites. Initially the Supreme Court ruled that the government's action was unconstitutional because it had not been passed by a two-thirds majority of both houses of Parliament sitting jointly, as the constitution provided. However, the NP government eventually succeeded in passing the Separate Representation of Voters Act after five years of legal manoeuvring, which included expanding the Senate and appointing a number of pro-apartheid judges to the Supreme Court. In the new system, coloureds were allocated four white MPs elected on a separate voters' roll.

When we consider the South Africa Act and the effects of the 1910 constitution in the following decades, we can understand how important a society's political structure is, and the role a constitution plays in limiting or protecting the rights of citizens.

THE REPUBLIC OF SOUTH AFRICA: THE 1961 CONSTITUTION

By 1960, international and local pressure was mounting on the South African government to reverse its policies of apartheid and to adopt a more democratic political structure. The need for a new order that recognised and protected basic human rights had grown in the 1950s, fuelled by international documents such as the Atlantic Charter and the United Nations Declaration of Human Rights, as well as South African documents like 'African Claims' and the Freedom Charter.

Up to this time, South Africa had been part of the British Commonwealth. But Prime Minister Hendrik Verwoerd was keen to create a South Africa that was completely independent of any British influence. In 1960 he called a whites-only referendum to decide whether the (white) electorate wanted South Africa to become an independent republic or continue as part of the British Commonwealth. By a very narrow margin, the majority decided on a republic.

On 31 May 1961 South Africa adopted a new constitution for the Republic of South Africa. Most of the clauses of the previous constitution remained unchanged, and the general political structure of government stayed the same. The only significant differences were that a State President replaced the Governor-General, and any powers held by Britain under the 1910 constitution were passed on to the government of the Republic.

In March 1961, 1 400 delegates representing the oppressed majority met in Pietermaritzburg at the All-In African Conference. They rejected the idea that a parliament representing the white minority of South Africans could create a constitution that applied to the entire population. The representatives called for a new national convention that would include male and female representatives from the entire population, black and white. Nelson Mandela was given the job of delivering these resolutions to Verwoerd. Predictably, the conference's resolutions were ignored.

The 1961 constitution reaffirmed parliamentary sovereignty by limiting the courts' power to review any laws. Ultimately the main aim of the 1961 constitution was to establish an independent republic dominated by the white minority. The constitution remained in place until 1983.

THE TRICAMERAL PARLIAMENT: THE 1983 CONSTITUTION

In the late 1970s and early 1980s the National Party experienced considerable internal and international pressure to abandon apartheid. In response, it devised the 1983 constitution in a bid to convince South Africa's people and the world in general that the country's political system was being reformed. It also tried to create divisions between the various sections of the black population by offering preferential treatment to the Indian and coloured populations.

The most significant feature of the 1983 constitution was the introduction of the Tricameral Parliament. Parliament was split into three houses, one each for the white, coloured and Indian populations – the House of Assembly (for whites), the House of Representatives (for coloureds) and the House of Delegates (for Indians). Africans were denied a chamber since, it was argued, they exercised their political rights in the bantustans. Voters would elect representatives from within their own group for each house, which would administer its group's 'own affairs'.

All three houses would vote together on important issues such as electing the State President. However, the houses did not hold equal power. A ratio of 4:2:1 governing the numbers of the white, coloured and Indian representatives ensured that whites always maintained power, even if the coloured and Indian representatives voted together. The 1983 constitution also merged the offices of State President and Prime Minister and gave the President supreme executive authority. The new constitution gave much more executive and legislative power to the President than the previous constitutions, thereby strengthening white power even further.

The 1983 constitution struggled to gain legitimacy. Most of the black population condemned it. A large majority of coloureds and Indians refused to take part in the elections to the new houses, which reduced the legitimacy of the Tricameral Parliament. The introduction of the constitution also played a role in the creation of the United Democratic Front (UDF), which was initially established to oppose it; the UDF was central to resistance struggles in the 1980s.

The 1983 constitution was scrapped in 1993, during the negotiations process, and was replaced by the interim constitution.

The Negotiated Peace: The 1993 Interim Constitution

After the unbanning of the liberation movements, the negotiations of the early 1990s largely centred on South Africa's new constitution. The National Party wanted those then involved in the negotiations to draft a new constitution for a democratic South Africa. Because they would be participating in this process, they would still have considerable control in the creation of the new order. The African National Congress (ANC) and other liberation organisations were keen to break with the 1983 constitution as soon as possible. However, they maintained that a constitution for the new South Africa could only be drawn up by the elected representatives of the entire South African population. Although the parties involved in the negotiations represented various sectors of society, they were not elected representatives.

The interim constitution agreed to in 1993 resolved the deadlock. It declared that a new, democratically elected Parliament had to draft a new constitution for South Africa. However, it was agreed that the new Parliament had to follow certain 'constitutional principles' which were set out in the interim constitution. These constitutional principles were agreed on by the different parties during the negotiations; they included one person one vote, a bill of rights, an independent judiciary, and the abolition of the bantustans.

The interim constitution laid the foundation of South Africa's constitutional democracy. It upheld the supremacy of the constitution and declared that all arms of government, including Parliament, were bound by the constitution. The interim constitution also created the Constitutional Court, which had to review and approve the text of the final constitution. The Constitutional Court had to make sure that the new constitution adhered to all the constitutional principles set out in the interim constitution.

The interim constitution came into force on 27 April 1994. It created a legal and political bridge between the old apartheid order and the new democratic constitution.

DEMOCRATIC SOUTH AFRICA: THE 1996 CONSTITUTION

On 27 April 1994 the first truly democratic elections took place in South Africa. The elected representatives formed a Constitutional Assembly and began drafting a new constitution that complied with the principles set out in the interim constitution. Unlike previous constitutions, all the clauses of the 1996 constitution were entrenched and thus could not be changed without a two-thirds majority in Parliament.

The Constitutional Assembly finalised the text of the new constitution in May 1996 and submitted it to the Constitutional Court for approval. The court rejected the draft because eight of the clauses did not comply with the constitutional principles. For example, the proposed new constitution did not protect the right of employees to engage in collective bargaining. The document was returned to Parliament, and the necessary changes were made. The Constitutional Court accepted the new version of the constitution on 4 December 1996. President Mandela signed the constitution on 10 December 1996 and it came into effect on 4 February 1997.

The constitution protects many liberal political rights such as the right to protest, the right of all people to be equal before the law, the right to be presumed innocent until found guilty by a court of law, the right to freedom of association, the right to freedom of speech, and the right to a free press.

In additional, the constitution protects a range of social and economic rights, including the right to universal basic education, the right of children to be cared for and protected, the right of workers to form or join a trade union, the right to strike, the right to freedom of movement, and the right to citizenship. The government has an obligation to take all reasonable measures to ensure that everyone has access to health care, food and water, and social security.

The 1996 constitution also attempts to guard against any excesses in the application or enjoyment of certain rights. That is, the constitution places limits on some rights where they conflict with other rights. For example, while the right to free speech is entrenched, this does not extend to incitement to violence or hate speech. Furthermore, while the constitution guarantees the right to property, it also provides for the right of redress to

Cyril Ramaphosa stands next to Nelson Mandela holding up a copy of the new South African Constitution, 1996. Source: Robbie Botha/Arena Holdings

people who lost land under colonialism and apartheid.

The right to restitution and redress for lost land became an important issue in 2017, when that year's ANC conference expressed its dissatisfaction with the slow pace of transformation of landownership in the country. In 2018 Parliament resolved that it would consider amending the constitution to allow for expropriation of land without compensation to the current owners. Some thought that a constitutional amendment was necessary to provide for land expropriation without compensation while others believed that the constitution already allowed for this. Parliament assigned the matter to a Constitutional Review Committee. In November 2018 this committee recommended to Parliament that the constitution should be amended to allow explicitly for expropriation of land without compensation.

Indeed, the section of the constitution dealing with land restitution had been the result of a compromise during the negotiations phase. The NP was determined to maintain property rights for whites, while the ANC and its allies demanded that the injustices of the past be addressed. As a result, the constitution protects individual property rights but allows the government to provide restitution to those who lost land owing to racist laws such as the 1913 Land Act, or who were forcibly removed during apartheid. However, land restitution can only involve cases that date back to 1913 and it does not address the question of land lost by African communities as a result of colonial or settler conquest.

The current constitution has also faced criticism for its handling of traditional leaders and customary law. While some people praise the constitution for incorporating this aspect of African culture, others argue that many of the principles of customary law or practice are inconsistent with the rights expressed in the constitution. For example, the practice of communal tenure of land is inconsistent with the right to private property, and the existence of hereditary chiefs is inconsistent with democratically elected leadership. The constitution's protection of traditional leaders was also a direct result of the negotiations of the early 1990s.

Overall, however, South Africa's final constitution has received much praise. It emphasises the individual human rights of dignity, equality and freedom, while trying to unify a society torn apart by a history of colonialism and apartheid. The 1996 constitution affirmed many of the checks and balances created by the interim constitution, which prevent any one arm of government from gaining too much power. The independence of the judiciary is vital, as it is responsible for ensuring that the legislative and executive arms of government uphold the constitution. Furthermore, Chapter Nine institutions such as the Public Protector, the Auditor-General and the South African Human Rights Commission are independent governmental bodies charged with protecting constitutional democracy and human rights.

CONCLUSION

When we trace the history of South Africa's various constitutions and the impact they have had on the majority of the population, we gain a deeper understanding of the processes that led to the creation of the current constitution. We can understand why the constitution entrenches so many rights. We can also understand why many South Africans rejected the idea of parliamentary sovereignty during the negotiated settlement, and opted for a constitutional democracy. Throughout post-apartheid South Africa, parties and organisations have relied on the constitution to hold government to account, to provide a framework for the functioning of the country's political and legal system, and to protect citizens' rights.

THEME 8: DISCUSSION QUESTIONS

General discussion questions

1. Explain what a constitution is in your own words. What are some of the functions of a constitution?

2. What role did British colonialism play in South Africa's constitutional history? Draw a mind map or make a list of the different ways in which British colonialism affected South Africa's constitutional history. In another colour, add the effects this had on Africans, coloureds, Indians and whites in South Africa.

3. What is your opinion of our system of constitutional democracy? What

are some of the disadvantages and advantages of this political system? As a group, draw up a list of advantages and disadvantages.

4. Draw up a list of groups of people that could be considered minorities. Remember that minority groups do not only have to refer to ethnicity, race or culture. Minorities could refer to language, wealth, political beliefs, religion and sexual orientation (to name a few). The 1996 constitution tries to protect the rights of individuals and minorities. Is this important? Why?

5. Does the 1996 constitution ignore the wishes of the majority at the expense of protecting individual and minority rights? Or does it allow for the wishes of the majority to have the final say? Provide factual reasons to support your answer. How should society balance the wishes of the majority with the rights of the minority?

SOURCE-BASED DISCUSSION QUESTIONS

For groups with access to the 1996 constitution, as well as earlier constitutions, if possible.

•   Read the Preamble of the 1996 constitution. What do you think about the ideas and hopes it expresses?

•   If you have access to any other constitutions, compare their preambles. What significant differences do you notice? Are there any similarities?

•   Read the Bill of Rights, which forms Chapter 2 of the 1996 constitution. Identify three rights that are currently the most important for you. Why are these rights so important? Are there any rights you would want to add to the constitution?

•   As a group, read Chapter 2: Section 25 of the 1996 Constitution, which deals with property. Do you think the 1996 constitution allows for land expropriation without compensation? Give reasons for your answer.

THEME 8: ADDITIONAL READINGS

Original text of the constitutions

United Kingdom (1909) The Union of South Africa Act. https://media.law. wisc.edu/s/c_8/jzhy2/cbsa1.pdf.

Republic of South Africa (1961) Constitution Act. *Wikisource*, https:// en.wikisource.org/wiki/Republic_of_South_Africa_Constitution_ Act,_1961.

Republic of South Africa (1983) Constitution Act, No. 110. https://www.gov.za/ documents/constitution/republic-south-africa-constitution-act-110-1983.

Republic of South Africa (1993) Interim Constitution. *South African History Online.* https://www.sahistory.org.za/article/interim-south-african-constitution-1993.

Republic of South Africa (1996) Constitution. Department of Justice and Constitutional Development. http://www.justice.gov.za/legislation/constitution/SAConstitution-web-eng.pdf.

Online readings

Constitutional History of South Africa. *ConstitutionNet.* http://www.constitutionnet.org/country/south-africa.

Ebrahim, Hassen (1998) *Soul of a Nation: Constitution-Making in South Africa,* (Chapter 2: Historical Background) http://www.sahistory.org.za/archive/chapter-2-historical-background.

Ebrahim, Hassen (2004) The South African Constitution: Birth Certificate of a Nation. In *Negotiation, Transition and Freedom.* Turning Points in History, Book 6. Johannesburg: STE Publishers. http://www.sahistory.org.za/archive/book-6-negotiation-transition-and-freedom-commissioned-department-education.

South African Constitutional Development Timeline 1902–1997. *South African History Online*, 30 March 2011, updated 11 April 2016. http://www.sahistory.org.za/topic/south-african-constitutional-development-timeline-1902-1997.

1909. [Union of] South Africa Act. O'Malley Archive. https://omalley.nelsonmandela.org/omalley/index.php/site/q/03lv01538/04lv01646/05lv01735.htm.

Online visual resources

Visit the following website for resources such as videos, posters and factsheets about South Africa's constitution: *The South African Constitution,* Department of Justice and Constitutional Development. http://www.justice.gov.za/legislation/constitution/index.html.

Books

Giliomee, H. and B. Mbenga (eds) (2007) *A New History of South Africa.* Cape Town: Tafelberg. (Chapter 9, A New South Africa in the Making; Chapter 15, Towards an Inclusive Democracy)

Ngcukaitobi, Tembeka (2018) *The Land Is Ours: South Africa's First Black Lawyers and the Birth of Constitutionalism.* Cape Town: Penguin Books. (Part III: Legacies)

International Solidarity against Apartheid

INTRODUCTION

International solidarity with oppressed groups in South Africa can be traced back to the late 1800s and early 1900s.[43] At the Pan African Conference held in 1900 in London, delegates from Europe, Africa and America met to promote racial equality for people under American and European control, including South Africa. The African National Congress (ANC) – called the South African Native National Congress (SANNC) until 1923 – established contacts with sympathetic people and groups in Britain and America after 1913. International solidarity increased after World War II as a growing number of African and Asian countries became independent and joined international organisations where they criticised South Africa for its racist laws. The Sharpeville massacre of 1960 focused international attention on South Africa, and more significant steps were taken in isolating South Africa and supporting its liberation movements.

The international campaigns expressed their solidarity in two ways. On the one hand there were campaigns to weaken the apartheid state by isolating it. On the other hand there were actions that directly supported and strengthened the liberation movements. Both the ANC and the Pan Africanist Congress (PAC) were recognised by international bodies like the Organisation of African Unity (OAU) and the United Nations (UN) as the legitimate representatives of the majority of the people in South Africa. However, over time the ANC received more support (internationally and internally) than the PAC, partly because it was better organised and more effective, and partly because its non-racial ideology, based on the Freedom Charter, was more attractive to those

---

43 This chapter draws substantially on Gregory Houston's 'Introduction' in *The Road to Democracy in South Africa*, Volume 3, edited by the South African Democracy Education Trust (SADET).

who opposed apartheid. Support was also given, in the late 1970s and 1980s, to anti-apartheid organisations operating mostly legally within South Africa such as the Black Consciousness Movement (BCM), the United Democratic Front (UDF), the Congress of South African Trade Unions (COSATU) and some of the churches.

LEVELS OF SUPPORT

The international campaign against apartheid was fought on many different levels. Some governments applied pressure on South Africa in international bodies like the UN, the OAU and the Commonwealth. Individual governments also took specific actions outside these bodies against South Africa or in support of the liberation movements. The Soviet Union and its Eastern European allies (also known as the Socialist Bloc), Cuba, China and most African, Asian, Caribbean and Latin American countries supported the liberation movements and opposed the apartheid regime, as did some Western European countries, notably the Nordic countries of Sweden, Denmark, Norway and Finland. Powerful Western governments, such as the United States and Britain, resisted attempts to isolate South Africa on any official level until the mid-1980s, when they came under growing pressure from the anti-apartheid movements in their countries and abroad.

The international anti-apartheid campaign took place within the context of the Cold War. Western, capitalist governments like the United States and Britain supported the apartheid regime because their companies had large investments in South Africa and because the country was anti-communist. Socialist countries such as the Soviet Union, the German Democratic Republic and Cuba supported the ANC, which was in alliance with the South African Communist Party (SACP). While the People's Republic of China provided most support to the PAC, it also gave limited political assistance to the ANC, especially in the 1950s.

Official support was merely one dimension of the solidarity movement. Civil society played a vital role, especially in Western countries, in the international anti-apartheid movements. Some organisations, like the British and Dutch Anti-Apartheid Movements or Africa Groups of Sweden, focused specifically on apartheid South Africa. Others, like the American Committee on Africa, focused on African liberation in general. Organisations like trade unions and student movements, or international bodies like the World Council of Churches, had broader aims but showed significant solidary with the anti-apartheid struggle. Civil society organisations helped create awareness of apartheid atrocities, criticised and boycotted their countries' businesses for their involvement in South Africa, raised funds for the liberation movements, or applied pressure on their governments to take a stronger official stance against apartheid South Africa.

In this theme we will explore some of the ways in which South Africa was isolated in an attempt to weaken it. Thereafter we will examine some of the ways in which the liberation movements were supported. The aim of this chapter is to provide a broad overview of various activities. Readers are encouraged to extend their knowledge of specific countries, organisations or individuals by consulting the Additional Readings list.

Campaigns to Isolate and Weaken the Apartheid State

Member states of the UN could not intervene in the domestic affairs of another country. However, they could show their disapproval of a country's policies by refusing to interact with it. Many governments refused to work with South Africa and cut all official diplomatic ties with the country. When governments such as those of Britain or the United States kept working with South Africa, people of those countries organised campaigns to put pressure on their governments and businesses which continued to operate in South Africa.

The subsections below look at three ways in which South Africa was isolated: politically, economically and socially.

Political isolation

Throughout the 1950s and early 1960s many African and Asian states gained independence from European colonisers. They formed new international alliances and organisations like the Organisation of African Unity and the Non-Aligned Movement (NAM). Many of these countries criticised apartheid and called for sanctions. The Socialist Bloc, as well as countries from Latin American and the Caribbean, also took steps to isolate apartheid South Africa.

Such countries were an important voice in intergovernmental bodies like the Commonwealth and the UN. They called for South Africa to be isolated and expelled from international bodies. For example, in 1960 at the Second Conference of Independent African States, a resolution was taken that all countries at the conference that were also part of the Commonwealth would try to remove South Africa from that body. To avoid being expelled, South Africa decided to give up its Commonwealth membership when it became a republic in 1961.

In 1962, the UN General Assembly condemned apartheid and called on all its members to break off diplomatic, economic, military and transport links with South Africa. This included refusing South African ships permission to enter their ports and forbidding South African aeroplanes to land at their airports. The General Assembly also set up a Special Committee against Apartheid. Furthermore, it asked the UN Security Council to hold South Africa accountable for violating the UN Charter. Many African, Asian and Socialist Bloc countries broke off their ties with South Africa as a result of this resolution, if they had not already done so. Most Western countries did not.

By the end of the 1960s South Africa had withdrawn or been excluded from several significant international bodies like the United Nations Educational, Scientific and Cultural Organisation (UNESCO) and the International Civil Aviation Organisation. Political isolation increased during the 1970s. In 1974, ten of the 15 UN Security Council members voted to expel South Africa from the UN, but Britain, France and the United States (who have veto powers) blocked the vote. However, while South Africa was not expelled, none of the UN agencies allowed South Africa to take part in any of their work.

The Soweto Uprising of 1976, the death in detention of Steve Biko in 1977 and the States of Emergency in the 1980s made it increasingly difficult for Western governments to openly support South Africa. By the late 1980s South Africa was excluded from almost all international governmental organisations, and by 1990 it had diplomatic links with only 28 countries.

Political sanctions played a role in reducing South Africa's international influence by refusing to give the apartheid government an official platform in the international arena. But their impact was limited as long as powerful Western countries like the United States and Britain continued to recognise South Africa. However, some argue that the fact that even these staunch allies called for negotiations, especially after the end of the Cold War in 1989, played a role in persuading the apartheid state to begin talks with the ANC.

Economic isolation

South Africa had various economic relationships with overseas countries. It exported its own goods to other countries, and imported products from them. Foreign companies set up factories or extended their operations to South Africa, and many invested their money in South African businesses. Foreign banks also loaned money to South African businesses and to the South African government. The international campaign to isolate South Africa economically tried to cut all these economic relations.

Many African, Asian, Latin American, Socialist Bloc and Caribbean states severed economic ties with South Africa, and consistently called for further sanctions in bodies like the UN. They refused to import South African goods and refused to export to South Africa. An important victory on this front occurred when most oil-producing countries refused to sell oil to South Africa from the early 1970s. By the 1980s South Africa was forced to buy oil on the black market, and as a result it had to pay much more money for oil at a time when its economy was already strained.

Economic isolation was a prime target for civil society mobilisation, especially in Western countries that resisted official sanctions against South Africa. Consumers boycotted South African goods such as fruit and wine, and trade union members refused to handle South African goods. In 1960 dock workers in Trinidad would not unload South African ships. In 1984 ten Irish shop workers went on strike for nearly three years because they refused to handle South African fruit. Activists in many countries picketed outside shops that continued to stock South African goods. The consumer boycotts gained momentum in the 1980s, causing decreased profits for South African businesses. Importantly, this reduced economic activity meant that South Africa received less foreign currency, which it needed to pay for the importation of oil and weapons.

Companies with assets in South Africa, or with shares in South African companies, were also targeted by civil society organisations, particularly in Western countries like the United States. Solidarity movements demanded that these companies disinvest (sell off their assets) from South Africa. At times companies were directly targeted and consumers were asked to boycott their products. For example, organisations were pressured to cancel their accounts with banks that provided loans to South Africa. Campaigners also put pressure on investors to withdraw their money from companies operating in South Africa. They further demanded that governments and financial institutions refuse to

Thousands of people joined the Anti-Apartheid Movement's March for Freedom, 28 June 1986.
Source: Tim Jarvis/AAM Archives

grant any more loans to South Africa. The governments of Sweden and Norway made it illegal to invest in South Africa after the 1976 Soweto Uprising.

The trade embargoes and disinvestment campaigns alone did not cripple South Africa, but they added to all the internal problems that its economy was facing in the 1980s. South Africa's financial crisis came to a head in 1985 when many foreign lenders refused to grant South Africa any further short-term loans. Banks like Chase Manhattan denied that this was a result of solidarity with the anti-apartheid movement, but claimed that their action was the result of South Africa's deteriorating economic conditions in the 1980s. However, anti-apartheid activists saw it as a victory, arguing that international financial institutions were finding it more and more difficult to justify their involvement in South Africa.

Social isolation

While the South African government and businesses might feel the effects of political and economic isolation, these were not everyday concerns for the majority of white South Africans. Campaigns that tried to isolate South Africa's social interactions probably had a much greater psychological impact on the white population. Social isolation included sport, cultural and academic boycotts.

The sports boycott was perhaps the most significant form of social isolation. South Africa was excluded from the Tokyo Olympics in 1964 and the Mexico City Olympics

In London, a 'Boycott Apartheid' bus sponsored by the Anti-Apartheid Movement, 1989.
Source: R. Barraez D Lucca

in 1968, and was expelled from the Olympic Committee in 1970. Pressure from anti-apartheid movements in Western countries and by some governments helped the sports boycott to develop. Sports teams and individuals were asked to refuse to play with their South African counterparts. By the late 1970s and early 1980s many countries had broken their sporting ties with South Africa. In 1981 the UN Special Committee against Apartheid began to publish reports of people who were involved with South Africa at a sporting level. Many authorities like city councils in Britain and other Western countries would not allow people named in these reports to use their sporting facilities.

The cultural boycott included international boycotts of white South African artists, as well as pressurising international artists to refuse to perform in South Africa. Groups of playwrights from Britain and Ireland refused to grant permission for any of their plays to be performed in South Africa in the mid-1960s. In 1965 about sixty American cultural personalities openly declared their refusal to work with South Africa. In 1980 the UN General Assembly passed a resolution calling all its members to institute a cultural boycott. A register of artists who performed in South Africa was also published, in an attempt to mobilise public opinion against these artists.

The academic boycott was first launched in 1965 by a group of British academics. In doing so, they tried to prevent South African academics from collaborating with other scholars in their fields, or publishing works outside South Africa, and even to limit their access to research. This boycott was largely centred in Western countries. Desmond Tutu argued that the academic boycott helped to create awareness among liberal white academics at home that they could not ignore their own role in apartheid South Africa.

Support to Help and Strengthen the Liberation Movements

Apart from trying to weaken the apartheid state, various organisations and governments actively supported the liberation movements directly involved in the fight against apartheid. The liberation movements were supported in many ways, by various governments, organisations and individuals. Broadly, the support can be categorised as support for the armed struggle, support for ANC and PAC non-military activities, and support for the broader anti-apartheid movement in South Africa.

Support for the armed struggle

Both the ANC and the PAC waged an armed struggle against the apartheid state from the 1960s, and relied on help from foreign governments to continue their campaigns. The ANC's military wing was Umkhonto we Sizwe (MK), and the PAC had the Azanian People's Liberation Army (APLA, formerly known as Poqo). Both MK and APLA needed training for their members, military material such as weapons and ammunition, and military bases where they could train and house their soldiers. Lastly, the liberation organisations needed the support of the governments of South Africa's neighbours so that they could launch their campaigns from neighbouring states.

African countries like Ethiopia, Egypt, Ghana, Libya and Morocco provided military training for groups of cadres from both liberation movements in the 1960s. Syria and China helped to train a large group of PAC members in 1976 and 1977. Between 1977 and 1988 hundreds of MK cadres underwent military training in the Soviet Union, the German Democratic Republic and Czechoslovakia. Furthermore, between 1979 and 1991 the Soviet Union sent over 200 specialists and interpreters to help train and support the Angolan armed forces and also provided training to MK forces in Angola. Cuban troops, who were in Angola at the request of the Angolan government to assist it in confronting the threat from South Africa, also provided training to MK cadres.

The front-line states – Angola, Botswana, Lesotho, Mozambique, Swaziland (eSwatini), Tanzania, Zambia and (after 1980) Zimbabwe – played an important role during the armed struggle. The PAC originally set up its headquarters-in-exile in Lesotho and during the 1960s it had military camps in Tanzania and, briefly, in Zambia. In 1964 the ANC established its first military base outside South Africa in Tanzania, but by 1971 most of the MK cadres had been moved to camps in Zambia. From the late 1970s Angola became the main MK training ground when the government of newly independent Angola welcomed them. Military camps were set up there as thousands of young people joined Umkhonto we Sizwe after the 1976 Soweto Uprising. The South African Defence Force fought in Angola in the 1970s and 1980s precisely because the South African and Namibian liberation movements had bases here.

Front-line states like Botswana, Swaziland and Lesotho were not strong enough to confront South Africa openly, and could not offer military bases to the ANC or PAC. However, Botswana could, and did, offer South African refugees and exiles a safe haven and also transport to African countries further north. Lesotho welcomed thousands of refugees, and provided many opportunities for refugees to study at Lesotho's university.

Swaziland allowed the ANC to infiltrate into South Africa from within its borders, and after independence Zimbabwe's government was a vocal critic of the apartheid regime and turned a blind eye to the use of its territory by the liberation movements. Front-line states risked their own security for the sake of the liberation struggle. The South African military conducted many cross-border raids, assassinations, bombings and open war (in Angola) in an attempt to reduce the threat of the ANC and PAC presence there.

Most Western governments and solidarity movements did not contribute directly to the armed struggle. Material needs like weapons, tents and food as well as military advice tended to come from countries like the Soviet Union, the German Democratic Republic, Czechoslovakia, Cuba and Vietnam for the ANC, while the PAC received some weapons in the 1960s from Egypt and Libya. Both organisations were recognised by the OAU, and received money or material support from the OAU's Liberation Committee.

Support for ANC and PAC non-military activities

Both the ANC and PAC set up missions in exile after they were banned in South Africa in 1960. They became involved in a variety of projects which needed much financial and material aid to succeed: offices for their staff and money to enable members to travel. Activists needed to support their families and ensure that their children were schooled. Money and materials were also needed for awareness campaigns. Furthermore, the PAC and ANC set up humanitarian projects – particularly around education, health and food production – to assist South African refugees and exiles. As mentioned earlier, while the PAC did get some support from organisations and governments, most of the material support by the 1970s and 1980s went to the ANC, as it became increasingly apparent that the ANC commanded overwhelming support among black people inside South Africa.

Support for the liberation movements' activities came in a variety of ways. It could be through direct money grants or through donations of materials such as stationery, medicine, food and clothing. Funds such as the United Nations Development Programme (UNDP) or the OAU's Assistance Fund for the Struggle against Colonialism and Apartheid provided support to the liberation movements. Various countries and organisations donated money or material to these funds, which then made their way to the ANC or PAC.

Individual governments also gave direct grants to the movements. For example, the United Arab Republic and China both gave money to the PAC, while the Soviet Union and the Nordic countries gave financial grants to the ANC. Non-governmental organisations (NGOs) in various countries also raised funds and sent material to the liberation movements. Often the support from Western governments and organisations was for humanitarian projects rather than for the armed struggle.

Countries also supported the liberation movements' social and economic projects by offering their services. Anti-apartheid groups and governments in Nigeria, Ghana, Tanzania, the German Democratic Republic, Sweden, Denmark, Norway, the Netherlands, Britain and Australia recruited and paid for people to work for the ANC's projects in exile, including at its school, the Solomon Mahlangu College (SOMAFCO) in Tanzania. Many countries from around the world sent educational material as well as food, clothing and medical assistance. All the Socialist Bloc countries, Cuba, and many African countries and India granted scholarships to young South African exiles to study in their countries. In many Western countries, scholarships were provided mainly by organisations associated with the broad anti-apartheid movement.

Support for the broader anti-apartheid movement in South Africa

The International Defence and Aid Fund for Southern Africa (IDAF) began as a fund to help defend anti-apartheid activists during the Treason Trial (1956–61). IDAF grew, and over the years was able to provide legal support for many activists in South Africa who were prosecuted by the apartheid regime. It also helped to maintain the families of activists who were jailed or had been executed. In addition, IDAF provided money to pay for lawyers to be present at the inquests of murdered activists such as Steve Biko.

While IDAF was an important source of support for political prisoners, their families and political refugees, there were other organisations who offered similar assistance. These included Amnesty International, the World Council of Churches and the UN Trust Fund for South Africa. Various organisations and governments donated money to these funds. Western solidarity movements often pressured their governments to contribute money to this cause.

The financial support available for activists who were arrested played an important role in maintaining the momentum of the anti-apartheid struggle. Activists often had to make difficult choices between taking up struggle activities or working to support their families. Knowing that funds were available to help their dependants if anything happened to them enabled many activists to continue their struggle work.

Support for the broader anti-apartheid struggle included awareness campaigns to highlight the atrocities of apartheid. An international campaign calling for the release of Nelson Mandela from prison gained much momentum during the 1980s and made people aware of apartheid injustices.

International governments and solidarity organisations did not only help the ANC and the PAC. They also helped other anti-apartheid movements working in South Africa such as Black Consciousness organisations, the UDF and COSATU. Support ranged from financial grants to help with the day-to-day running of the organisations, to assistance for humanitarian and development projects, including bursaries for South African students.

CONCLUSION

The international solidarity movement gained momentum during the 1960s and reached its peak in the 1980s. It was one of the largest sustained international solidarity movements ever to have existed, involving governments and NGOs from across the globe. It played an important role in isolating and weakening the apartheid state, and strengthening

Free Nelson Mandela protest in Berlin

the liberation movements, both in exile and in South Africa. Any understanding of resistance to apartheid needs to include an appreciation of international solidarity, and the considerable sacrifices of countries such as the front-line states, in contributing to South Africa's liberation.

THEME 9: DISCUSSION QUESTIONS

1. What was your opinion or knowledge of the international solidarity movement before you read this Theme? Did the information contained here change any of your perceptions? If so, how? If not, did you learn anything new? What was the most interesting new information you learned?

2. How important were the international solidarity campaigns? Which activities or campaigns do you think were the most important? As you discuss this, refer to the effects and results of:
    a. political, economic and social isolation;
    b. support for the liberation struggle.

3. As a group, make a list of all the African countries that supported the anti-apartheid movement and jot down what they did. Put a star next to countries that were part of the front-line states.

a. How important were the contributions of African countries to the liberation struggle?

b. What effect did their involvement in anti-apartheid activities have on the front-line states?

c. Foreign nationals from other African countries have experienced violent attacks and even murder at the hands of South Africans in the recent past. Does the knowledge of African support for the liberation struggle change the way you view the attacks? Why or why not?

4. The international solidarity movement cut across many levels of society in many countries. It involved individuals, local and international organisations and governments. What role do civil society and government in modern South Africa play in speaking out and taking action against injustices in other countries? Should we take a leading role in such matters? Is our civil society politically conscious about human rights violations in other parts of the world? How does this reflect on us as a people and on our status in the world?

THEME 9: ADDITIONAL READINGS

Online readings

Barnes, Catherine (2008) International Isolation and Pressure for Change in South Africa. *Conciliation Resources*, Accord Issue 19. http://www.c-r.org/accord/incentives-sanctions-and-conditionality/international-isolation-and-pressure-change-south.

Houston, Gregory (2008) *The Road to Democracy in South Africa*, Volume 3: *International Solidarity*, edited by the South African Democracy Education Trust. Pretoria: Unisa Press. (Chapter 1). http://www.sadet.co.za/road_democracy_vol3.html#part2.

The Union of Soviet Socialist Republics (USSR) and the Anti-Apartheid Struggle (2012) *South African History Online*, 13 November 2012, updated 3 February 2017. http://www.sahistory.org.za/topic/union-soviet-socialist-republic-ussr-and-anti-apartheid-struggle.

Online visual resources

Multimedia: South Africa, the United Nations and Apartheid (2014) Brand South Africa, 23 June 2014. https://www.brandsouthafrica.com/people-culture/history-heritage/multimedia-south-africa-the-united-nations-and-apartheid.

Nordic Documentation on the Liberation Struggle in Southern Africa (n.d.) (interviews, stories, photos and videos about Nordic campaigns against apartheid). http://www.liberationafrica.se/.

Simpkins, Chris (2014) US Anti-Apartheid Movement Helped Bring Change to South Africa. *Voice of America*, April 2014. https://www.voanews.com/a/us-anti-apartheid-movement-helps-bring-change-to-south-africa/1900704.html.

United Nations General Assembly (1963) The Policies of Apartheid of the Government of the Republic of South Africa. United Nations Dag Hammarskjöld Library. http://repository.un.org/handle/11176/204132.

Books

Some of the chapters from *The Road to Democracy in South Africa* (Volume 3, International Solidarity and Volume 5, African Solidarity) are available online. This series is very comprehensive. Different chapters deal with various countries and their contributions. Try to get the print books for further readings.

South African Democracy Education Trust (2008) *The Road to Democracy in South Africa*, Volume 3: *International Solidarity.* Pretoria: Unisa Press. http://www.sadet.co.za/road_democracy_vol3.html#part2.

South African Democracy Education Trust (2013) *The Road to Democracy in South Africa*, Volume 5: *African Solidarity.* Pretoria: Unisa Press. http://www.sadet.co.za/road_democracy_vol5.html.

Appendix for Teachers

How to use the Text Engagement Activities

The discussion questions at the end of every chapter aim to promote thoughtful analysis of South Africa's historical context, as well as its present challenges. A good understanding of content is necessary to ensure that a discussion is focused on facts rather than vague ideas and misconceptions. The Text Engagement Activities, found in this section of the book, are tasks that aim to help readers make sense of the information in the Themes in a systematic way, while also generating some basic analysis to stimulate a more critical reading of the content.

The Text Engagement Activities can be done in the book itself, or photocopied, or done on a separate piece of paper. It is up to the individual to determine her needs and resources. The Text Engagement Activities will be particularly useful in a classroom context or one in which readers and group members have varying levels of reading proficiencies. By completing these common tasks, it can allow more members to read for meaning effectively, and thus more members can participate with greater confidence in group discussions. By expecting members to bring completed Text Engagement Activities to discussion sessions, it can also help to ensure that participants have done the requisite reading.

There are nine Text Engagement Activities, one for each of the Themes. At the very end of this section are the memoranda, or answers, for each of the activities. Groups can decide whether they want to go over the tasks as a group or whether individuals should check their own understanding against the activity's memorandum before the discussion.

Text Engagement Activities

THEME 1: THE SOUTH AFRICAN ECONOMY

Many factors affect a country's economic development, including government policies and actions. Governments identify certain demands or needs, and take action to try to meet those needs. The following table tracks some of the South African state's policies and actions, as well as the effects they have had.

We first present an example of how to carry out the activity. The first column in the table shows the time period. The second column identifies demands and needs that the state recognised. The third column shows what actions the government took to meet the demands or needs. The last column shows some of the effects which the government's actions had. Some of the information has been left out. Refer to the foregoing text of this theme to help you fill in the missing information in each row. Sometimes you need to supply missing words and at other times you need to fill in the information for the whole block.

Example

Era	Demand/Need	Government Action	Effect
1870–1910	Labour shortages on mines and white commercial farms	• •	More African men took up wage labour on farms and mines

Answer

Era	Demand/Need	Government Action	Effect
1870–1910	Labour shortages on mines and white commercial farms	• **Restricted African people's access to land** • **Imposed taxes**	More Africans took up wage labour on farms and mines

The table starts on page 299.

Government Reactions to Certain Economic Demands

Era	Demand/Need	Government Action	Effect
Union government: SAP, 1910–1924	More labour needed on mines and white commercial farms	•	Africans were no longer allowed to be sharecroppers; many Africans became farm wage labourers; poorer white farmers lost sharecropping income; African agriculture declined
Pact and Fusion: 1924–1939	Mining companies were losing profits and wanted to cut white wages and employ more black workers in semi-skilled positions	*Government sided with the mine owners *Smuts crushed the Rand Revolt	• • •
	Money needed to develop agricultural and manufacturing industries	•	More money was made available to develop agriculture and manufacturing
	Need to provide support for white farmers	Government introduced supportive measures for white farmers including: • • •	*More farmers mechanised but agricultural input did not increase significantly *Foundation was laid for the improvement of white commercial farming during apartheid
	•	*Colour bar expanded across more industries *40 per cent of manufacturing labour was reserved for whites	White workers legally protected from competition with black workers for certain skilled and semi-skilled jobs
	Need to create employment for white workers	• •	White employment increased, especially in manufacturing so that by 1949 there were more jobs available in industry than whites to fill them
	South African exports suffered during Great Depression	Devalued the South African pound by going off the gold standard	• •

Era	Demand/Need	Government Action	Effect
	Need to expand South African industry	•	*Manufacturing protected from foreign competition *Manufacturing expanded rapidly and employment in this sector grew by 60 per cent between 1933 and 1939
World War II	Demand for black workers increased in industry during World War II	•	• Rapid black urbanisation • Industry continued to expand •
National Party, early apartheid: 1948–1970s	Need to regulate African labour and create an unskilled, rurally based pool of cheap labour	Measures included: • Expansion of colour bar • Restrictions on black trade unions • • •	• Black urbanisation slowed • More black people were forced to take up wage labour on white farms • An unskilled, rurally based pool of cheap labour was created • Migrant labour entrenched • Poverty increased in bantustans
	Need to modernise white commercial agriculture	•	• Maize yields increased • Farmers needed fewer workers, thereby contributing to a growing surplus of rurally based unskilled workers who struggled to find employment
	Desire to grow Afrikaner stake in economy beyond agriculture	NP government promoted and supported Afrikaner financial institutions and businesses •	Afrikaner share of ownership increased between 1949 to 1970 in: • Mining (1 per cent to 30 per cent) • •
	Need to break the cycle of poverty in the white population by creating a new generation of skilled whites	•	•

Era	Demand/Need	Government Action	Effect
National Party, late apartheid: 1970s–1994	Skilled, urbanised black labour needed to maintain economic growth	Limited reforms made to segregationist legislation: • Colour bar relaxed • •	*Reforms were too limited and ineffective *Economic growth slowed and declined

THEME 2: SOUTH AFRICA'S BANTUSTANS

1. In the space provided below, list at least seven different economic challenges that the bantustans faced.

Bantustan Economic Challenges
•   •   •   •   •   •   •

2. Only the apartheid state and the bantustan governments considered the bantustans independent states. Why did so many people, both inside and outside South Africa, reject the idea that bantustans were fully independent countries?

3. The following graph shows the population of QwaQwa in three different years. Column 1 records QwaQwa's population as 24 000, but it does not show the year for this statistic. Consult the section 'Conditions in the Bantustans' to find out when QwaQwa's population stood at 24 000 people and fill in the date under column 1. Do the same for columns 2 and 3.

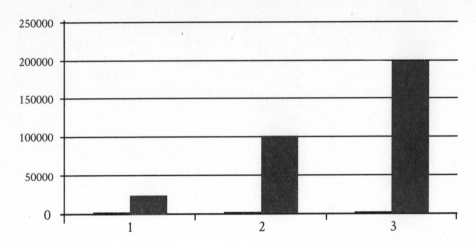

4. Find the year in which the events below occurred by referring to the text of this Theme, and insert it in the blank space next to the event. The events are not in chronological order. Your next step is to put them in chronological order by placing them onto the timeline that follows. The timeline also includes events that are mentioned briefly in the Theme in order to provide further historical perspective. You can also fill in any other significant events on your timeline that you might come across in the Additional Readings or from your own knowledge.

Year	Event
_____	Defiance Campaign
_____	Ciskei 'independence'
_____	Transkei 'independence'
_____	Transkei unbans ANC and PAC
_____	Bantu Authorities Act
_____	Pondoland Revolt
_____	Bisho Massacre
_____	Promotion of Bantu Self-government Act
_____	Bophuthatswana 'independence'
_____	Venda 'independence'
_____	End of bantustans
_____	Bantu Homeland Citizenship Act
_____	Transkei gains self-government
_____	KwaZulu gains self-government

Timeline

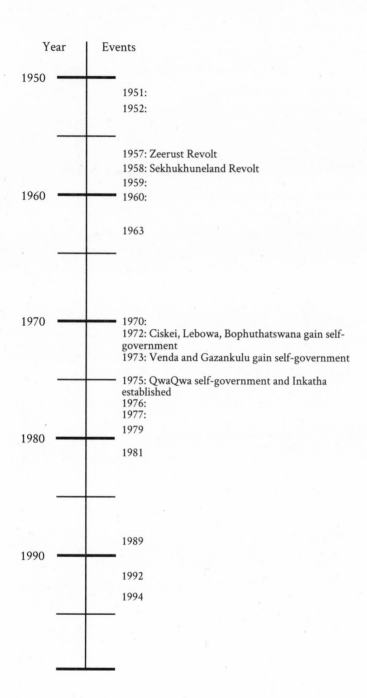

Year	Events
1950	
	1951:
	1952:
	1957: Zeerust Revolt
	1958: Sekhukhuneland Revolt
	1959:
1960	1960:
	1963
1970	1970:
	1972: Ciskei, Lebowa, Bophuthatswana gain self-government
	1973: Venda and Gazankulu gain self-government
	1975: QwaQwa self-government and Inkatha established
	1976:
	1977:
	1979
1980	
	1981
	1989
1990	
	1992
	1994

THEME 3: A HISTORY OF SCHOOLING IN SOUTH AFRICA

The following questions and activities are designed to help you understand some of the information that you have read. You can fill in your answers on this sheet or on your own paper.

1. Compulsory schooling was introduced for white children in the early 1900s. In what year did schooling become compulsory for:

a)   Indian children?   _____

b)   African children?   _____

c)   coloured children?   _____

2. Name two conditions that schools had to accept if they wanted financial aid from the Cape government in the 1800s. Write your answer in the space provided.

First condition:

Second condition:

3. Provide at least three examples from the text to prove that racial discrimination existed in schools and in government education policies before apartheid.

-
-
-

More examples:

4. What were the language policies for African schools in the following periods?

Time period	Language policy in African schools
1935–1955	

1955–1974	
1975–1976	
1976–1978	Afrikaans no longer compulsory (July 1976). Either English or Afrikaans used as language of instruction from Standard 5.
1979–1994	

5. The following table shows per capita expenditure on education in South Africa in ratio form. The original numbers are rounded off to the nearest rand. Use the reading to fill in the missing information for the years 1977–1978 and 1988–1989.

Year	African	Coloured	Indian	White
1953–54	R1	R2	R2	R8
1969–70	1	4	5	17
1975–76	1	3	5	14
1977–78	1			
1980–81	1	2	4	7
1982–83	1	3	5	8
1984– 85	1	3	5	8
1986–87	1	2	5	6
1988–89	1			

Source: P. Christie, The Right to Learn, p. 110

6. Fill out the following table to help you compare the various school protests during apartheid.

Protest	Demands or reasons for the protest	Was the protest successful? Provide reasons for your answer.
1955 boycotts		
1976–1978 uprising		
1980s boycotts		

THEME 4: POVERTY AND INEQUALITY

1. The Theme you have just read mentions various statistics. It often helps to see statistics in a visual way, such as in a graph. Below are some bar graphs that reflect some of the statistics mentioned in the reading. Some of the bars need to be coloured in to show the statistic they reflect. Find the information in the text and fill it in on the bar graphs below.

   1.1. Show on the bar graph below what percentage of South Africa's total income is earned by the richest ten per cent of the population. The first bar has been filled in for you. You have to fill in the second bar.

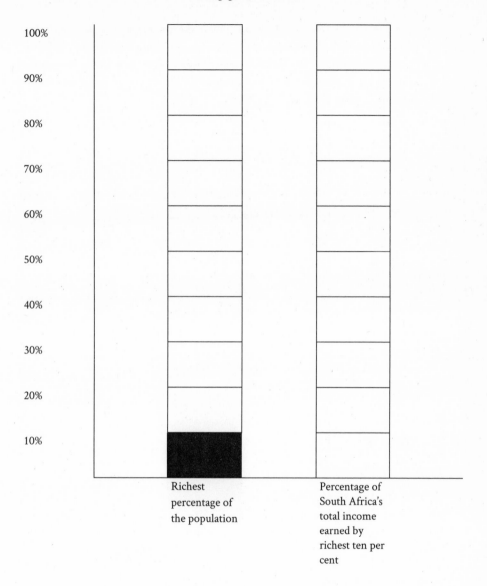

1.2 The bar graph below shows the historical categories of African, coloured, Indian and white. Each bar represents what percentage of the group lived in poverty in 2016. The bar for the Indian population has been filled in for you as an example. Fill in the bars for Africans, coloureds and whites, and write down the percentage below each bar.

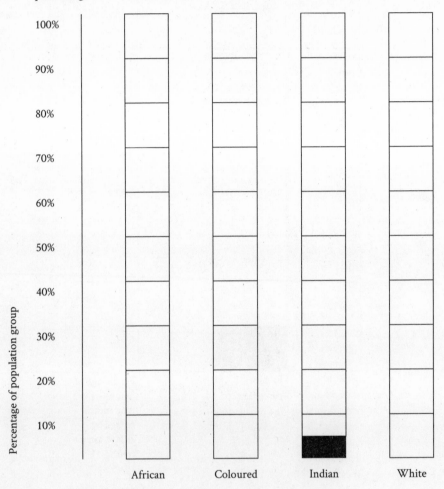

5%

Percentage of Africans, coloureds, Indians and whites living in poverty in South Africa

2. The white minority governments took some key political decisions that had lasting effects on the wealth and poverty of blacks and whites in South Africa.

2.1. The various white minority governments of the twentieth century clearly privileged white people and exploited and oppressed black people and especially Africans. Fill in the blanks in the table below (action or effect) to get a better idea of the different ways African and white people were treated, and the long-term effects this had.

Group	General state of group in late 1800s, early 1900s	Colonial or white minority government policies, actions and laws (include the results of the actions – look at first point for an example)	General state of group by 1970s and 1980s
African	• Largely self-sufficient before conquest. Societies did not really need money for food, since most food was farmed. • Wage labour (before conquest) was optional. • Conquest caused loss of land but many African families entered into sharecropping or cash tenancy contracts with white farmers.	• **Action:** Taxes imposed that had to be paid in cash. **Effect:** Wage labour or farming for profit became necessary. • **Action:** Limited access to land after conquest, especially after the 1913 Natives Land Act. **Effect:** • **Action:** **Effect:** People were prevented from finding work in the towns. • **Action:** Job reservation or the colour bar. **Effect:** African people had access only to lowest-paying work. • **Action:** Pay discrimination and 'civilised labour policy'. **Effect:**	• Majority of the African population still lived in rural areas, especially the bantustans. Independent African farming virtually destroyed and most relied on migrant labour remittances for survival. More families also became dependent on state pensions. • Africans prevented from developing the skills needed for an industrial economy that needed fewer unskilled and more skilled labour. Unemployment increased • In the 1980s intra-racial inequality increased, as job reservation eased and some African workers gained sought-after skills and an urban middle class slowly expanded. However, the middle class made up a tiny minority of the African population

Group	General state of group in late 1800s, early 1900s	Colonial or white minority government policies, actions and laws (include the results of the actions – look at first point for an example)	General state of group by 1970s and 1980s
		• **Action:** **Effect:** Prevented most blacks from gaining skills necessary for skilled work. • **Action:** Trade unions were not recognised until 1979. Workers did not have the right to strike or negotiate for higher wages. **Effect:** • **Action:** Some access to disability grants and pensions, but much less so than for other groups. **Effect:**	
White	Growing number of unemployed or 'poor whites'. Nearly a third of the Afrikaner population was considered poor by 1930.	• **Action:** **Effect:** No longer competing for work with Africans, even if an African person could do the job better • **Action:** Civilised labour policy – white workers earned more than all other groups. Pressure from the government and society to employ more white workers. **Effect:** • **Action:** 40% quota in manufacturing. A large number of jobs reserved purely for whites. **Effect:** • **Action:** State support for white farmers. **Effect:**	White poverty and unemployment largely removed. Most whites became part of the middle class. Most were able to afford private pension schemes and medical aid, and no longer relied on the state for these services. New generation of skilled and educated workers.

Group	General state of group in late 1800s, early 1900s	Colonial or white minority government policies, actions and laws (include the results of the actions – look at first point for an example)	General state of group by 1970s and 1980s
		• **Action:** **Effect:** Large number of unskilled 'poor whites' became employed. • **Action:** White education and training promoted, which improved skills of majority of white population. **Effect:** • **Action:** Welfare grants provided relief for needy and poor whites. White grants were significantly higher than grants for Africans. **Effect:**	

2.2 Government policies affected all groups. How did government policies affect the wealth or poverty of the coloured and Indian populations, particularly when compared to African and white people? Jot down some thoughts in the space provided below:

Government policies regarding coloured and Indian people and their impact:

THEME 5: LIFE UNDER APARTHEID: URBAN AND RURAL EXPERIENCES

1. Conditions in the bantustans

    1.1. Below is a diagram that shows the specific aspects of betterment planning mentioned in Theme 5 and their results. Fill in the blanks.

Betterment Planning   Result of betterment planning

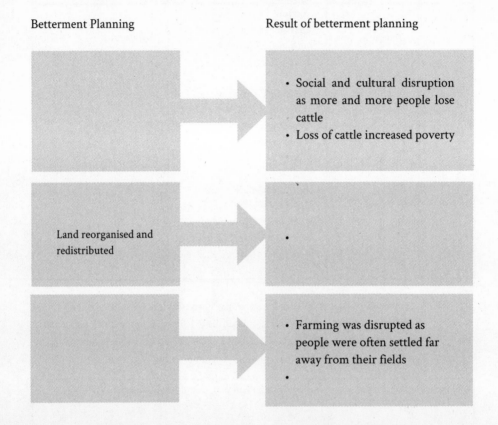

- Social and cultural disruption as more and more people lose cattle
- Loss of cattle increased poverty

Land reorganised and redistributed

-

- Farming was disrupted as people were often settled far away from their fields
-

1.2. The conditions experienced in the bantustan relocation camps were appalling. Fill in the detail for each of the relevant points in the spider diagram below. 'Municipal services' has been filled in as an example.

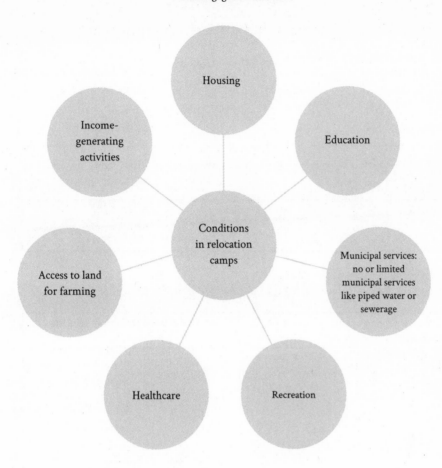

2. Conditions on white-owned farms

   2.1. Fill in the table below.

Living conditions of the majority of farm workers (mainly African)	Living conditions of many white farmers

   2.2. Working conditions on white-owned farms were often horrendous. Identify some of the poor working conditions many black workers experienced, and write them down in the space provided.

2.3. Identify two reasons why black families were evicted from white-owned farms under apartheid.

-
-

3. Conditions in the urban areas
    3.1. Fill in the information for the table below.

Black urban living conditions under apartheid	White urban living conditions by 1980s

3.2. Decide whether each of the statements listed below is true of false. Write 'True' or 'False' in the space provided under each statement. If the statement is false, you need to correct it. The first statement has been filled in as an example.

1	Before the 1940s most African workers lived in multiracial neighbourhoods like Sophiatown. **False: Before the 1940s most urban African workers lived in single-sex hostels or in servants' quarters. A minority lived in multiracial neighbourhoods.**
2	African people needed permission to live and work in an urban area, which was reflected in their pass books.

3	The apartheid state built thousands of new houses for black people in the 1950s.
4	Violent crime, alcoholism and domestic abuse are symptoms of social despair.
5	Around 100 000 people, mainly African, were forcibly removed as a result of the Group Areas Act of 1950.
6	District Six and Chatsworth were multiracial neighbourhoods before the forced removals of the 1960s.
7	The living conditions of many coloured and Indian people improved during the 1970s and 1980s, compared to the African population.
8	The African youth of the 1980s experienced a similar childhood to the youth of the 1960s.

Theme 6: Women's Struggles

1. The chapter includes a number of abbreviations, which can be confusing. Fill out the table below to help familiarise yourself with the different abbreviations.

Acronym	Full Name	Brief Description
ANCWL		
BWL		
CCAWUSA		

Acronym	Full Name	Brief Description
FEDSAW		
FCWU		
GWU		
NOW		
UWO		
WNC		

2. Women often participated in political campaigns, even if they did not make up the majority of the activists or were not represented in leadership structures. Identify at least four different resistance campaigns or demonstrations where women participated together with men in the first half of the twentieth century.

-
-
-
-

3. Why is the 1913 Bloemfontein anti-pass campaign significant?

4. Apart from the 1956 Women's March, how else were women involved in anti-apartheid demonstrations during the 1950s and early 1960s? Identify at least four events or campaigns.

-
-
-
-

5. Read the preamble of the Women's Charter of 1954. Write down your opinion about the Charter. Do you agree with its principles? Do you think they are realistic? Are they still relevant today?

6. Identify at least four ways in which women mobilised against apartheid during the 1970s and 1980s.

-
-
-
-

7. What three aims did the National Coalition of Women prioritise during the negotiation process in the early 1990s?

-
-
-

8. Write down a list of challenges and obstacles that women still face today. What could you do to help remove these challenges?

Challenges:

What I can do:

THEME 7: THE TRADE UNION MOVEMENT

Fill out the following table to help you to become familiar with the different federations and their abbreviations or acronyms. The first row has been filled out as an example.

Date Established	Body Name		Membership	Years Active	Cause of decline
1919	ICU	Industrial and Commercial Workers' Union	160 000 members at its height; mainly African but also included a few thousand coloureds and some whites	1919–1930	Divisions in leadership regarding direction of ICU led to a loss of militancy and support (CPSA members expelled)

Date Established	Body Name	Membership	Years Active	Cause of decline
1928	FNETU		1928– early 1930s	Depression of 1930s weakened bargaining power of workers, and caused many black unions to collapse
1941		158 000 workers by 1945 from 119 affiliated trade unions		
		Formed when members of Trades and Labour Council (TLC) and CNETU united. At start 20 000 members from 19 affiliated unions; grew to 55 000 from 51 affiliated unions by early 1960s	1955– early 1960s	
1979			1979– 1985	
	CUSA	Most militant affiliate was NUM	1980– 1986	

Date Established	Body Name		Membership	Years Active	Cause of decline
1985			460 000 at founding	Still active	Still active
1986			CUSA and smaller trade unions with BCM sympathies merged, with 150 000 members at founding	Still active	Still active

THEME 8: SOUTH AFRICA'S CONSTITUTIONS

1. Match the columns. Write down the letter from Column B that matches the phrase in Column A. An answer sheet is provided on page 322.

Column A		Column B	
1	National Convention	A	Can only be changed by a significant majority, usually two-thirds, in Parliament
2	Constitution of 1961	B	1 400 representatives who met in 1961 and called for a new national convention made up of elected representatives from the entire adult population to draw up a new constitution for South Africa
3	Franchise	C	The ratio of representatives from the different so-called racial groups who negotiated the interim constitution
4	1996 constitution	D	Created the Constitutional Court
5	Governor-General	E	Parliament was split into three houses representing whites, coloureds and Indians
6	Entrenched clauses	F	The right to vote
7	Cape franchise	G	Parliament holds the most power and can make most laws with a simple majority

Column A		Column B	
8	Constitutional principles	H	Parliament can only make laws that are consistent with the constitution
9	1983 constitution	I	Parliament added three houses representing the coloured, Indian and African populations
10	Parliamentary sovereignty	J	Met in 1955 in Kliptown and adopted the Freedom Charter
11	4:2:1	K	Created the Union of South Africa
12	All-In African Conference	L	Created by representatives who were elected in South Africa's first democratic election, and approved by the Constitutional Court
13	Interim constitution	M	Met to oppose the racist 1910 constitution and approached the British Parliament directly
14	Constitutional supremacy	N	Specific rights set out in the interim constitution that the new constitution had to follow
15	South African Native Convention	O	Established in 1912 to oppose the 1913 Natives Land Act
16	South Africa Act, 1909	P	All men with a certain amount of property or wealth could vote, regardless of race
		Q	Based largely on the 1910 constitution; any powers held by the Governor-General or the British monarch were transferred to the State President or the South African government
		R	White, male representatives from the four self-governing colonies drew up a constitution for the Union of South Africa
		S	All adults have the right to vote
		T	The voting ratio used by the Tricameral Parliament to determine important questions
		U	The belief that the constitution is perfect
		V	Represented the British monarch

Write your answers next to the relevant number.

1	_____	9	_____
2	_____	10	_____
3	_____	11	_____
4	_____	12	_____
5	_____	13	_____
6	_____	14	_____
7	_____	15	_____
8	_____	16	_____

2. Compare the various reasons why South Africa had five constitutions in the twentieth century, as well as some of the effects or implications of these constitutions. The first row has been filled in for you as an example.

Constitution	Reasons for new constitution	Significant effects or implications
1910	Four separate self-governing colonies wanted to form a new, united country	Only white men (and, later, women) had the vote Parliament could pass almost any law through a simple majority Allowed for many racist laws to be passed
1961		

Constitution	Reasons for new constitution	Significant effects or implications
1983		
1993		
1996		

THEME 9: INTERNATIONAL SOLIDARITY AGAINST APARTHEID

On the next page is a graphic that breaks down the different types of international solidarity campaigns. Some of the information has been filled in, but you need to fill in the blanks. You can either write on the graphic provided, or redraw a similar graphic on your own paper. Where possible, include some examples for each activity.

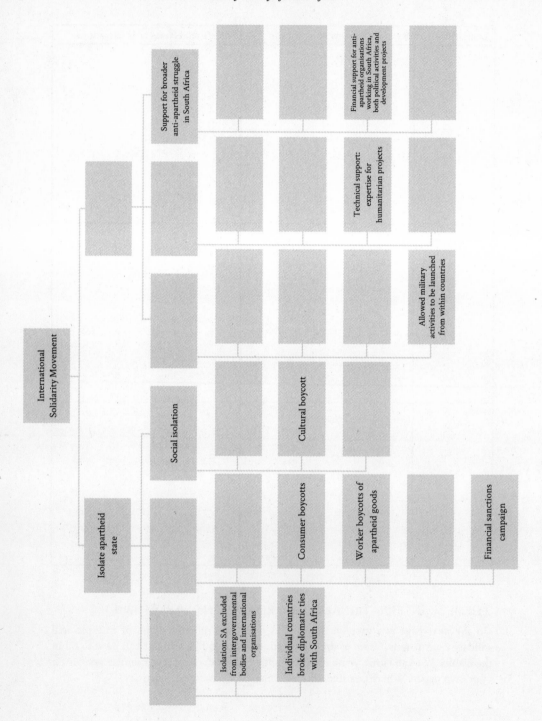

The chart presents the structure of the International Solidarity Movement. Its two main branches are "Isolate apartheid state" and "Support for broader anti-apartheid struggle in South Africa."

Under "Isolate apartheid state":
- Social isolation
  - Isolation: SA excluded from intergovernmental bodies and international organisations
  - Individual countries broke diplomatic ties with South Africa
- Cultural boycott
  - Consumer boycotts
  - Worker boycotts of apartheid goods
  - Financial sanctions campaign

Under "Support for broader anti-apartheid struggle in South Africa":
- Allowed military activities to be launched from within countries
- Technical support: expertise for humanitarian projects
- Financial support for anti-apartheid organisations working in South Africa, both political activities and development projects

Memoranda for Text Engagement Activities

THEME 1: THE SOUTH AFRICAN ECONOMY

Era	Demand/Need	Government Action	Effect
Union government: SAP, 1910–1924	More labour needed on mines and white commercial farms	**1913 Natives Land Act**	Africans were no longer allowed to be sharecroppers; many Africans became farm wage labourers; poorer white farmers lost sharecropping income; African agriculture declined
Pact and Fusion: 1924–1939	Mining companies were losing profits and wanted to cut white wages and employ more black workers in semi-skilled positions	*Government sided with the mine owners *Smuts crushed the Rand Revolt	• **White mine wages cut by 25 per cent** • **More black workers employed in semi-skilled work** • **More black workers employed in place of whites**
	Money needed to develop agricultural and manufacturing industries	**Pact government taxed mines more heavily than the SAP had done**	More money was made available to develop agriculture and manufacturing

Era	Demand/Need	Government Action	Effect
	Need to provide support for white farmers	Government introduced supportive measures for white farmers, including **(any three)**: • **Farm subsidies** • **Drought grants** • **Cheaper railway rates for agricultural products** • **Capital works** • **Loans**	*More farmers mechanised but agricultural input did not increase significantly *Foundation was laid for the improvement of white commercial farming during apartheid
	Need to protect white workers from black competition	*Colour bar expanded across more industries *40 per cent of manufacturing labour was reserved for whites	White workers legally protected from competition with black workers for certain skilled and semi-skilled jobs
	Need to create employment for white workers	• **State employed many whites, especially in railways and harbours** • **Support given to grow manufacturing industry, e.g. by establishing ISCOR**	White employment increased, especially in manufacturing so that by 1949 there were more jobs available in industry than whites to fill them
	South African exports suffered during Great Depression	Devalued South African pound by going off the gold standard	• **South African products became cheaper and exports expanded** • **Gold price soared**
	Need to expand South African industry	**State implemented import-substitution policy**	*Manufacturing protected from foreign competition *Manufacturing expanded rapidly and employment in this sector grew by 60 per cent between 1933 and 1939

Era	Demand/Need	Government Action	Effect
World War II	Demand for black workers increased in industry during World War II	**Segregationist legislation such as the colour bar and pass laws relaxed during World War II**	• Rapid black urbanisation • Industry continued to expand • **More black workers in semi-skilled and skilled positions**
National Party, early apartheid: 1948–1970s	Need to regulate African labour and create an unskilled, rurally based pool of cheap labour	Measures included: • Expansion of colour bar • Restrictions on trade unions • **Extension of passes to black women** • **Forced removals to the bantustans** • **Bantu Education**	• Black urbanisation slowed • More black people were forced to take up wage labour on white farms • An unskilled, rurally based pool of cheap labour was created • Migrant labour entrenched • Poverty increased in bantustans
	Need to modernise white commercial agriculture	**State aid to white farmers so they could mechanise**	• Maize yields increased • Farmers needed fewer workers, thereby contributing to a growing surplus of rurally based unskilled workers who struggled to find employment
	Desire to grow Afrikaner stake in economy beyond agriculture	NP government promoted and supported Afrikaner financial institutions and businesses	Afrikaner share of ownership increased between 1949 to 1970 in • Mining (1 per cent to 30 per cent) • **Manufacturing and construction (6 per cent to 25 per cent)** • **Finance (6 per cent to 15 per cent)**

Era	Demand/Need	Government Action	Effect
	Need to break the cycle of poverty in the white population by creating a new generation of skilled whites	**Universal quality education provided to all white children**	**White working class declined and white middle class expanded**
National Party, late apartheid: 1970s–1994	Skilled, urbanised black labour needed to maintain economic growth	Limited reforms made to segregationist legislation • Colour bar relaxed • **Increased spending on black (especially African) education** • **Pass laws relaxed and influx control abolished in 1986** • **Black trade unions recognised**	*Reforms were too limited and ineffective *Economic growth slowed and declined

THEME 2: SOUTH AFRICA'S BANTUSTANS

1. In the space provided below, list at least seven different economic challenges that the bantustans faced.

Bantustan Economic Challenges

- Inherited underdeveloped state of reserves
- Poor agricultural conditions
- Little commerce (few shops and businesses)
- No industrial centres
- Small tax base – most families were poor and relied on migrant labour
- Fragmented land areas
- Some bantustans were very small
- Skills shortages
- Coastal bantustans had no established ports
- Pretoria prevented them from taking own development initiative
- Pretoria's funding not enough to address challenges

---

2. Only the apartheid state and bantustan governments considered the bantustans independent states. Why did so many people reject the idea that bantustans were fully independent countries?

> - They understood that the bantustans were a ploy of the apartheid government to deflect international criticism of its racist policies.
> - The government used the bantustans to deprive the majority of people of their South African citizenship.
> - Bantustans had very weak economies and could not act independently since they were economically dependent on South Africa and relied on grants from Pretoria.
> - South African security forces worked with bantustan governments to suppress any opposition.

3. The following chart shows the population of QwaQwa in three different years. Consult the text of the Theme and fill in the correct date under the corresponding column.

   Column 1: 1970, Column 2: 1975, Colum 3: 1980

4. Timeline activity:

Year	Event
1952	Defiance Campaign
1981	Ciskei 'independence'
1976	Transkei 'independence'
1989	Transkei unbans ANC and PAC
1951	Bantu Authorities Act
1960	Pondoland Revolt
1992	Bisho Massacre
1959	Promotion of Bantu Self-government Act
1977	Bophuthatswana 'independence'
1979	Venda 'independence'
1994	End of bantustans
1970	Bantu Homeland Citizenship Act
1963	Transkei gains self-government
1977	KwaZulu gains self-government

Timeline

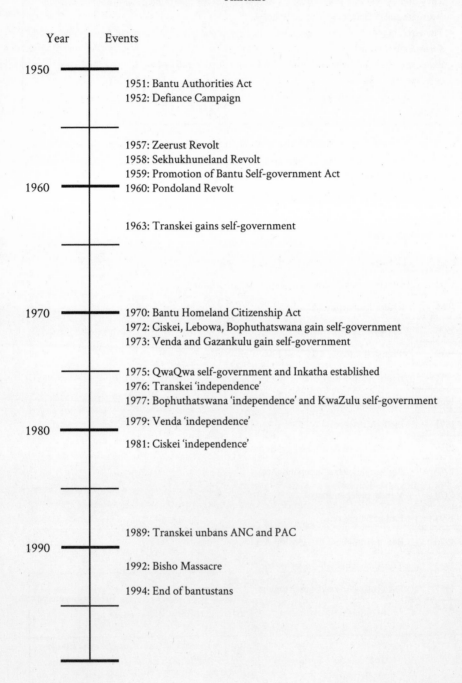

Year	Events
1950	
	1951: Bantu Authorities Act
	1952: Defiance Campaign
	1957: Zeerust Revolt
	1958: Sekhukhuneland Revolt
	1959: Promotion of Bantu Self-government Act
1960	1960: Pondoland Revolt
	1963: Transkei gains self-government
1970	1970: Bantu Homeland Citizenship Act
	1972: Ciskei, Lebowa, Bophuthatswana gain self-government
	1973: Venda and Gazankulu gain self-government
	1975: QwaQwa self-government and Inkatha established
	1976: Transkei 'independence'
	1977: Bophuthatswana 'independence' and KwaZulu self-government
	1979: Venda 'independence'
1980	1981: Ciskei 'independence'
	1989: Transkei unbans ANC and PAC
1990	
	1992: Bisho Massacre
	1994: End of bantustans

THEME 3: A HISTORY OF SCHOOLING IN SOUTH AFRICA

The answers in this memorandum are answers that readers would get from the text. Answers are presented in bold.

1. Compulsory schooling was introduced for white children in the early 1900s. When did schooling become compulsory for:
   a. Indian children? **1965**
   b. African children? **1996**
   c. Coloured children? **1963**

2. Name two conditions that schools had to accept if they wanted financial aid from the Cape government in the 1800s.

First condition:
Schools had to teach in English.

Second condition:
African children had to do manual labour as part of the school day.

3. Provide at least three examples from the text that show that racial discrimination existed in schools and in governmental education policies before apartheid.

- **During the 1800s, black and white children at the same boarding school had to eat at separate tables and sleep in different dormitories.**
- **Black schools had a different curriculum from white schools – for example, it included manual labour, and the Transvaal drew up a separate curriculum after Union.**
- **Education was compulsory for white children from 1918, but not for other children.**
- **Per capita spending was unequal for white and black children. For example, in 1940 state expenditure per capita on white children was £26 compared to £2 for African children.**

4. What were the language policies for African schools in the following periods?

Era	Language policy in African schools
1935–1955	**Mother-tongue instruction for first four years and an official language (usually English) for the rest of primary and high school**
1955–1974	**Mother-tongue instruction up to Standard 6 (end of primary school); dual-medium policy in high school with both English and Afrikaans used**

Era	Language policy in African schools
1975–1976	Mother-tongue instruction up to Standard 4; English and Afrikaans used from Standard 5 until the end of high school
1976–1978	Afrikaans no longer compulsory (from July 1976). Either English or Afrikaans used as the language of instruction from Standard 5.
1979–1994	Compulsory Afrikaans removed as a language of instruction. Schools taught in mother tongue for the first four years and, if they wished, they could introduce one official language (English or Afrikaans) in Standard 3.

5. The following table shows per capita expenditure on education in South Africa in ratio form. The original numbers are rounded off to the nearest rand. Use the text to fill in the missing information for the years 1977–1978 and 1988–19989. [Answers in bold]

Year	African	Coloured	Indian	White
1953–54	R1	R2	R2	R8
1969–70	1	4	5	17
1975–76	1	3	5	14
1977–78	**1**	**3**	**5**	**12**
1980–81	1	2	4	7
1982–83	1	3	5	8
1984–85	1	3	5	8
1986–87	1	2	5	6
1988–89	**1**	**2**	**3**	**4**

Source: P. Christie, The Right to Learn, p. 110

6. Fill out the following table to help you to compare the different school protests during apartheid.

Protest	Demands or reasons for the protest	Was the protest successful? Provide reasons for your answer.
1955 boycotts	• Protest against implementing Bantu Education Act	• Unsuccessful: Bantu Education was implemented Some success with cultural clubs but these were eventually shut down

Protest	Demands or reasons for the protest	Was the protest successful? Provide reasons for your answer.
1976–1978 uprising	• Protest against Afrikaans in upper primary and high schools • Demand for better resources	• Successful in that Afrikaans was removed as a compulsory language of instruction and more money was spent on black education and more schools were built; Bantu Education Act was also scrapped • Unsuccessful because conditions in most black schools remained inferior and there was still unequal state spending per capita; racial discrimination and different education departments continued
1980s boycotts	• End of apartheid, and rejection of racist, segregated system as a whole • Better learning conditions • More democratic school structures • Alternative education and curriculum – People's Education	• Successful to some extent: eventual end of apartheid; private schools allowed to admit black pupils in 1986, and in 1990 'open' schools were allowed

THEME 4: POVERTY AND INEQUALITY

1. The Theme you have just read mentions various statistics. It often helps to see statistics in a visual way, such as in a graph. Below are some bar graphs that reflect some of the statistics mentioned in the reading. Some of the bars need to be coloured in to show the statistic they reflect. Find the information in the text and fill it in on the bar graphs below.

    1.1. The bar graph below shows what percentage of South Africa's total income is earned by the richest ten per cent of the population. The first bar has been filled in for you. You have to fill in the second bar.

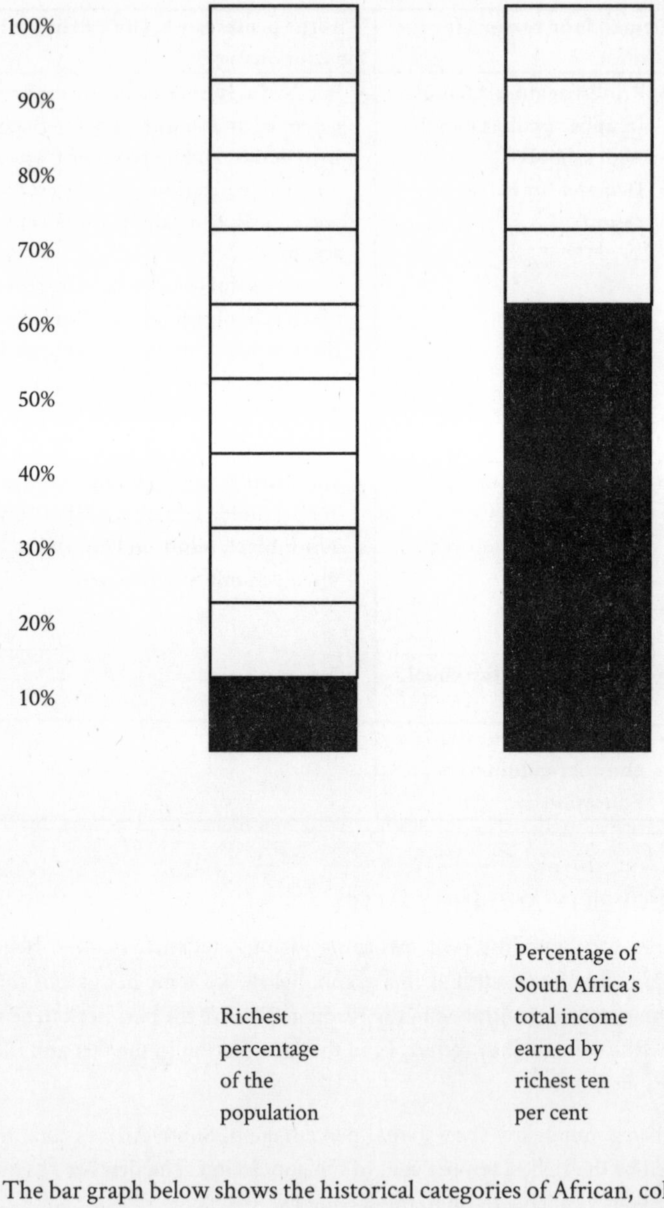

100%

90%

80%

70%

60%

50%

40%

30%

20%

10%

Richest
percentage
of the
population

Percentage of
South Africa's
total income
earned by
richest ten
per cent

1.2 The bar graph below shows the historical categories of African, coloured, Indian and white. Each bar represents what percentage of the racial group lived in poverty in 2016. The bar for the Indian population has been filled in for you as an example. Fill in the bars for African, coloured and white, and write down the percentage below each bar.

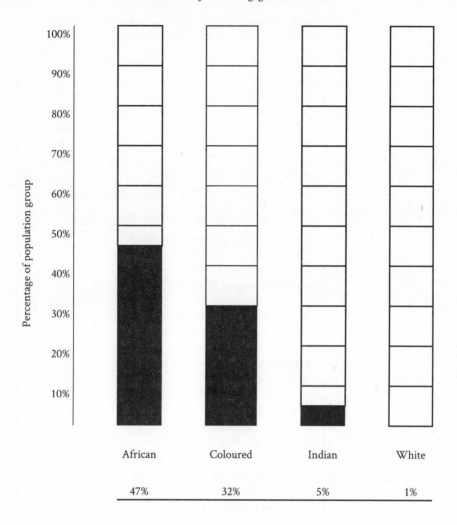

Percentage of Africans, coloureds, Indians and whites living in
poverty in South Africa

2. The white minority governments took some key political decision that had lasting effects on the wealth and poverty of blacks and whites in South Africa.

   2.1. The various white minority governments of the twentieth century clearly privileged white people and exploited and oppressed black people and especially Africans. Fill in the table below to get a better idea of the different ways African and white people were treated, and the long-term effects this had.

Group	General state of group in late 1800s and early 1900s	Colonial or white minority government policies, actions and laws (include the results of the actions – look at first point for an example)	General state of group by 1970s and 1980s
African	• Largely self-sufficient before conquest. Societies did not really need money for food, since most food was farmed. • Wage labour (before conquest) was optional. • Conquest caused loss of land but many African families entered into sharecropping or cash tenancy contracts with white farmers.	• **Action:** Taxes imposed that had to be paid in cash. **Effect:** Wage labour or farming for profit became necessary. • **Action:** Limited access to land after conquest, especially after the 1913 Natives Land Act. **Effect: Reserves became overcrowded. Not enough resources for the number of people forced to live and farm in reserves. Poverty and malnutrition increased.** • **Action: Pass laws (especially under apartheid) prevented many people from leaving the rural areas.** **Effect:** People were prevented from finding work in the towns. • **Action:** Job reservation or the colour bar. **Effect:** African people had access only to lowest-paying work. • **Action:** Pay discrimination and 'civilised labour policy'. **Effect: Africans were paid less than white, coloured and Indian workers for the same job.** • **Action: Inferior education and limited access before apartheid, and inferior Bantu Education during apartheid.** **Effect:** Prevented most blacks from gaining skills necessary for skilled work. • **Action:** Trade unions not recognised until 1979. Workers did not have the right to strike or negotiate for higher wages. **Effect: Wages were kept low, especially in comparison with other groups.**	• Majority of the African population still lived in rural areas, especially the bantustans. Independent African farming virtually destroyed and most relied on migrant labour remittances for survival. More families also became dependent on state pensions. • Africans prevented from developing the skills needed for an industrial economy that needed fewer unskilled and more skilled labour. Unemployment increased. • In the 1980s intra-racial inequality increased, as job reservation eased and some African workers gained sought-after skills and an urban middle class slowly expanded.

Group	General state of group in late 1800s and early 1900s	Colonial or white minority government policies, actions and laws (include the results of the actions – look at first point for an example)	General state of group by 1970s and 1980s
		• **Action:** Some access to disability grants and pensions, but much less so than for other groups. **Effect: Provided some relief but ensured that African people remained the poorest of all groups.**	• However, the middle class made up a tiny minority of the African population.
White	• Growing number of unemployed or 'poor whites'. Nearly a third of the Afrikaner population considered poor by 1930.	• **Action: Colour bar ensured skilled and semi-skilled work was reserved for whites.** **Effect:** No longer competing for work with Africans, even if an African person could do the job better. • **Action:** Civilised labour policy – white workers earned more than all other groups. Pressure from the government and society to employ more white workers. **Effect: White wealth increased at expense of blacks.** • **Action:** 40% quota in manufacturing. A large number of jobs reserved purely for whites. **Effect: Whites had more access to work, even if they were less skilled or able. White workers faced less competition.** • **Action: State support for white farmers.** **Effect:** White farmers were able to mechanise and improve their farming skills. • **Action: Job creation: work for poor whites in harbours, railways, and state-owned enterprises.** **Effect:** Large number of unskilled 'poor whites' became employed.	• White poverty and unemployment largely removed. Most whites became part of the middle class. .

Group	General state of group in late 1800s and early 1900s	Colonial or white minority government policies, actions and laws (include the results of the actions – look at first point for an example)	General state of group by 1970s and 1980s
		• **Action:** White education and training promoted, which improved skills of majority of white population. **Effect: Fewer unskilled white workers competed for work with unskilled black workers. General earnings of white population increased, and white middle class expanded.** • **Action:** Welfare grants provided relief for needy and poor whites. White grants were significantly higher than grants for Africans. **Effect: Even in poverty whites remained privileged, ensuring needy whites got more than blacks.**	• Most were able to afford private pension schemes and medical aid, and no longer relied on the state for these services. New generation of skilled and educated workers

2.2. Government policies affected all racial groups. How did government policies affect the wealth or poverty of the coloured and Indian populations, particularly when compared to African and white people? Jot down some thoughts in the space provided below:

Government policies regarding coloured and Indian people and their impact:

Accept any relevant answers. Students are encouraged to draw on information gained from further readings or their own knowledge.

Points that could be included:

Job reservation: Indians and coloureds could enter many skilled and semi-skilled occupations from which Africans were barred. Many jobs were reserved for whites only and thus discriminated against all other workers.

It was easier for Indians and coloureds than it was for Africans to own businesses although there were laws restricting their businesses to certain areas and excluding them altogether from 'white' areas.

Pay discrimination: Coloured and Indian workers received less than white workers but more than black workers for doing the same work.

Education: More money was spent on coloured and Indian education than on African education, resulting in better educational outcomes and qualifications for them. White education had by far the largest education budget.

Movement: Coloured and Indian people were largely able to move around the country to live or search for work, unlike Africans, whose movement was severely restricted by the pass laws. An exception was the ban on Indians living in the Free State or even travelling through it without a permit. Whites were prohibited from entering African townships without special permission.

THEME 5: LIFE UNDER APARTHEID: URBAN AND RURAL EXPERIENCES

1. Conditions in the bantustans

1.1. Below is a diagram that shows the specific aspects of betterment planning mentioned in Theme 5 and their results. Fill in the blanks.

Betterment Planning

Result of betterment planninng

Betterment Planning	Result of betterment planninng
Africans forced to limit cattle herds through: • Selling off cattle • Culling	• Social and cultural disruption as more and more people lost cattle • Increased poverty as a result of loss of land
Land reorganised and redistributed	• People lost access to land without sufficient compensation. Less access to land caused people to rely even more on igrant labour remittances.
Villagisation	• Farming was disrupted as people were often settled far away from their fields • Social disruption as communities were broken up and settled next to strangers. Criminality increased.

1.2. The conditions experienced in the bantustan relocation camps were horrendous. Fill in the detail for each of the relevant points in the spider diagram below. 'Municipal services' has been filled in as an example.

2. Conditions on white-owned farms

    2.1. Fill in the table below.

Living conditions of the majority of farm workers (mainly African)	Living conditions of many white farmers
• No electricity • Limited or no access to piped water • No modern toilets • Shacks or huts • Inferior or no education for children	• Electricity • Piped water • Sewerage • Large, sturdy farmhouses • Good education available for children

2.2. Working conditions on white-owned farms were often appalling. Identify some of the poor working conditions and write them down in the space provided.

- Farm wages much lower than mining or urban wages
- Workers were exploited
- White farmers were often verbally and physically abusive
- Black children were used for labour
- 'Dop' system

2.3. Identify two reasons why black families were evicted from white-owned farms under apartheid.

- Apartheid state clamped down on cash tenancy and sharecropping.
- Mechanisation of white farms meant fewer workers were needed.

3. Conditions in the urban areas

3.1. Fill in the information for the table below.

Black urban living conditions under apartheid	White urban living conditions by 1980s
• Overcrowding • High levels of violence • Few facilities, services or amenities • Many resorted to shack-dwelling • Political unrest, violence, protest action, military presence in many townships in 1980s	• Houses or flats in low-density suburbs • Generally safe and peaceful • Well-serviced with many able to afford private facilities like swimming pools

3.2. Decide whether each of the statements listed below is true of false. Write 'True' or 'False' in the space provided under each statement. If the statement is false, you need to correct it, using the space provided.

1	Before the 1940s most African workers lived in multi-racial neighbourhoods like Sophiatown. **False: Before the 1940s most urban African workers lived in single-sex hostels or in servants' quarters. A minority lived in multiracial neighbourhoods.**
2	African people needed permission to live and work in an urban area, which was reflected in their pass books. **True**
3	The apartheid state built thousands of new houses for black people in the 1950s. **True**

4	Violent crime, alcoholism and domestic abuse are symptoms of social despair. **True**
5	Around 100 000 people, mainly black, were forcibly removed as a result of the Group Areas Act of 1950. **False: Over 850 000 people, mainly coloureds and Indians, were forcibly removed as a result of the Group Areas Act of 1950.**
6	District Six and Chatsworth were multiracial neighbourhoods before the forced removals of the 1960s. **False: District Six was a multiracial neighbourhood but Chatsworth was not.**
7	The living conditions of many coloured and Indian people improved during the 1970s and 1980s, compared to the African population. **True**
8	The African youth of the 1980s experienced a similar childhood to the youth of the 1960s. **False: There was much more mass political resistance to apartheid in the 1980s, with clear and direct challenges to the state.**

THEME 6: WOMEN'S STRUGGLES

1. The chapter includes a number of abbreviations, which can be confusing. Fill out the table below to help familiarise yourself with the different abbreviations.

Acronym	Full Name	Brief Description
ANCWL	**African National Congress Women's League**	**Founded in 1943, as the women's wing of the ANC**
BWL	**Bantu Women's League**	**Founded in 1913, with Charlotte Maxeke as first president**
CCAWUSA	**Commercial, Catering and Allied Workers' Union of South Africa**	**Second-largest affiliate of COSATU with 50 000 members**
FCWU	**Food and Canning Workers' Union**	**Created in 1940s in the Cape, also dominated by women**
FEDSAW	**Federation of South African Women**	**Established in 1954, adopted the Women's Charter, made up of affiliates (mainly ANCWL and trade unions); organised 1956 Women's March to Union Buildings**

GWU	Garment Workers' Union	Trade union in clothing industry dominated by women, already active in 1930s; Lilian Ngoyi and Lucy Mvelase prominent in it
NOW	Natal Organisation of Women	Women's organisation set up in the 1980s in Natal, aligned with UDF
UWO	United Women's Organisation	Women's organisation set up in the 1980s in the Cape, aligned with UDF
WNC	Women's National Coalition	Women's movement established during the transition that incorporated women from all sections of the political spectrum; agitated for women's representation in the negotiation process and for non-sexism in the final constitution

2. Women often participated in political campaigns, even if they did not make up the majority of the activists or were not represented in leadership structures. Identify at least four different resistance campaigns or demonstrations where women participated together with men in the first half of the twentieth century.

- 1913 Indian passive resistance campaign
- 1919 (Witwatersrand) and 1928–9 (Potchefstroom) anti-pass campaigns
- Squatter movements
- Alexandra bus boycott
- 1946 Indian passive resistance campaign

(any 4 mentioned in the chapter)

3. Why is the 1913 Bloemfontein anti-pass campaign significant?

- Women mobilised on their own, without reference to men
- An example of mass mobilisation among Africans and coloureds long before ANC considered these tactics
- Persuaded authorities to treat passes for women with caution
- Led to the creation of the Bantu Women's League

4. Apart from the 1956 Women's March, how else were women involved in anti-apartheid demonstrations during the 1950s and early 1960s? Identify at least four events or campaigns.

- Defiance Campaign
- Bantu Education boycott
- Congress of the People and Freedom Charter
- 1955 Black Sash march to Union Buildings
- 1959 Cato Manor riots
- Sharpeville protest
- Rural women's revolt
- Indian women's march to Union Buildings

5. Read the preamble of the Women's Charter of 1954. Write down your opinion about the Charter. Do you agree with its principles? Do you think they are realistic? Are they still relevant today?

Accept any reasonable response.

6. Identify at least four six ways in which women mobilised against apartheid during the 1970s and 1980s.

- Formed BC organisations like Black Women's Federation and Black Parents' Association
- Participated in student uprisings
- Participated in trade union activities
- Part of organisations aligned with the UDF or that supported trade union activities
- Participated in street and area committees

7. What three aims did the National Coalition of Women prioritise during the negotiation process in the early 1990s?

- To be part of the negotiating teams during the multi-party talks
- For non-sexism to be a basic constitutional principle
- For women's right to equality to supersede traditional and customary law

8. Write down a list challenges and obstacles that women still face today. What could you do to help remove these challenges?

Open. Accept any reasonable responses.

THEME 7: THE TRADE UNION MOVEMENT

Date Established	Body Name		Membership	Years Active	Cause of decline
1919	ICU	Industrial and Commercial Workers' Union	160 000 members at its height; mainly African but also included a few thousand coloureds and some whites	1919–1930	Divisions in leadership regarding direction of ICU led to a loss of militancy and support (CPSA members expelled)
1928	FNETU	**Federation of Non-European Trade Unions**	**Mainly Africans; about 10 000 workers initially from 5 trade unions**	1928–early 1930s	Depression of 1930s weakened bargaining power of workers, and caused many black unions to collapse
1941	**CNETU**	Council of Non-European Trade Unions	158 000 workers by 1945 from 119 affiliated trade unions	**1941–1955**	**Suppression of 1946 strike effectively destroyed AMWU and weakened African trade union movement. By 1949 many African trade unions no longer existed, thus weakening CNETU. CNETU dissolved into SACTU.**

Date Established	Body Name		Membership	Years Active	Cause of decline
1955	**SACTU**	**South African Congress of Trade Unions**	Formed when members of Trades and Labour Council (TLC) and CNETU united At start 20 000 members from 19 affiliated unions; grew to 55 000 from 51 affiliated unions by early 1960s	1955– early 1960s	**Repression by state made it difficult to function by the 1960s**
1979	**FOSATU**	**Federation of South African Trade Unions**	**45 000 at founding with 120 000 by 1984 and 8 affiliated unions**	1979– 1985	**Dissolved into the newly formed COSATU**
1980	CUSA	**Council of Unions of South Africa**	Most militant affiliate was NUM	1980 – 1986	**Dissolved into NACTU but NUM joined COSATU**
1985	**COSATU**	**Congress of South African Trade Unions**	460 000 at founding	Still active	Still active
1986	**NACTU**	**National Council of Trade Unions**	CUSA and smaller trade unions with BCM sympathies merged, with 150 000 members at founding	Still active	Still active

THEME 8: SOUTH AFRICA'S CONSTITUTIONS

1. Match the columns. Write down the letter from Column B that matches the phrase in Column A.

1	National Convention	R	White, male representatives from the four self-governing colonies drew up a constitution for the Union of South Africa
2	Constitution of 1961	Q	Based largely on the 1910 constitution; any powers held by the Governor-General or the British monarch were transferred to the President or the South African government
3	Franchise	F	The right to vote
4	1996 constitution	L	Created by representatives who were elected in South Africa's first democratic election, and approved by the Constitutional Court
5	Governor-General	V	Represented the British monarch
6	Entrenched clauses	A	Can only be changed by a significant majority, usually two-thirds, in Parliament
7	Cape franchise	P	All men with a certain amount of property or wealth could vote
8	Constitutional principles	N	Specific rights set out in the interim constitution, which the new constitution had to follow
9	Tricameral Parliament	E	Parliament was split into three houses representing whites, coloureds and Indians
10	Parliamentary sovereignty	G	Parliament holds the most power and can make most laws with a simple majority
11	4:2:1	T	The voting ratio used by the Tricameral Parliament to determine important questions
12	All-In African Conference	B	1 400 representatives who met in 1961 and called for a new National Convention made up of elected representatives from the entire adult population to draw up a new constitution for South Africa
13	Interim constitution	D	Created the Constitutional Court
14	Constitutional supremacy	H	Parliament can only make laws that are consistent with the constitution
15	South African Native Convention	M	Met to oppose the racist 1910 constitutional clauses and approached the British Parliament directly
16	South Africa Act 1909	K	Created the Union of South Africa

2. Compare the various reasons why South Africa had five constitutions in the twentieth century, as well as some of the effects or implications of these constitutions. The first row has been filled in for you as an example

Accept any reasonable answer not included in this memorandum.

Constitution	Reasons for new constitution	Significant effects and/or implications
1910	Four separate self-governing colonies wanted to form a new, united country	Only white men (and, later, women) had the vote Parliament could make almost any law through a simple majority Allowed for many racist laws to be passed
1961	South Africa became a republic	Continued the racist regime of previous constitution without any formal links to Britain
1983	Attempted to reform apartheid system and to divide blacks, and tried to align the interests of coloureds and Indians with whites	Africans denied any representation Attempted to divide coloured and Indian population, while continuing white supremacy
1993	Result of negotiated settlement; an attempt to create a stable transition from apartheid to democracy; protected certain rights while still allowing the elected representatives to draw up the final constitution	Created legal equality between all people Provided for a process for drafting the final constitution Implemented constitutional supremacy Set out specific 'constitutional principles' Created the Constitutional Court
1996	The first constitution drawn up by elected representatives of the entire adult population	Reaffirmed legal equality between all people Entrenched fundamental human rights Reaffirmed constitutional supremacy

THEME 9: INTERNATIONAL SOLIDARITY AGAINST APARTHEID

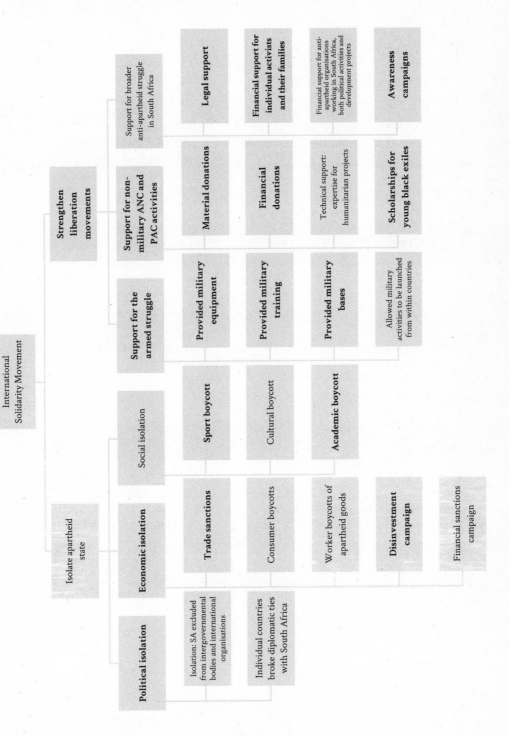

Index

This index is arranged word by word. Page numbers that refer to illustrative material are given in italics.